Comparable to the long-successful
Gerry Frank's Where to Find It, Buy It, Eat It in New York
(over 1,000,000 copies sold), you will indeed see where to
find it, buy it and eat it–this time, though, in OREGON.
A contributor to *The Oregonian* for many years, enjoy
reviewing many of Gerry's travel columns and much more.

Explore these seven regions with Gerry: Greater Portland,
Willamette Valley, Coast, Columbia Gorge and Mt. Hood,
Central, Eastern and Southern, where you will discover....

Hotels in various price categories
Bed & breakfasts
State parks & camping options
Wine & dine favorites
Gourmet to comfort food
Killers & millers (of grains & breads)
Bridal gowns & mother-of-the-bride
(& groom) dresses
Hardware selections, knickknacks & gifts
Museums & interpretive centers
Bakeries
(including Gerry's own Konditorei restaurant)
Brew pubs
Shoes! (especially for women)
Maps of 7 Oregon regions
Esoteric historic tidbits
And hundreds of other Oregon gems

Gerry's Frankly Speaking
800/692-2665 • 503/585-8411 • PO Box 2225, Salem, Oregon 97308
E-mail: gerry@teleport.com • oregonguidebook.com

Gerry Frank's
Oregon

Printed in Portland, Oregon, United States of America
by Printing Today

ISBN: 978-1-879333-23-9
First Edition, 2012

Gerry Frank's
Oregon

Gerry's Frankly Speaking, Inc.

P.O. Box 2225

Salem, OR 97308

503/585-8411

800/692-2665

email: gerry@teleport.com

oregonguidebook.com

JOHN A. KITZHABER, MD
GOVERNOR

Gerry Frank's Oregon is a must read for anyone who loves this state. Woven by Oregon's first citizen and master story teller this book is a rich fabric of practical information and fascinating details about our state and its history. In many ways Gerry Frank has become almost synonymous with Oregon and has dedicated his life to public service and to enriching our state and its people. Gerry Frank's Oregon is his latest contribution to the Oregon story.

John A. Kitzhaber, M.D.
Governor

254 STATE CAPITOL, SALEM, OR 97301-4047 (503) 378-3111 FAX (503) 378-4863
WWW.GOVERNOR.OREGON.GOV

To the reader,

Gerry Frank must know more Oregonians than just about anyone. In his years of public service and community leadership, Gerry has traveled Oregon – all of Oregon. The combination of those two facts leads us to a certain conclusion: For sure, he knows more about Oregon's best places to eat, drink, stay and play than most of the rest of us combined.

N. Christian Anderson III
President and Publisher, The Oregonian

Gerry's travels and his vast following of readers who give him tips about the good things of Oregon inform his weekly column in The Oregonian, Gerry Frank's Picks. Whether it's something as big and as well-known as the Oregon Shakespeare Festival or as small as the Oxbow Restaurant & Saloon in Prairie City, Gerry knows about it and shares his insight.

So there may be some guidebooks to Oregon, but none as comprehensive as this one. And it's not just about food and drink, though there's plenty of that. Now you know about where to buy quilts in Tillamook and how to watch a dogsled race in Wallowa County (and where to eat and stay while you're there).

All of this information comes to be shared with Oregonians and people everywhere because Gerry Frank is a cosmopolitan fellow who cares about this state and its people. He may be a big city guy – he does have a definitive guidebook to New York City, after all – but he loves all the corners of Oregon. He knows how to enjoy those places, too.

When he used to travel across the state with his friend, our former governor and Sen. Mark Hatfield, Gerry knew where to go to get a bite to eat or soak in some history and culture. We're fortunate that he's able to reflect all that knowledge so the rest of us can enjoy the bounties of Oregon as well.

Contents

Columbia Gorge and Mt. Hood 255

Central Oregon 287

Eastern Oregon 333

From the author

Dear readers, all,
and especially fellow Oregonians!

It's been my pleasure and honor to have written for *The Oregonian* for decades, and now share many of the people, places and things that I've discovered since my column has evolved into a weekly Sunday travel piece. One might say that this volume is an Oregon version of my New York guidebook, *Where to Find It, Buy It, Eat It in New York* (now in its 17th edition).

However, this book is much more personal, an amalgamation of a travel book that hopefully will help readers in and out of Oregon's many interesting nooks and crannies, as well as a personal tome of the Frank family and the former Meier & Frank department store (so entwined, separating family and department store history is almost impossible). I hope you will enjoy perusing fascinating vignettes, historical tales and legends, photographs, little-known hot spots and interesting trivia.

I am a proud fourth-generation native Oregonian (with seven generations to date) and a storied Oregon family background. I have been cajoled and asked and flat-out been demanded upon that I get something on paper. This book is a compromise, combining the fun of my *Oregonian* column and the reminisces of what turned into an eclectic life I'd not imagined as a young man.

The twists and turns that happen to everyone came as somewhat of a shock to me, especially as it related to my chosen profession. I assumed (without question) that I would follow in the footsteps of my father, my grandfather and my great-grandfather in managing the family store. This was not to be, but, as it's said, when a door closes, a window opens; sure enough, I continued to be blessed with a career that took me from Portland public schools to Stanford University, interrupted with duty-bound service with the U.S. Army Field Artillery in Europe during WWII, followed by further higher education (Bachelor and Masters) at Cambridge University in England; then, after the contentious sale of M&F, to the U.S. Senate to work with Senator Mark Hatfield as his chief of staff. I traveled abroad to some 150 countries, with off-shoots into other vocational and avocational interests.

This anthology could not have happened without my fine staff and periphery conduits. First, I must thank Linda Chase who carried the lion's share of its production. Cheryl Johnson and Linda Wooters were also integral players. Nancy Chamberlain, a fine graphic artist, fashioned the cover, and event planner Diana Miller helped lead me around the state to various book signing events. Terry Myers of Printing Today took the manuscript and made it into a book. Todd Davidson, director of Travel Oregon, kindly cooperated in several ways, including providing Oregon maps used in this book. Kris Stalnaker of Stalnakers Photo Studio expertly assisted in the reproduction of the book photo section. Last but not least, *The Oregonian*, led by editor, Peter Bhatia and presentation editors, Randy Mishler and Wesley Uno, fully cooperated with formatting and production. My sincere thanks goes to each person.

Open this book for a peek into our state, its celebrated history and that of many people who are chronicled as having a hand in it; gain appreciation for our entrepreneurial spirit and Oregon's unprecedented natural and varied beauty. Most of all, get out and enjoy this great place we call Oregon!

Gerry Frank, Author

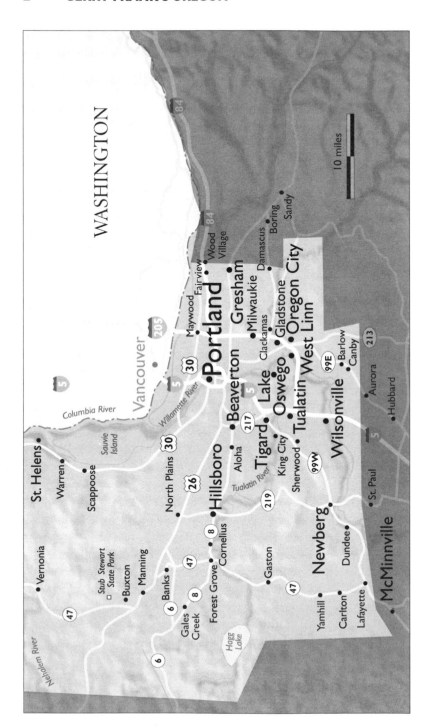

Greater
Portland

BEAVERTON

DECARLI

4545 SW Watson Ave   503/641-3223
Dinner: Tues-Sun   decarlirestaurant.com
Moderate

Jana and Paul Decarli are talented and attentive hosts at their Italian ristorante. With a wealth of cooking experience, Chef Paul creates sophisticated and rustic dishes influenced by his Swiss-Italian-American background amalgamated with Northwest fresh bounty. The daily-changing menu includes wonderful salads and pasta, meat, fish and seafood entrees. Fascinating and delicious ingredients and accompaniments turn ordinary offerings into gourmet fare. Happy hour selections and desserts receive similar treatment. The warm dining room is lighted by a large brass chandelier which, in another life, illuminated the historic Benson Hotel; private dining room available.

JIN WAH SEAFOOD RESTAURANT

4021 SW 117th Ave, Suite E   503/641-2852
Daily: 10 a.m.-10:45 p.m.

8001 SE Powell Blvd, Portland   503/788-3113
Daily: 10 a.m.-midnight   jinwah.com
Dim sum: Mon-Fri: 10-2:30; Sat, Sun: 10-3
Moderate

Indulge in Chinese or Vietnamese food at this large restaurant just off of Canyon Road. The menu is huge with plenty of noodle, rice, meat, seafood and vegetable choices. Chef's specialties, clay pot dishes and dim sum add to the dilemma of what to order.

MONTEAUX'S PUBLIC HOUSE

16165 SW Regatta Lane, #1000   503/439-9942
Lunch, Dinner: Mon-Sat   monteauxs.com
Moderate

Larry Crepeaux's pub could also be described as an international public house. Bring the entire family to this fun spot for express lunches or flavorful house favorites of étouffée, schnitzel, Mongolian beef and burgers or housemade soup and salad for lunch or dinner.   Other highlights include a burger of the week (interesting toppings and combinations), happy hour drinks and eats (don't miss the housemade corn dog or red-eye BBQ pork sliders) and more entrees and house favorites (dad's spicy meatloaf and butternut squash ravioli); many items may also be prepared gluten-free. Lest the menu get mundane, specials from around the world are highlighted each month, one region at a time (call or check website for specifics). South African, German or Australian dishes may be featured and then back home to shine the spotlight on New Orleans or Kansas City. Larry keeps his restaurant lively and folks from the 'burbs coming back for comfortable dining inside and on the fair-weather patio (well-mannered pooches welcome).

STOCKPOT BROILER

8200 SW Scholls Ferry Road   503/643-5451
Lunch, Dinner: Daily; Brunch: Sat, Sun   stockpotbroiler.com
Moderate

When you want a delicious meal, don't forget the always-busy Stockpot for an elegant lunch or dinner. Chef **Brett Tuft** features a consistently good menu using Northwest ingredients. Entree salads are filling, soups are fresh and meals are made to order. In addition to lunch sandwiches and burgers, you may enjoy a chicken and waffle entree, fish tacos and seasonal seafood pot pie. You won't be disappointed with dinner from the grill, especially the tender, flavorful steaks. On weekends, a trip to a buffet of fresh fruit, rich pastries and other treats accompanies brunch favorites like German pancakes, build-your-own omelets, duck hash and other creative vittles.

GLOBAL TYCOON

The name **Phil Knight**, the genius behind **NIKE** (nike. com), is well known and highly respected across the world, but nowhere more so than in our state and at the University of Oregon where it all began. What is not widely recognized is that Phil's father, **William "Bill" Knight**, was the long-time influential publisher of the *Oregon Journal* newspaper in Portland; in fact, he was the final publisher before the paper merged through acquisition by *The Oregonian*. The William W. Knight Law Center at the University of Oregon was named by Phil in his father's honor. (The Matthew Knight Arena is so named for the Knight's son who tragically lost his life while scuba diving.) The Knights have generously given millions to the university and a multitude of other educational and charitable organizations.

DAMASCUS

CARVER CAFE

16471 SE Hwy 224   503/658-3206
Mon-Fri: 6:30-2; Sat: 7-3; Sun: 8-3   carvercafe.com
Inexpensive

Breakfasts are the real deal at **Sarah Long** and **Kris Stafford**'s quaint restaurant. Fans of the *Twilight Saga* will recognize the 1950s-style cafe from the blockbuster flick. The Carver is particularly known for hearty early-morning meals of chicken-fried steak, crisp bacon and superb biscuits and gravy plus traditional fare and lighter options. You can count on no-nonsense burgers and other sandwiches for lunch. Commemorative *Twilight* T-shirts proclaim "I got a BITE at the Carver Cafe."

FOREST GROVE

MAGGIE'S BUNS
2007 21st Ave   503/992-2231
Mon-Fri: 6-5:30; Sat: 7-2   maggiesbuns.com

The slogan at Maggie's Buns is "Too Hot to Handle." The restaurant offers exciting full breakfast and lunch menus; breakfasts and a limited lunch menu are available on Saturday. Sandwiches are made on Maggie's freshly-baked breads, salads are healthy and tasty, the variety of homemade soups changes daily and lunch entrees run the gamut from pasta dishes to pork loin and salmon. Giant

CONTENTED COWS, HAPPY FOLKS

One of the great family names in Oregon is Cadonou, who own and operate **Alpenrose Dairy** (alpenrose.com) in southwest Portland. Since its beginning in 1891 when Florian Cadonou began delivering milk in a horse-drawn wagon, this family has provided top-quality dairy products. In 1916 during the next-generation operation that included Florian's son, Henry, who married into a family of Swiss descent, the business was officially named "Alpenrose" after the national Swiss flower. Family entertainment became an integral part of the business, including the annual Easter Egg Hunt that generations of children fondly remember; Dairyville is a replica frontier town; the Alpenrose Stadium provides baseball facilities for Little League and the girls' Little League Softball World Series; the Alpenrose Velodrome (bicycle race track) is Olympic-class and one of only 20 in the United States and a Quarter Midget Racing arena attracts speedster enthusiasts. All recreational facilities offer free admission. Based on the Alpenrose long history, effective commercials make anyone want to visit this unique family farm-and-more venture.

cinnamon buns are always served piping hot straight from the oven — as advertised. Maggie's also offers catering and specializes in corporate and wedding events. Come as you are; this is a favorite "gal pal" coffee-and-more spot.

SAKÉONE

820 Elm St   503/357-7056
Daily: 11-5   sakeone.com

This is a different kind of craft brewery. SakéOne brews saké for America, based on more than 500 years of Japanese history and traditions. Production includes six traditional ginjo rice wine sakés (premium grade, including two organic), a super-premium saké called "G Joy" and fruit-flavored infused sakés under their Moonstone brand. All are available nationally and, increasingly, internationally. In the tasting room, choose from three saké tasting flights; you will also find imported saké sets and diverse saké glasses as well as logo apparel. Enlightening guided tours are conducted daily at 1:00, 2:00 and 3:00. *Kanpai!*

GALES CREEK

OUTAZABLUE MARKET & CAFE

57625 NW Wilson River Hwy   503/357-2900
Breakfast, Lunch, Dinner: Thurs-Tues   outazablue.com
Moderate

Chef **Gabriel Barber** has chosen a tiny Washington County spot to perform his European-honed culinary talents. The menu is ambitious with everything from inspired sandwiches and wraps to pizza, pastas, burgers, steaks, fish and poultry dishes; all are attractively presented. AZA breakfasts are advertised as extraordinary; sweets and healthy breads are homemade; pizzas and calzones are fashioned on fresh pizza skins with unique ingredients. Youngsters feel grown up when they are offered a choice of kid-favorite ingredients and sauces for their special pasta dishes. Chef Gabriel says that the meaning behind OutAZABlue is "to create anything from A to Z." Catering is available off-site and for intimate on-site events. This countryside market also sources take-home organic produce, breads, meats and dairy products.

HILLSBORO

HELVETIA TAVERN

10275 NW Helvetia Road
Lunch, Dinner: Daily
Inexpensive to moderate

503/647-5286
helvetiatavern.com

Helvetia Tavern opened the day that the Prohibition Era came to a close. Decades later, beer continues to flow; domestic, imported, draft and micros by the pint or pitcher. While the rustic, rural locale is part of the draw, foremost are burgers that would make Popeye's pal Wimpy a daily customer. All burgers are made with freshly ground beef, cooked to perfection and finished with the usual fixings and special sauce (bacon, jalapenos and ham are extra). Don't pass on an order of hand-cut fries and onion rings (or both). This is a popular gathering spot for any-occasion parties and rehearsal dinners; outdoor patio for family dining; live music always brings a crowd. Check out the collection of ball caps tacked to the ceiling.

RICE NORTHWEST MUSEUM OF ROCKS AND MINERALS

26385 NW Groveland Dr
Wed-Sun: 1-5
Nominal

503/647-2418
ricenorthwestmuseum.org

This educational attraction, founded in 1953 by Richard and Helen Rice, has one of the world's best collections of crystals and petrified wood, plus a fascinating showing of fluorescent minerals. The working collection of over 20,000 specimens includes the

OFT IT'S STOTT

Julie and Peter Stott are often mentioned as one of Portland's top "power couples." Peter is a self-made, tough businessman who went from driving trucks to owning (and selling) one of the area's major trucking companies. Julie is an interior architect and a highly-talented hostess. Both are philanthropically involved community leaders, especially with Portland State University and the Portland Art Museum.

"Alma Rose" Rhodochrosite, dinosaur eggs, meteorites, an impressive chunk of gold and breathtaking exotics. Don't miss what is perhaps Oregon's largest state rock, a one-ton thunder egg. The gift shop is like no other museum outpost; high-end faceted gemstone jewelry and five-figure carvings from the Myrickite collection, as well as rare books and $1 polished stones.

SYUN IZAKAYA JAPANESE RESTAURANT AND SAKÉ CLUB

209 NE Lincoln St   503/640-3131
Lunch: Mon-Sat; Dinner: Daily   syun-izakaya.com
Moderate

Stupendous sushi is the feature at this quaint Japanese restaurant in Hillsboro's former Carnegie Library. Sushi lovers will find a large selection of dishes: raw fish, sashimi, sushi rolls and delicious daily specials. Patrons unfamiliar with the cuisine on this expansive menu are well-served by the knowledgeable and attentive staff; recommendations for food are on the mark. They'll also steer you toward fine sakés or you may opt for your familiar favorite from the full bar. Enter the brownstone under the green awning; seasonal outdoor seating.

LAKE OSWEGO

CLARKE'S RESTAURANT

455 2nd St   503/636-2667
Dinner: Mon-Sat   clarkesrestaurant.net
Expensive

Sophisticated surroundings and delicious dinners make **Laurie and Jonathan Clarke**'s upscale restaurant the go-to spot in Lake Oswego. Rack of lamb is a reliable favorite and is as good as I've tasted anywhere; lobster and shrimp risotto is also popular. Beef, fish and pork entrees are seasonally prepared to benefit from the freshest fruits, vegetables and herbs befitting this gourmet fare. Among several appetizer choices, you won't go wrong with the artisan cheese platter. The bar area is a cheerful stop for late afternoon happy hour with moderately priced casual bar grub. Banquets and private dining venues are easily accommodated.

Busy Laurie pulls double duty with her artistic celebration cake business (503/662-2533; laurieclarkecakes.com).

OSWEGO GRILL AT KRUSE WAY
7 Centerpointe Dr   503/352-4750

OSWEGO GRILL AT WILSONVILLE
30080 SW Boones Ferry Road   503/427-2152
Lunch, Dinner: Daily   oswegogrill.com
Moderate

Experienced ownership is evident with the winning ingredient of well-trained and friendly wait staff. Happy hour bargains, fresh salads, burgers, a first-rate prime rib sandwich, pot pie, the usual run of steaks and more American classics await. The hardwood grill's distinctive smoky flavor is found on the romaine lettuce salad, meats, chicken and fish with Cajun, Southwest and Thai influences spicing up the menu. Desserts like rich and gooey molten chocolate lava cake with French vanilla ice cream or just-baked warm cookies finish a tasty meal. Both locations are equally attractive and as charming as hardworking owners **Christie and David Burnett** and **Kathy and Bud Gabriel**.

TERRACE KITCHEN
485 2nd St   503/699-1136
Lunch, Dinner: Tues-Sat   terracekitchen.com
Moderate

Marlene and Fernando Divina, along with their son, Zoey, are capably behind this fine restaurant. The attractive century-old building is divided into cozy rooms (and warm weather terrace with Mt. Hood view) emanating a romantic ambience. Influenced by the family's Old and New World and Asian ancestry, the handcrafted American cuisine features favorites like scallops, pheasant, beef and in-season ingredients. Chef Fernando is known for seafood offerings; his Northwest seafood chowder is full of fish, clams and crab, a satisfying lunch especially when paired with seasonally-topped American grill bread. Monthly communal dinners (reservations required) focus on various regions or celebrations.

KIDS' ACTIVITIES: IN AND AROUND PORTLAND

Gaston

Tree to Tree Adventure Park
(503/357-0109, treetotreeadventurepark.com): seasonal

Hillsboro

Rice Northwest Museum of Rocks & Minerals
(503/647-2418, ricenwmuseum.org)

Milwaukie

North Clackamas Aquatic Park
(503/557-7873, ncprd.com/aquatic-park)

Portland

Oaks Amusement Park (503/233-5777, oakspark.com)

OMSI (503/797-4000, omsi.edu)

Oregon History Center & Museum (503/222-1741, ohs.org)

Oregon Zoo (503/226-1561, oregonzoo.org)

Portland Aerial Tram (503/494-8283, portlandtram. org)

Portland Art Museum (503/226-2811, portlandartmuseum.org)

Portland Children's Museum (503/223-6500, portlandcm.org)

Portland Public Parks (503/823-7529, portlandparks. org): Jamison Square (11th Avenue and Johnson Street) and Keller Fountain (3rd Avenue and Clay Street) are summertime favorites.

Portland Spirit Cruise (503/224-3900, portlandspirit. com)

World Forestry Center's Discovery Museum
(503/228-1367, worldforestry.org)

Sauvie Island

Sauvie Island (sauvieisland.org)

TUCCI

220 A Ave   503/697-3383
Lunch: Wed-Fri; Dinner: Daily   tucci.biz
Moderate

Tucci is a delightful casually elegant dining spot featuring modern Italian fare prepared in an open kitchen. Lunch standouts are warm spinach salad made with pancetta and heartier veal ragu (Grandma Tucci's original recipe). The evolving menu changes seasonally and features homemade pastas, quality meats, fresh seafood and local Italian-style foods; the Dungeness crab bruschetta on grilled ciabatta is superb. A late-winter menu listed roasted deboned half chicken, prawns cooked in terra cotta and lamb and beef transformed into impressive entrees with the addition of vegetables, herbs and wonderful sauces. Plates of assorted sweet bites eliminate the dilemma of dessert selection, although the salted caramel chocolate cake is difficult to resist. Private dining is accommodated in the Bacchus Room (14 to 28

AMONG THE BEST IN THE METROPOLITAN AREA

Bridal

Bridal Exclusives (8942 SE Sunnyside Road, Clackamas, 503/659-3766 and 16850 SW 72nd Ave, Tigard, 503/213-1292; bridalexclusives.com): accessories, bridesmaids dresses, trunk shows

Divine Designs (512 NW 17th Ave, Suite B, Portland, 503/827-0667; divinedesignsbridal.com): by appointment

Rosewood Bridal (11545 SW Durham Road, #B1, Tigard, 503/603-0363; rosewoodbridal.com): unique and flattering designs

Jewelers

LaRog Jewelers (9225 SW Hall Blvd, Tigard; 503/684-4824 and 13033 SE 84th Ave, Clackamas; 503/774-8991; larog. com): family-owned and -operated, full service

Margulis Jewelers (800 SW Broadway, 503/227-1153; margulis.com): original creations; repairs and examinations

guests); alfresco dining is offered in summer and artisanal Italian wines are noteworthy.

MILWAUKIE

BOB'S RED MILL WHOLE GRAIN STORE
5000 SE International Way   503/607-6455, 800/349-2173
Mon-Fri: 6-6; Sat: 7-5 (restaurant till 3)   bobsredmill.com

Charlee and Bob Moore have been grinding out flours, mixes, cereals, vegetarian-friendly products and other good-for-you eats (including gluten-free goods) since 1978. Under one roof of the 15,000 square-foot red barn is a popular retail store that features all of Bob's Red Mill foods (packaged and bulk) and culinary related items, a casual restaurant and in-house bakery. Nutritious recipes and essential techniques are taught in weekly cooking classes also emphasizing whole grains. It's mighty difficult to resist the bakery which turns out dozens of healthy breads, muffins, cookies and vegan goodies; you'll spot them on the breakfast and lunch menus as well as other choices made with Bob's products. Beautifully landscaped grounds, super products, helpful suggestions and knowledgeable employees make this a true Oregon winner. The state-of-the-art milling, packaging and distribution operations are one mile down the road (15321 SE Pheasant Court). Guests learn the ins-and-outs of the business with a smattering of the industry's history on a free tour of the facility conducted each Wednesday at 10 a.m.

DAVE'S KILLER BREAD
5209 SE International Way   503/335-8077
Mon-Fri: 7:30-6; Sat: 8-5; Sun: 9-5   daveskillerbread.com

Dedicated to baking the highest quality, best tasting, organic bakery products possible, Dave's Killer Bread, founded in 2005, has revolutionized the healthy bread industry. Raised in a bakery business, **Dave Dahl** took the wrong road one too many times and spent 15 years incarcerated. Upon his release, he desired to make a positive impact on the world and with his brother, Glenn, and nephew, Shobi, they developed this bread phenomenon. Breads are currently available in nine states at large and small retailers as well as the bakery/store location (great samples). All 16 bread varieties are vegan and packed with grains, nuts and seeds; no artificial preservatives. Not only are they nutritious, but also make fabulous toast and super sandwiches. Dave is humble, inspiring, a true role model and is helping others make a positive difference in their lives; see his motivational story on the website.

MIKE'S DRIVE-IN

3045 SE Harrison St	503/654-0131
1707 SE Tenino St, Portland	503/236-4537
905 7th St, Oregon City	503/656-5588

Daily: 10-9 (or later)
Inexpensive

When mealtime dictates a quick stop for a burger, fries and milkshake, think Mike's. Hard ice cream flavors vary during the year and are excellent as cones, sundaes, parfaits, splits and floats. Specialty sandwiches, baskets and dogs top off the menu.

OREGON CITY

THE VERDICT BAR & GRILL

110 8th St	503/305-8429
Lunch, Dinner: Daily	verdictbarandgrill.com

Moderately expensive

Owner **Ryan Smith** remodeled Oregon's oldest commercial building and created his friendly Verdict restaurant across from the Clackamas County Courthouse. The reasonably priced lunch and dinner menus are broken down as "Opening Statements" (delicious bacon-wrapped shrimp and hot artichoke dip), "Lighter Sentence" (soups and salads), "In the Jury Box" (classic sandwiches and burgers) and "Order in the Court" (fish and chips, fish tacos, pasta). "Guilty as Charged" refers to the fresh dessert options. Flat screen TVs, free Wi-Fi, hand-crafted cocktails and Oregon brews and spirits round out the docket. Smith's next door casual coffee shop, the **Caufield House**, is convenient to downtown workers for breakfast, lunch and a quick cuppa joe. Banquet and private party space are available at The Verdict and **The Holding Cell**, appropriately named for its location between the two entities.

Meier & Frank & macy*s

The year was 1857 — two years before Oregon was admitted into the Union. **Aaron Meier** opened his mercantile store in Portland, joining nine other shops that serviced a population of 1,300! By all accounts, the business should have failed, but the 26-year-old entrepreneur's store near Yamhill and Front streets thrived.

By 1873, the Frank family was integrated into the company, and the enduring store name became Meier & Frank's (later Meier & Frank Co., known as Oregon's Own Store). **Emil Frank** was a partner, but left the store in 1885, giving his brother, **Sigmund Frank** (married to Aaron Meier's only daughter, **Fannie Meier**) the opportunity for a partnership in 1885.

Tragedy struck in 1878 when a large city fire burned the store to the ground, but it was immediately rebuilt. By 1881, more space was rented giving the store walk-through space from Front to First Street. In 1885, Meier & Frank had its own more modern two-story building built on Taylor Street between First and Second. The first weekly "Friday Surprise" event was held on April 29, 1887, becoming a very popular, long-running store tradition of bargains and bargain hunting. In 1894, what is known as the Great Flood, doused the ground floor with over three feet of water; nevertheless, the store remained open and customers shopped via rowboats and raised walkways! The final location of the Portland downtown M&F was at 5th and 6th avenues between Alder and Morrison streets (now **Macy's**).

With two elevators and other mechanical efficiencies, the store was designated as "One of America's Great Stores." In a span of 40 years from its founding, the store grew by 68 times its original size to 120,000 square feet. Lewis and Clark played an important role in the store's further growth with the Lewis and Clark Centennial Exposition in 1905; thousands of people visited Portland, and M&F was there to help accommodate them with modern facilities and its famous customer service. By 1915, the store had been demolished and rebuilt on the same site to a 16-story department store (the 17th floor was added by 1932). In the early part of the 20th century, a state-of-the-art, in-store switchboard telephone system was installed, the largest in the Western United States.

During the Roaring Twenties, one of the greats of yesteryear's motion picture industry, **Clark Gable**, lived in Portland and was employed as a necktie salesman — not hard to imagine the debonair young man in this capacity. (As a sidebar, my late brother, **Dick Frank**, was color blind and he also sold neckties at M&F. One time a customer thought he was being rude when he pulled out a red tie instead of the green she had requested; she promptly reported him to the store manager, our father, Aaron Frank. It was a sort of blessing in disguise as no one previously had an inkling that Dick suffered from this anomaly.)

Other memorable men and women graced our family store with loyalty and dedication.

Vivian Cooley was one of the great M&F characters of the 20th century, a wisp of a lady who ran the book department. What a mess the stock was in that department! Only Vivian knew where every one of the thousands of books was located - she was the most sought after "bookworm" in all of Oregon!

Another, **Ed the Doorman** (as he was always known), faithfully stood at Meier & Frank's 6th Avenue entrance during the mid-1950s. He would kindly open the door, greet customers by name and dependably retrieve parked vehicles, even knowing most individuals' car make and model!

Audrey Joy was another co-worker who gained a

fine reputation for her tie-flying abilities for the sporting goods department (well known as the most extensive in the West and overseen by my brother, Dick). She was even perched in a display window so passersby could watch her craft, which proved highly popular.

Whether customers bought a single fly, a spool of thread, groceries, or a truckload of furniture, the legendary super-polite delivery men happily delivered purchases citywide in their M&F green trucks.

Speaking of green, the Green twins (Bernice and Beatrice) were beautiful young ladies and models for the store in the mid-20th century. (2011 marked their 95th birthdays — still going strong.)

Ames Hendrickson, a close family friend and effective merchant, was in charge of the housewares department, masterfully turning it into one of the largest in the nation. In those days, if housewives couldn't find what was needed here, it probably couldn't be found anywhere. He later became a senior executive for the store.

During the trying 1930's Depression era, banks were closing or on the verge of it. To show support, Meier & Frank took a full-page ad in *The Oregonian* simply stating: **CONFIDENCE** in bold letters. Even so, many people were scared and brought any cash they had, their life savings, into Meier & Frank for "safekeeping." No company in Oregon, or the people who owned it, were more trusted; that trust was rewarded with every penny being later returned to the rightful owners.

M&F served as much as a retail operation as Portland's social outlet. The Georgian Room (also known as the Tea Room) became a highly popular ladies' luncheon haven. The famous Meier & Frank Cobb salad was a standout and longtime standby (that has been resurrected in **Gerry Frank's Konditorei** in Salem).

From 1941 to 1945 with World War II at the front and center of everyone's attention, Meier & Frank was cited as the most patriotic retail operation in the country. No merchandise was advertised during this period; instead, 1,207 continuous daily full-page ads showed only support for the war and urged citizens to buy war bonds; all window displays were also devoted to the war effort.

Christmastime at Meier & Frank was a production! Many a family tradition centered around visiting the "real" Santa Claus at "Murphy & Finnegan's," the nickname moniker somehow attached to M&F; decorations could only be termed "no-holds-barred." A monorail was later installed giving kids rides around the tenth-floor ceiling. Springtime brought the flower show to the first floor where it came alive with extravagant arrangements along with one of the twice-yearly fashion shows in the store's tenth-floor auditorium.

1950 brought the prestige and notoriety of having the longest "up" and "down" escalator in the world (from the basement to the 12th floor). There was a sudden influx of customers who came just to ride the new attraction!

In December, 1955, in the midst of a Friday Surprise sale, a loud explosion rocked the men's third-floor restroom. The event coordinated with an extortion note for funds, delivered to store president, **Aaron Frank** in his office. Several attempts by authorities to make contact with the perpetrator were unsuccessful. Finally, through a State Police team and postal inspectors, the culprit was identified as blind chemist, **William Clarence Peddicord**. He was apprehended, eventually found guilty and sentenced to 20 years in the state penitentiary. This episode was the beginning of a nationwide epidemic of bombing for extortion.

Also in 1955, the first branch operation opened in Salem, which is when your author arrived in the capital city to manage the new store. The Lloyd Center store opened in 1960.

Under my watch as manager of the Salem store, we formed a family of co-workers, the result of which is too many memories to include here. I will share a few:

What first comes to mind is the annual college and back-to-school fashion shows that were anticipated with bated breath, always held on the store's rooftop. (Never once was the fashion show rained out!) In 1961, however, we staged the show at **Timberline Lodge**, touting it as the 205-mile-long fashion show with 600 collegians and the supporting audience arriving on chartered buses for the Mt. Hood "Fashion Fireside" extravaganza. The fashion show and dance, with a special free box supper provided on the bus trip to the mountain, was by ticket only. Dressed to the nines, bands and all manner of fun folderol greeted the busloads of people.

All summer long for several years, the Village Internationale was held on the patio, a conglomeration of tiny shops with everything from vitamins to spices and flowers to entertainment and food. This mini-mall was the talk of the town with people going to and from this fun event over its 91-day run.

Christmas was a magical time in Salem, too. One year, the Salem store commissioned a train to and from Albany to bring kids into Salem for the Santa Claus Parade.

The stories and treasured memories go on and on. If you lived in Oregon, particularly on the west side of the state, during the 20th century, Meier & Frank was a familiar and beloved institution. At M&F, there was no question that *the customer was always right*. Returns were accepted on their word alone. Once a customer (falsely) insisted that his dentures were purchased at the store and he was unhappy with them; at the customer's request, credit was given. Another customer's comment epitomized the policy when she errantly asked, "Where else would I have bought this?"

No longer do folks say, "I'll meet you under the clock," a phrase that referenced M&F without the store name ever being mentioned. It was located in the center of the Portland downtown store's first floor at the "up" elevator entrance, a decor item duplicated in Salem. The large clocks hung as sentinels for generations, the phrase repeated ad infinitum over the hundred-plus years of Meier & Frank's existence.

In 1966, Meier & Frank left family hands under a contentious sale to the May Co.; **Macy's** purchased the operation in 2006, and the Meier & Frank name disappeared from Oregon signage — an understandable decision, but also a sad day for the Meier and Frank families, all of our personnel and Oregonians who remain so proud of the department store's heritage. Meier & Frank Co. contributed mightily to the fabric of the communities as well as to the state of Oregon, but all things come to an end — and so it was for our family store. We are proud that Macy's is now doing its very best to re-create the famous service and selections associated with the original store.

Macy's (macys.com) and **Meier & Frank** have a long history of togetherness, with both department stores established during the mid-19th century. My late older brother, **Dick Frank**, was an intern in the Macy's Executive program, and Meier & Frank worked for decades with Macy's in overseas purchasing. Nearly 900 Macy's stores around the state and country provide outstanding values and selection, led from the top by the nation's leading retailer and CEO, **Terry Lundgren**, and his superb staff. Store locations in Oregon: Bend, Eugene, Hillsboro, Medford, North Bend, Portland (3), Roseburg, Salem (2) and Tigard; Southwest Washington: Vancouver.

PORTLAND

3 DOORS DOWN CAFÉ & LOUNGE
1429 SE 37th Ave   503/236-6886
Dinner: Tues-Sat   3doorsdowncafe.com
Moderate

This Italian sanctuary is serious about two things: wine and food. Proseco is on tap and some wines-by-the-glass are straight from the barrel. The list of imported and Northwest bottled wines, sparkling wines and champagnes is impressive; specialty cocktails are artfully composed. You can cut to the chase and order full-bodied pasta dishes and flavorful roast chicken or linger over reasonably priced antipasto, appetizers and happy hour small plates while you navigate the bar offerings. Bring this bite of Italy to your next party with group-size appetizers, entrees and desserts (arrange in advance).

23HOYT
529 NW 23rd Ave   503/445-7400
Dinner: Daily; Brunch: Sun   23hoyt.com
Moderate

Trendy New American tavern, 23Hoyt (so named for its location at 23rd and Hoyt), has a birdseye view of this hip neighborhood. The two-story front windows bathe the first floor bar and upstairs dining room in natural light. It's no secret that this is a hot spot for daily happy hour snacks (priced between $1 and $9). Segue to dinner and choose from the chef's seasonal farm-to-table menu of interesting soups and salads, housemade charcuterie and entrees accompanied by seasonal sides given an updated twist (duck fat French fries, cauliflower mousse). Brunch kicks off with eye-openers ($2 mimosas) and delivers punched up doughnut holes, lamb or beef burgers, omelets and sandwiches.

a CENA
7742 SE 13th Ave   503/206-3291
Lunch: Tues-Fri; Dinner: Daily   acenapdx.com
Expensive

Dinner at a Cena (Italian meaning come to supper) is reminiscent of an Italian country kitchen. Freshly-baked bread, pizzas and cured meats are favorites. Fabulous pasta dishes are made in-house; lasagna varieties change daily and tender ravioli are stuffed with housemade ricotta cheese. Second courses of duck, braised short ribs, lamb and seafood are equally enticing with exquisite fresh ingredients. For the finale, enjoy espresso or after-dinner coffee drinks and savor affogato, gelato or tiramisu; all desserts are made daily from scratch.

ANDINA

1314 NW Glisan   503/228-9535
Lunch, Dinner: Daily   andinarestaurant.com
Moderate to expensive

Another standout restaurant in the Pearl is a *novo* Peruvian entry celebrating the country's culture and cuisine; the space is bold, warm and beautiful and masterfully appointed to showcase the wine rack and atrium. A large menu lists various Andean tapas — meats, fish, vegetables and cheeses. Plates are offered in three sizes — small, medium or large, to savor or share. You won't be disappointed with the extensive wine list (Northwest, Spanish, South American) and imaginative cocktails served in the lounge or dining room. Gussied-up family recipes and traditional entrees are served for lunch and dinner; each presentation is a visual masterpiece. Meat and fish headliners are deliciously married with herbs, spices, quinoa and sundry elements creating unforgettable flavors as demonstrated with the double rack of lamb served with a Peruvian potato side and roasted pepper demi-glace. The wait staff is knowledgeable and gracious; their Spanish pronunciation of menu items is music to my ears.

BAR MINGO

811 NW 21st Ave   503/445-4646
Sun-Thurs: 4-11; Fri, Sat: 4-midnight   barmingonw.com
Moderate

Looking for a bar that specializes in casual Italian fare? Look no further than Bar Mingo for a daily happy hour with specials between 4 and 6. There are plenty of easy-priced hot and cold sharable plates. Substantial dinner choices are listed on the giant chalkboard featuring several fresh pasta dishes. This attractive

---

PORTLAND FAST BREAKS

Boyd's Coffee (19730 Northeast Sandy Blvd, 503/666-4545; boyds.com)

Steven Smith Teamaker (1626 NW Thurman St, 503/719-8752; smithtea.com)

Stumptown Coffee (128 SW 3rd Ave, 503/295-6144; 4525 SE Division St, 503/230-7702; 3356 SE Belmont St, 503/232-8889 and 1026 SW Stark, 503/224-9060; stumptowncoffee.com)

Voodoo Doughnut (22 SW 3rd Ave, 503/241-4704 and 1501 NE Davis, 503/235-2666; voodoodoughnut.com): dozens of varieties (weird names, combinations and shapes); worldwide following

---

watering hole offers sidewalk seating, perfect on warm evenings. Come early, it is always crowded!   Next door, **Caffe Mingo** (503/226-4646) is open daily for dinner with comforting pizzas and calzones.

BEACHES RESTAURANT AND BAR
Portland International Airport
7000 NE Airport Way   503/335-8385
Daily: 5 a.m.-11 p.m.   beachesrestaurandandbar.com
Moderate

Beaches serves innovative and satisfying meals at the Portland airport.   Owner/operator **Mark Matthias** has a superbly trained wait staff that operates efficiently and makes customers feel welcome.   The Asian-, American-, Italian- and Mexican-influenced menu has something for everyone's taste (Molten Smokin' S'Mores are my favorite sweet temptation) including an inexpensive kids' menu. The long hours accommodate travelers' breakfast, lunch and dinner appetites; breakfast is offered all day, ideal for coping with jet lag. If you're in a hurry, stop by their quick-service **Beach Shack** (5 a.m.-9 p.m.) on the airport's main concourse for to-go food to take aboard your flight. Both outlets have delicious options and marvelous caramel corn that is made fresh daily. The main Beaches location is on the Columbia River in Vancouver (1919 SE Columbia River Drive, 360/699-1592).

BEAKER & FLASK

727 SE Washington St   503/235-8180
Mon-Sat: 5-11   beakerandflask.com
Moderate

   The name perfectly describes this bustling enterprise. If it is mixed in a beaker or poured from a flask, chances are that it is served at this bar. Cocktails are imaginative, as are their monikers. Requisite bar food is not the usual deep-fried variety. Drink accompaniments may include chicken liver mousse, smoked beef short rib, or black lentil salad small plates. Large-plate entrees emphasize meats and fish paired with sometimes unlikely ingredients, resulting in unique flavor combinations. Cheers!

BEAST

5425 NE 30th Ave   503/841-6968
Dinner: Wed-Sat; Brunch: Sun   beastpdx.com
Expensive

   If you've had a beast of a week, a relaxing dinner or brunch at BEAST restaurant may just be what the doctor prescribes. It is best to plan ahead if you want a table; diners are offered a choice of two seatings (6 p.m. or 8:45 p.m.) four nights a week for a six-course *prix-fixe* menu (one menu for the week; substitutions politely declined). Scrumptious meals are inspired by fresh and intriguing ingredients from local sources; the charcuterie plate (braised duck, beef cheeks, terrines) is generous and immensely flavorful. Main courses are at the chef's whim according to the season and varying cuts from whole lambs, pigs and other beasts. Vegetable garnishes and accompaniments are oh-so-good. Special dinners are offered twice each month including vegetarian meals and meals with special cocktail pairings. Cheese and dessert courses warrant saving room and wine pairings are carefully chosen to best complement each course. Four-course Sunday brunches (10 a.m. or noon) are similarly composed. What a feast!

THE BENSON HOTEL

309 SW Broadway   503/228-2000, 800/663-1144
Moderate and up   bensonhotel.com

The Benson is one of Portland's most elegant landmarks where guests are greeted by debonair doormen. Since 1913 it has been the "residence of the presidents," graciously accommodating each U.S. president from William Howard Taft to Barack Obama (and many celebrities, too). The AAA four-diamond property features original Austrian crystal chandeliers, Italian marble floors and now-extinct Circassian walnut imported from the forests of Imperial Russia. Guests unwind in 287 sophisticated rooms and suites. Tempur-Pedic beds are standard in most rooms; specially designed eight-foot pillow-top mattresses are optional in select rooms and suites. Luxurious amenities include organic bamboo bathrobes and slippers, umbrellas, in-room safes and modern technology (complimentary Wi-Fi, flat-screen HDTV, dual-line speakerphones and iPod docking system). Lavish ballrooms have been the scene of memorable soirees for Portland's elite and the setting for impressive business meetings. Upscale **El Gaucho** steakhouse offers old-school tableside service perfect for special occasions while **The Palm Court Restaurant and Lobby Bar** offers a sumptuous breakfast buffet, lunch and dinner as well as happy hours and weekend live entertainment. Exemplary accommodations and service are first-class.

A bit of history: **Simon Benson** broke ground on the Oregon Hotel in 1912, which opened in 1913, and changed the name to The Benson Hotel in 1914. An innovative lumberman, he is also remembered for his public service and philanthropy. One such act was his $10,000 donation to the city to install 20 bronze drinking fountains around town, also known as the iconic **Benson Bubblers**, which still grace Portland's city streets.

BLUEHOUR

250 NW 13th Ave   503/226-3394
Lunch: Mon-Fri; Dinner: Daily   bluehouronline.com
Expensive

Portland restaurateur **Bruce Carey** has made an indelible imprint on the local dining scene. Five diverse restaurants (23Hoyt,

Saucebox, Clarklewis, Via Tribunali) are in his current portfolio with Bluehour wowing patrons for the past dozen years. The setting is modern yet intimate; there is casual fare at the bar, superb dinners in the dining room and a private room for group occasions. To capture the essence of seasonal Northwest bounty, the classic Mediterranean-inspired menu changes daily. Expect terrines, salads, pastas, fish and seafood, pork belly and more. "Happy Bluehour" eats are interesting and range from blue cheese stuffed olives to charcuterie and the signature burger. You can't go wrong with the assorted chocolates for dessert. Keep up the great work, Bruce!

BUFFALO GAP SALOON & EATERY

6835 SW Macadam Ave   503/244-7111
Daily: 7 a.m.-2:30 a.m. (open Sat at 8 a.m., Sun at 9 a.m.)   thebuffalogap.
com
Moderate

Every neighborhood deserves a place like the Gap: fun, laid-back, long open hours, consistently good food and a jam-packed menu. Breakfast choices are hearty (pork chop with eggs and Hang Town frittata) or sensible (fresh fruit and yogurt parfait). Soups are made from scratch; specialty salads are indeed special and laden with lots of tasty ingredients and intriguingly named sandwiches and burgers are served with a choice of sides. Not to be overlooked are the pizza, pasta and full-meal-deal dinner platters. There's plenty of seating inside and out, upstairs and down, live music Tuesday through Saturday nights, billiards and every saloon beverage you can think of.

CASTAGNA RESTAURANT

1752 SE Hawthorne Blvd   503/231-7373
Dinner: Wed-Sat
Expensive

CAFÉ CASTAGNA

Dinner: Daily   503/231-9959
Moderate   castagnarestaurant.com

Thank you, **Monique Siu**, for creating one of my favorite fine dining houses in Portland. Elegantly presented courses take center stage in this sleek, modern establishment where service reigns supreme. Choose from *prix-fixe* or tasting menus with optional wine pairings, a la carte options are also available. The chef defines the cuisine as "seasonal and progressive" with unexpected twists created by incorporating uncommon ingredients. Next door, Café Castagna offers casual renditions of sandwiches, pasta, pizza, steak and a three-course dinner. Seasonal outdoor dining is delightful; restaurant reservations are recommended (cafe reservations for groups of five or more).

CHRISTIE'S RESTAURANT

5507 N Lombard   503/289-6111
Breakfast, Lunch, Dinner: Daily   christiesofportland.com
Moderate

North Portland has a reliable neighborhood diner serving family-favorite meals made from scratch with the finest ingredients. It's no wonder that folks line up for award-winning weekend breakfasts. The draws are French toast variations (New Orleans-style with strawberries and whipped cream, toffee bark, caramel apple), omelets and scrambles that are made with everything but the kitchen sink; all are served until 2 p.m. Light or hearty lunches are under $10 — healthy salads, homemade soups, pasta and over 20 specialty sandwiches and gourmet burgers (also available for dinner). The transformation to dinner brings fancier comfort fare — beef stroganoff, meatloaf, salmon, scampi and pasta dishes. Bring the kids (milkshakes are made with real ice cream) or friends and relax on the patio with your four-legged best friend and a selection from the full-service bar.

DAN & LOUIS OYSTER BAR

208 SW Ankeny St   503/227-5906
Lunch, Dinner: Daily   danandlouis.com
Moderate to expensive

Five generations of the Wachsmuth family have been shucking oysters at this landmark since 1907. A prominent green and red striped awning over the gleaming brass and glass front doors and large windows frame the interior. What to eat? Oysters, of course — on the half-shell, Rockefeller, in stew, as a sandwich, broiled, fried or combined with other fresh seafood. A specialty of the house is cioppino which blends the best of the ocean: fresh fish, mussels, clams, prawns and calamari in a delicious broth. For decades, this has been a go-to restaurant for client dinners, company parties and celebrations. The future looks strong for the next generation.

POTPOURRI OF ATTRACTIONS

Among Portland's myriad attractions, here are a few of my favorites:

International Rose Test Garden (850 SW Rose Garden Way, 503/227-7033, rosegardenstore.org/thegardens): beautiful in bloom; fragrant

Lan Su Chinese Garden (239 NW Everett St, 503/228-8131, lansugarden.org): traditional

Pittock Mansion (3229 NW Pittock Dr, 503/823-3623, pittockmansion.org): 1914 home of Henry and Georgiana Pittock; tours

Portland Japanese Garden (611 SW Kingston Ave, 503/223-1321, japanesegarden.com): authentic

Portland Saturday Market (North Waterfront Park & Ankeny Plaza, 503/222-6072, portlandsaturdaymarket.com): outdoor arts and crafts market, March through Dec. 24

THE DAPPER FROG

915 NW Davis St   503/224-4000
Mon-Fri: 10-6 (Sun till 5); Sat: 9-6   dapperfrog.com

Since it has been open, your author has frequently wandered in and out of The Dapper Frog at **The Shops at Salishan**. Their latest outpost is in Portland which brings a new dimension to the array of galleries in the Pearl District. The high-quality, large and eclectic mix of fun pieces for the home or office is enjoyable to peruse. Displays are eye-appealing, whimsical and showcase critters (including frogs), collectibles, functional items, jewelry, teaware, prints, figurines and home decor. Works by artists from Oregon and around the world are made of art glass, ceramic, wood and more. Other alluring locally-owned and -operated Dapper Frog shops are in Dundee, Pacific City and Newport.

EL GAUCHO PORTLAND

The Benson Hotel
319 SW Broadway   503/227-8794
Dinner: Daily   elgaucho.com
Expensive

Impress your clients or main-squeeze with an extraordinary evening at El Gaucho where no detail is overlooked. The well-orchestrated exhibition kitchen is in full swing turning out melt-in-your-mouth dry-aged prime steaks, meats, poultry, seafood and poultry expertly prepared on a charcoal grill or rotisserie. Elaborate tableside preparations include Caesar salad, carved chateaubriand, sirloin or porterhouse. The showmanship continues with flaming swords of brochettes of tenderloin or lamb shish kabobs. Flambéed desserts of Bananas Foster and cherries jubilee turn any occasion into a special occasion. A nice touch: a fruit and cheese dish served "on the house" after your table finishes their entrees. Enjoy nightly live music in the bar or retire to the clubby **Cigar Lounge** for single malt scotches, after-dinner drinks and imported cigars from the humidor. The tab will be pricey, but when only the best will do…

FILSON

526 NW 13th Ave   503/246-0900
Mon-Sat: 10-6; Sun: 12-6   filson.com

Since 1897, "might as well be the best" is the creed and motto that this company has lived up to. The recreational outdoorsman and -woman or those whose profession puts them in the elements will find high-quality clothing and accessories at Filson's flagship store. Customized orders are available to fit any body type. If you have a favorite Filson garment that has been discontinued, it may still be replaceable; boots and shoes can be re-soled, along with other garment repairs (contact customer service; 866/860-8906). Filson luggage can proudly be handed down for generations. Only the finest from Filson for canines, too: coats, beds, car seat covers, leashes and even dog dishes are made from Filson's proprietary Tin Cloth.

FINK'S LUGGAGE & REPAIR CO.
517 SW 12th Ave   503/222-6086
Mon-Fri: 8:30-6; Sat: 9-5

For over 40 years, travelers have been outfitted with Fink's savvy packing products. Luggage brands in every price range, wallets, briefcases, handbags and other travel necessities are offered, plus outstanding repair service, knowledgeable staff and personal attention. **Alex Fink** and crew repair all makes of luggage and leather jackets, replace linings, recondition leather items and work magic on handbags and briefcases. Service, service, service — they are the best!

FOSTER & DOBBS
2518 NE 15th Ave   503/284-1157
Mon-Sat: 10-8; Sun: 11-6   fosteranddobbs.com

Luan Schooler and **Tim Wilson** oversee a delightful spot in the Irvington District which features artisanal foods and products. You'll find superb European and domestic cheeses and cured meats, as well as sandwiches and charcuterie platters accompanied by craft beers and wine. Other fine groceries

---

PETAL POWER IN THE ROSE CITY

Portland's century-plus-old **Rose Festival** (rosefestival.org) was named the Best Festival in the World in 2011. This annual celebration is a source of pride and community spirit that brings millions of dollars to Portland and surrounding communities. The event kicks off each year in March with court selections from city high schools with one of the princesses being named Queen of Rosaria at the highly-anticipated coronation event. Fun runs and walks, the Starlight Parade, dragon boat and milk carton boat races, fireworks, Naval fleet participation, the Junior Parade and many more activities make up the four-month celebration, culminated, for all intents and purposes, with the fantastic Grand Floral Parade. Jeff Curtis is the able chief executive officer — and it's a big job!

include breads, crackers, condiments, pastas, grains, sauces, sweets, meats and fish and essential ingredients for a well-stocked kitchen. Buster's Biscuits are a grain-free treat for canines and felines made especially for Foster & Dobbs; each batch offers a unique flavor. Generous samples, weekly wine tastings and classes are excellent introductions to the bounty in this gourmand's paradise.

GARTNER'S COUNTRY MEAT MARKET

7450 NE Killingsworth St   503/252-7801
Tues-Sat: 9-6; Sun: 10-4   gartnersmeats.com

More than 50 years ago, Jack Gartner opened his butcher shop with the mission statement of "People come for what's inside the case. They come back for the service behind the counter." From Jack's parents to his children, they all pitched in over the years; **Jerry Minor** came on as a business partner in 1965. The company has passed along generationally and today **Sheri Gartner Puppo** and **Rick Minor** (the "kids") continue the operation with the same commitment. It's a busy and popular spot for always-fresh beef, pork, poultry, lunch meats and cheeses along with Traeger grills and pellets for just-right barbecuing; custom cutting and game processing are also offered. Three smokehouses turn out the best sausages (many also fresh or unsmoked), hams, bacon and specialties.

GENOA

2832 SE Belmont St   503/238-1464
Dinner: Tues-Sun   genoarestaurant.com
Expensive

Classic! Award-winning! Elegant! For over 40 years Genoa has wowed customers with elaborate multi-course dinners and has propelled talented chefs onto celebrated careers. In 2008, Chef **David Anderson** stepped in to make a good thing even better. Gourmet *prix-fixe* dinners are now five courses, updated to reflect his interpretation of traditional, pescatarian and vegetarian menus. Genoa's emphasis continues in the Italian vein integrating seasonal Northwest delicacies. Fine wines are primarily French and Italian labels with a few Oregon varietals selected by sommelier/manager **Michael Garofola**. Today's Genoa continues the reputation as a special occasion destination.

GILDA'S ITALIAN RESTAURANT

1601 SW Morrison St   503/224-0051
Lunch: Mon-Fri; Dinner: Daily   gildasitalianrestaurant.com
Moderate

Grandma Gilda's home cooking influenced chef-owner **Marco Roberti** to pursue his passion for Italian food and entertaining. That enthusiasm led him to Italy where he immersed himself in cuisine, culture and cooking family dishes with his aunts and cousins, ultimately earning his master's degree in Italian Culinary Arts. With those experiences under his belt, he returned to Portland with the goal of owning a restaurant featuring his beloved grandmother's signature family dishes. Daily fare includes meatball paninis (lunch), various pasta and risotto dishes and meat, poultry and fish entrees prepared with the finest ingredients. If *braciole* is on the menu, by all means, order this flavorful stuffed beef roll; desserts are interesting and delicious. Gilda's Old World specialties will leave you satisfied and enamored with this family business.

GOOSE HOLLOW INN

1927 SW Jefferson St   503/228-7010
Daily: 11 a.m.-midnight (Fri, Sat till 1 a.m.)   goosehollowinn.com
Inexpensive

The history of the Goose Hollow Inn is as interesting as its proprietor, **Bud Clark**, Portland's colorful mayor between 1985 and 1992. Bud's first tavern venture was the Spatenhaus (which was replaced by the Ira Keller Fountain). Spatenhaus' limited menu was largely inspired by customers' favorites and suggestions. The soul and simplicity of those days has been retained as Goose Hollow has evolved to match today's modern palates and interests. The Reuben sandwich is still referred to as "the best on the planet," meats are cooked on premise and frying is not an option. Soups are homemade and fresh as are the salads (crab and shrimp Louis, spinach) with homemade dressings. Hard liquor and wine join the lineup of a baker's dozen of beers on tap. Outside, the Portland Timbers Army has found a welcome watering hole on the deck; inside, framed historical photos and posters add to the cabin atmosphere. Bud's other notorieties are his enthusiastic "Whoop, Whoop" greeting and as the trench coat-clad model for an infamous poster entitled *Expose Yourself to Art*.

BIG MAC

Portland's **Multnomah Athletic Club** (themac.com) is the largest (in terms of membership) private athletic club in the world. With over 20,000 members and eight levels encompassing 550,000 square feet over a two-block area, this facility offers three pools; multiple tennis, handball and racquetball courts; three gyms (one for rock climbing); an indoor track; batting cage; exercise rooms; three restaurants, private dining, a grand ballroom and more. The MAC has been a focal point of the city since 1891; by invitation, non-members are always welcome for dining and at the many social and political events held at the club. The location overlooking **Jeld-Wen Field** (jeldwenfield.com) — home of the **Portland Timbers** (portlandtimbers.com) — offers special stadium views. Although membership is at capacity, periodic admission lotteries are held. Prima Chef **Philippe Boulot**, long associated with the dining room at **The Heathman Hotel** (heathmanhotel.com), oversees the exceptional club food operations.

GRAND CENTRAL BAKERY

2230 SE Hawthorne Blvd	503/445-1600
3425 SW Multnomah Blvd	503/977-2024
Mon-Fri: 7-7; Sat, Sun: 7-6	

1444 NE Weidler St	503/288-1614
7987 SE 13th	503/546-3036
714 N Fremont	503/546-5311
Daily: 7-6	

2249 NW York	503/808-9860
Mon-Fri: 6:30-4; Sat, Sun: 7-4	grandcentralbakery.com

These artisan bakeries are conveniently situated around town and at local farmers markets. They craft breads to perfection: crusty on the outside, chewy on the inside and are at their prime when eaten warm and generously buttered. Muffins, croissants, fruit tarts, cookies, pies and cakes are sweet choices; purchase one or be a hero and bring treats for the office. Ingredients for all breads and pastries are natural and top-quality. All locations serve sandwiches for breakfast and lunch, from-scratch soups, salads and seasonal specials; sack lunches are a specialty. Busy home cooks get a helping hand with balls of U-Bake pizza dough, rolls of puff pastry, pre-formed cookie dough and disks of pie dough ready to be transformed into "homemade" meals and desserts.

GRÜNER

527 SW 12th Ave   503/241-7163
Lunch: Mon-Fri; Dinner: Mon-Sat   grunerpdx.com
Moderate

Hearty eaters are always on the lookout for German restaurants, where portions are usually large and the food filling. Grüner is no exception. Talented Chef **Chris Israel** has been involved with a number of restaurant reincarnations and now assembles an attractive array of snacks, appetizers, salads and entrees. I particularly like the Liptauer cheese, radish, celery and pretzel croutons nibble; if the butternut squash soup is on the menu, go for it. It's tough to choose from so many delicious main dishes: housemade sausages, unusual roasted trout stuffed with all manner of vegetables and a touch of red wine sauce, beef goulash and what every true German appetite loves — späetzle (with braised chicken and mushrooms).

THE HEATHMAN HOTEL

1001 SW Broadway   503/241-4100, 800/551-0011
Expensive and up   heathmanhotel.com

HEATHMAN RESTAURANT & BAR

Breakfast, Lunch, Dinner: Daily; Brunch: Sat, Sun   503/790-7752
Moderate

Service is still an art at this luxurious downtown property. Built in 1927, for the past 26 years The Heathman has earned four diamonds from AAA. This independently-owned 150-room luxury boutique hotel recently completed a $4 million landfill-free "green" restoration and is a proud member of Preferred Hotel Group as well as Historic Hotels of America. The classically-elegant guest rooms are tastefully furnished with modern accents, technology and amenities; a full array of upscale services is offered including a floor dedicated to guests with four-legged companions. Exquisite artwork is exhibited throughout the building; works from the Vanderbilt Estate grace the charming Tea Court. Unbeknownst to many Portlanders, overnight guests of the property have access to a cataloged lending library of books signed by author-guests. **Heathman Restaurant & Bar** Executive Chef **Michael Stanton** blends fresh-daily Northwest cuisine into elegant meals. The menu changes to accommodate seasonal choices and may offer bouillabaisse, local beef, pork, poultry, fish and seafood — all prepared with panache. Casual fare is served in the Marble Bar, Tea Court (live jazz Wednesday through Saturday evenings) and seasonal sidewalk cafe. Culture and beauty permeate the ten-story brick landmark under the leadership of talented GM **Chris Erickson**.

HILTON PORTLAND & EXECUTIVE TOWER

921 SW 6th Ave   503/226-1611
Moderate and up   hilton.com

BISTRO 921

Breakfast, Lunch, Dinner: Daily   503/220-2685
Moderate   bistro-921.com

PORTO TERRA TUSCAN GRILL & BAR

830 SW 6th Ave   503/944-1090
Breakfast, Lunch, Dinner: Daily   portoterra.com
Moderately expensive

Your author has spent many a night away from home as a guest in this downtown hotel. The management and staff are wonderful ambassadors — cheerful, helpful and provide quick service. That is no small feat considering this is Oregon's largest hotel; 782 rooms in two separate buildings. The main building was constructed in 1963 and was remodeled in 2006. The on-site restaurant, **Bistro 921**, offers casual American fare; the lounge remains open until 11 p.m. (midnight on weekends). Across the street is the Executive Tower which was completed in 2002, the rooms are more contemporary and spacious with business king suites outfitted with a printer/copier/fax/scanner. **Porto Terra Tuscan Grill**

& Bar is the Tower's diners' choice for traditional breakfasts and Italian lunches and dinners; lounge until midnight. Both entities offer underground self- or valet-parking, complimentary fitness center with pool and free Wi-Fi in the lobbies. All guest rooms and suites are equipped with 37-inch HDTVs, work desks, luxurious bath amenities and coffeemakers. Elegant ballrooms and more intimate conference rooms accommodate momentous meetings and informal occasions; the incredible staff will work magic to make your event memorable.

HOTEL MONACO PORTLAND

506 SW Washington St   503/222-0001, 888/207-2201
Expensive   monaco-portland.com

   Spend a luxurious night in downtown amid museums, boutiques and large shops, amazing restaurants, nightclubs and entertainment. A vibrant, ornate lobby, the site of morning coffee and tea service, greets guests at this Kimpton Hotel property. Each of the 221 rooms and suites are awash with a tasteful assortment of colorful furnishings and Italian Frette linens atop deep pillow top beds. Classy French doors separate sleeping and living areas in the roomy suites, a nice touch when enjoying in-room spa services. Standard conveniences include flat-panel TVs, private mini-bars, personal

---

LAND GRANT

   The spectacular setting of **Lewis & Clark College** (lclark.edu) in Portland is a twisted tale within the Frank family. The **Frank Manor House** and surrounding grounds was once the home of **Lloyd Frank** (brother to my father, **Aaron Frank**), designed by famous architect **Herman S. Brookman** and built in 1924. The short version is that Aaron acquired the property due to troubled family circumstance and in a show of generosity, **Fir Acres**, as the 63-acre estate was called, was more or less gifted (sold at a rock-bottom price) in the early 1940s to the college (originally Albany College). The Manor House, looking to southwest Portland and Mt. Hood, now serves as the president's and other administrative offices.

coffeemakers, laptop compatible safes and fun animal print bathrobes. Complimentary to guests are a hosted evening wine reception, 24/7 fitness center, newspapers, morning coffee in the lobby and use of bicycles (seasonal). Guests with four-legged companions are welcome on the pet-friendly floor with special services. Adjacent to the Monaco, **Red Star Tavern & Roast House** (503/222-0005, redstartavern.com) provides round-the-clock room service; but to experience the Portland vibe, head on over for phenomenal American cuisine and impressive scotch and bourbon selections.

HOTEL VINTAGE PLAZA

422 SW Broadway   503/228-1212, 800/263-2305
Expensive   vintageplaza.com

PAZZO RISTORANTE

627 SW Washington   503/228-1515
Breakfast, Lunch, Dinner: Daily; Brunch: Sat, Sun   pazzo.com
Moderately expensive

PAZZORIA BAKERY & CAFE

625 SW Washington
Mon-Fri: 7-4; Sat, Sun: 9-3   pazzo.com

Luxury and romance go hand in hand at this Kimpton hotel. Guest rooms and suites feature custom furnishings, private bars and mini-refrigerators, modern touches and views of the City of Roses. Unique accommodations include rooms with overhead conservatory windows to allow stargazing; rooms with two-person Fuji-style jetted tubs and three rooms have private balconies with two-person hot tubs. The 1,000 square foot townhouse suite affords privacy in the upstairs bedroom with jetted tub; a separate living and entertainment area is on the first floor. A second two-story suite connects the floors with a spiral staircase and includes a dining area. Enhance your experience with in-room spa services or room service during restaurant hours. **Pazzo Ristorante** is exceptional; Italian cuisine is influenced by the best Northwest flavors for breakfast, lunch, dinner and weekend brunch. The brick pizza oven is behind many of the delicious choices. The casual **Pazzoria Bakery & Cafe** is ideal for a quick bite in the morning or for lunch, coffee to-go or baked goodies.

HUBER'S CAFE

411 SW 3rd Ave   503/228-5686
Lunch: Mon-Sat; Dinner: Daily   hubers.com
Moderate

Huber's was established in 1879 and is Portland's oldest-operating restaurant. The original location was at the corner of First and Alder and named The Bureau Saloon; this domain with a magnificent arched leaded-glass ceiling is on the ground floor of the Historic Oregon Pioneer Building. The history is an interesting read and stars **Frank Huber**, **Jim Louie**, turkey sandwiches, Prohibition and Spanish Coffee. The latest chapter of Huber's continues the Louie family's involvement, a tradition of turkey (sandwiches and turkey cuisine are prominent on the menu) and Spanish Coffee (the signature drink) is still prepared tableside. Each week about 1,000 pounds of roasted turkey is served as entrees (picatta, marsala, enchiladas, wings, drumsticks) along with salads made with organic field greens, Certified Angus Beef steaks, seafood and pasta. Interesting fact: Huber's uses more Kahlua than any other independent restaurant in the United States.

CELEBRATED ATHLETICISM

The **Oregon Sports Hall of Fame** (oregonsportshall.org) honors Oregon's sports arena greats. From auto racing to wrestling with 30 other sports and related athletic contributions in between, this museum has come a long way since its 1978 inception; however, it is currently looking for a new bricks and mortar home in the Portland metro area where the achievements of Schollander, Baker, Prefontaine, Fosbury, Salazar, Drexler, Sitton, Walton, Schonely, Jacobsen and many others will again be publically showcased for all time. The museum is dedicated to education and continues to award collegiate scholarships annually. The underlying message that hard work and dedication reaps benefits for any life path is at the heart of this organization.

IRVING ST. KITCHEN

701 NW 13th Ave   503/343-9440
Dinner: Daily; Brunch: Sat, Sun   invingstreetkitchen.com
Moderate

Joining the Pearl District's growing list of eateries is Irving St. Kitchen for New American cuisine. The space is large and airy; nice weather brings outdoor dining. Interesting snacks along with a reasonably priced mix of charcuterie are good meal-starters; there are about a dozen delicious first courses like meatballs with Yukon Gold mashed potatoes and sauce au poivre, barbecued shrimp or a tasty Bibb lettuce salad with Rogue blue cheese dressing. For the main course, Draper Valley fried chicken is a standout, as is the olive oil-baked Alaskan halibut (seasonal). Desserts are inspired, including the butterscotch pudding with sherry caramel sauce and the molasses whoopie pie and ice cream. Waiters leave attitude at the door and there is enough space to carry on conversation.

JAKE'S FAMOUS CRAWFISH

401 SW 12th Ave   503/226-1419
Lunch: Mon-Sat; Dinner: Daily   jakesfamouscrawfish.com
Moderate to expensive

I love Jake's crawfish! Just the thought makes my mouth water! If I've set my heart on a big 1½-pound bowl of the freshwater crustaceans boiled in a spicy broth, I call ahead to make sure they are fresh and on the menu (the season is roughly Easter to Halloween). Other delicious preparations are in pasta, cooked and chilled, Cajun-style or "popcorn" fried tails. The best, however, is the famous live crawfish boil. Lunch and dinner menus are printed daily to reflect the freshest bivalves, seafood and steaks; fresh catch is listed with the source of origin. Check out the daily Blue Plate lunch special and catch of the day priced at $8.95. Jake's clam chowder is legendary and you can't go wrong with a fabulous crab or shrimp cocktail or salad for lunch or dinner; sandwiches (turkey, crab, shrimp, chicken) are served for lunch. Dinner steaks are superb with the option of adding a lobster tail or jumbo scampi prawns to create a surf and turf combo to your liking. Chocolate truffle cake and bread pudding with bourbon *anglaise* have become famous in the dessert department. If you want just a bite, consider

Jake's dessert trio with mini-portions of berry cobbler, truffle cake and a cream puff. The bar is a very popular downtown after-work watering hole and this hot-spot is a supreme venue for groups and banquets. Jake's has rightfully earned a spot in the top ten seafood restaurants in America and has been a Portland fixture since 1892.

JOY'S UPTOWN STYLE
1627 NW Glisan St   503/223-3400
Mon-Fri: 10-6; Sat: 10-5   joysuptown.com

Joy Walker has an eye for fashion, especially mother-of-the-bride (or groom) dresses and formal attire. Most ensembles may be ordered in a full spectrum of brilliant or subdued colors. An expert seamstress can take a tuck here or there, reposition buttons, raise hemlines or modify sleeves and collars to customize the piece for the desired look. Just as attractive are the unique and classy daytime, casual fashions and accessories that fill the lovely boutique. The seemingly lost art of personalized customer service is superb!

KENNY & ZUKE'S DELICATESSEN
1038 SW Stark St   503/222-3354
Mon-Thurs: 7 a.m.-8 p.m.; Fri: 7 a.m.-9 p.m.;
Sat: 8 a.m.-9 p.m.; Sun: 8-8   kennyandzukes.com

There are delis, then there is Kenny & Zuke's! They arguably have the best pastrami sandwich in town, made with brisket that is cured for a week, smoked for ten hours and steamed for three hours. It is served between slices of housemade rye bread on toast, or with chopped liver and cole slaw. The most popular version is a glorious Reuben with sauerkraut, Swiss cheese and Russian dressing, then grilled and served with K&Z's pickles and potato salad. Other hearty hot and cold sandwiches round out the lunch and dinner menu — meatloaf, pot roast and create-your-own double deckers. There's much more: smoked and pickled fish, noodle kugel, rugelach, Sabrett hot dogs, burgers and fries, salads and homemade desserts. Breakfasts feature deli case meats with eggs, bagels or in omelets as well as latkes, blintzes and weekend

Benedicts and biscuits. Eat in, take out, rent the deli for your private event or arrange for the crew to cater your party; any way you slice it, this place is a winner.

KEN'S ARTISAN BAKERY

338 NW 21st Ave   503/248-2202
Mon-Sat: 7-6; Sun: 8-5

KEN'S ARTISAN PIZZA

304 SE 28th Ave   503/517-9951
Mon: 5 p.m.–9 p.m.; Tues-Sat: 5 p.m.–10 p.m.;   kensartisan.com
Sun: 4 p.m.–9 p.m.

Boulangerie and patisserie proprietor, **Ken Forkish**, has honed his craft as an artisan baker exceptionally well and has justifiably been recognized in the local and national media for his rustic breads and luscious pastries. The latter are jaw-dropping creative works of art, handmade with real butter, fresh fruits, rich chocolate and other fine ingredients. Lunch fare (sandwiches, soups, salads) is served in the cafe (11-3) in addition to the anytime bakery items and coffee drinks. Ken thoroughly researched flours and settled upon a local, sustainable product for his breads, croissants and pizzas. The popular pizzas are a Monday night (5:30-9:30) offering at the bakery. A separate pizzeria was opened to accommodate the demand for the Italian pies — thin, crisp and baked in a wood-fired oven. You'll find Ken's breads on the tables of some of Portland's best restaurants and at select retailers. For the best selection, visit the bakery.

LAURELHURST MARKET

3155 E Burnside St   503/206-3097
Restaurant: Dinner: Daily: 5-10
Moderate

Butcher shop: Daily: 10-10   503/206-3099
                                                    laurelhurstmarket.com

Don't be misled by this enterprise's name; it is not where you shop for eggs, butter or bread. Most of the day it is a first-rate butcher shop featuring all-natural, and hormone- and antibiotic-free meats plus sausages, cured meats, duck confit, housemade lard and other uncommon items. Special requests are not a problem. Fried chicken is prepared only on Tuesday, and Wednesday is the day designated for a barbecue plate lunch. The steakhouse inspired brasserie serves an intriguing selection of hors d'oeuvres, including a charcuterie plate, marrow bones, steak tartare and crispy veal sweetbreads. Steaks and chops, though, are the signature dishes with varied a la carte side dishes.

LE PIGEON

738 E Burnside St   503/546-8796
Dinner: Daily   lepigeon.com
Expensive

True to Portland's persona is fine dining in a hole-in-the-wall establishment. Cuisine is French-inspired and features inventive game dishes such as rabbit, venison and quail as well as beef, fish and pork. Chef **Gabriel Rucker** offers five- and seven-course tasting menus. Every nook and cranny of the small restaurant is used with pigeonholed wine bottles becoming part of the decor.

TOE TO HEAD

Forty-plus years after the genesis of M&F, Swedish immigrant **John Nordstrom** invested his Klondike gold-mining fortune ($13,000) to start a shoe store with Carl Wallin in Seattle, Washington. After the retirements of both partners by 1929, the store was in the hands of Nordstrom's descendants and expanded to eight stores in Washington and Oregon; by 1960 the Seattle flagship store was the largest independent shoe store in the country. It wasn't until 1963 that apparel was added and in 1971 the company went public. As expansion occurred, the company remained true to the mission of maintaining exceptional service, selection, quality and value. Today 225 **Nordstrom** (shop.nordstrom.com) stores are located in 29 states; international online shopping is offered. Nine Nordstrom and Nordstrom Rack (sale, off-season) stores are located in Oregon: Portland, Beaverton, Clackamas, Happy Valley, Tigard and Salem.

The open kitchen is in full view and best observed from the Chef's Counter; reservations are accepted for three communal tables. Sister restaurant, **Little Bird** (219 SW 6th Ave, 503/688-5952; littlebirdbistro.com) is open daily for lunch and dinner — fine dining in more refined surroundings.

MADE IN OREGON

Pioneer Place	
340 SW Morrison St, Suite 1300	503/241-3630
Lloyd Center	
1017 Lloyd Center	503/282-7636
Washington Square Mall	
9589 SW Washington Rd	503/620-4670
Clackamas Town Center	
12000 SE 82nd Ave	503/659-3155
Portland International Airport	
Oregon Market	503/282-7827
Concourse C	503/335-6563
Concourse D	503/493-5970
Salem Center	
480 Center St, #242, Salem	503/362-4106
342 SW Bay Blvd, Newport	541/574-9020
	madeinoregon.com

It's all about Oregon! Since 1975 Made in Oregon has been *the* source for the best Oregon products under one roof. The product mix is fabulous; Pendleton blankets and clothing, gourmet foods (cheese, candies, nuts, salmon, cookies, jams and jellies), wines, jewelry, home accessories, books, T-shirts, Oregon State University and University of Oregon paraphernalia, souvenirs and gifts. Many of these items are assembled into attractive boxes and baskets which are ideal for gift giving; customize your choices for specific occasions or buy a single item (order online or from eye-catching mail order catalogs). At the helm of Made in Oregon is legendary **Sam Naito**. The Naito family has a long history of community service, philanthropy and commerce in Oregon (previously Norcrest China Company). Share the love and bounty of Oregon with gifts from this notable Oregon company.

MAMA MIA TRATTORIA

439 SW 2nd Ave   503/295-6464
Lunch, Dinner: Daily   mamamiatrattoria.com
Moderate

No doubt you've driven past this busy downtown trattoria just off the Morrison Bridge. Crystal chandeliers, marble-top tables and gilded mirrors create a comfortable dining spot. Food is traditional Italian — slow-cooked, made from scratch and plentiful. Housemade mozzarella is one of many items that are made daily. Lunch choices include salads, paninis, Italian gourmet burgers, sandwiches, pizza, homemade pastas and parmigiana and cioppino entrees (portions are regular or *molto grandi*). As the sun sets, offerings include chicken milanese, chicken and veal parmesan, jumbo prawns scampi and traditional pastas with marinara sauce simmered to perfection and married with cheeses, sumptuous meatballs and other fine additions. From the bar menu choose Chianti, prosecco, Northwest wines, beers and specialty cocktails; happy hour eats are value priced. Desserts are also homemade and range from sinful amaretto cheesecake to delicate sorbets.

THE MEADOW

3731 N Mississippi Ave   503/288-4633, 888/388-4633
Sun-Thurs: 10-7; Fri, Sat: 10-8   atthemeadow.com

Question: If you mix artisan salt, some of the world's great chocolates, throw in an interesting selection of Oregon and European wines, gourmet products and flowers, what do you get? Answer: A very personal business plan that has produced The Meadow. **Jennifer and Mark Bitterman** turned their love of food and travel into this unusual shop. Exploring the properties of salt varieties (there are many!), an array of more than 300 (mostly dark) chocolate bars and delicious Oregon pinot noirs (so good with chocolate) makes for quite a mix-and-match experience. Tastings and classes are held at the shop from time to time. If you're in New York City, the Bitterman's second Meadow location is in Manhattan's West Village (523 Hudson Street, 212/645-4633); sans wine.

YOUR NORTHWEST

Northwest bounty from Oregonian **Robert B. Pamplin Jr.**'s Columbia Empire Farms is made into delicious preserves, syrups, jams, jellies and sauces. These products, attractive gift baskets and packs, hazelnuts, and wine from Pamplin's Anne Amie winery are marketed at Portland International Airport's five **Your Northwest Travel Mart** outlets and through the online store (yournw.com). Aebleskiver pancake kits, baking mixes, cookbooks and candies make super gifts. Bob Pamplin is a successful businessman (construction, media and textiles) and philanthropist following in his father's footprints. The stores and more are supervised by able **Linda Strand**.

MEHRI'S BAKERY & CAFE

6923 SE 52nd   503/788-9600
Mon-Fri: 7-7; Sat: 8-5; Sun: 8-2   mehris.com

Check out Mehri's for specialty cakes and desserts just like mom used to make: banana, pumpkin and zucchini breads; apple, berry and lemon meringue pies; fruit cobblers and company's coming chocolate fudge cake. Not only does Mehri produce spectacular sweets (and custom wedding cakes), but she also offers the unusual twist of Persian delights (pomegranate chicken stew, shish kabobs and crusty bottom rice to name a few), along with more traditional fare for breakfast and lunch.

MOTHER'S BISTRO & BAR

212 SW Stark St   503/464-1122
Breakfast, Lunch: Tues-Sun; Dinner: Tues-Sat   mothersbistro.com
Moderate

Mother alwa`ys said to eat all your dinner before dessert. Fortunately, this mother does not make that admonishment! The oh-so-good pies vary according to the season and are baked fresh — as are all of the desserts using rich butter, cream, local fruits and quality ingredients. The devil's food cake with chocolate ganache is good and gooey! Mom would approve of the comfort food meals, often updated to appease more sophisticated tastes. For example;

wild salmon hash, chicken salad, macaroni and cheese, meatloaf, beef pot roast and greens (salads and side dishes). Successful chef-owner **Lisa Schroeder** brings a wealth of experience from her training and experience on the East Coast, the Mediterranean and Europe. Specials change monthly to reflect the background cuisine of assorted mothers. This is a comfortable and dependable breakfast, lunch or dinner spot to take business associates, family and mom for people-pleasing meals "made with love."

PROFESSIONAL LEGACY

Who was mainly responsible for the astounding rebirth of the **Portland Art Museum** (1219 SW Park Ave, 503/226-2811, portlandartmuseum.org), raising millions of dollars to improve the facilities and bring verve to the institution? Answer: the late John Buchanan and his wife, Lucy (who acted as money-raiser-in-chief). **Lucy and John Buchanan** were a force to be reckoned with; we lament John's much-too-soon passing. Moving on, Director **Brian J. Ferriso** now very capably leads the West Coast's oldest art museum. It is a must see!

NEW SEASONS MARKET

7300 SW Beaverton-Hillsdale Hwy	503-292-6838
3495 SW Cedar Hills Blvd	503/641-4181
15861 SE Happy Valley Town Ctr Dr	503/558-9214
1214 SE Tacoma St	503/230-4949
14805 SW Barrows Road, Suite 103, Beaverton	503/597-6777
1453 NW 61st Ave, Hillsboro	503/648-6968
3 SW Monroe Pkwy, Lake Oswego	503/496-1155
2100-B SE 164th Ave, Vancouver	360/760-5005

Daily: 8 a.m.-10 p.m.

6400 N Interstate Ave	503/467-4777
5320 NE 33rd Ave	503/288-3838
4034 SE Hawthorne Blvd	503/236-4800
1954 SE Division St	503/445-2888

Daily: 8 a.m.-10 p.m. (summer till 11 p.m.)   newseasonsmarket.com

On Leap Day 2000, Raleigh Hills welcomed an upstart grocer to their community. Now, a dozen years later, a dozen New Seasons

Markets in Oregon and Southwest Washington are committed to providing an easy, fun and friendly neighborhood shopping experience — one that meets customers' needs for both national brand staples and local sustainable products. You'll find quality merchandise in all departments: bakery, beer and wine, bulk, cheese, deli, floral, grocery, meat, pastry, produce, seafood and wellness. By supporting New Seasons and the local economy, they, in turn, give grants and donations back to the community while their employees volunteer throughout the area.

NEWMAN'S FISH MARKET

City Market
735 NW 21st Ave   503/227-2700
Mon-Sat: 9:30-7; Sun: 10-7   newmansfish.com

Inside this cooperative market of independent vendors is a fresh fish market that has earned the patronage of discriminating customers and wholesale accounts. Newman's operation started in the fish business in 1890 in Eugene and expanded north to Portland a century later in 1986. **Newman's Fish Company** (1545 Willamette St, 541/344-2371) still thrives in Eugene. Both locations shine in their selection of fish, seafood, warm water fish, crab and lobster (live tank systems maintain freshness) and custom-smoked fish. Many items are sourced from the Northwest as well as Alaska, Hawaii, the East Coast and other countries and cut to order whenever possible. For the "fresh fish report" call 503/286-5950 after 4 p.m. daily. Other City Market vendors peddle meats, produce, florals and upscale groceries.

THE NINES

525 SW Morrison St   877/229-9995, 800/325-3589
Moderate and up   thenines.com

DEPARTURE RESTAURANT & LOUNGE

Dinner: Mon-Sat   503/802-5370
Dinner: Moderately expensive   departureportland.com

URBAN FARMER

Daily: 6 a.m.-10 p.m. (Fri, Sat till 11 p.m.)   503/222-4900
Dinner: Expensive   urbanfarmerrestaurant.com

Having spent a good part of my life in the block in downtown Portland now known as Meier & Frank Square, it's natural that I had a keen interest in the major renovations a few years ago. In 2008 The Nines opened a modern luxury hotel, filling the floors above **Macy's** retail space with 331 guest rooms and 13 suites, meeting facilities, an atrium, fitness center, library and rooftop dining. It is spectacular and a great addition to Portland's downtown. Oregon artists are featured in the eighth-floor lobby, also the location of a charming library. Guest rooms and suites are tastefully appointed, sleek and tranquil. Guests on the 12th-floor club level receive light breakfasts, snacks and evening libations. The one bedroom Meier and Frank Suite affords spectacular city views from the comfortable living room and accommodates up to eight in the dining room. During the summer, it's hard to beat the two patios that add to the spectacular ambience at **Departure Restaurant & Lounge**. Enjoy modern Asian cuisine in the rooftop setting. Diners can also enjoy the comfortable indoor bar or more private, classy seating. Dim sum, with specialties like crystal shrimp dumplings, is usually available. Chef **Gregory Kushiyaki**'s grill and wok dishes feature a variety of chicken and meats; a favorite is the Ishiyaki steak, a stone-grilled Wagyu strip steak served on a sizzling

TV TIMES

Marty Brantley, my good friend and civic icon, capably led television station KPTV in Portland for decades. Marty provided the opportunity for me to do fun weekly segments (1992 to 2001) on **Northwest Reports** and later **Good Day Oregon**. It was a fascinating experience, learning more about the state and getting a taste for television reporting. One of the most memorable parts of that show was working with the host of Northwest Reports, **Lars Larson**. Since our TV days, Lars is still based in Portland, but now hosts a popular conservative radio talk show on KXL. He is highly controversial, skilled in his profession and an individual who has earned a reputation as one of the most able debaters in the Northwest. A word to the wise: the guy with the microphone always wins; don't get into an argument with Lars Larson if you don't have your facts in order! In real life, he is as opinionated as ever, but a most interesting person with whom to chew the fat!

hot stone. The **Urban Farmer** steakhouse is also first-rate with inviting country-chic decorative touches. A huge table in the middle seats dozens of single diners. Make a friend at breakfast, lunch, dinner or Sunday brunch. Yes, my friends, the top floors of my family's department store have been spiffed up "to the nines."

NOISETTE RESTAURANT
1937 NW 23rd Pl   503/719-4599
Tues-Sat: Dinner   noisetterestaurant.com
Moderately expensive

Portland diners of years back will remember cozy Couvron, a tiny establishment adjacent to the Lincoln High School athletic field. Alas, **Tony Demes**, the talented chef/owner pulled up stakes and moved to New York City. After this experience, plus interim travels and a marriage, he returned to the city that he loves. Noisette (translation: hazelnut) is the dream operation for both **Debbie and Tony Demes**. It is not just another "small plate establishment;" the dozen or so hot and cold appetizer-size offerings are superb, each with sublime taste and outstanding eye appeal. Choose from fabulous butternut squash soup, scallops, white sturgeon, steelhead mignon, duck liver or breast, New York strip steak and Painted Hills braised short rib (extraordinary) and more. Eliminate the stress of decision-making and let Chef Tony present his eight-course gourmet tasting extravaganza adapted to seasonal availabilities. The soufflé offerings (house, Grand Marnier, chocolate) are especially worthy dessert choices.

NOSTRANA
1401 SE Morrison St   503/234-2427
Lunch: Mon-Fri; Dinner Daily   nostrana.com
Moderate

Nostrana is large and extremely busy, with an energy level as high as any dining spot in Portland. This rustic Italian eatery, meaning "ours" in Italian, features a daily changing menu of locally grown produce and tasty homemade dishes. Antipasti choices may include Dungeness crab bruschetta, house charcuterie and roasted beet salad followed by salads and interesting pastas (made in-house). Fish, seafood, chicken, pork and beef platters are delicious and accompanied by polenta, lentils or other Italian preparations. In traditional style, uncut pizzas are delivered to your table along with a pair of scissors for cutting (fun for kids). Fine wines and baked-to-order seasonal fruit crisps complete the meal.

OBA RESTAURANT

555 NW 12th Ave   503/228-6161
Dinner: Daily   obarestaurant.com
Moderate

   Chef **Scott Neuman** knows Nuevo Latino cuisine and he knows the best way to serve it is in a full-on festive environment. OBA is renowned for tableside-prepared guacamole, grilled fresh fish, scallop ceviche and an abundance of jalapenos, tomatoes, chilies, spices, fresh fruits and vegetables; all are natural, organic and regional, as available. Special dietary requests are accommodated; nutritious, low-fat options are suggested on the menu. Latin street food is served in the lounge where spirited conversations are fueled by potent potables and wines from south of the border and around the world. Several rooms accommodate private dining groups, or inquire about delivery to your door. Request a warm fireside table.

OREGON HISTORY MUSEUM

1200 SW Park Ave   503/306-5198
Tues-Sat: 10-5; Sun: noon-5   ohs.org

   Located in Portland's Park Blocks, the Oregon History Museum is a required stop for anyone wanting to understand the Oregon story. Operated since 1898 by the Oregon Historical Society, the museum includes the award-winning "Oregon My Oregon" permanent exhibit that traces Oregon's history from the first Native Americans to the Lewis and Clark expedition to the iconic Conestoga wagons of the Oregon Trail. A much-anticipated new interactive "Oregon Voices" exhibit, highlighting 20th century history, opened in June 2012. The museum also houses the Oregon Historical Society Research Library, which contains one of the country's most extensive collections of state history materials, including approximately 25,000 maps, 30,000 books, over 8 million feet of film and videotape, and more than

UNDER COVER

In 1923, the original plans by **Ralph Lloyd** for his property on Portland's east side included a grand residential hotel, but economic conditions did not allow his vision to come to fruition. After Lloyd's death, **Richard Von Hagen**, husband of one of the four Lloyd daughters, announced plans for the **Lloyd Center** (lloydcenter.com), which opened August 1, 1960 with the second Portland area **Meier & Frank** as the anchor store. The center took in nearly 1.5 million square feet. and, at that time, was the largest covered mall — including an ice rink — in America. Today, the Lloyd Center has over 130 stores and 35 restaurants.

2 million photographic images. OHS also sponsors an extensive series of educational programs and lectures. Executive Director **Kerry Tymchuk** is also an Oregon one-of-a-kind.

OREGON ZOO

4001 SW Canyon Road
Daily
Nominal

503/226-1561
oregonzoo.org

Lions and tigers and bears—oh, yes! And an elephant named Packy! You, your family and friends will want to visit all of the animal friends at the Oregon Zoo. The zoo's origins date back to 1888 with a few animals collected from a Portland pharmacist's seafaring friends. Today, the menagerie has grown from one "she grizzly" to over 2,200 animals. The zoo encompasses 64 acres of exhibits (Great Northwest, Fragile Forests, Asia, Pacific Shores, Africa), exotic plants, a one-mile loop railway, eateries, gift shops and a petting zoo for the pint-size set. The zoo's focus centers on animal enrichment, zoological knowledge, education, sustainable operations and conservation. Over 1.5 million folks visit this animal kingdom each year; other popular events include summertime concerts on the lawn and the annual holiday ZooLights extravaganza. Back to Packy; in 1962 he was the first elephant to be born in this country in over four decades and overnight became the zoo's star attraction. His 60th birthday party was fit for a king!

PACIFIC FISH & OYSTER

3380 SE Powell Blvd   503/223-4891
Mon-Fri: 9-6   pacseafood.com

Is the fish fresh? You know it is if you shop here. The folks at Pacific Seafood own and operate nearly 40 fish and seafood processing and distribution facilities from Alaska to Texas. From those plants and worldwide imports, customers enjoy one of the largest selections in this area. In addition to shrimp for your salad or salmon for the grill, they supply Dungeness crabs for fundraising crab feeds and ship Northwest fish and seafood across the country. If you're a restaurateur you may already know them as a reliable wholesale source.

PALEY'S PLACE

1204 NW 21st Ave   503/243-2403
Dinner: Daily   paleysplace.net
Expensive

Portland's culinary duo, **Kimberly and Vitaly Paley**, perfected their roles as general manager and executive chef at fine establishments in New York and France. The lure of this area's sustainable and seasonal products brought them to Portland to launch their own restaurant. A beautiful house with two dining rooms and a wide front porch serves as a showcase for their talents. Picture perfect charcuterie (order a single serving, or tastes of three, five or one of each) and desserts are also delicious. Superb entrees are planned factoring in seasonal availability of main and complementing ingredients. To bring out the best flavors and qualities, preparations are braised, roasted or grilled. Relax and unwind at the cozy full-service bar with Oregon and French wines, handcrafted cocktails and the always-popular Paley's Burger. Paley is expanding to downtown Portland in summer 2012 with **Imperial** and **Portland Penny Diner** connected to Hotel Lucia.

PARK KITCHEN

422 NW 8th Ave   503/223-7275
Dinner: Mon-Sat   parkkitchen.com
Moderate

Chef **Scott Dolich**, Executive Chef **David Padberg**

and their crew do wonders with the dishes that come out of the open kitchen at the far end of the dining room. Scott is a true genius in the kitchen. Small hot plates (chickpea fries with pumpkin ketchup and asparagus soup with marinated mushrooms), small cold plates (duck ham, halibut carpaccio, lamb tartare), large plates (seared salmon, sorrel, potatoes, leeks) and desserts (apple butter crepes or a selection of cheeses) are uniformly delicious. The seasonal cuisine incorporates original compositions and updated favorites. Visit on a warm evening, when you can sit outside and enjoy a view of the park and busy bocce ball court.

PEARL BAKERY

102 NW 9th Ave   503/827-0910
Mon-Fri: 6:30-5:30; Sat: 7-5; Sun: 8-3   pearlbakery.com

Bread is the staff of life, especially when it comes from Pearl Bakery. Pugliese is the signature variety, characterized by its chewy crust and dense holes. Unique flavors and textures are achieved through different leavening methods and the addition of specialty flours and sweet and savory ingredients. The fragrant fresh loaves vary in size and shape from petite French rolls up to the four-pound pugliese and are sold as baguettes, rounds and in decorative shapes. In addition to the daily breads, bakers turn out diet-breaking breakfast pastries, cookies and shortbreads, cupcakes, tarts, layer cakes and bundt cakes like mom made. At the top of my list are the oh-so-elegant Parisian macarons; cookie and filling flavors are ever-changing. For lunchers on the run, the retail case is filled each morning with sandwiches made with Pearl's breads and natural meats, imported cheeses and organic greens; stop in anytime for coffee and sweet treats. This busy bakery has been on the fringe of the trendy Pearl District since 1997 and has grown with the influx of businesses and residents.

PEARL SPECIALTY MARKET & SPIRITS
900 NW Lovejoy St   503/477-8604
Mon-Sat: 9 a.m.-10 p.m.; Sun: noon-7   pearlspecialty.com

Here's a liquor store on steroids! By the numbers it has 1,000 spirits, 400 wines, 500 beers and 300 cigars. Those are labels, not actual pieces! They carry an impressive array of top-shelf bottles and imported and locally-produced wines, spirits and beers; champagnes; sakés; bitters; syrups and barware. The more exclusive (read very expensive) products, including a bottle of Remy Martin Louis XIII cognac, are behind lock and key; special orders are welcome. Unlike run-of-the-mill Oregon Liquor Control Commission outlets, Pearl Specialty stocks all these items including craft beers and wines under one roof. They also have a glass-walled walk-in humidor that pairs well with the extensive bourbon and scotch selection. Check their Facebook page for updates on First Thursday events, tastings and other parties.

PETITE PROVENCE
1824 NE Alberta   503/284-6564
4834 SE Division   503/233-1121

LA PROVENCE BAKERY AND BISTRO
16350 SW Boones Ferry Road, Lake Oswego   503/635-4533
Daily   provencepdx com

Originally from France, the owners are bent on bringing a nostalgic French atmosphere to their establishments and becoming an integral part of neighborhoods. Hours vary by location; menus are similar, but chefs operate in creative styles. Omelets, French toast, Benedicts, hash and more for breakfast; lunch can spill over into the dinner hour with salad, sandwich and soup choices. Throughout the day

ANGEL

Known to them or not, many people have reaped the spiritual goodness of **Carolyn Winter**. She not only heads up the Providence Health Systems major philanthropy efforts, but administers to many a hospital patient and others and once served as a nun. "St." Carolyn is not far off the mark!

enjoy wonderful fresh bakery choices from cases filled with yummy croissants, chocolate treats galore and fruit tarts. A sister location, **Petite Provence of the Gorge**, is in The Dalles (408 E 2nd St, 541/506-0037).

PIAZZA ITALIA
1129 NW Johnson St   503/478-0619
Lunch, Dinner: Daily   piazzaportland.com
Moderate

For an authentic Italian meal, visit this fun Pearl District eatery. In 2000, the late Gino Schettini, who hailed from Rome, along with **Kevin Gorretta**, a fellow Italian descendant, realized their dream. Gino's family carries on his vision of providing fantastic food from a large menu (try Gino's favorite — linguine squarciarella), good friendly service, lively Italian conversations and an obvious bent for celebrating soccer. A large selection of Italian wines and a deli counter to stock your fridge add to the appeal. You're sure to meet some interesting people here (like **Serge D'Rovencourt**, a retired Portland hotelier). Ciao!

PINE STATE BISCUITS
3640 SE Belmont St   503/236-3346
Daily: 7-2

2204 NE Alberta St   503/477-6605
Daily: 7-2; Fri, Sat: 6 p.m.-1 a.m.
Inexpensive   pinestatebiscuits.com

Don't miss these sumptuous buttermilk biscuits!   Order just one (I dare you) or a dozen, then slather on butter, honey or jam. The sausage gravy is out of this world, and so are the biscuit sandwiches made with bacon, housemade sausage, ham, fried chicken, flank steak, eggs and assorted greens, cheeses and sauces. You'll probably tackle your towering concoction (multi-layers dripping with melted cheese atop creamy gravy) with a knife and fork. Southern food extras and housemade pecan pie are hard to resist. Just when you thought it couldn't get better, Pine State opened a location on Alberta Street. The good news continues; that locale is also open Friday and Saturday evenings with beer, cocktails and a year-round outdoor patio alongside the acclaimed biscuit meals.

POK POK

3226 SE Division St   503/232-1387
Lunch, Dinner: Daily   pokpokpdx.com
Moderate

Accolades to Chef **Andy Ricker** who mastered the art of Thai cooking during a lengthy sojourn in Southeast Asia. His hard work has not gone unrecognized; he earned the James Beard Award for Best Chef Northwest and continues to add to his realm. Specialties of the house include flavorful rotisserie roasted game hen, papaya Pok Pok salad and deep-fried Vietnamese fish sauce wings; all are best enjoyed with sticky rice. Other authentic dishes utilize pork belly and ribs, sausage, boar collar and fish; preparations may be grilled or incorporated into noodle dishes. **Pok Pok Noi** (1469 NE Prescott, 503/287-4149) is a counter-service/take-out operation. New Yorkers have descended upon the recently-opened **Pok Pok Wing** (137 Rivington St, 212/477-1299) in Manhattan.

PORTLAND MARIOTT DOWNTOWN WATERFRONT

1401 SW Naito Pkwy   503/226-7600
Moderate to expensive   marriott.com

For those visiting downtown Portland for business or pleasure, this luxury hotel is for you. The hotel is ideally located in the heart of the city at the waterfront with easy to-and-from freeway access. Rooms are beautifully decorated, enhanced with plush beds, up-scale bathrooms and intelligent technology. Large windows afford

AMONG THE BEST IN THE METROPOLITAN AREA

Shoes

Mario's (833 SW Broadway, 503/227-3477 and 17031 SW 72nd Ave, Tigard; 503/601-7310; marios.com): high-end for men and women

Zelda's Shoe Bar (633 NW 23rd Ave, 503/226-0363; zeldaspdx.com): upscale women's boutique

Florists

Crystal Lilies (134 SE Taylor St, 503/221-7701; crystallilies. com): unique and interesting

Sammy's Flowers (2280 NW Glisan St, 503/222-9759 and 1128 NW Lovejoy St, 503/281-0310; sammysflowers.com): fresh-cut local and exotic flowers

Gifts

Occasions Fine Gifts (7515 SW Barnes Rd, 503/384-0269; occasionsfinegifts.com): affordable treasures

Linens

French Quarter Linens (1313 NW Glisan St, 503/282-8200; frenchquarterlinens.com): European bed and bath linens and accessories

Stationery

Uptowne Papers (9 NW 23rd Pl, 503/224-8266; uptownepapers.com): stationery, home accessories, gifts

picture postcard views of the Willamette River, Mt. Hood and the City of Bridges. Relax in the indoor saltwater swimming pool and whirlpool or stay in shape at the modern fitness center. Executive Chef **Andrew Arndt** oversees **Truss**, the newly-concepted destination restaurant, which is open daily for breakfast, lunch and dinner. Truss embraces the Portland tradition of sourcing the best local and seasonal products, supporting the surrounding neighborhood's local artisans to create familiar American favorites. Truss provides a timeless epicurean experience, where the simple and familiar are done extraordinarily well. The menu is moderately priced and designed to offer shareable choices for a perfect meal. The casual **Lobby Cafe & Bar** becomes a favorite gathering spot for travelers and locals from early morning to late night for coffee, light meals, appetizers and cocktails. A unique feature transforms the coffee bar into a contemporary bar where bartenders create exciting cocktails using freshly squeezed juices and local liquors. The recent $6.5 million renovation includes the addition of over 2,000 square feet of dividable premier meeting space on the second floor, complemented with outstanding views; very nice, indeed.

POPCORN, ANYONE?

Is there any former Lincoln High School graduate (who attended in the former Park Blocks location) who doesn't remember legendary Paul, the popcorn man?

POWELL'S BOOKS

1005 W Burnside   503/228-4651
3723 SE Hawthorne Blvd
3747 SE Hawthorne Blvd (Home and Garden)
7000 NE Airport Way (3 outlets at PDX)
3415 SW Cedar Hills Blvd, Beaverton
Hours vary by location   powells.com

One could say if it is printed on paper, it may just be at Powell's. **Alice and Michael Powell**'s operation has been a Northwest Portland fixture since 1971 and has expanded numerous times to make room for more shelves of every ilk of book — new and used, fiction, non-fiction, hard back, soft cover, rare, reference, collectible, signed and audio, plus toys and gifts. Over 1 million tomes are housed in the Burnside flagship location; each genre shelved in the labyrinth of rooms. The popularity of Powell's and the burgeoning supply necessitated growth to other buildings; its technical book store is adjacent to the main Burnside building. Convenient to Washington County readers, the Beaverton store has over a half million selections. Travelers appreciate the three shops at PDX for last minute reading material before boarding flights or to grab a quick gift on the way in or out of town. Two neighboring businesses are on Hawthorne Boulevard, one dedicated to home and garden material as well as cooking utensils, accessories and related merchandise; the other store carries a full spectrum of reads.

Powell's is a leader in book-buying and selling; in stores or online. This is another quintessential Portland institution!

RIFFLE NW

333 NW 13th St
503/864-8978
Dinner: Daily
rifflenw.com
Moderate

Owners **Jennifer and Ken Norris** have a great food background and it shows in the unusual dishes they offer. The sophisticated, catch-inspired menu changes to capture the essence of each season; fresh-daily elements are featured in nightly specials. I must admit that I am not a great octopus fan, but my fellow diners gave it rave reviews! Seafood is sourced from around the globe and so are wines, most affordably priced. Fun drink menus are creatively stowed in a slot in the table. Another nice touch is the hand-cut ice, shaped to complement customized cocktails. Seating is inside, outside, at the chef's table or raw bar; a private dining room accommodates 16 diners.

RINGSIDE STEAKHOUSE DOWNTOWN

2165 W Burnside
503/223-1513
Dinner: Daily

RINGSIDE STEAKHOUSE
GLENDOVEER GOLF COURSE

14021 NE Glisan
503/255-0750
Lunch: Mon-Fri; Dinner Daily
ringsidesteakhouse.com

RINGSIDE FISH HOUSE

838 SW Park Ave
503/227-3900
Lunch: Mon-Fri; Dinner: Daily
ringsidefishhouse.com
Moderate and up

The RingSide has been a Portland tradition for nearly 70 years. After decades of providing great steaks, fabulous onion rings and other delectables, refurbished digs live up to the superior food. Gone is the dark and mysterious atmosphere; the new space is airy and cozy with a welcoming fireplace, one of the few remnants of yesteryear. Service, as always, is highly professional.

The 10,000-bottle wine cellar is fabulous. Across town, expect the same fine dining and impeccable service in a relaxed, clubby atmosphere. In an era of chain restaurants, it is refreshing to boast about a homegrown winner; great credit goes to the three members of the Peterson family who keep watchful eyes on every phase of the business. Branching out from its historic Portland custom of providing the "best steaks in town" and celebrating Oregon's proximity to fresh fish and seafood is RingSide Fish House in the Fox Tower downtown. You'll find a raw bar, seafood platters, sandwiches (including non-seafood) and changing entrees of halibut, cioppino, lobster, trout and many other fish choices with a sprinkling of beef, pasta and poultry. This space is warm, classy and inviting and offers early and late happy hours in the busy bars; private dining.

RISTORANTE ROMA
622 SW 12th Ave   503/241-2692
Lunch: Mon-Fri; Dinner: Mon-Sat   ristoranteromaportland.com
Moderate

You hardly notice the entrance to this tiny restaurant where the platters are quite tasty. This is not a fancy establishment; a dozen or so tables enhance the intimate and friendly atmosphere. The antipasti choices range from salads and minestrone soup to seafood plates. The authentic Italian dishes combine shrimp, clams and mussels in a variety of impressive dishes. Pastas are wide-ranging: rigatoni, fettuccine, ravioli, gnocchi, spaghetti and more. A filet steak is available, as well as beef tenderloin and chicken; from-scratch sauces are made daily. Conversation is easy in this casual trattoria where prices are also easy on the wallet. Reservations are recommended for busy Thursday through Saturday nights.

RIVERPLACE HOTEL
1510 SW Harbor Way   503/228-3233, 800/227-1333
Moderate to very expensive   riverplacehotel.com

THREE DEGREES WATERFRONT BAR & GRILL
Breakfast: Mon-Fri; Lunch, Dinner: Daily; Brunch: Sat, Sun 503/295-6166
Moderate to expensive   threedegreesportland.com

This is one of Portland's finest settings — downtown Portland along the Willamette River. The city and river vistas are stunning, but never more so than on a sunny day when watercraft navigate the sparkling river. Miles of walking paths front the RiverPlace connecting pedestrians with bustling or tranquil neighborhood eateries and shops (complimentary guest use of hotel bicycles). Consider staying here when you attend events at adjacent Tom McCall Waterfront Park or book a riverview room for the annual parade of Christmas ships alternating between the Willamette and Columbia rivers. Luxury abounds in the 84 spacious rooms and suites at this Kimpton Craftsman-style boutique hotel; upscale in-room features are the norm as well as refrigerators stocked with local and organic snacks, yoga mats, umbrellas and electronic conveniences. Seasonal cooking has diners looking forward to meals at **Three Degrees**.

DOUBLE ACT

One of the most effective husband and wife teams in Oregon is the **Tom Walsh/Patricia McCaig** couple. Tom, former head of TriMet and a leader in dozens of civic projects, is the epitome of a leader "flying under the radar." Patricia was chief of staff to former Governor Barbara Roberts, and later served as a top advisor for the 2010 Kitzhaber for Governor campaign; she is a skilled political insider. Oregon profits enormously from this capable and talented pair.

ROSE'S EQUIPMENT AND SUPPLY
207 SE Clay St   503/223-7450, 800/898-7450
Mon-Fri: 8-5; Sat: 9-2   rosesequipment.com

Most folks associate this business with the food service trade. That it is, but anyone who wants to cook like a pro shops here, too. Rose's sells new and refurbished equipment and works with businesses to design efficient work areas. The inventory includes necessities for the kitchen, dining area, bar, catering and concessions and janitorial equipment along with large and small items for cooking, baking, serving, preparation and storage. Home cooks will find kitchen items such as meat thermometers, cutlery, dishes, specialized bakeware and hard-to-find gadgets used by celebrity chefs. Rose's also sells hot dog grills, popcorn machines and waffle makers. The list keeps going — it's an amazing place.

RUTH'S CHRIS STEAK HOUSE

850 SW Broadway   503/221-4518
Dinner: Daily   ruthschris.com
Expensive

This prestigious steak house chain does things in a big way; Portland's warm, comfortable location is no exception. The beefsteak tomato salad is superb, baked potatoes are gigantic and other potato dishes are more than generous. Beef lovers have their choice of USDA Prime cuts; tender, juicy and delicious every time. My preference, though, are the grilled lamb chops; cut extra thick and very flavorful. Fresh lobster is always on the menu as are other seafood and fish selections. Desserts (there's always room for dessert, right?) include homemade cheesecake, crème brûlée, chocolate cake, ice cream and seasonal berries. Weekday happy hours are between 4 and 7, a very pleasant way to ease into the evening.

SALTY'S ON THE COLUMBIA

3839 NE Marine Dr   503/288-4444
Lunch: Mon-Sat; Dinner: Daily; Brunch: Sun   saltys.com/Portland
Moderate

The mighty Columbia flows past this local landmark restaurant. Alfresco dining on the wraparound deck is spectacular in summer

CITY FATHERS

Who were the movers and shakers in Portland from early in the 20th century to the 1960s or even beyond? It was a small group of businessmen, each owning or running major companies, unselfishly devoting time and resources to making the city vibrant. The five: **David Simpson** (Norris, Beggs & Simpson — real estate); **E.C. "Ed" Sammons** (United States National Bank); **E.B. MacNaughton** (First National Bank); **E. Palmer Hoyt** (*The Oregonian*) and **Aaron Frank** — my dad (Meier & Frank Co.).

and window seats are coveted when the Christmas ships sail past in December. Salty's arguably presents the busiest and best Sunday champagne brunch buffet in the state. Prawns, Dungeness crab, salmon, clams, mussels, omelets, crepes, waffles, fruit, cheeses, baked ham (excellent), prime rib and much more make choosing a real dilemma; a four-foot tall fountain of gurgling chocolate sauce awaits for dipping fruits and cookies (kids love to swirl marshmallows). The impressive sea and land lunch and dinner menus feature entries such as sustainable seafood, live Maine lobster, cioppino and Painted Hills beef. Lighten up during the bar's weekday happy hours with great bar eats and drinks or join in the fun at Salty's entertaining cooking classes and special events.

SERES RESTAURANT AND BAR

1105 NW Lovejoy St   971/222-0100
Mon-Sat: 11-10; Sun: 3 p.m.-10 p.m.
Moderate   seresrestaurant.com

Tasty Szechuan and multi-regional Chinese cuisine are served at this Pearl District restaurant. The surrounds are modern, neat and clean and the staff is informed. Start your meal with the chicken and lotus lettuce wraps or scallion pancakes — delicious. Classic dishes made with fresh ingredients (free of hormones, antibiotics and MSG) come off the flaming woks. Eat in, take out or have your order delivered through **Portland Pedal Power** (503/764-1415, portlandpedalpower.com), a bicycle delivery service. While you're in the area, enhance your cultural experience with a visit to the remarkable **Lan Su Chinese Garden** (503/228-8131, lansugarden.org) in Old Town Chinatown before or after your meal.

SERRATTO

2112 NW Kearney St   503/221-1195
Lunch, Dinner: Daily   serratto.com
Moderately expensive

Serratto is a busy Alphabet District favorite recognized for Mediterranean and Northwest fare. The extensive, eclectic menu features homemade pastas, family-pleasing delicious pizzas, risottos, locally-sourced meats, Idaho trout and falafel. Portland's best artisan bakeries provide the breads. On the dessert menu is a bittersweet chocolate cobbler served warm with vanilla bean gelato; other seasonal sweets and a cheese plate are also satisfying. You'll feel like part of the neighborhood at this cozy corner spot; the outside tables are charming.

SHERATON PORTLAND AIRPORT HOTEL

8235 NE Airport Way   503/281-2500, 800/325-3535
Moderate   sheratonpdx.com

This hotel completed an $8 million renovation in 2008; meeting space was increased and state-of-the-art technology was added to the 15 meeting and conference rooms. Restaurant space was redesigned for **Columbia Grill and Bar** which offers appealing meals from 6 a.m. to 1 a.m.; room service too. The 213 guest rooms were not overlooked in the makeover; new furnishings were installed in a more contemporary color palette. If you've stayed at a Starwood property, you know about the ultra-comfortable Sheraton Sweet Sleeper beds, standard in all rooms. Starwood Preferred Guest rooms contain oversize desks, fax/copier/printer machines and high-speed Wi-Fi. Hardworking, civic-minded hotelier **Harold Pollin**'s portfolio includes two other airport properties. Next door to the Sheraton is **Hampton Inn Portland Airport** (8633 NE Airport Way, 503/288-2423; hamptoninn.com) and **Aloft Portland Airport** (9920 NE Cascades Parkway, 503/200-5678; alofthotels.com) at Cascade Station. Complimentary shuttle service to the airport runs 24/7 making these convenient stays for travelers in and out of PDX; also great, too, as jumping-off-points for exploring Southwest Washington or the Gorge.

ST. HONORÉ BOULANGERIE

2335 NW Thurman St   503/445-4342
Daily: 7 a.m.-8 p.m.

315 1st St, Lake Oswego   503/496-5596
Mon-Fri: 7-7 (till 8 in summer);
Sat, Sun: 7 a.m.-8 p.m.   sainthonorebakery.com

Cruising down northwest Thurman Street, be on the lookout

BATTER UP!

When you're onto a good thing, it's best to stick with it. Such is the case at **Slappy Cakes** (4246 SE Belmont St, Portland; 503/477-4805; slappycakes.com) where scratch pancakes and a lot more breakfast items are the order of the day. Emphasis is on organic and their own garden supplies many ultra-fresh ingredients. Pick a batter (buttermilk, whole grain, sweet potato, etc.); then the fixins (chocolate or butterscotch chips, fruits, nuts); add a lavender honey, peanut butter, lemon curd or maple syrup topping – and you'll have a memorable pancake breakfast made at your table. A host of additional creative breakfast choices, including eye-opening cocktails, are available every day from 8 a.m. to mid-afternoon.

for flags which identify this traditional French bakery evocative of the French countryside. The wonderfully rustic establishment sets the stage for specialty items (raisin and fennel benoitons, rolls, the signature Miche Banal loaves and cranberry hazelnut bread and rolls), baguettes and other breads. Not to be overlooked are the pain au chocolat (chocolate-filled croissant) and other decadent pastries. Croissant and other sandwiches, quiches, soups, salads and oh-so-good desserts are served in these neighborhood cafes at communal harvest or Parisian-style tables; the atmosphere is truly delightful. **Stephanie and Dominique Geulin**'s Lake Oswego cafe is elegant; both locales provide warm customer service.

STEPPING STONE CAFE

2390 NW Quimby St   503/222-1132
Mon-Tues: 6 a.m.-7 p.m.; Wed-Thurs: 6 a.m.-10 p.m.;
Fri: 6 a.m.-3 a.m.; Sat: 7:30 a.m.-3 a.m.;
Sun: 7 a.m.-10 p.m.   steppingstonecafe.com
Inexpensive

Breakfast! All hours, every day! Enter hungry and leave stuffed! Here's another Portland eatery that has earned a national reputation. Casual Stepping Stone is famous for its dinner-plate-size mancakes (aka pancakes); one will probably do, but order a stack if you dare. There are plenty of other choices, some with interesting names like the Grazing Goat and Neo Bobcat omelets and One-Eyed Jack burgers. Lunch sandwiches, soups and salads are served starting at 10:30 a.m. and comfort food dinners begin at 5 p.m.; meatloaf and chicken-fried steak are full-meal-deals. You'll probably need a shoe horn to get into this small quirky cafe on weekends!

SUSHI MAZI

2126 SE Division St   503/432-8651
Lunch: Tues-Fri; Dinner: Tues-Sun   sushimazipdx.com
Moderate

Chef Marc takes great pride in preparing and presenting sushi using fresh fish and vegetables to create culinary works of art. The coconut shrimp roll, real grasshopper sushi and a tuna and avocado roll sprinkled with Pop Rocks are appealing and interesting. Sushi, mazi and chicken platters are served with miso soup; beer and wine are available. Expect friendly service and a casual and quiet atmosphere.

TORO BRAVO

120 NE Russell St   503/281-4464
Dinner: Daily   torobravopdx.com
Moderately expensive

There are plenty of choices at this Spanish-inspired restaurant. For a tiny bite, order toasted almonds, cheese and salads from the Pinchos section. Tapas selections of griddled shrimp, sauteed spinach, grilled flat bread and other small plates are great for sharing or a light meal. Several whole meals are offered; paella, meatballs, fish and seafood and vegetable options. For a special evening order the chef's choice for your table, complemented with Spanish wine and dessert such as olive oil cake or churros and chocolate.

TRADER VIC'S

1203 NW Glisan St   503/467-2277
Dinner: Daily; Brunch: Sat, Sun   tradervicspdx.com
Expensive

Longtime Portlanders fondly recall the original Trader Vic's, tucked away in the **Benson Hotel** from 1959 until 1996.

Oh, the stories that went away with it! In 2011, local booster **Clayton Hering** wooed this Polynesian escape back to Portland. Order a famous mai tai or other exotic cocktail that is sure to bring visions of a Tahitian vacation. The splendid bar is open every day between 3 and 10 (till midnight on Friday and Saturday). Traditional pupus like beef cho cho, the cosmo tidbit platter and bongo bongo soup are very good. A custom-built Chinese wood-fired oven turns out tasty fish and seafood, beef, pork and chicken permeated with the classic sweet, smoky flavor. The Indonesian lamb loin chop is the star of the menu, complemented with Bali fried rice and a trio of sauces. Sweet cravings are satisfied with rum ice cream or passion fruit mousse. Service is exceptional in this tiki-adorned, Polynesian-style hot spot with plenty of seating inside and out.

VERITABLE QUANDARY

1220 SW 1st Ave   503/227-7342
Lunch: Mon-Fri; Dinner: Daily; Brunch: Sat, Sun   veritablequandary.com
Moderately expensive

Legions of loyal patrons affectionately refer to this delightful restaurant as the "VQ." The fare is fresh from Northwest farms and prepared with a nod to Chef **Annie Cuggino**'s New Orleans and

New York culinary experiences. What to order? Bacon-wrapped dates, housemade pierogi, seafood stew, osso bucco and other dishes from around the world; try the shrimp and grits for weekend brunch. You'll find a large selection of superb desserts such as a peanut butter banana split, tarts, soufflés and housemade ice creams and sorbets. The patio's sensational spring and summer blooms are sure to release pent-up endorphins, stagnant from rainy days; a table in the glass-walled dining room is the next best seating. Classy private dining for up to eight friends is available in the wine cellar.

WEST CAFE

1201 SW Jefferson St   503/227-8189
Lunch: Mon-Fri; Dinner: Mon-Sat; Brunch: Sun   westcafepdx.com
Moderate

Chef **Sean Concannon** and partner **Doug Smith** offer brunch, lunch and dinner at their contemporary New American restaurant. Great selections of scrumptious small-plate appetizers (or make a meal of them) are reasonably priced, ditto the soups and salads. Dinner choices such as chicken molé, lamb stew with coffee and red wine, Asian spice-rubbed beef tenderloin and various chicken preparations are joined by daily fish and vegetarian specials; all are served with interesting fresh and seasonal accompaniments. A little of this and that is

NO SMALL POTATOES

It's a long haul from making superb potato salad to becoming one of the nation's leading manufacturers of high-quality refrigerated food brands. From humble beginnings, Cornelius native (the late) **Al Reser** (**Reser's Fine Foods, Inc.**; resers.com) came to a position of fame and fortune after taking the reins from his parents, Mildred and Earl (who could not have envisioned a nearly billion dollar company while hand-making potato salad from 50-pound sacks of spuds). **Pat and Al Reser** never forgot their debt to educations at Oregon State University (Reser Stadium). (*No Small Potatoes* is Al's legacy book, available at the company website.)

on the sweets menu — assorted mini-cupcakes, housemade chocolate truffles and cookies, bread pudding, crème brûlée and other desserts. Stop in on Saturdays for live jazz or anytime for handcrafted cocktails featuring local distillers.

THE WESTIN PORTLAND

750 SW Alder St   503/294-9000, 800/937-8461
Moderate to expensive   westinportland.com

A $6.5 million renovation upgraded guest rooms, meeting and other public spaces in 2011. The 205 tranquil guest rooms and suites were redone with a color palate of brown, gray, saffron and lavender and stocked with spa-like bath products; Westin's famous Heavenly beds and baths are standard in all rooms. Original art works from a private collection embellish the lobby and common areas. A full range of features and amenities are offered including concierge service, multilingual staff, valet parking, free Wi-Fi in the lobby, 24-hour room service from the next-door **Daily Grill** and other courtesies. You may want to take a seat at **The Lobby Bar** for a refreshing drink and use one of the built-in iPads or step outside into the center of Portland. The MAX light rail, museums, concert halls and shopping at **Nordstrom**, **Macy's**, outdoor markets and fashionable boutiques are within a short walk.

WHOLE FOODS MARKET

3535 NE 15th Ave   503/288-3414
4301 NE Sandy Blvd   503/284-2644
2825 E Burnside St   503/232-6601
1210 NW Couch St   503/525-4343
19440 NW Cornell Road, Hillsboro   503/645-9200
7380 SW Bridgeport Road, Tigard   503/639-6500
Daily: 8 a.m.-10 p.m.   wholefoodsmarket.com

Whole Foods is big, beautiful and busy! It is also the nation's leading natural and organic food retailer. If you can't find a particular food item here, it probably doesn't exist. These grocery superstores have huge deli, bakery and floral sections, as well as sushi, seafood, fresh juices and all kinds of carryout items. Takeout dishes are as fine as any in the region. Their mission emphasizes customer satisfaction and health.

WICHITA FEED & HARDWARE

6089 SE Johnson Creek Blvd   503/775-6767
Mon-Fri: 8-6; Sat: 8-5:30

I'll be honest with you, I don't do my own home repairs, but I like gadgets and gizmos. Those who are handy swear by the customer service at Wichita. These guys know what it takes to fix things around the house, and better yet, they know where to find the correct parts. A stop here may save you a trip to an expensive specialty store and you're sure to have fun perusing the crowded shelves stocked with electrical, plumbing and repair supplies; tools; pet supplies and whatchamacallits. Their expertise and advice have steered many a homeowner onto the right track of ridding their yard of moles or having the lushest lawn on the block. Seems like there's a gizmo or gadget in the store for just about any purpose!

WILDWOOD RESTAURANT

1221 NW 21st Ave   503/248-9663
Lunch: Mon-Sat; Dinner: Daily   wildwoodrestaurant.com
Expensive

Perennial favorite Wildwood is synonymous with Portland thanks to the talents and labors of founder **Cory Schreiber** and Executive Chef **Dustin Clark**. New American-style menus influenced by ethnic cuisines are driven by local farms and purveyors who also practice environmentally sound agriculture and sustainable farming; therefore, it's obvious that the menu is ever-changing. Lunch menus may include fennel braised pork manicotti,

THE CONTROVERSY CONTINUES

Have you heard of Dr. **Ruth Barnett**? For decades during the first half of the 20th century, Dr. Barnett was a nationally recognized, highly-skilled naturopath who reportedly performed abortions at her office in the Broadway Building in the heart of downtown Portland; rich and poor, it's said that her clientele came from across the West Coast. While illegal, Dr. Barnett operated in the open with a highly successful practice until a 1951 crackdown when legal battles and incarceration ensued.

a house-ground lamb or beef burger on housemade buns or outstanding Dungeness crab cakes. A selection of lighter lunch fare also appears as dinner starters before entrees of grilled fish, coal-roasted lamb chops, game or assorted cuts of beef. Don't overlook the exquisite desserts and assemblage of local distillers, brewers and vintners. This is the personification of an A-Team. Schreiber has deep family roots in Portland's restaurant scene.

ZUPAN'S MARKETS

2340 W Burnside	503/497-1088
3301 SE Belmont St	503/239-3720
Daily: 6 a.m.-10 p.m.	

7221 SW Macadam	503/244-5666
16380 Boones Ferry Road, Lake Oswego	503/210-4190
Daily: 7 a.m.-10 p.m.	zupans.com

Founded by the late **John Zupan** in 1975, Zupan's is a locally- and family-owned market that serves Portland's food-loving community. Likened to farmers markets, Zupan's focuses on quality, selling everything from the best meats and wines to the freshest produce, baked goods, gourmet deli products, specialty foods, flowers and more. Touting a unique grocery shopping experience, Zupan's stores are meant to indulge the senses, inviting customers to see, smell, taste and learn. Regularly scheduled beer, wine and cheese tastings are among customer favorites. Full-service floral departments (Burnside, Boones Ferry and Macadam locations) have beautiful fresh-cut flowers year-round and provide custom design, wedding and event services. The deli features handmade, home-style items with grab-n-go meals, gourmet sandwiches and catering. Bakery items are delivered from 35 of the best bakeries around the Portland area.

SAUVIE ISLAND

BLUE HERON HERBARY

27731 NW Reeder Road	503/621-1457
March-Nov: Wed-Sun: 10-5; Dec: Sat, Sun	blueheronherbary.com

Take a trip to Sauvie Island and explore the meandering roads passing by farms and wildlife refuges. Blue Heron Herbary is worth a stop to learn about the magic of herbs. Nearly 300 unusual and household herbs are planted in specialty beds: Mediterranean, salad, tea, bee and butterfly. You'll find great-smelling lavenders of a myriad of varietals, medicinal herbs, culinary additives and ornamentals grown under the loving care of the Hanselman family. In the gift shop you'll find herbal plants for home growing (over 350 varieties of herbs and more than 100 lavender variations), plus pottery, wind chimes, birdhouses, honey, spices and seasonings. Herbal and/or lavender wreaths, bath and beauty products, herbal cookies for dogs, catnip for felines and home decor and accessories (many items also available online) are crafted at the farm. Plan a wedding or reception on the beautiful grounds that are abuzz with bees, butterflies and songbirds.

SHERWOOD

SLEIGHBELLS FARM AND GIFT
23855 SW 195th Pl   503/625-6052, 866/857-0975
Daily: 10-6   sleighbells.biz

Although the name implies Christmas, nary a season or holiday goes by without attractive displays of decorative (traditional, whimsical, stylish) merchandise: Easter, patriotic, St. Patrick's, Valentines, Hanukkah, Halloween and especially Christmas. The best lines are represented: Christopher Radko, Department 56, Jim Shore, Papyrus, Yankee Candle, Byers Carolers and others. A tradition for many families is searching the 75-acre tree farm for the perfect Noble, Grand or Douglas fir Christmas tree. Starting in September, customers may preselect trees and have them ready on the predetermined day; of course, tromping through the farm with kids and dog in tow and saw in hand is also an option. Sleighbells is delightful any time of the year.

ST. HELENS

HOULTON BAKERY
2155 Columbia Blvd   503/366-2648
Tues-Sat: 9-4

This small town bakery has much going for it.   Maybe it's

THERE'S NOTHING LIKE A GOOD STEAK

For years, wise steak-lovers have made one-of-a-kind **Sayler's Old Country Kitchen** (105th and SE Stark, Portland, 503/252-4171; saylers.com) crowded every day of the week. Reasonable prices for top quality eats bring customers back again and again. Although steaks are in the main here, those who prefer seafood or chicken can find a number of entrees. The crab Louis is especially attractive and delicious. Don't miss the fabulous onion rings – right at the top of any offered in the Portland area. Steak offerings include filet mignon, top sirloin, T-bone, porterhouse, ribeye (bone-in or not), New York and ground sirloin steak. Since 1948, the 72 oz. top sirloin dinner has been served free to anyone who can eat the steak and trimmings within one hour (weekdays only). (Why – or how – anyone could do this is beyond me.) Senior dinners (value-priced) are offered, as well as prime rib plates and sandwiches. Sayler's is a true quality Portland tradition open seven days a week, varying hours.

the bread or fine desserts or some specialty food that you've been trying to find. If so, waste no time in getting to owner **Gainor Riker**'s establishment that features breads and pastries, chocolate-dipped shortbread, pecan-topped sticky buns, fresh berry tarts, cupcakes, specialty cakes, and on and on. Stop by for great sandwiches made on one of the daily baked breads (dill, dark rye, challah, potato rosemary, etc.) stuffed with satisfying fillings or opt for fresh salads and homemade soups. Just off of Highway 30, this is a convenient stop to fill up your coffee mug (and curb a sweet craving); outside seating in good weather.

SEAWRIGHT HOUSE

134 N 2nd St   503/366-3035
Moderate   seawrighthouse.com

You or your group will be the only (very spoiled) guests during your stay. This restored home, built in 1910, offers a 1,700 square-foot private suite with a complete kitchen, living room with fireplace, dining room, a spacious master bedroom, second bedroom, Jacuzzi tub, full laundry room, mini-office area, sunroom and inviting sundeck with private hot tub, water garden and views of Mt. St. Helens, the Columbia River and marina. **Melinda Beville** offers exceptional hosted, extended-stay or vacation rental accommodations; rented by the week, month or longer. Gracious hostess Melinda will help you begin a relaxing vacation with a "she thought of everything" feeling upon your arrival at this well-appointed home.

TIGARD

BRIDGEPORT VILLAGE
7455 SW Bridgeport Road   503/968-1704
Daily   bridgeport-village.com

Fashionistas, take note! This premier location offers unparalleled shopping with more than 60 fine shops and boutiques. Bridgeport is home to Oregon's only **Crate & Barrel**, **Tommy Bahama**, **Eileen Fisher**, **Z Gallerie**, **Container Store** and **Saks Fifth Avenue OFF 5th**. Hungry visitors have a dozen eateries from which to choose including **PF Chang's China Bistro**, **McCormick & Schmick's Grill** and **California Pizza Kitchen**. First-class amenities include valet parking, free Wi-Fi, strollers, wheelchairs and an enjoyable playground for kids. Catch a first-run flick at Regal Cinema; 18 screens and a 3-D IMAX. Additional big-name

LIKE FATHER, LIKE SON

Father and son **Wendell** and **Bill Wyatt** have served with excellence in various capacities throughout the state of Oregon. The late Wendell Wyatt called Astoria home following World War II and became a popular member of the U.S. House of Representatives after a special election in 1964, going on to win four succeeding terms; he was a close confidant of President **Gerald Ford.** Bill was a state representative from 1974 to 1977 for the north coast area, served as chief of staff during Governor **John Kitzhaber**'s first two terms and was appointed Executive Director of the busy Port of Portland in 2001, a position he presently holds.

FINE AND FRESH!

The vision of having a year-round farmers market in Portland brings back memories of the open-air stalls that once dotted southwest Yamhill Street when well-known food purveyors like **Isaac Hasson** (vegetables) and **"Jasper"** (who later operated a produce truck that covered the West Hills), endeared themselves to generations of Portland families. **Jack Luihn**, whose Sealey-Dresser was Portland's top gourmet food store, later became one of the prime movers in the **Sunshine Division** (sunshinedivision.org), still the charity arm of the Portland Police Bureau. Plans for the **James Beard Public Market** are underway at the western edge of the Morrison Bridge; convenient to public transportation and downtown.

shopping venues are in the immediate area. This is retail therapy at its best! The only drawback is the confusing and crowded traffic pattern.

THE GRAND HOTEL AT BRIDGEPORT

7265 SW Hazel Fern Road   503/968-5757, 866/968-5757
Moderate to very expensive   grandhotelbridgeport.com

Travelers and shoppers call The Grand Hotel their home away from home in this Portland suburb; the location is ideal for business or pleasure. Package deals combine superb lodging with golf, hot air balloon adventures, shopping and romantic stays. The 124 luxurious rooms and suites offer first-class service and amenities and complimentary covered parking, Internet service, shuttle service and a delicious breakfast buffet. Within easy walking distance is **Bridgeport Village** offering splendid local, regional and national retailers, irresistible boutiques and adjacent complexes with additional stores and services. Unwind after a flurry of activities in comfortable rooms, conveniently furnished with leather couches and coffee tables, microwaves, refrigerators, coffee stations, work desks with ergonomic chairs and the outstanding hospitality of The Grand Hotel. **Steve Johnson**, president of parent company VIP's Industries, is an expert in the hospitality arena.

THIRSTY LION PUB AND GRILL

10205 SW Washington Square Road   503/352-4030
Lunch, Dinner: Daily   thirstylionpub.com
Moderate

Head here if you are hungry as a lion. Burgers start with a half-pound of ground beef, then grilled and dressed with different cheeses, sauces, onions, bacon, guacamole, peppers or mushrooms. Slaw, salad or hand-cut fries accompany burgers and other great sandwiches (chicken, turkey club, pulled pork, French dip, Reuben) with delicious components. The grilled pear and gorgonzola starter salad is superb and fresh entree salads (ahi, chicken Caesar, Cobb) are a full meal. Eclectic

---

ENDURING QUALITY

Certainly one of the best known names in Oregon manufacturing is the **Pendleton** (pendleton-usa.com) brand. Originally the maker of high-quality woolen blankets with Native American themes and tough men's shirts, the company branched out to include the same quality in additional men's and women's clothing and home goods. Founded in 1909 by brothers, Clarence, Roy and Chauncey, the Bishop family (also associated in early days with the Thomas Kay Woolen Mills, now the site of **The Willamette Heritage Center at The Mill** (willametteheritage.org) in Salem) has been a leader in the commercial and social life of both Portland and Pendleton. Fourth-generation **Mort Bishop III** now heads the close-knit, hands-on family management team. The company is long admired for its corporate citizenship, participating in countless civic activities. The Pendleton label and the Bishop family are true Oregon treasures. The Portland metro area offers four retail stores, including clothing at the downtown and Lake Oswego locations, Pendleton Home, and The Woolen Mill store; Lincoln City, Pendleton and Seaside have outlet stores; and you can find the Pendleton brand in many top-quality retailers throughout the United States and in Canada.

sharable appetizers include nachos, Scotch eggs, garlic sesame edamame and favorites like pretzels and artichoke spinach dip. Entrees are also varied: mac and cheese, artisan pizzas, pastas, chicken and fish dishes, ribs, steaks and more. Fare is seasonal and made from scratch; daily specials emphasize local ingredients. They pride themselves on a large offering of craft beers; signature cocktails are pretty tasty, too.

TUALATIN

FIORANO RISTORANTE
18674 SW Boones Ferry Road   503/783-0727
Lunch: Mon-Thurs; Dinner: Mon-Sat   fioranos.com
Moderate

Inviting Tualatin Commons Lake is the setting for this traditional and infused Italian ristorante. For starters, order one of Chef Shan's daily appetizer specials. Robust pasta dishes are enhanced with traditional red or cream sauces, chili flakes or optional chicken, shrimp, Italian sausage or meatballs. Entrees are accompanied by pasta or polenta and are priced easy on the wallet. Choose a sunny midday or a balmy evening to enjoy lakeside dining; catering at your site or theirs.

HAYDEN'S LAKEFRONT GRILL
8187 Tualatin-Sherwood Road   503/885-9292
Breakfast, Lunch, Dinner: Daily   haydensgrill.com
Moderate

Hungry? Pop into Hayden's, adjacent to the **Century Hotel**, for quality meals in a relaxed atmosphere (inside or outside seating along the man-made lake). Breakfast choices appeal to light or hearty eaters and are served until 3 p.m. each day; lunches include meal-size salads and generously-portioned sandwiches with fries. Classic comfort food dinners of meatloaf, pork tenderloin, pastas and stews are made with fresh local ingredients and updated for today's palates; Hayden's three-course dinner is priced just right. Kudos to the chef for offering entrees in two sizes — small or regular and desserts that are also full-size or mini!

VERNONIA

COASTAL MOUNTAIN SPORT HAUS

66845 Nehalem Hwy N   503/429-6940
Moderate   coastalmountainsporthaus.com

Load up your friends and bikes for a great escape to this European-style inn offering four spacious guest rooms, a bunk room, custom outdoor soaking spa and a yoga session. Great biking trails abound, or simply enjoy the peaceful surroundings; laid-back or active — you choose. Built in 1999, this locale easily accommodates retreats, girls' getaways, man-cations and family groups. The tariff includes well-prepared breakfasts, lunches and dinners using fresh and local ingredients. (Two-night minimum; children 14 and older; no pets.) Mention *Gerry Frank's Oregon* when you book your stay and save 10% during March and April, based on availability.

WEST LINN

(FIVE-0-THREE)

21900 Willamette Dr, Suite 201   503/607-0960
Lunch: Tues-Fri; Dinner: Daily   restaurant503.com
Moderately expensive

A dinner at (five-0-three) is a pleasant experience. Note that the restaurant's name is its area code and represents their commitment to source local ingredients. Not only is the food very good, but the service is personal, the atmosphere cordial and the prices are on the easy side. The menu changes seasonally and many favorites come and go. If available, try the blue cheese butter and red wine pommes frites, roasted beet salad or other bites from the small plate menu. Recommended entrees include the fish of the day (perhaps crispy potato-crusted trout), pork or the signature burger (house-ground chuck, white cheddar, housemade bacon and caramelized onions on an artisan bun). For dessert, a slice of the rich 12-layer chocolate cake with homemade ice cream is a must.

Oregon late treasures and defining tidbits

At the mention of Oregonians who've made their mark in one way or another, fond memories come to mind.

Harry Banfield: Iron Fireman Manufacturing CEO, provided strong leadership in helping build the Oregon highway system; the Banfield Freeway is named in his honor.

Jack Burns, Bob Burns: both fresh out of the Navy with honorable discharges in 1947, opened the first Burns Bros. Truck Stop in Portland with the assistance of their parents Mr. and Mrs. E.V. "Bobby" Burns. The late Bobby Burns was Portland District Manager of Standard Oil Company for 30 years and a great civic booster.

Truman Collins: shy and gentle lumberman with a quiet demeanor that somewhat overshadowed his brilliant mind and the great philanthropic actions that forever framed his life

Ken Ford: One-of-a-kind early forester who never forgot his roots. The Ford Family Foundation (tfff.org) has benefitted thousands of Oregonians, especially in education.

Ted Gamble: Theater owner, promoter and the man who successfully sold more World War II war bonds than anyone in America.

John Hampton: outstanding lumberman and civic leader who once kicked a troublesome competitor out of a meeting in front of a highly approving governor of Oregon.

Loretta and Ira Keller: both feisty and smart, brought renewed vigor to the Portland business and social communities as "outsiders;" The Keller Fountain Park and the Ira Keller Fountain are named after Ira.

Dorothy McCulloch Lee: hardworking Portland mayor who liked nothing better than (for hours) bending the ears of other Portland leaders on how to clean up the city

Herb Lundy: Editorial page chief at *The Oregonian* commented on the news and events of the day from what came his way within the confines of his office (pre-instant communications era!).

Wayne Morse: Oregon senator, compelling conversationalist who loved the political spotlight (and raising prime Oregon cattle)

Frank Branch Riley: storyteller, lecturer, who never had enough resources to stay in first-class digs, when traveling would ask, "Do you want me to stay at the YMCA?"

E.C. "Ed" Sammons: United States National Bank legendary tough head honcho and civic leader; enjoyed personally distributing new, crisp $100 bills to his board for director fees

Lee Schlesinger: Personal troubles drove Olds, Wortman & King department store CEO to be taken for drowned after purposely running his car into the Columbia River; he turned up years later in South America under an assumed name.

Harold Schnitzer: universally respected, who, with his wife, Arlene, set a new standard for philanthropy in our community

Edgar Smith: another personable speechmaker, had to start all over if his canned Oregon presentation was interrupted

Ernie Swigert: ESCO industrialist extraordinaire whose talented offspring (Nani, E.C. "Ernie," deceased; Henry "Hank;" Elizabeth "Betty," deceased) also made history in their native state in various ways.

Moe Tonkon: smart, worldly and largely responsible for breaking down religious discriminatory barriers in Portland's private clubs

Sig Unander: **Simon Benson** family member, once the darling of the very "republican" Arlington Club, was defeated for the gubernatorial nomination by upstart republican **Mark Hatfield** who became Oregon's most celebrated politician.

Howard Vollum: shy, brilliant, made Tektronix history with **Jack Murdock** starting their tech business in a garage. Through benevolent planning both men and their families have made major contributions to civic good works.

Sam Wheeler: Willamette Industries' lumber executive, personal benefactor to many causes, proud father of State Treasurer **Ted Wheeler** and three other sons

Duke Wieden: superb advertising man, father of **Dan Wieden** (Wieden+Kennedy); fun, uplifting Portland treasure

Your notes

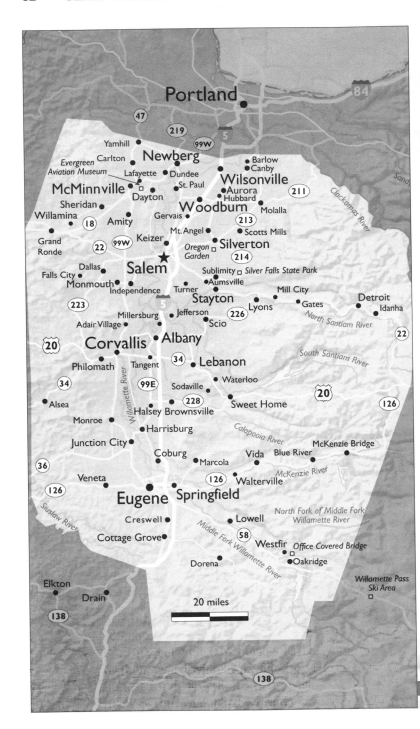

2. Willamette Valley

ALBANY

NICHOLS GARDEN NURSERY

1190 Old Salem Road NE
Mon-Sat: 9-5

541/928-9280, 800/422-3985
nicholsgardennursery.com

A treat for gardeners awaits at this longtime Willamette Valley nursery. Two generations of the family-run business continue to take pride in the fact that they never buy or sell genetically-engineered seeds or plants. All garden varieties are home tested so vegetables grown from Nichols' seed or stock are delicious and healthy. Their picture-perfect herb garden is a mid-summer delight; visitors are welcome and photographers are encouraged to snap away. In addition to new and unusual seeds (vegetable, herb and flower), plants, bulbs and roots, Nichols markets discontinued seeds, lawn mixes, books and other garden essentials. Non-garden products include beer, wine and cheese-making supplies, herbs and spices, oils, soaps and lotions.

SYBARIS
442 1st Ave W
Dinner: Tues-Sat
Moderate

541/928-8157
sybarisbistro.com

What was once a historic industrial building in downtown Albany is now a spacious, upscale dining establishment. A new menu is created each month using the freshest goods from growers and farmers in the heart of the Willamette Valley. The Northwest cuisine is an innovative and eclectic interpretation of classic meat, seafood and poultry dishes. Seasonally-adapted choices may include chilled pea soup, Hawaiian fried chicken with potato and macaroni salads, risotto of summer vegetables, pork rillettes or winter vegetable Wellington. Housemade is the rule, not the exception, right down to catsup and daily bread. Chef **Matt Bennett**'s outstanding reputation led him in 2008 and 2011 to prepare dinner at New York's legendary James Beard House where he was named one of the best Northwest chefs. The restaurant's decor is always fresh, too; wife, Janel, arranges displays of local artists' works.

ALSEA

LEAPING LAMB FARM STAY
20368 Honey Grove Road
Moderate

541/487-4966, 877/820-6132
leapinglambfarm.com

Scottie and Greg Jones continue the original 19th-century Honey Grove Farm homestead tradition as a working farm growing hay, raspberries and blueberries, grapes, plums, pears, apples and garlic and raising turkeys and sheep. A unique aspect to this farm is the two-bedroom rental cabin for bed and breakfast guests. The kitchen comes fully stocked with breakfast items (seasonally fresh) for guests to prepare as they wish. Guests have the option to help feed the farm animals, harvest fruits and vegetables, collect fresh eggs or wander the trails throughout the 64 acres. Of course, lazing by the creek or curling up with a good book is always an option. Urban kids dig the opportunity to be on the farm for a taste of rural life.

BLOOMING FIELDS

The brilliant colors of Oregon's flower industry are manifested in these Willamette Valley fields. Some farms celebrate the peak of the season with special events (family activities, festivals, barbecues). Cut flowers are for sale during bloom season and varieties are shown in catalogs for convenient ordering throughout the year. Bring your camera (and perhaps boots).

Canby
Swan Island Dahlias (503/266-7711, dahlias.com): August and September

Salem
Schreiner's Iris Gardens (schreinersgardens.com, 503/393-3232): May to early June
Adelman Peony Gardens (503/393-6185, peonyparadise. com): May to mid-June

Woodburn
Wooden Shoe Tulip Farm (503/634-2243, woodenshoe. com): April

AMITY

THE BLUE GOAT RESTAURANT
506 S Trade St   503/835-5170
Lunch, Dinner: Wed-Sun (seasonally adjusted)   amitybluegoat.com
Inexpensive to moderate

Along a stretch of Highway 99W dotted with wineries is a wee restaurant offering affordable upscale simple dining with Old World eclectic charm. Owners **Cassie and Dave VanDomelen** source local products for the daily-changing menu. You'll find soups, salads and other starters, sandwiches and pizza on the lunch menu; dinnertime brings some of the same with added scrumptious entrees (maybe braised beef gnocchi and housemade pasta), many prepared in a special wood-fired earthen oven. Several gluten-free dishes are also available. Diet-splurge desserts range from chocolate caramel tart to fresh fruit atop housemade pastries. Fresh daily rustic bread, a diverse selection of local wines and eight taps pouring Northwest microbrews complete your meal.

BLUE RAEVEN FARMSTAND

20650 S Hwy 99W   503/835-0740
Spring, summer, fall: Daily; winter: Tues-Sun (hours vary)
                                                    blueraevenfarmstand.com

Step inside this farmstand and you'll be greeted by tantalizing aromas emanating from freshly-baked bread and pies. Regular white and wheat are always on the racks joined by different specialty breads each day. One day it may be cheddar jalapeno loaves, another day cinnamon raisin or the baker's choice. For sweet-seekers, dozens of varieties of 5- and 9-inch pies will fulfill the hankering; many are seasonal to capture the essence of the freshest fruits. Berries and fruits are enveloped in golden crust, sometimes solo or in interesting and delicious combinations. There is also a generous list of cream pies; on request, most pies can be prepared sugar-free. (It's best to call ahead if you're craving a certain flavor.) Fresh produce, jams, jellies, syrups and other local products and gifts round out the merchandise selection.

AURORA

ANNA BECKE HOUSE BED & BREAKFAST

14892 Bobs Ave   503/678-6979
Moderate   annabeckehouse.com

Anna and Charles Becke likely could never have imagined that their dream home (circa 1910) would become a welcome travelers' accommodation in the form of a bed and breakfast inn. This Craftsman-style home has kept its original exterior and offers two guest rooms (no children or pets). The house has beautiful grounds and vintage and antique furnishings and collections. After a day of shopping in this heart of Oregon's antiquing capital, your hosts provide afternoon and evening refreshments in the

KIDS' ACTIVITIES: WILLAMETTE VALLEY

Brooks
Antique Powerland Museum (503/393-2424,
antiquepowerland.com)

Eugene
Science Factory Children's Museum (541/682-
7888, sciencefactory.org)

McMinnville
Evergreen Aviation & Space Museum (503/434-
4185, evergreenmuseum.org) and **Evergreen Wings
& Waves Waterpark** (503/434-4185,
evergreenmuseum.org/waterpark)

Mollala
Molalla Train Park at Shady Dell (503/829-6866,
pnls.org): seasonal
Rosse Posse Acres (503/829-7107, rosseposseacres.
com)

Salem
A.C. Gilbert's Discovery Village (503/371-3631,
acgilbert.org)
Salem's Riverfront Carousel (503/540-0374,
salemcarousel.org)

Silverton
Oregon Garden (503/874-8100, oregongarden.org)
Silver Falls State Park (800/551-6949,
oregonstateparks.org)

Turner
Enchanted Forest (503/371-4242, enchantedforest.com)

comfortable guest lounge. Depending on the weather, you may choose to cozy up to the parlor fireplace or rest on the charming front porch to speculate on life in the early days in Oregon's first designated National Historic District. A full gourmet breakfast awaits in the attractive sunlit dining room in preparation for a day of exploring this wonderful north Willamette Valley area.

TIMELESS ANTIQUES & COLLECTIBLES

14988 2nd St   503/678-6987
Daily: 11-5   timelessantiquesonline.com

A building that served as Aurora's post office until the late 20th century is now home to **Barbara Johnson**'s plethora of first-rate antiques and elegant vintage and Depression glassware. Beautiful oak pieces showcase colorful collections of glassware by Fostoria, Heisy, Cambridge, Imperial, Hocking and Carnival. There are ample lines of china, pottery and dinnerware such as Hall, Limoges, Haviland, Franciscan, Homer Laughlin, Spode and Irish Belleek. Mid-century modern pieces have been added to the merchandise mix.

BLUE RIVER

HOLIDAY FARM RESORT

54455 McKenzie River Dr   541/822-3725
Moderate to expensive   holidayfarmresort.com

The secluded resort is ideally situated on the scenic McKenzie River and is a mecca for fly-fishing, drift boating, bird watching, hiking and nearly unlimited outdoor recreation. Five cottages are on the

DID YOU KNOW ...?

... that the **myrtlewood** crafted in Southern Oregon is not genuine myrtle (found only in the Old World), but a California laurel?

... that former Secretary of State **Norma Paulus** has the unusual distinction of being the only woman, or perhaps person, accepted into an Oregon law school with only a high school diploma (Burns, Oregon high school graduate) and was also the first woman in Oregon history to win a statewide office (elected Secretary of State, 1977-1985)?

... that the unspoiled Northeastern Oregon **Wallowa Mountains**, approximately 350 square miles, contain some 100 lakes, literally teeming with (mostly stocked) fish that await your hook, line and sinker?

property; eight others are scattered up to 16 miles away. Each accommodation is a bit different and individually named to reflect its character: log house, historical, Mediterranean-style, rustic, cozy or spacious; capacity ranges from two to 14 occupants. Wood-burning fireplaces, kitchenettes and decks are standard in most units. Golfers may want to book a tee time at the 18-hole **Tokatee Golf Course** (tokatee.com), a Giustina family enterprise in nearby Rainbow; views are incredible when not eyeballing your shot. This stretch of the McKenzie is dotted with little burgs, parks and trails and a splendid region to explore for a day or longer.

PACIFIC TREE CLIMBING INSTITUTE

541/461-9410, 866/653-8733
Prices vary   pacifictreeclimbing.com

If there's one thing that Oregon has an abundance of it is trees, and with the coaching of these well-trained professionals, you can learn the art of tree climbing (while having the experience of your life). Go on an old-growth expedition using state-of-the-art equipment specifically designed for this activity; the low guest-to-guide ratio provides plenty of individual attention. You will bed down high among the branches in a comfortable canvas hammock fitted with a two-inch thick air mattress. Day climbers relish the organic lunch; more adventurous overnighters are rewarded with dinner, morning hot beverage and refreshing peppermint-aroma hot towel, followed by an organic breakfast back on terra firma. Melodic forest sounds are sure to lull insomniacs into dreamland. No particular age or experience is required.

BROWNSVILLE

THE LIVING ROCK STUDIOS

911 W Bishop Way   541/466-5814
Tues-Sat: 10-5 (or by reservation)   livingrockstudios.org
Free (donations accepted)

Take a short detour off of I-5 for a look back into history with a fabulous showing of rocks, historic artifacts, carvings of Oregon native woods, life-size bird paintings, hundreds of mineral specimens and other fascinating objects. Visionary artist and naturalist

Howard B. Taylor spent over 30 years creating this unique attraction, made with more than 800 tons of stone and concrete. Visitors marvel at seven biblical scenes made of translucent rocks, perhaps more beautiful than stained glass windows. A tree of petrified wood pieces, lined with sparkling crystals, reaches two stories high, crowned by a fiber-art canopy. Look high and low as many items are built into walls, ramps and the stairway; flashlights are provided to highlight special details and to make agates glow.

CARLTON

ABBEY ROAD FARM
10501 NE Abbey Road   503/852-6278
Moderate to very expensive   abbeyroadfarm.com

Owners **Judi and John Stuart** preside over an 82-acre farm, offering guests a choice of five tastefully appointed "silo suites" or a renovated three-bedroom farmhouse which works well for families or couples traveling together. The suites are unique in that they are built into units with windows on the curved walls that open to stunning views of the cherry orchard, vast grass seed fields, a neighboring vineyard and an English garden. Breakfast in the old farmhouse is served at 8:30, just a short stroll away. Animal lovers will be entertained with the collection of llamas, sheep, goats and chickens; it is possible that your breakfast eggs are produced from one of these colorful cluckers and you'll enjoy homemade chèvre cheese, courtesy of the goats. The inviting parlor and outdoor observation deck are conducive to sampling wines purchased in this wine region.

BROOKSIDE INN ON ABBEY ROAD
8243 NE Abbey Road   503/852-4433
Moderate to very expensive   brooksideinn-oregon.com

Expect first-class linens and amenities in the nine attractively appointed suites at this secluded country inn. Primarily furnished a la the Northwest, rooms feature Asian and Scottish touches and fine artwork by Northwest artists. Wine and food lovers will be in seventh heaven with Brookside's aim to provide a fine culinary experience for their guests. Breakfast is a three-course affair

ABOUT FACE!

One of Oregon's two former WWII training camps, **Camp Adair** honored war hero and Astoria native Lieutenant **Henry Rodney Adair** (killed in a Mexican border clash in 1916) and took in some 65,000 acres six miles north of Corvallis. (**Camp Abbot**, at what is now Sunriver, was the other training camp.) Governor **Charles Sprague** was instrumental in Adair's siting by identifying the necessary acreage (akin to German topography and climate where soldiers would likely be sent), good water supply, electrical power and railroad access; 8,000 laborers working with a $32 million budget to construct 1,800 buildings (some were full-scale models of European and Japanese towns) in a six-month period (a boon to the Oregon economy as well as the war effort). From 1942 to 1944, 100,000 soldiers trained for combat here; it was a POW camp for Italians and Germans from 1944 to 1946. In use as a military installation only for about six years, the buildings were demolished, salvaged, sold or took on new purposes over several years. Oregon State University was the beneficiary of large blocks of timberland and gained student and faculty housing; wildlife preserves were established. Today, a population of over 800 call Adair Village home.

inspired (and occasionally prepared) by Northwest chefs. Typical morning fare includes gourmet coffee, granola and fruit, pastries, artisan cheeses and cured meats and entrees bursting with fresh local bounty. Meandering trails, attractive gardens, streams, hand-built waterfalls and a catch-and-release trout pond beg visitors to stay a tad longer to enjoy the surroundings.

CARLTON WINEMAKERS STUDIO

801 N Scott St   503/852-6100
Daily: 11-5 (winter: 11-4)   winemakersstudio.com

While in Carlton, visit this cooperative winemaking facility where a dozen or so small, independent winemakers produce and sell bottles of some of the best that Oregon's wine country has to offer. Wineries represented may be as small as operations producing only 200 cases a year with treasures exclusive to this innovative location. Creative uses of repurposed, recycled and green materials in the building's design and construction led to its impressive status as the first winery to be registered with the U.S. Green Building Council. You'll see many of these features in the tasting room and in the production areas. The selection of reds and whites is large with prices ranging from $15 to $72 a bottle.

CUVEE

214 W Main St   503/852-6555
Lunch: Memorial Day to Labor Day: Sat, Sun;
Dinner: May-Dec: Wed-Sun; Jan-April: Fri-Sun   cuveedining.com
Expensive

Chef-owner **Gilbert Henry** from Alsace, France, wanted to find a place reminiscent of his hometown, a place where he could set up a fine country French restaurant. He decided that Carlton was just that locale. So he set to work to create a dinner house with a distinct French accent, a large wine list (French imports and Oregon favorites), classic cocktails and a restaurant drawing diners to his tables because of its sophisticated ambience. Lovers of true French cuisine will appreciate many traditional favorites such as bouillabaisse, escargots, coquille St. Jacques, steamed mussels and *boeuf bourguignon* with ingredients sourced from local farms and vendors. Two signatures of a real French dinner house are crisp *pomme frites* and warm, crunchy French bread with that just-out-of-the-oven aroma. In both cases, Cuvee excels. In-the-know diners head to Cuvee on Wednesday, Thursday and Sunday evenings for Chef Henry's scrumptious three-course *prix-fixe* dinner; it's a real bargain at $25 per person.

EQUESTRIAN WINE TOURS

                                                         971/241-1030
Year round, by reservation   equestrianwinetours.com
Prices vary

For a super family or romantic outing, head to the Dundee Hills and explore the wine country via horseback or carriage. **Shirley and Jake Price** and their son **Don Price** offer several options for a world-class scenic adventure. If you'd just like to sit back and enjoy yourself, opt for a carriage ride; choose from an antique surrey, a white "Central Park" carriage, a circa 1890 black carriage or a 12-passenger carriage (ideal for small groups). If you are more ambitious, climb atop one of their Tennessee Walkers and wind your way between vineyards on a two-hour guided tour and wine tasting. To complete your memorable outing, arrange with the Prices for a gourmet picnic served in high style. Extremely affable Jake is a world champion horseman and in 1995 represented the United States at the Equitana equestrian sports world fair in Germany.

SOCIAL BUTTERFLY

In the days of in-depth reporting on the social goings-on in communities, the *Oregon Statesman* (later merged with the *Capital Journal* to become the *Statesman Journal*) had **Jeryme English** on its staff. Jeryme relished her society position, attending any and every party that occurred in Salem and reporting on who wore what (*Mrs. so-and-so was resplendent in blue…*), who "poured" and perhaps who was not there! Known and liked by everyone, Jeryme didn't just report, she was always dressed like a lady going to a party and mingled with guests for the latest scoop (whether for print or kept to herself). Reminiscent of "ladies who lunch" while at the same time holding a professional position in a time when that wasn't so common, surely Jeryme English is a historic Salem figure. (**Mary Louise VanNatta-Gail's** *Out and About* column, now seen in the Sunday *Statesman*, is a fine adaptation of Jeryme's *Around Town* features.)

THE HORSE RADISH

211 W Main St   503/852-6656
Lunch: Daily; Dinner: Fri, Sat (till 10)   thehorseradish.com
Inexpensive to moderate

Superb artisan cheeses from around the Northwest reign at The Horse Radish, a restaurant and wine and cheese bar. I love great cheese and there are no shortage of sweet and savory choices made with milk from cows, goats or sheep. The knowledgeable staff assists customers in creating custom meat and cheese platters from any of the offerings to take along on a wine tasting sojourn or enjoy in-house with wine or a meal. Standard soup, salad and sandwich fare prevails on the brief lunch menu, and dinner specials are offered Friday and Saturday nights in conjunction with weekly live music performances. Yes, horseradish is on the menu in a smoked salmon dip.

LOBENHAUS BED & BREAKFAST & VINEYARD

6975 NE Abbey Road   503/864-9173
Moderate   lobenhaus.com

Carlton's Abbey Road is dotted with bed and breakfast inns and lodges. This resting place is in a tri-level rustic home built as a B&B in 2001 and recently updated and refreshed. Each of the six guest rooms contains a private bathroom and opens onto an outside deck or patio. Gracious hosts **Shari and Joe Lobenstein** offer a beautiful breakfast spread and around-the-clock refreshments, fine linens and robes, tasting certificates to nearby wineries and free Wi-Fi. The common area has a

REMARKABLE TWOSOME

The next time you are sitting in a dental chair (probably wishing you were not there) cheer up by knowing that the chair and all the other nearby tools and paraphernalia were likely manufactured by a highly-successful Oregon firm. Talented engineer Ken Austin and his ace financial partner and wife, Joan (JoAnn), founded **A-Dec, Inc.** (us.a-dec.com), an acronym for Austin Dental Company, in Newberg in 1964. **Joan and Ken Austin** originally met in Newberg and returned to begin what has turned into a world-renowned company employing nearly 1,000 people and approaching $300 million in annual sales. With hard-earned financial success and caring hearts, the Austins have liberally shared much of their wealth with all manner of causes throughout their community and our entire state. I tip my hat to this fine pair!

large-screen television and fireplace and the expansive porch is comfortable for sitting a spell. Viticulturist Joe established the vineyard at the same time the home was constructed and delights in sharing his grape wisdom with guests.

R.R. THOMPSON HOUSE BED & BREAKFAST

517 N Kutch St   503/852-6236
Moderate   rrthompsonhouse.com

Within walking distance of over two dozen Carlton wineries and tasting rooms, the R.R. Thompson House is a meticulously restored Colonial Revival 1930s estate. As visitors enter through a charming white picket fence lush gardens enhance the approach to the stately white home with green shutters. The historic home features five floral-themed guest rooms and suites with private marble and granite bathrooms, whirlpool tubs and luxurious mattresses for restful slumber. Breakfast in the dining room is a feast for the senses and morning appetites; the signature brie omelet or puffed apple pancakes may be the choice du jour. A thoughtful selection of light beverages from the well-stocked refrigerator is handy for guests to raid day or night.

CORVALLIS

BIG RIVER RESTAURANT

101 NW Jackson Ave   541/757-0694
Lunch: Mon-Fri; Dinner: Mon-Sat   bigriverrest.com
Moderate

Big River has been a big hit since it first opened featuring eclectic, fresh, Northwest cuisine using local organic produce, natural meats, sustainable seafood and Big River artisan breads from the on-site bakery. Sandwiches are extra delicious made on these breads and stuffed with pulled pork, turkey or house-cured beef brisket layered with sauerkraut. Seasonal martinis, single malt scotches and local and regional wines are featured at the bar; live jazz on weekends. The perfect end to your meal is dessert created by their award-winning pastry chef. The crew strives to bring good, honest food directly from the Valley with the menu supporting many of the area's hard-working farmers, ranchers and foragers.

THE BROKEN YOLK CAFE

119 SW Third St   541/738-9655
Breakfast: Daily: 7-3   broken-yolk.com
Inexpensive

Many Corvallis residents and Oregon State University alums fondly remember Burton's Sunny Brook Restaurant, a popular eatery spanning five decades. With a nod to the nostalgic past, the current owners retained Burton's familiar booths and tables when they renovated and upgraded their acquisition. This building is now a home-style breakfast spot. Eggs, of course, take top billing in skillet and scramble dishes or alongside or atop crispy chicken-fried steak or hobo hash. Creamy sausage gravy complements just about any entree, and grandma's strawberry jam is the perfect topper for toast or fluffy hotcakes. A special touch is a fun play area for young kids in this family-friendly and collegiate favorite.

HANSON COUNTRY INN

795 SW Hanson St   541/752-2919
Moderate   hcinn.com

One of the Valley's oldest country inns enjoys a charming knoll-top setting. The five-acre estate was built in 1928 by J.A. Hanson and also functioned as a poultry breeding ranch. The home has been brought back to its original style and class by the Covey family and adorned with attractive antiques and art. Four spacious guest rooms feature original built-ins, sitting rooms and private baths; a cozy two-bedroom cottage is equipped with a private kitchen and modern electronic conveniences. The aroma of homemade muffins entices guests into the sunny dining room to partake in a full gourmet breakfast; a well-stocked library beckons bookworms. The facilities are ideal for garden weddings, receptions, parties and meetings.

LUC

134 SW 4th St   541/753-4171
Dinner: Wed-Sun   i-love-luc.com
Moderate

It's all about food and wine at this casually elegant eatery. Chef **Ian Hutchings** often changes the menu, featuring inventive yet

FAMOUS BUT NOT EQUAL

When famed African-American singers **Marian Anderson** and **Paul Robeson** appeared in concert at Willamette University in Salem during the 1950s, there were no accommodations because of the city's discriminatory restrictions. They were forced to travel to Portland for hotel rooms, driven by none other than **Mark Hatfield**, then a Willamette student. Mortified by this disgraceful social insult, Mark did not forget and went on to successfully campaign for change as a state legislator. (Anderson's nephew is the great Maestro **James DePreist** who so ably led the Oregon Symphony for years.)

down-to-earth savory gourmet delights; **Adrienne Marler** oversees the vino. Their partnership turns out great tasting meals such as pork shoulder au poivre with creamy polenta, Dungeness crab fritters and goat cheese tiramisu. House-cured bacon is a tasty addition to several dishes. Come for a special wine-paired dinner, or just because, and enjoy the results of these serious foodies.

NEARLY NORMAL'S

109 NW 15th St   541/753-0791
Breakfast, Lunch, Dinner: Mon-Sat   nearlynormals.com

We all like to think we're normal, or at least nearly so and Nearly Normal's makes the case with its mission of in-house cooperation, unique style and "growth through challenge" at its eatery. The vegetarian restaurant with its five owners has been evolving since 1979, producing "gonzo cuisine" — the outcome of using the freshest, often organic, ingredients, many original recipes and careful preparation and presentation. The large menu offers choices that may make you forget the vegetarian bent: eggs, potatoes, pancakes, soups, salads, veggie burgers (try the famous Sunburger), falafel and a "nearly nasty" burrito; kids' menu, too.

BREWERIES – DISTILLERIES – WINERIES

Oregon has seen an amazing growth in the beer, wine and distillery industries. Go to "See and Do" under **Travel Oregon**'s (traveloregon.com) website. You'll find specific details for beer and breweries, distilleries and wineries and wine. Additional websites that provide excellent information with search by area, by features and/or interactive maps, include:

oregonbeer.org

oregondistillersguild.org

explorer.oregonwine.org

oregonpinotnoirwine.com

winesnw.com

COTTAGE GROVE

APPLE INN BED AND BREAKFAST

30697 Kenady Lane   800/942-2393
Moderate   appleinnbb.com

Kathe and Harry McIntire's family home and tree farm is tucked into 270 acres. They offer two comfy guest accommodations, appropriately named the Apple Orchard and Tree House rooms (each with a private bath and either a claw-footed tub or rain shower), a common area and decks for relaxing and appreciating the natural vista. Creature comforts include in-room refrigerators and microwaves, board games, cozy socks, fluffy robes and flax and lavender neck wraps. Professional home economist Kathe exhibits her culinary skills each morning with a delicious breakfast and in the evening with home-baked treats delivered to your room. Explore the great outdoors with a walk through the woods or arrange with expert forester Harry for a field trip.

STACY'S COVERED BRIDGE RESTAURANT & LOUNGE

401 E Main St   541/767-0320
Lunch: Tue-Fri; Dinner: Mon-Sat (Sun: March-Sept)
Moderate

Stacy's is in downtown Cottage Grove next to the Centennial

Covered Bridge in a building that originally housed the Bank of Cottage Grove. With just 14 tables, the dining area fills up quickly for lunch and dinner. Owner **Stacy Solomon** prides himself on good service and comfortable prices and a menu of fresh seafood, prime rib, pastas and fresh salads. A good selection of appealing lunch sandwiches, reasonably-priced early-bird specials and outdoor seating in nice weather adds to the appeal.

VICTORIANA ANTIQUES & COSTUMES
538 E Main St   541/767-0973
Tues-Sat: 10-5

When you're poking around Cottage Grove, browse through **Lesley Neufeld**'s unusual shop. Lesley traded life in Hollywood, where she was a costume designer, for a quiet spot in small-town America. Her high-end vintage clothing with a customer base of Civil War aficionados and other hobbyists is a unique business indeed!

DAYTON

RED RIDGE FARMS
5510 NE Breyman Orchards Road   503/864-2200
Lodging: Expensive to very expensive

OREGON OLIVE MILL
Daily

RED RIDGE STORE
Tues-Sun: 9-5   redridgefarms.com

Red Ridge Farms is a 2001 creation of **Penny, Ken and Paul Durant**'s 40-year involvement with the Oregon farming community. The family began growing wine grapes in the early 1970s; today they farm over 60 acres of prime wine grapes and tend to approximately 13,000 olive trees. In 2005, they began growing cold hardy olive trees which started the olive oil industry in Oregon. The **Oregon Olive Mill** building houses a state of the art Italian Alfa Laval press and bottling facilities where olives are pressed mid- to late-November. The weekend before Thanksgiving, the Durants host an Olio Nuovo party open to the public with tastings of fresh olive oil, bruschetta and samples of their wines, also available for sale in the gift shop. Other products include specialty vinegars, gourmet salts, teas, local products and houseplants. Lavender and rosemary plants, other perennial and annual herbs, shrubs and trees are available from the nursery. Lodging accommodations include a charming guest suite above the gift shop and a beautiful new cottage in the vineyard.

STOLLER VINEYARDS

16161 NE McDougall Road   503/864-3404
Expensive to very expensive   stollervineyards.com

This generational family property was once the largest turkey operation in Oregon. In 1993, with the collapse of Oregon's turkey market, **Cathy and Bill Stoller** (Cathy passed away in 2011) took the plunge and purchased the property with a vision of a world-class vineyard. It is now 200 acres devoted to pinot noir and chardonnay grapes. The vineyard's three diverse vacation homes are ideal for a romantic weekend or week long group outing. Each rental (at or near the winery) offers a fully-equipped kitchen, laundry facility and free Wi-Fi. You'll also find a bottle of flagship SV Pinot Noir on arrival. A complimentary tasting is part of any stay; tours available by appointment.

WINE COUNTRY FARM
BED & BREAKFAST AND CELLARS

6855 Breyman Orchards Road   503/864-3446, 800/261-3446
Moderate to expensive   winecountryfarm.com

Although this is a working farm where delicious grapes are grown and beautiful Arabian horses are raised, guests come for peace, quiet and relaxation. Nine rooms and suites with private entrances are available, all with private baths, down comforters and Wi-Fi. Guests are welcomed at check-in with a glass of wine as they familiarize themselves with their queen- or king-bed room and discover the beautiful views and grounds from the decks. Breakfast is a superlative start to the day. At their adjacent boutique winery and cellars, guests receive a complimentary tasting of the estate wines. Spend an hour or all day on the property wine tasting, wandering the lovely grounds or exploring the trails on foot or on one of **Jake Price**'s **Equestrian Wine Tours** (equestrianwinetours.com).

MCGRATH'S FISH HOUSE

The first **McGrath's Fish House** opened in 1980 in downtown Salem on Chemeketa Street; the popular fresh-catch restaurant soon added a second, then a third location. There are now 13 waterfront-style restaurants in Oregon, Washington, Idaho and Utah. **Debbie and John McGrath** have stayed true to the mission of supplying the freshest seafood at the lowest prices and have added steaks, pork ribs, chicken entrees, pasta selections, great clam chowder and delicious crab and shrimp salads to their full-service lunch and dinner menus.

Beaverton	3211 SW Cedar Hills Blvd	503/646-1881
Bend	3118 N Hwy 97	541/388-4555
Corvallis	350 Circle Blvd	541/752-3474
Eugene	1036 Valley River Way	541/342-6404
Medford	68 E Stewart Ave	541/732-1732
Milwaukie	11050 SE Oak St	503/653-8070
Salem	350 Chemeketa NE	503/362-0736
	3805 Center St NE	503/485-3086

DETROIT

BREITENBUSH HOT SPRINGS
5300 Breitenbush Road   503/854-3320
Daily   breitenbush.com
Inexpensive

One of the Northwest's gems is tucked in 154 acres in the Willamette National Forest about ten miles upstream from Detroit. This sanctuary along the Breitenbush River offers a rustic retreat for singles, couples or groups (reservations required). Make a day trip or pitch a tent (good weather) or stay in the lodge or geothermally heated cabins. While there, enjoy vegetarian organic cuisine; take advantage of daily well-being offerings (yoga, meditation, massage); a monthly Inipi Ceremony (sweat lodge);

concerts, readings and dances and the natural hot springs for soaking away any worries (to garb or not to garb, that is *your* question). Overnighters should check the website for a list of personal items to bring and what to leave at home. This escape is off the grid in many ways and yours to experience. Caution: Don't rely on GPS or Mapquest for directions, especially in winter months when snow-covered roads are tricky.

DUNDEE

BLACK WALNUT INN & VINEYARD

9600 NE Worden Hill Road   503/538-8663, 866/429-4114
Expensive to very expensive   blackwalnut-inn.com

Italy's Tuscan region meets Oregon's wine country at this jewel set in Dundee's Red Hills. The inn is a labor of love for the **Karen and Neal Utz** family and special care and attention to detail is evident throughout the eight suites with upscale Italian linens, quality bath amenities, spa soaking tubs and meticulously decorated suites. Rooms are both spacious and restful. Organic vegetable gardening has been Karen's passion since she was a child. Now her impressive gardens yield fresh herbs and fruits that are part of the full gourmet breakfast; she considerately provides several selections. A brood of hens is the source of fresh eggs used in the delicious egg dishes. Don't end your memorable stay without purchasing a bottle or so of their estate-grown pinot noir and chardonnay wines (Black Walnut Inn and Utz Family). Consult the innkeepers for superb concierge services and intimate weddings at the inn.

CANDIDATE AND COACH

The name Bowerman has deep roots in the annals of Oregon history. Senate President **Jay Bowerman** was a forward-thinking politician, assuming the office of acting governor (1910-1911) when Governor **Frank Benson** became ill. Jay Bowerman never won election to Oregon's top spot, being defeated by **Oswald West**. Jay's son, **Bill Bowerman**, is a legendary figure in the history of University of Oregon track and field; among other well-known track athletes, he coached **Phil Knight** and co-founded **NIKE**.

DUNDEE BISTRO

100-A SW 7th St   503/554-1650
Lunch, Dinner: Daily   dundeebistro.com
Moderately expensive

PONZI TASTING ROOM AND WINE BAR

Daily: 11 till closing   503/554-1550
                                                        ponziwinebar.com

Mention the name Ponzi in Oregon and it will probably receive instant recognition as one of the leaders in the Oregon wine industry. It is no surprise that Ponzi's Dundee Bistro and Tasting Room and Wine Bar are winners as well. With more than a decade's success hosting locals and the ever-increasing number of wine country visitors, the Bistro's kitchen continues to present fresh ideas and dishes inspired and executed by Executive Chef **Christopher Flanagan**. The Bistro consistently sources ingredients from neighboring farms, ranches, orchards, fishermen and wild mushroom foragers; the result is a constantly changing menu. Wines are showcased, properly presented and served in varietally correct Reidel crystal. Designed and built by the Ponzi clan, the Italianate complex features murals and artwork by Oregon artists. Guests enjoy cozy fireside seating and summer courtyard dining; a private dining room accommodates up to 50 people.

DUNDEE MANOR

8380 NE Worden Hill Road   503/554-1945, 888/262-1133
Expensive   dundeemanor.com

Well-traveled hosts **Brad Cunningham** and **David Godfrey** put fond memories and experiences from around the globe to good use in their Edwardian estate built in 1908. Accommodations consist of four rooms with Asian, European, African and North American motifs and accessories acquired on their journeys. Upon arrival, guests are welcomed with a glass of local wine; a thoughtful prelude to the afternoon appetizer; in-room snacks and refreshing beverages are offered; and a sweet treat is provided with the nightly turndown service. Carve out some time to enjoy the wooded and landscaped areas with gazebos, pergolas and private sitting areas, complete with attractive lighting and soothing music. En suite amenities are sure to please even finicky guests: down comforters, extra comfy queen beds, luxury linens, fleece spa robes and daily fresh flowers. The seemingly unending pampering continues at candlelit breakfasts — wonderful gourmet courses, beautiful presentation and special attention by your hosts.

RED HILLS PROVINCIAL DINING

276 N Hwy 99W   503/538-8224
Dinner: Tues-Sun   redhills-dining.com
Expensive

A changing seasonal menu in a charming restored Craftsman-style house is the forte of **Nancy and Richard Gehrts**. The attractive setting becomes more resplendent in the spring when massive rhododendrons are in bloom; the classy dining room is pleasingly done in black and taupe, setting off crisp white tablecloths. Nancy warmly welcomes diners at the front of the house while Richard prepares soups, sauces, stocks, desserts, breads, charcuterie and ice creams from scratch, relying upon family recipes for inspiration. Richard pulls double duty tending organic gardens at the restaurant locale and at Gehrts Vineyard in the hills of Dundee. The fruits (and herbs and vegetables) of his labor often find their way onto the menu. For example, you may find smoked duck breast with marionberry catsup, tenderloin of pork with riesling sauce and späetzle, pastas and game dishes. Definitely delightful!

TINA'S RESTAURANT

760 Hwy 99W   503/538-8880
Lunch: Tues-Fri; Dinner: Daily
Expensive   tinasdundee.com

Twenty years ago, husband and wife team, **Tina and David Bergen**, found happiness through mutual love of food and its preparation. Their passion continues to shine in the small 50-seat restaurant whose customers often return to the two intimate dining rooms and familiar bar. Weekday lunches include salads, sandwiches, risottos, stews and soups; dinner entrees include duck, salmon, lamb, beef, vegetarian or gluten-free offerings. All are prepared primarily using European techniques. The menus are developed around organic, healthy, high-quality, fresh and regional foods from nearby farmers and neighbors. Unsurprisingly, offered wines are from vintners just a stone's throw away.

EUGENE

BEPPE & GIANNI'S TRATTORIA

1646 E 19th Ave   541/683-6661
Dinner: Daily   beppeandgiannis.net
Moderate

This bustling trattoria is in a remodeled house that is as comfortable as a well-loved Prada handbag. Just south of the University of Oregon campus, it is an oft-frequented spot for families visiting away-from-home students. Aromatic roasted garlic is especially good with Cambozolo cheese and grilled bread as an appetizer. Most pastas are fresh and handmade; shapes, fillings, sauces and accompanying meats and seafood are paired into delicious combinations. Before you order, ask about the special ravioli flavor of the day. Chicken, fish, lamb, eggplant and other familiar mainstays are also made into Italian dishes. Additionally, there is a special menu for youngsters and seasonal alfresco dining. Always busy; reservations for groups of eight or more.

CADDIS FLY ANGLING SHOP

168 W 6th Ave   541/342-7005
Mon-Fri: 9-6; Sat: 10-5; Sun: 10-3   thecaddisfly.com

Novice or professional fishermen (and fisherwomen) head to this amazing 4,000-square foot emporium for fishing gear. With more than three decades of service to those who love the outdoors, this Eugene institution not only offers the best brands of equipment (Orvis, Winston, Bauer, Rio, Sage and more), but also provides advice on just about anything you'd want to know about one of Oregon's greatest recreational activities. As a fly-fishing shop, they specialize in flies and stock patterns for all types of fish and an amazing selection of supplies and materials for tying your own. Don't go near the water without the appropriate waders, inflatable watercraft, clothing, books and accessories that you may not have known even existed (convenient online shopping, too). Lastly, book a trip with one of their licensed and experienced guides for an unforgettable experience — rain or shine.

CAFÉ 440

440 Coburg Road   541/505-8493
Lunch, Dinner: Mon-Sat; Brunch: Sun   cafe440eugene.com
Moderate

When you're in the mood for a relaxed lunch or dinner at a friendly place, head over to this area clustered with strip malls. You'll find top-notch comfort food like burgers, meatloaf and other sandwiches, delicious salads with housemade dressings, soups and "gourmet" mac and cheese. The dinner menu expands to include steaks, chops, cornflake-encrusted fried chicken, pastas and more. There is plenty of action on Sundays for the brunch offerings of omelets, Benedicts, homemade biscuits and gravy (topped with Tillamook cheese) and shrimp and grits. The sizable menu is bursting with old-standbys, many given updated treatment with unexpected and tasty ingredients. Owner **Todd Scheutz** adheres to his philosophy "keep it simple and make it better than everyone else." I say he has the right idea.

CAFE SORIAH

384 W 13th Ave   541/342-4410
Dinner: Daily   cafesoriah.com
Moderate

This longtime south-Valley dinner house continues to please patrons with Mediterranean dishes inspired by chef and owner **Ib Hamide**. Old World spice blended with Northwest-fresh is Soriah's trademark on its varying menu. You might find Greek and Middle Eastern favorites like souvlaki (marinated beef skewers) or fattoush (romaine lettuce mix) that pair nicely with chicken, steak, fish and seafood, lamb entrees or vegetarian plates of spanakopita (spinach pastry) or aubergine (eggplant). Hamide enjoys mingling with his diners; order a flambé entree or dessert, and he will dazzle you tableside. The cafe's backyard garden provides a great seating venue (heated to ward off a bit of chill if necessary).

CASCADES RAPTOR CENTER

32275 Fox Hollow Road   541/485-1320
Nov-March: Tues-Sat: noon-4; April-Oct: Tues-Sun: 10-6   eraptors.org
Nominal

For educational fun, take your children to this nature center and wildlife hospital. Over 60 non-releasable birds of 30 native species are viewable in roomy outdoor aviaries as part of the permanent exhibition. Elsewhere on the property, and away from public view, are other injured, ailing or orphaned birds of prey which are rescued, rehabilitated and released back into the wild. A combination of special permits, exemplary medical care and following stringent standards, have allowed the dedicated staff and volunteers to return over half of their patients to their rightful environments.

CREATIVE CLOCK

730 Conger St   541/344-6359, 800/887-3445
Mon-Sat: 10-5:30   creativeclock.com

My fascination with watches and clocks (Remember "Meet Me Under the Clock" at Meier and Frank in downtown

Portland?) of all kinds makes me a booster of this timepiece emporium which features one of Oregon's biggest and best selections of new, rare and traditional clocks. The shapes and sizes are seemingly endless: cuckoo, grandfather, mantle, wall, gallery, anniversary, nautical and animated clocks. Handsome Black Forest cuckoo clocks can cost up to a staggering $10,000. The adjoining **Conger Street Clock Museum** is a popular destination for all ages with fascinating window exhibits: clocks (of course), cameras, pigeon timers, telephones, toys and many other intriguing treasures from the past.

FIDDLER'S GREEN
91292 Hwy 99N   541/689-8464, 800/548-5500
Daily: 8-8 (spring, summer)   fiddlersgreen.com

Between Junction City and Eugene is every golfer's dream stop — the "largest on-course golf pro shop in America." If it is golf-related, it can be found at this family-owned and — operated business. To dress the part, there is a full array of men's and women's apparel, shoes, rainwear and accessories. To equip yourself for the sport, clubs, carts, balls, bags, books and everything you might possibly need is here, too. They carry well-priced, impressive lines of merchandise for novices and pros, including themed goods for neighboring Beaver and Duck fans. To play the game, sign up for individual or group lessons, participate in popular clinics or initiate customized instructions. The on-property 18-hole executive course and driving range are open year round, ideal for testing the latest equipment. Fiddler's also provides service, repair and an online store.

FISHERMAN'S MARKET RESTAURANT
830 W 7th St   541/484-2722
Daily: 11-8   eugenefishmarket.com
Restaurant: Moderate

Ask about the catch of the day and you're sure to hear where it was caught, by whom and perhaps a fish tale or two. The owners have long been part of the Alaskan fishing scene and are proud to have supported local fishing families for over 30 years. They know fresh fish and the best ways to prepare cod, halibut, salmon, clams,

While there are two sides to the coin, our addiction to gambling in support of tourism and the state coffers has generally proven worthwhile. With a statewide lottery and nine Oregon communities sporting Indian casinos that incorporate hotels and resorts, there's as much gaming as Oregonians and our visitors would like to play.

Burns
The Old Camp Casino (oldcampcasino.com)
Canyonville
Seven Feathers (sevenfeathers.com)
Chiloquin
Kla-Mo-Ya Casino (klamoyacasino.com)
Coos Bay
The Mill Casino (themillcasino.com)
Florence
Three Rivers Casino & Hotel (threeriverscasino.com)
Grand Ronde
Spirit Mountain Casino (spiritmountain.com)
Lincoln City
Chinook Winds Casino Resort (chinookwindscasino. com)
Pendleton
Wildhorse Resort & Casino (wildhorseresort.com)
Warm Springs
Indian Head Casino (indianheadgaming.com)

oysters, scallops and other ocean denizens. The restaurant serves tasty appetizers, fried or grilled combos with criss-cut fries, tacos and chowders. Crab salads are loaded with succulent Dungeness morsels and fresh veggies accompanied by housemade Louis dressing. If you'd rather prepare fish your way, shop at the well-stocked fish counter; there are plenty of options for seafood gift baskets and samplers, too.

GLENWOOD RESTAURANT

1340 Alder St	541/687-0355
Daily: 7 a.m.-9 p.m.	
2588 Willamette St	541/687-8201
Mon-Fri: 6:30 a.m.-9 p.m.;	
Sat, Sun: 7 a.m.-9 p.m.	glenwoodrestaurants.com
Moderate	

Where does one go for breakfast all day in TrackTown, USA? Glenwood, of course. The two locations are slightly different in nature and menus but serve casual, healthy fare for the daily three squares. Pick from Glenwood hazelnut French toast, a long list of three-egg omelet combos, burgers (named after local rivers), sandwiches, salads and meat entrees. South-of-the-border flavor fans will find plenty at each meal, too. Value-priced dinners-to-go are offered Monday through Friday and designed to feed a family of four.

INN AT THE 5TH

205 E 6th Ave	541/743-4099, 855/446-6285
Moderate to expensive	innat5thmarket.com

It's been decades since Eugene has seen a Class A hotel rise. With former Eugene Mayor **Brian Obie**'s dream for a high-end resort realized in 2012, the 70-room boutique hotel offers the city's downtown core an infusion of business and panache. It is ideally positioned across a courtyard from the **5th Street Public Market** (5stmarket.com), a crafters' destination since 1976 and home to unique shops and eateries. The sophisticated and sumptuous decor features Oregon artworks melded with interesting glass fixtures and artfully rustic furniture. Window seats and balconies afford striking views of the Emerald City and grounds; gas fireplaces are thoughtfully placed in most guest quarters. Room service is proficiently handled by the neighboring **Marché** restaurant (marcherestaurant.com) through an unobtrusive butler door. Like we did for snacks in tree houses of our youth, guests can lower baskets from balconies for a grown-up choice of bottles of wine from the **LaVelle Vineyards Tasting Room** (lavellevineyards.com). If that isn't enough pampering, relax and rejuvenate at **Gervais Salon and Day Spa** for professional body, hair, nail, waxing and makeup treatments; in-room services also offered. The staff is extra friendly!

LAND OF THE EMPIRE BUILDERS

Mike McMenamin and **Brian McMenamin**, more commonly referred to as the McMenamin brothers, have a tiger by the tail, turning their mostly historic **McMenamins'** (mcmenamins.com) menagerie of properties into brew pubs, full-blown restaurants, breweries, wineries, distilleries, coffee-roasting houses, spas, hotels and entertainment centers. (With a vision in mind, some buildings have been reincarnated and literally saved from the wrecking ball.) Currently, over 60 interests are strewn across the Willamette Valley and touching the Oregon Coast at Lincoln City, into Central Oregon at Bend and include many Washington state holdings. These entrepreneurs show no signs of slowing up and are fast becoming a hospitality dynasty. Check the website for good grub and pub stops and overnight options in your own neighborhood or on car trips.

KING ESTATE WINERY

80854 Territorial Road   541/942-9874, 800/884-4441
Visitor Center: Daily: noon-5
Restaurant: 541/685-5189
Lunch, Dinner: Daily (seasonal variations); Brunch: Sat, Sun
Moderate (brunch, lunch), Expensive (dinner)   kingestate.com

For a special occasion in a very impressive Oregon setting, make plans to enjoy this family-owned, 1,000-plus-acre certified organic wine operation. The stunning European-style winery in the main facility sits on the rolling south Willamette Valley hills offering breathtaking vistas. Sustainable and organic farming practices are used in the vineyards and also in gardens which produce fruits, vegetables and flowers, to protect and nourish this prime agricultural land. Daily informative tours of the production facilities depart on the hour from the visitors center or you may choose to settle into the expansive tasting room to sample flights of their award-winning wines. Oenophiles will surely want to stop in the wine library to appreciate King Estate standouts from past vintages (difficult to find at retailers). Culinary Institute of America-trained chef **Michael Landsberg** oversees the culinary branch and turns out superlative gourmet fare incorporating estate and local ingredients. What a winning combination: excellent food, a phenomenal setting and world-class wines!

MARCHÉ
5th Street Public Market
296 E 5th Ave, Suite 226   541/342-3612
Breakfast, Lunch, Dinner: Daily   marcherestaurant.com
Moderate (breakfast, lunch), Expensive (dinner)

MARCHÉ PROVISIONS
Next to the fountain in the Market: Daily   541/743-0660

MARCHÉ MUSEUM CAFÉ
Jordan Schnitzer Museum of Art   541/346-6440
Inexpensive

Marché is *the* place to go for French market fare that is well-prepared, beautifully presented, fresh, healthful, seasonal and regional. Start with a signature artisan cocktail or glass of European or American vino and perhaps share a Provisions charcuterie plate while choosing from the mouthwatering fish, seafood, duck, beef and pork entrees flavorfully seasoned and accompanied by special

OUR HATS ARE OFF TO YOU

Since the renowned leadership of Dr. **John Byrne** (1984-1995), **Oregon State University** (oregonstate. edu) is again blessed with one of its most effective presidents in modern times. Since his 2003 arrival, Dr. **Ed Ray** and his charming wife, Beth, have won legions of friends at one of Oregon's major educational institutions. At the time of this publication, under Ed's leadership and that of co-chair **Jim Rudd** and others working on the Campaign for OSU, the lofty goal of over $1 billion is within grasp. Formerly a member of the economics faculty at Ohio State, Dr. Ray is a quiet and effective voice in the transformation of Oregon State from a mainly agricultural and natural resources scholastic base to an outstanding engineering and business university.

vegetables, roots, grains, pastas and cheeses. The likes of mussels, steelhead, and pizzetta are even better prepared in the wood-fired oven. The expanded bar serves a casual bar menu all day — a smashing success. The house steak dish is superb. **Provisions** encompasses an artisan bakery and emporium for wines, gifts, specialty foods, pantry goods, a casual eatery (morning pastries, pizzas and more) and a fun spot for popular cooking classes. The **Museum Café**, on the UO campus, is the scene of a small plate, quiche and sandwich casual eatery and a convenient meeting place for espresso and dessert. *Bon appétit!*

OFF THE WAFFLE

2540 Willamette St   541/515-6926
Sun-Thurs: 7 a.m.-8 p.m.; Fri, Sat: 7 a.m.-11 p.m.   offthewaffle.com
Inexpensive

Off The Waffle is a reasonably priced authentic Liège waffle house. These yeast-based treats are prepared with Belgian pearled sugar that caramelizes to produce a delicious flavor in the cooked batter as well as a distinctive crispy texture. The brothers who began this operation are picky about ingredients and use high-quality, local and organic options as much as possible. You can order original Liège waffles or one of the signature waffles made with unique and delicious combinations of ingredients. They also offer omelets, organic salads, tea infusions, wood-roasted coffee and freshly squeezed orange juice. This is a one-of-a-kind restaurant!

OREGON ELECTRIC STATION

27 E 5th Ave   541/485-4444
Lunch: Mon-Fri; Dinner: Daily   oesrestaurant.com
Expensive

When you have a yen for juicy prime rib or fresh seafood, the Oregon Electric Station will fill the bill. The large menu offers much more, from starters such as deep-fried mozzarella or prawn cocktails to soups, salads, poultry and pasta. Generously portioned desserts are homemade; Dutch apple pie a la mode and decadent carrot cake are worth the extra calories. Warm brick and paneled walls, gleaming brass and replica light fixtures evoke memories of the station's heyday; an antique railcar doubles as the wine cellar. Located in Eugene's historic depot area, the Oregon Electric Station served the Great Northern and Northern Pacific Willamette Valley electric train system, circa 1912. Well-known Portland architect **A.E. Doyle** designed the building which has pulled duty as an office, storage space and museum. Fortunately, renovations made to correct the prior owners' adaptations resulted in a building that Doyle would be proud of once again.

OSTERIA SFIZIO

105 Oakway Center (in the Heritage Courtyard)   541/302-3000
Lunch, Dinner: Daily; Brunch: Sat, Sun   sfizioeugene.com
Moderate

Sfizio's wide-ranging menu is termed modern Italian with the taste of Northwest fresh; the bounty of locally sourced food and drink (Oregon wines, micro-distilled spirits and brews) is evident. For a quick lunch, choose from a satisfying list of main dishes and housemade pastas featuring traditional sauces and fillings of fennel sausage, rabbit, clams, elk, prawns, squid and ubiquitous fresh vegetables. A selection of lunch favorites joins veal sweetbreads, duck breast, hanger steak and pork, fish and seafood dinner offerings. *Affogato* (espresso over a scoop of vanilla gelato) or warm Sfizio doughnuts with *crema inglese* are sinfully good for dessert. Weekend brunch with egg and breakfast dishes prepared the Italian way, and a pitcher of prosecco punch are an enjoyable pre-game or Duck-win celebratory meal. A private dining room is ideal for special events, family gatherings or business meetings.

PRINCE PÜCKLER'S GOURMET ICE CREAM

1605 E 19th Ave   541/344-4418
Daily: noon-11   princepucklers.com
Inexpensive

Sprint, don't walk, to this longtime really cool ice creamery that has been satisfying locals since 1975. Top quality ingredients are blended into best-selling and unusual flavors such as Galaxy (chocolate malt with white and chocolate chips), Chai Tea (Oregon Chai), sorbets and frozen yogurt. Euphoria Chocolate Company's ultra-chocolate sauce is the crowning touch to just about any ice cream dish, sundae or pie that you concoct from the 40 awesome flavors; seasonal variations, of course, to feature fresh Oregon fruits and berries.

MEMORABILIA

I've long been a philographer; i.e., a collector of autographs. My most prized collection is that of all the U.S. presidents (currently through President **Barack Obama**) beginning with leaders from the Continental Congress (some of whom were not literate and signed their names only with an "X"). I also have a celebrity compendium of photographs by the famous portraitist, **Philippe Halsman**. I purchased one of his books years ago and proceeded to send it or take it to various celebs and simply asked that they inscribe a notation with their signature on the book's photo. Many kindly accommodated my request (**Dustin Hoffman, Audrey Hepburn, Carol Channing, Lucille Ball, Mickey Rooney, Marlon Brando, Shirley Temple, Bob Hope, Johnny Carson, Sammy Davis, Jr., Richard Nixon** and others). After over a year's absence and many, many follow-up calls and letters, the book finally arrived home. It was then that I decided it best to keep it in my possession; today, the signed and framed Halsman's and many other works are displayed in my office where I enjoy and share them every day.

THE RABBIT BISTRO AND BAR

2864 Willamette St, Suite 300
Dinner: Daily
Moderate

541/343-8226
rabbitbistro.com

After years of culinary experience that began in his grandmother's kitchen and took him to top New York, Portland, Santa Fe and Los Angeles restaurants, Chef **Gabriel Gil** ventured into the Eugene restaurant scene. The unpretentious Rabbit Bistro offers seasonal dinner menus reflecting classic French choices like escargot, Niçoise salad, hanger steak frites and foie gras. Gil adds a personal flair — you'll find Northwest and French blending in chicken, pork, duck, lamb, game, fish and seafood dishes. Patrons enjoy value pricing in a casual atmosphere. Chef insists that there are no substitutions and no ketchup!

SCIENCE FACTORY CHILDREN'S MUSEUM AND EXPLORATION DOME

2300 Leo Harris Pkwy   541/682-7888
Wed-Sun: 10-4   sciencefactory.org
Nominal

Kids will want plenty of time to navigate and discover the fascinating Exploration Dome (pre-recorded, full-dome educational movies and seasonal star gazing shows), exhibits and rotating informative hands-on entertainment at this 50-year-old museum in Alton Baker Park. Activities are continuously changed and upgraded to encourage youngsters' fertile minds as they explore science, technology and humanity. Renegade, the resident iguana, is popular with all visitors; the lizard terrarium encompasses even more exotic critters and flora from around the world. Camps, classes and special events present opportunities to delve into all sorts of subjects with a bent to kids. This is also a fun birthday party locale.

SWEET LIFE PATISSERIE

755 Monroe St   541/683-5675
Mon-Fri: 7 a.m.-11 p.m.; Sat, Sun: 8 a.m.-11 p.m.   sweetlifedesserts.com

As the sole judge of the annual chocolate cake contest at the Oregon State Fair, I feel qualified to pass opinion on sweets throughout the state. This bakery passes muster, in spades! There is a magnificent selection of handmade cakes, tortes, scones, sticky buns, muffins, croissants and other delectables that help make life a bit sweeter. A few savory choices complete the menu. Favored cake flavors include black bottom, chocolate salted caramel, Bananas Foster and maple bacon. Each month features a quartet of specials: cakes, cheesecakes, petit sweets and pies or tortes are often made with exotic or only-in-season ingredients. Consultants at their **Wedding Cake Salon** (775 Monroe St, 541/686-2633) meticulously provide cake tastings and top-notch service to couples planning one of the most important occasions of their lives.

FALLS CITY

THE BREAD BOARD
404 N Main St   503/787-5000
Fri, Sat: 9-9; Sun: 9-8; Mon: 4-8   thebreadboard.net

Falls City may be a trek for a loaf of bread, but **Keith Zinn** and **John Volkmann**'s artisan bakery in a revamped storefront is worth the detour if you're in the vicinity. The ever-changing varieties are made with the owners' special wild yeast sourdough starters and baked in the largest wood-fired bread oven in the state. Frequently appearing in the rotation of loaves are country sourdough, roasted garlic and sundried tomato, olive and rosemary, walnut sourdough, fennel with raisins and more. Sweet sticky buns, pastries and scones delight early-morning customers. Later in the day a limited quantity of wood-fired pizzas are prepared starting at 4 p.m.; the crust is crunchy, thin and scattered with fresh, seasonal toppings. A retail location is open in Silverton (206 S Water St.) Thursday through Saturday. You may happen across The Bread Board's hearth-baked products at select farmers markets throughout the Valley.

GERVAIS

BAUMAN'S FARM & GARDEN
12989 Howell Prairie Road NE   503/792-3524
Spring, summer: Mon-Fri: 9-6, Sat: 9-5;
fall: Mon-Fri: 9-6, Sat, Sun: 9-5; winter: Mon-Sat: 9-5   baumanfarms.com

This is a year-round operation, with each season showcasing the best there is to offer. In the original buildings are mouthwatering displays of fresh fruits and vegetables; shelves of fresh baked pies, breads, muffins and cookies; flavorful concoctions of fudge and tempting doughnuts (apple cider, strawberry, pumpkin, etc. depending on the season). Tastes of the bakery's freshest goods are strategically placed for sampling; fudgy bites are cheerfully offered at the coffee counter. Packaged gourmet products and a vast array of gifts and housewares are strategically integrated. Step into the greenhouse for an overwhelming profusion of colorful seasonal plants, already planted in attractive containers and ready to dress up patios and porches or buy individual plants for do-it-yourself gardening. Exciting and fun family events are scheduled throughout the year with something for everyone: food, produce, nursery items, classes, activities and so much more.

INDEPENDENCE

THE PINK HOUSE CAFE
242 D St   503/837-0900
Breakfast, Lunch, Dinner: Wed-Sun
Inexpensive to moderate

Just across from the Independence Cinema is a charming pink and white house adorned with gingerbread trim where service is always friendly. Inside are several rooms which create an intimate, relaxing ambience. The appealing, consistently good menu is filled with hearty breakfasts (a generous side of pan-fried spuds is included), lunches, dinners and desserts. Not-your-ordinary soups, salads, sandwiches and burgers are offered for both lunch and dinner; a serving of a green or homemade potato salad accompanies sandwiches; movie patrons will find other tasty comfort food choices for date night with fish, Mt. Angel Sausage Co. bratwurst, ravioli or short rib entrees. There's always room for berry cobbler, bread pudding or other desserts at this Victorian beauty.

RAGIN' RIVER STEAK CO.
154 S Main St   503/837-0394
Lunch: Tues-Fri; Dinner: Tues-Sun; Brunch: Sat, Sun   raginsteakco.com
Moderate

Pleasant lunch and dinner menus (as well as super happy hour specials weekdays between 3 and 7) draw folks into this Polk County steak (and more) house. There are several items not to miss: prime rib sliders, crispy onion strings, Chinese chicken salad, jambalaya and create-your-own pasta combinations. The lunch crowd enjoys housemade soups, salads, pasta dishes and a variety of char-broiled burgers (such as classic, spicy, or topped with peanut butter and cheddar cheese). Dinner seafood options change weekly but certified Angus steaks are always just an order away. Weekend brunches, attractive seasonal patio dining, a full bar and comfortably-sized and -priced meals for seniors and small-fries round out the offerings at this establishment.

KEIZER

CARUSO'S ITALIAN CAFE & WINE BAR

5745 Inland Shores Way N   503/393-8272
Tues-Sun: Dinner   carusositaliancafe.com
Expensive

A perennial favorite for diners in the Salem/Keizer area is **Angie and Jerry Phipps**' classy northern Italian cafe. The cuisine is delicious, service superb and the Staats Lake setting is beautiful, especially at sunset. You can't go wrong with the house special ravioli of the day, veal scaloppini, mac n' cheese with crab and shrimp, ossu buco, garlicky jumbo prawns or a New York steak topped with rosemary-garlic compound butter. As a bread lover, I especially like the never-ending bread basket. To wholly enjoy Chef Jerry's authentic fare, include an appetizer and homemade dessert with your dinner in the dining room, wine bar or on the terrace. The owners are a charming couple!

LYONS

OPAL CREEK ANCIENT FOREST CENTER

                                                   503/892-2782
Seasonal   opalcreek.org

Take a one-hour, scenic drive east of Salem for a green experience at Jawbone Flats. Recreational opportunities beckon in the largest remaining low-elevation old growth forest left in Oregon. This Willamette National Forest center includes lore of Native American inhabitants, forest fires, the Shiny Rock Mining Company and a rich conservation history. Rusty remnants from the ore mining camp are still recognizable just off the gravel road to Jawbone Flats, where rustic cabins, a lodge (group lodging up to 18 people), commissary and the education center are nestled along Battle Ax Creek and the North Santiam River. Environmental workshops, camps, courses, hearty meals and seasonal lodging (cabins sleep four to 16 and are equipped with kitchens and bathrooms) are offered. Visitor vehicular traffic is not permitted past the locked gate; area guests are encouraged to walk the three miles to the center; overnight guests will appreciate the gear shuttle.

THE DEVIL'S IN THE DETAILS!

Both Senator **Wayne Morse** and Governor **Douglas McKay** were great Oregon boosters — with one glaring failing (particularly for politicians): remembering names of constituents. Fortunately for both men, their wives (**Mildred "Midge" Morse** and **Mabel McKay**) were at their right arms most of the time and made it their business to be experts in the recognition department. Mrs. Morse was responsible for an outstanding office reference file detailing individuals' data important to the senator.

MARQUAM

MARKUM INN
36903 S Hwy 213   503/829-9853
Daily: 11-10 (Fri, Sat till 11)
Inexpensive (lunch), moderate (dinner)   markuminn.com

Marquam? It's a tiny spot on Highway 213 northeast of Silverton heading toward Oregon City. Now that you've located it, plan a lunch or dinner laden with comfort foods. MarKum burgers (Jumbo and Double Jumbo) and fries will fill the hungriest stomachs, as will the hot roast beef or turkey sandwiches with real mashed potatoes and gravy. Full steak, liver and onions, fish and chicken dinners include a choice of starch, vegetables, roll and soup or salad; spaghetti, with a dare to consume a second helping, is always an option. The Challenge Burger and fries weigh in at 6 ½ pounds, costs about $30, and is free if finished by one person within the timeframe. Prices are super-friendly; even Sunday's prime rib dinner comes in around $18. Young ones, 12 and under, have a special menu and eat free on their birthday.

MCMINNVILLE

3RD STREET PIZZA CO.

433 NE 3rd St   503/434-5800
Daily: 11-9 (Fri till 10)   3rdstreetpizza.com
Inexpensive

Because they are made in a traditional stone oven, these New York-style pizzas are among the best you can find. House specialty toppings are added to create Thai, Mexican, Greek and barbecue flavor blends; pizza aficionados can also choose from traditional alternatives. The expanded menu includes salads, sandwiches on homemade bread and chicken wings. Eat in or take along an order for a Sunday afternoon drive through wine country.

ADAMS ST. ANTIQUES

1101 NW Adams St   503/560-1438
Mon-Sat: 10-5

For an eclectic glimpse into the past, visit **Howard Converse**'s Adams Street shop where he has been collecting this and that for more than 20 years. The assortment includes items and rarities pertaining to aviation, advertising, Native Americans, vintage paintings by Oregon and California artists, lamps and much more. Howard describes the assemblage as "good unusual stuff." You may find just what you've been searching for or something you didn't even know you needed.

BISTRO MAISON

729 NE 3rd St   503/474-1888
Brunch, Lunch: Wed-Fri, Sun; Dinner: Wed-Sun   bistromaison.com
Expensive

It's like a journey to France as you step inside this tiny bistro in the heart of Oregon wine country. Classic French onion soup gratinée paired with a Croque Monsieur sandwich and a glass of wine evoke fond memories of a quaint countryside lunch in France. European-influenced entrees are enhanced with seasonal elements and Northwest flavors such as Emmentaler and Tillamook cheddar cheeses in the white truffle fondue, classic Coq au Vin and cassoulet. The charmingly remodeled home-turned-bistro is furnished with comfortable banquettes and chairs (crisp white linens set an elegant tone); the front porch and garden patio are equally appealing. Dessert standouts are profiteroles au chocolat, tartes and local fruit clafoutis. An unlikely but yummy dessert treat is the build-your-own s'mores (customer participation required).

CRESCENT CAFE

526 NE 3rd St   503/435-2655
Breakfast, Lunch: Wed-Fri; Brunch: Sat, Sun
Inexpensive to moderate

Wheel in to **Michael McKenney** and **Danny Wilser**'s wonderful breakfast, brunch and lunch spot for fine daytime cuisine sourced as locally and freshly as possible. To get the day properly started, try chicken hash (a plate of crispy potatoes and large, tender pieces of chicken), an omelet or Benedict, fresh coffeecakes, buttermilk pancakes, pastries, breads and incredibly flaky and flavorful biscuits. The same attention is given to homemade soups

ONCE UPON A TIME

Governor **Mark Hatfield** was always interested in monarchies and distressed that no reigning ruler had ever visited Oregon. In 1960 to amend this situation, he invited His Majesty **King Mahendra** of Nepal to pay a visit to discuss mutual timber issues. The king, of course, was given a grand tour of Salem, including the **Meier & Frank** store. Of utmost interest was the store's then-novel butterfly-designed parkade where the king directed his 20-car motorcade up and down its several levels. The evening's state dinner at the former Marion Hotel was a first for Salem; M&F furnished the chef and complete dinnerware and highly-trained waiters were brought in from Portland's **Benson Hotel**. After the governor welcomed guests, he presented the king with a beautiful silver dish in a special presentation box. To the amazement and embarrassment of the host and his guests, the king (who could speak English) did not look at the gift or respond in any way. Always able to react to unforeseen circumstances, the governor quickly summoned the wait staff and asked the king to greet each one, visibly easing tension.

and sandwiches for lunch. Be patient, there are only about a dozen tables which fill quickly (alas, they don't accept reservations), but you will be treated well in this ultra-friendly and popular downtown neighborhood destination. Michael and Danny have high regard for the first meal of the day and provide a fine setting with fresh flowers, classical music and impeccable attention to detail.

EVERGREEN AVIATION & SPACE MUSEUM

500 NE Captain Michael King Smith Way   503/434-4180
Daily: 9-5
Moderate

EVERGREEN WINGS & WAVES WATERPARK

Winter: Mon, Thurs, Fri: 3-8; Sat, Sun: 10-8;
Memorial Day to Labor Day: Daily: 10-8
Expensive   evergreenmuseum.org

The home of **Howard Hughes**' Spruce Goose is one of Oregon's premier family attractions, inspiring, educating, promoting and preserving aviation and space history. Besides this mammoth plane, there are other historic collections of general aviation, military aircraft (SR-71 Blackbird), space flight (replicas of the Lunar module and Rover), helicopters, firearms and more. Tours are self-guided or docent-led; knowledgeable docents are also stationed throughout the museum to enlighten visitors about these prized beauties. Continuing in a big way, the six-story tall digital 3-D theater engrosses viewers with daily aviation-themed showings (additional admission fee). The newest attraction is the splendid waterpark with ten water slides departing from the rooftop Boeing 747 (appropriately named Tail Spin, Sonic Boom, etc.), pools, a play structure, an arcade, and the educational H_2O Hands-on Science Center. Quite the place that Oregon aviator and entrepreneur **Del Smith** has assembled!

GOLDEN VALLEY BREWERY & RESTAURANT

980 NE 4th St   503/472-2739
Lunch, Dinner: Daily   goldenvalleybrewery.com
Moderate

This brewery-eatery is in a historic setting with a gorgeous bar purported to be from Portland's famous Hoyt Hotel. Brews are given names with seasonally descriptive and local connections. Choose from the huge appetizer selection, soups and salads, sandwiches, seafood, pork schnitzel, pastas and steaks; the cuisine is fresh, local and made in-house. Owners **Celia and Peter Kircher**'s 76-acre Angus Springs Ranch provides much of the restaurant's meat and produce. (An interesting side note is that the beef herd is fed on Golden Valley Brewery grain which provides a diet especially high in protein and fiber.) A second location with similar offerings recently opened in Beaverton (1520 NW Bethany Boulevard, 503/972-1599).

HONEST CHOCOLATES

575 NE 3rd St	503/474-9042
312 E 1st St, Newberg	503/537-0754
Tues-Sat: 11:30-6	honestchocolates.com

Candies are crafted (even marshmallows) using high-quality, taste-tested chocolate, cooked in small batches and hand-dipped. What's not to love about (dark or milk) chocolate honey caramels with French sea salt or (dark, milk or white) brickle bark with crumbled bits of honeycomb? A niche they have deliciously filled is chocolates to pair with Oregon's special wines. Oregon wines are used as flavorings (the alcohol evaporates) resulting in a perfect chocolate candy to accompany a glass of pinot noir or your favorite wine.

LA RAMBLA RESTAURANT & BAR

238 NE 3rd St	503/435-2126
Lunch, Dinner: Daily (Jan-March, closed Tues, Wed)	
Moderate	laramblaonthird.com

If you like cuisine with a Spanish flair, then this 1884 downtown brick building (the oldest in town) is for you. The full-service copper bar lists over 400 local and Spanish wine labels and cocktails made from house-infused liquors. Imported and domestic cheeses are offered as cold tapas or added to salads. Among the vegetable, seafood and meat tapas are more than enough choices to assemble a tasty *la comida* prepared with the finest Northwest ingredients from local purveyors. The average tapas price is under $10, thus your tab depends upon your choices and appetite.

Linger over light tapas and sangria if you opt for Spanish paella that is chock-full of shrimp, clams, sausage, chicken or vegetables; it is made to order and as is often the case, good things come to those who wait. A few lunch specials and assorted desserts are an amalgamation of Spanish and Northwest inspiration. P.S.: The entire upper level of the building is a nicely refurbished luxury vacation rental; details at the restaurant or online.

NICK'S ITALIAN CAFE

521 NE 3rd St   503/434-4471
Lunch, Dinner: Tues-Sat   nicksitaliancafe.com
Inexpensive to moderate

You will not go away hungry from Nick's! This is a renowned pasta house where local, sustainable produce and hormone- and antibiotic-free eggs and meats dominate the menu. For lunch, who can turn down crab and pine nut lasagna, authentic thin-crust pizzas, classic minestrone soup or interesting paninis with housemade potato chips? At lunch or dinner, you'll likely rub elbows with local vintners as well as guests from Yamhill County's numerous country inns. They know that choices from the a la carte fare or the special five-course tasting menu will be excellent and satisfying. Select from ragùs, pastas, seafood and vegetarian dishes or ask about the daily wood-fired oven lamb and pork preparations. Familiar folks enter through the back door for the ambience of the comfy bar to enjoy their preferred wine and antipasti and perhaps a game of pool. No wonder Nick's has been a gem on the McMinnville dining scene since 1977.

RED FOX BAKERY
328 NE Evans St   503/434-5098
Mon-Sat: 7-4; Sun: 8-2   redfoxbakery.com

Red Fox is Yamhill County's first independent artisan bakery, using local fresh ingredients as much as possible (even growing many of their own herbs), offering housemade jams and handcrafting breads and pastries. Flour is milled, produce grown and butter churned within miles of the bakery. Lunchtime (11-3) brings filling sandwiches, soups and salads. The bakery turns out coconut macaroons, with daily fresh batches sold on-site or shipped; brownies, too. Cinnamon rolls, coffee cakes and more make up the daily-changing pastry menu and "everything" scones are only baked on Thursday. Loyal customers return to Red Fox for homemade goodness and incredible goodies.

RIBSLAYER BBQ TO GO
575 NE 2nd St   503/472-1309
Tues-Sat: 11-7   ribslayer.com
Inexpensive to moderate

You'll know that you're near Ribslayer by the mouthwatering aroma emanating from the 9,000-pound custom-built behemoth smoker. This is one of the largest smokers in the area and can cook over 1,000 pounds of chicken, beef or pork at one time; all carefully seasoned and roasted long and slow. Homemade slaw, chips and pickles accompany orders of a half or whole bird, beef brisket and Carlton Farms pulled pork or country-style spareribs. If you're really famished, sink your teeth into the "XXX" sandwich:

THE REAL DEAL

Car dealerships are not a common entry in a guidebook; however, **Withnell Motor Company** (withnellauto. com), led by patriarch and semi-retired, **Dick Withnell** and son, **David Withnell**, are exceptional businessmen and community stewards. Dick started in the banking industry, but left a sure paycheck to try his hand at entrepreneurship when he purchased the Salem Dodge dealership years ago. He worked extraordinarily hard and overcame personal challenges as well. Along with professional boards, including service as president of the National Automobile Dealers Association, Dick has served on countless boards and commissions especially keying on children and families. Dick would be the first to say that his accomplishments would not have happened without his wife, **Gayle**, by his side. With all of **Gayle and Dick Withnell**'s hard-earned success, they illustrate their community appreciation as generous philanthropists and stand at the helm of Salem's action-oriented couples. **Gracie's Place**, a part of **Family Building Blocks** (familybuildingblocks.org), is just one entity on a showcase of legacy achievements. The Withnell family and organization are the real deal!

a juicy combination of thinly sliced beef brisket, pulled pork and corned beef. Other housemade sides and salads round out the menu. Owners **Theresa and Craig Haagenson** also operate **Haagenson's Catering** (503/550-7388, haagensonscatering. com), a full-service (and barbecue) catering business.

YOUNGBERG HILL VINEYARDS & INN

10660 SW Youngberg Hill Road   503/472-2727
Moderate to very expensive   youngberghill.com

This luxurious inn and organic vineyard is perched upon picturesque rolling hills. The four king suites and four queen en suite guest rooms are tastefully decorated and loaded with amenities; most have gas or electric fireplaces, perfect on a chilly evening or early morning. In-room MP3 docking stations, spa robes and complimentary Wi-Fi throughout the house are thoughtfully provided. All guest rooms have inspiring views of the vineyard and valley; three rooms have private decks. Breakfast is a two-course gourmet affair, enhanced with regional bounty. Favorite dishes come and go from the menu and may include salmon hash, pancetta tarts, Cornish baked eggs and piping hot fresh muffins. Don't think about departing without sitting a spell on the expansive wrap-around deck and tasting their award-winning pinot noir and pinot gris wines, all the while gazing at not-too-distant Mt. Hood, Mt. Jefferson and the Coast Range.

WHEN CANNERIES WERE KING

"Tough as nails" was the reputation of **F.M. "Farmer" Smith**, for 30 years the general manager of the giant **Stayton Canning Company** (now **Norpac**). Underneath the outer façade, was a very soft heart; Farmer was the glue that held this rural community together, being a prime mover in every good cause. His widow, **Bula Smith**, celebrated her 100th birthday in 2012 and passed away later in the year.

MONMOUTH

MAMERE'S BED & BREAKFAST
212 Knox St   503/838-1514
Inexpensive to moderate   mameresbandb.com

Book a stay at MaMere's if you're visiting a Western Oregon University student, touring wineries or taking a B&B break in the mid-Willamette Valley. The historic Howell House serves as the framework for this New Orleans-style accommodation, full of R&R and attentive service by owner **Terri Gregory**, who bravely took on the renovation process. Vibrant color schemes and room names taken from the Crescent City create a lively ambience; only two of the five rooms have private bathrooms. Borrow a bicycle and cruise through the quiet streets or plan a route to a winery or lavender field. Further relaxation is across the street in the Main Street Park gazebo.

MONROE

THE INN AT DIAMOND WOODS

96096 Territorial Road   541/510-2467
Moderate   theinnatdiamondwoods.com

This relatively new large facility features four en suite bedrooms and meeting rooms. Views of the Willamette Valley and **Diamond Woods Golf Course** are captured through the soaring windows and from the expansive patio and sprawling lawn (ideal for large weddings or corporate events; catering available). Individual, group and whole-house reservations are accepted with special rates for several couples who would like to have the entire place to themselves for a football weekend, wine excursion or special occasion. Guests receive 50% discount on golf at the 18-hole Diamond Woods Golf Course.

MT. ANGEL

GLOCKENSPIEL RESTAURANT & PUB

190 E Charles St   503/845-6222
Lunch, Dinner: Daily   glockenspielrestaurant.net
Moderate

Mt. Angel comes alive every September for its annual Oktoberfest and German cultural activities; however traditional cuisine is not just autumnal fare in this Bavarian-themed village. Start your meal by sharing a pot of fondue, twirling apple slices and baguette chunks in the melted Swiss national dish. Sweet and savory braised red cabbage accompanies platters of schnitzels, späetzle, wursts, potato pancakes and other specialties. While German lunch selections are hard to beat, salads, hearty homemade soups and sandwiches (Reuben, sausage and schnitzel) are equally as tempting, especially when washed down with German and Northwest brews and wines. Fish lovers show up on Friday evenings for Glockenspiel's popular weekly Fish Fry featuring beer-battered fish, German slaw and potato pancakes. It goes without saying that any time is the right time for delicious apple strudel. Before leaving, be sure to notice the unique clocktower; bells chime hourly as figures dance above the entrance. It's quite a place!

MT. ANGEL SAUSAGE CO.

105 S Garfield St   503/845-2322
Mon-Fri: 11-8; Sat: 8-8; Sun: 8-6 (seasonal variations)   ropesausage.com

Robust Old World-style artisan sausages are expertly handmade by the Hoke family and served at their on-site restaurant. Chicken, beef, pork and assorted spices, cheese and loads of garlic are added to create distinctly flavored sausages that are then cured. Only high-quality natural products are used; no chemicals, fillers or by-products. This casual eatery offers over a dozen varieties of wursts in sandwiches or on a stick, schnitzel entrees, fondue and hearty dinners. Good food, German and domestic brews, wines, cocktails and refreshing Mt. Angel Brewing Company's root beer attract patrons to the comfortable outdoor deck on warm summer afternoons and evenings. Weekend breakfasters come for the German pancakes, omelets and heaping platters of schnitzel and fried potatoes. Their products are a staple at many nearby fairs and events. If you're not in the area, but need a bratwurst fix, they gladly fill and ship orders each week. *Prost!*

NEWBERG

THE ALLISON INN & SPA

2525 Allison Lane   503/554-2525, 877/294-2525
Expensive to very expensive

JORY

Breakfast, Lunch, Dinner: Daily; Brunch: Sun   theallison.com
Moderate to very expensive

Words cannot properly describe this magnificent haven built by Oregon entrepreneurs **Joan and Ken Austin**. The genius of this world-class retreat is in the attention to details. For instance, comfy throws on "living room" couches beg for nappers; there is a fabulous spa with every amenity, including a treatment room with an overhead "rain" feature; fireplaces are on automatic timers. Every guest room in this 85-room wine country boutique resort has an outside view terrace; gorgeous landscaping blends with the setting. The casually elegant in-house **Jory** restaurant is of the same high caliber and honors Oregon's wine, microbrew, hand-

POWERHOUSE

For most of the period from 1975 to 1997 Oregon's Congressional delegation was one of the most powerful in the union. Representative **Al Ullman** was the chair of the House Ways and Means Committee, that body's most potent panel (1975-1981); Senator **Mark Hatfield** served as chair of the Appropriations Committee, the most prestigious job in the Senate (1981-1987 and 1995-1997) and Senator **Bob Packwood** served as chair of the Senate Finance Committee (1985-1987 and 1995), a commanding assignment. While these plum appointments resulted from seniority, Oregonians were made proud by each man's skill and knowledge; it's unlikely that such a trifecta of power and influence will ever again come to our state (or any other).

crafted distilled spirit and agricultural industries with outstanding Oregon wine country cuisine. For special occasions there are private dining rooms to accommodate small gatherings; the private chef's table for eight affords a catbird seat inside the working kitchen. Any meal is a guaranteed palate pleaser especially the brioche French toast with berry compote at breakfast or midday interesting salads and charcuterie; the dinner menu wood-grilled Wagyu New York steak is as good as you will find anywhere. Superlative, indeed!

CHEHALEM RIDGE BED AND BREAKFAST
28700 NE Mountain Top Road   503/538-3474
Moderate   chehalemridge.com

Perched high above the Willamette Valley floor is this appropriately named bed and breakfast with inspiring vistas. The four bedrooms offer queen beds and private baths (some with jetted tubs and fireplaces) and private decks. If you oversleep or depart early you'll miss the three-course breakfast extravaganza. Experienced as a professional chef and baker, **Kristin Fintel** is busy each morning baking fresh pastries, preparing fresh fruits and impressing guests with hazelnut waffles, crepes, salmon quiche or amazing Benedicts. No worries if you have special dietary needs;

food allergies are pleasantly accommodated (Chehalem Ridge earned the "Best B&B if you have a special diet" award). The library offers reading material and HDTV (if you must); but first make a slight detour to the cookie jar full of home-baked goodies.

PRESIDENTIAL LUNCH

What is dished up to the President of the United States when he comes to your home for lunch? **Antoinette Hatfield** (wife of Senator **Mark Hatfield**) served President **Richard Nixon** string beans. I wasn't in charge of the menu, but string beans? He loved them!

CRITTER CABANA

516 E 1st St   503/537-2570
Mon-Sat: 10-8; Sun: noon-6   crittercabana.com

You'll be absolutely amazed when you walk into this pet-and-more store. It is a charming place full of interesting products and lovable pets. You'll find dogs, cats, birds, fish, snakes, frogs, tortoises, lizards, panda bear hamsters, rabbits and exotics such as hedgehogs or perhaps armadillos, plus other curious creatures. There is no shortage of high-quality pet supplies for your critters including food, toys, treats and everyday necessities. The fact that such a well-stocked and well-maintained store exists on the main street of one of Oregon's smaller communities is proof that we have viable enterprises in unusual places. You have to see this menagerie to believe it; and keep your eyes open for the giant strolling tortoises! Here's a great idea for birthday parties: they will open at special hours or take their pets on the road. The store closes one hour earlier from October through May.

FANUCCHI OILS

2401 E Hancock St, Suite B-4   503/537-9774
Wed-Sun: 12-5   fanucchioils.com

Skip the butter and dressing and dip into more healthful extra virgin olive oil. You can bring the Mediterranean into your kitchen with flavored oils, balsamic vinegars, olives, pastas and other antipasto and sweets. Founder **Gina Fanucchi** is passionate about her products and offers classes on this ancient health food as well as tasting parties at your home (you provide the guests and she brings along samples, recipe ideas and merchandise). Related culinary accessories and luxurious bath and beauty items containing these important oils are ideal gifts, especially when paired with the edible offerings.

THE LIONS GATE INN BED AND BREAKFAST
401 N Howard St   503/476-2211
Moderate   distinctivedestination.net

Built in 1911, this historic Craftsman home was once known as the Maggie Littlefield home and was considered to be one of the original mansions in Newberg. This property was remodeled by owner **Loni Austin Parrish** in 2006 and designed as a luxury inn with the amenities of a fine hotel. Restoration began with special care taken to reuse or refurbish the original historical elements of the house while also adding environmentally-friendly aspects wherever possible; the B&B doors opened in 2008. Concierge services are provided by the staff and a complimentary custom wine loop tour with tasting passes are some of Distinctive Destination's special services. Guests enjoy afternoon wine and cheese on the outdoor covered seating area, in the lovely gardens or fireside in the common living area. Guests are offered the choice of a gourmet savory or sweet breakfast along with locally roasted coffee. Each of the four spacious suites has its own stunning private bath and three of the suites boast gas fireplaces. An additional touch of elegance is the vintage sparkling leaded glass throughout the home. Stately bronze lions stand sentinel on the front steps to bid guests welcome or farewell. The Lions Gate Inn coordinates reservations for its two nearby rural sister properties, **The Lake House** and **Vineyard Ridge**.

THE PAINTED LADY
201 S College St   503/538-3850
Dinner: Wed-Sun   thepaintedladyrestaurant.com
Expensive

Great things often come in small packages and this Willamette Valley dinner house is arguably one of the best in all of Oregon (awarded AAA's four diamond rating in 2011). Classy consistency with innovative cuisine and top-notch service continue to make this tiny Victorian home a huge winner. Owners **Jessica Bagley** and her husband **Allen Routt** are a model team: Jessica mainly takes care of the front of the house and Allen does magical things in the kitchen creating classic dishes updated for a modern, refined palate. Everything in the intimate 35-seat home-cum-gourmet-restaurant, from the initial greeting to the superb service, makes for a special experience. Your party can choose from two four-course menus, one of which is vegetarian or intermix the two. Chef Allen offers a seven-course menu with his creations of the day; optional local wine pairings are available with all menus. Hint: If the sweet-and-sour Black Tiger prawns are on the menu, they are fabulous. If it's not on the evolving selections, I'm confident something equally tasty won't disappoint from a menu grounded on seasonal, local, quality ingredients. Don't leave without trying the chocolate lava torte with white Russian ice cream, if available. Reservations are nearly a must unless you are very lucky…and tell Jessica and Allen that Gerry sent you!

RECIPE, A NEIGHBORHOOD KITCHEN

115 N Washington St   503/487-6853
Lunch, Dinner: Tues-Sat   recipeaneighborhoodkitchen.com
Moderate

As comfortable as supping in a good friend's kitchen is how guests are made to feel at Recipe. **Paul Bachand** and **Dustin Wyant** personally remodeled a home into a restaurant and then morphed back into their other roles — Bachand as chef and Wyant in charge of operations. In the shade of a gigantic tree lies the fruits of their labor; a Victorian that radiates charm and offers a fresh, seasonal and local menu. Riddlers Room is a fun gathering place; dine at a no-reservation communal table between the bar and the main dining area, or be seated in the main dining room. Menu choices range from homemade pastas, soups, sandwiches and salads for lunch to dinnertime fine dining. The changing dinner menu includes entrees such as sirloin of spring lamb with pesto-basted potatoes and tapenade vinaigrette, wild-caught steelhead, Cascade natural beef in a peppercorn sauce or perhaps a game or seafood offering.

ALL AROUND ATHLETE!

Only one Oregonian has been honored with the prestigious Heisman Trophy for outstanding accomplishments on the gridiron. **Terry Baker**, quarterback for Oregon State University from 1960 to 1962 with an undergraduate engineering degree, went on to a successful law career. Beyond the Heisman celebrated honor, Terry played in the NCAA basketball Final Four in 1963; he was also a gifted baseball player.

OAKRIDGE

BREWERS UNION LOCAL 180

48329 E 1st St   541/782-2024
Lunch, Dinner: Daily (hours vary)   brewersunion.com
Inexpensive to moderate

This Anglo-American public house and brewery is lauded as Oregon's only real ale pub and brewery. When you ask for a pint you will receive the proper measure; it is served in a 20-ounce oversized, lined glass (certified with the Honest Pint Project) in the bar. Ales are conditioned in firkins (casks) and pumped from six beer engines; other beers, ciders and perry are tapped from a keg or sold in bottles. For nourishment, try fish and chips, assorted sandwiches, soups and salads, vegetarian options or satisfying daily specials. Families and kids are welcome at all times in the pub or on the outdoor patio. Come on in, lift a full pint, tell a tall tale and enjoy free pool, books and games.

RICKREALL

CHERRY COUNTRY

6200 Oak Grove Road   503/835-0347, 877/324-3779
Mon-Fri: 11-4 or by appointment   thecherrycountry.com

Royal Ann cherries are at the heart of this family-affair business 15 miles west of Salem. Royal Ann, Tart, Regina and other hardy varieties are marketed fresh or dried without adding any preservatives, sulfites, sugars or oils. The cherry varieties are sold dried *au natural* or enrobed in decadent chocolate (their signature product).   More cherry goodness comes in the form of triple cherry and pistachio (or almond) chocolate bark, cherry jams and pepper jellies that are sold individually or assembled into gift crates. Looking for a cherry pitter? They have those, too. You may find these tasty products at retailers around the state or order online.

Head of State

It took some doing to make Salem our capital city.

In 1844, provisional government legislation chose Oregon City. When Salem was proclaimed the governmental seat in 1850, you can imagine the ruckus this caused; the matter was settled by an act of Congress in 1852.   However, in 1855, the Oregon Territorial Legislature made a move to designate Corvallis as the capital city, though blocked by noting that it would take another congressional act to do so. When the statehouse burned down, also in 1855, the question was reopened and it was decided to put it to the people, giving the two cities receiving the most votes a runoff.   Eugene and Corvallis won, but many ballots were invalidated putting Salem back in the running.

Even though Eugene won the runoff election, the turnout was so low that the election was ignored. After 1859 statehood, the legislature put the question to popular vote, and Salem was officially declared Oregon's capital city. Another fire disrupted state business in 1935 when only the outer walls remained of the building that had stood since 1876. Citizens and multiple community firefighters rushed to help (including then 12-year-old **Mark Hatfield**, who went on to become a two-term governor, five-term U.S. senator and one of our state's most beloved politicians).

Oregon's current structure is the fourth newest in the U.S., dedicated on October 1, 1938, with President **Franklin D. Roosevelt** attending. The 1993 "Spring Break Quake" damaged the Capitol, which was repaired at a cost of several million dollars.   In 2008, another fire did heavy damage to the governor's offices, which have since been repaired. Little known and keeping with Oregon's "green" culture, the Capitol is the first to produce solar power through the use of photovoltaic panels. The art, architecture and history of our state Capitol is worthy of many visits.

Guided tours are available or just stop in and wander the magnificent House and Senate chambers, ceremonial Governor's Office and grand Rotunda; weather permitting, hike the 121 steps to the observation deck to visit our Golden Pioneer and enjoy the view!

SALEM

ALCYONE CAFÉ & CATERING
315 High St SE   503/362-5696
Breakfast, Lunch: Mon-Fri: 8-5; Brunch: Sat: 8-2   alcyonecafe.com
Moderate

Tucked in downtown's Pringle Park Plaza is this small, casual bistro. Rain or shine, outside dining is available year round under the canopy of the parkade. Breakfasts of tender, made-from-scratch croissants, authentic scones, muffins, oatmeal, egg dishes and fruit start the day; soups, salads, sandwiches and daily specials follow. Tasty pastries (including gluten-free, housemade selections) tempt customers for morning starters (or make them dessert), best accompanied by an artfully prepared steaming hot latte. Parking is easy and the location is convenient to Riverfront Park and downtown businesses.

ASSISTANCE LEAGUE GIFT SHOP
AT THE DAUE HOUSE
1095 Saginaw St S   503/364-8318
Mon-Sat: 10-4

ENCORE FURNITURE
1198 Commercial St SE   503/581-3300
Mon-Fri: 11-4; Sat: 10-4   assistanceleaguesalem.org

Savvy shoppers who frequent the Assistance League's two retail stores have a variety of choices in quality merchandise.

The Daue House, on the Historic Register, has well-priced antiques, collectibles, gifts and quality women's used clothing and accessories. Merchandise includes china, wall decor and pictures, glassware, tchotchkes, fine and costume jewelry and small furniture pieces. A block away, Encore is in a large building with an eclectic selection of consigned furniture, decorating accessories and bargain-priced books. At both stores, unique pricing shows automatic price reductions of up to 75%. Most goods are consigned, some are donated; new merchandise, at the gift shop, is purchased to augment the product mix. These shops are the main fundraising activity of the Assistance League of Salem whose endeavors support philanthropies benefitting children, most notably Operation School Bell® which provides impoverished school age children with clothing. Other programs aiding children and adults are capably operated by the League ladies; this is an all-volunteer, nonprofit organization and recently celebrated 50 years of good works in Salem. The Salem chapter is part of a national organization of 120 chapters.

CAFÉ 22 WEST

5152 Salem-Dallas Hwy   503/363-4643
Mon-Thurs: 7-3; Fri-Sun: 7 a.m. - 8 p.m.   cafe22west.com
Inexpensive to moderate

The Aspinwall clan has tended the soil on this 40-acre property for over 100 years. Hard working **Clyde Aspinwall** combines fresh produce from his next-door market with great comfort food. For hearty breakfasts, try fruit-topped pancakes and waffles with a mound of whipped cream, a heaping platter of chicken-fried steak with taters or the Big Rig (biscuit, creamy sausage gravy, eggs, breakfast meat and taters). Platters, sandwiches and burgers with fries or beer-battered onion rings get afternoons off to a satisfying start and are tasty dinner choices, too. On weekends, the star attraction is the slow-roasted baby back ribs dinner special; sides of mac and cheese and baked beans can't be beat. If you're still hungry, there is always dessert, or saunter across the parking lot to **Aspinwall's Nursery & Produce** for summertime-favorite strawberry shortcake and ice cream. The restaurant is open year round and the market and greenhouse are seasonal. Aspinwall peaches are top-notch!

ENTERTAINMENT CENTRAL

Car buying is not what it used to be! In the **Capitol Auto Group**'s (capitolauto.com) new digs at Salem's northernmost city entry, owner **Scott Casebeer**, showcases Chevrolet, Cadillac, Toyota, Subaru and other brands. Turns out it's nothing short of an entertainment center for customers and drop-bys alike. The lakefront property features a walking/jogging area, doggie park (give your pooch a break), a sixty-foot lighted fountain, a floating green to practice your swing (or your aim) and a fishing ramp for fisher-people of all ages to catch and release from the pond. It may be hard to remember you're there to buy one of Capitol's new or used cars!

COURT STREET DAIRY LUNCH
347 Court St   503/363-6433
Mon-Fri: 6 a.m.-2 p.m.
Inexpensive

If you want to check the pulse of Salem, pop in any weekday for breakfast or lunch. You'll see folks from every walk of life ordering their "regular" and holding court with their cronies. At times, it seems like as much business is conducted at this legendary cafe as in offices around town. Breakfast, served until 11, consists of sweets, omelets, fresh cottage-fried potatoes and egg dishes. Soups are homemade; one for each day of the week. Great juicy burgers and special sandwiches are served with a choice of sides. There are also daily lunch specials, and satisfying fried ham and egg, meatloaf (warm or cold) and PB&J sandwiches. Sweet daily goodies include ice cream, sundaes, milkshakes, malts, ice cream sodas and floats (dairy products were the mainstay of this business when it was founded in 1929).

ET CETERA ANTIQUES AND ART GALLERY
3295 Triangle Dr SE, #140   503/581-9850
Tues-Sat: 11-5   etceteraantiques.com

Dynamic owner **Cindy Day** has a loyal following of customers at her shop bursting with antique furniture, glassware, china, silver and collectibles. The artwork features American and European artists from the 18th, 19th and 20th centuries and Oregon art from 1850 to 1970. You'll also find wood carvings by Oregon's renowned late Leroy Setzoil. Estate sales and buying and selling treasures from the past keep the merchandise fresh and intriguing. Cindy is the widow of the legendary L.B. Day, a state legislator, labor chief and civic powerhouse. She grew up in Portland, took art courses at the Portland Art Museum and had early experiences with Oriental art and various furniture styles. All of this background has served her well. The real joy of visiting her establishment is the chance to converse and learn from her wealth of knowledge.

E.Z. ORCHARDS

5504 Hazel Green Road NE   503/393-1506
Mon-Fri: 9-6; Sat: 9-5; Sun: 11-5 (Oct only)   ezorchards.com

Friendly farmer **John Zielinski** leads his capable team and family business on the eastern outskirts of Salem. Much of the fresh produce comes from the family's orchards and other farms from around the Valley. Smart retailer that he is, upon entering the store customers are assailed with the aroma and samples of just-out-of-the-fryer seasonal doughnuts (apple cider, strawberry, blueberry and pumpkin). The merchandise displays are full of mixes, sauces, seasonings, ingredients, condiments and gourmet staples to stock your pantry, plus housewares and gifts to outfit any kitchen. A new addition to the product mix is Cidre, a tasty Normandy French-style hard cider. Outside, the Shortcake Stand (open May to October) is a beehive of activity selling strawberry, raspberry, blueberry, marionberry and peach desserts with hand-scooped ice cream and/or whipped cream. Activities are held throughout the year; the harvest festival with a corn maze, pumpkin patch and lots of wholesome fun is many a family's tradition. You can count on John for great customer service and a willingness to accommodate special orders.

GERRY FRANK'S KONDITOREI

310 Kearney St SE   503/585-7070
Breakfast, Lunch, Dinner: Daily   gerryfrankskonditorei.com
Moderate

This is my favorite lunch spot in Salem! Alright, I'm prejudiced! My good friend **Barney Rogers** (now retired) and I opened the sweet venture on June 24, 1982 (alas, we ran out of cake the first day and had to close the doors early!). For 30 years, cake-lovers from across the country have descended upon the 40-seat cake shop for a slice of decadent dessert made with the finest ingredients. Temptations include cheesecakes, cookies, bars, tortes and other delicious baked goods; be assured that every recipe has been personally tasted by a panel of discerning experts before they are sold to our customers. Many a customer has lingered at the display cases to make the biggest decision of their day: choosing from the 50 available layer cakes. Choices include Gerry's Chocolate, Barney's Blackout, carrot, champagne, Mounds, poppy seed, seasonal preferences such as pumpkin and strawberry and others. In addition to goodies, cake by-the-slice and whole cakes to go, we offer breakfast, lunch and dinner (beer and wine, too), plus catering. The famous **Meier & Frank** Cobb salad and old-fashioned Konditorei ribbon loaf (ham, turkey and egg salads layered on white and wheat bread and wrapped with cream cheese!) are Konditorei exclusives and favorites; daily quiche and soup specials are always offered, along with sandwiches, lasagna and more. Come join us; we have earned a recommendation from AAA and are a consistent *Best of the Mid-Valley* multi-category winner.

THE GRAND HOTEL
201 Liberty St SE   503/540-7800, 877/540-7800
Moderate to expensive   grandhotelsalem.com

BENTLEY'S GRILL AND LOUNGE
291 Liberty St SE   503/779-1660
Lunch, Dinner: Mon-Sat; Sun: Dinner   bentleysgrill.com
Moderate

Grand, it is, and provides Salem's most elegant lodging and flawless customer service. The prime downtown location is contiguous to the **Salem Conference Center**; this combination is a major draw for visitors, meetings and conferences throughout the year. The nearly 200 rooms and suites are spacious, classically appointed and very comfortable. Suites are thoughtfully planned with separate bedrooms, microwave ovens and refrigerators; some suites have gas fireplaces, Jacuzzi tubs and wet bars. A complimentary full breakfast buffet is included with an overnight stay. Sharing the complex, **Bentley's** offers Northwest ingredients on its regional fine dining and bar menu. Light appetizers, salads, pizzas and sandwiches are served beginning at lunch with fresh seafood a prominent element; steaks, chops, chicken, pasta and ocean fare are on the dinner menu. This highly visible corner has served as a hospitality center since the Marion Hotel was completed in 1870. (I have dined on hundreds of meals in this location's various banquet halls since I moved here in 1955, the most memorable in 1960 for His Majesty **King Mahendra** of Nepal.)

HALLIE FORD MUSEUM OF ART

Willamette University
700 State St   503/370-6855
Tues-Sat: 10-5; Sun: 1-5   willamette.edu/arts/hfma
Nominal (free on Tues)

This museum supports the liberal arts curriculum of Willamette University with primarily regional historical and contemporary art, collections and objects. Works by Carl Hall, Ruth Dennis, C.S. Price and other well-known mid-century Oregon modernists are permanently on display in the gallery named for Willamette University art professor **Carl Hall** (consult the website for other collections and rotating exhibitions). **Willamette University** has a long presence in Salem, founded in 1842 by Methodist missionaries as the first university in the West. The inviting campus setting between **Willamette Heritage Center at the Mill** and the State Capitol invites folks to take a stroll through campus. The **Mark O. Hatfield Library** is in the middle of campus overlooking the millrace.

KWAN'S ORIGINAL CUISINE

835 Commercial St SE   503/362-7711
Lunch, Dinner: Daily   kwanscuisine.com
Moderate

My long association with **Bo and Kam Sang Kwan** goes back to the 1960s. "Kwan's" roots and work ethic started in Asia well before he ran the household of yours truly. In 1976 Kwan's Kitchen debuted in Salem and in 1982 his restaurant moved down the street to a new 300-seat restaurant with a landmark pagoda,

Salem gem

What we know today as **Historic Deepwood Estate** (historicdeepwoodestate.org), a Queen Anne Victorian home, was completed in 1894 as a private residence for Dr. Luke A. Port at the astronomical cost of $15,000. (The average home price of the era was $1,000.)

Lauded architect, William C. Knighton, designed the home, and it was his first residential commission. (Knighton went on to become Oregon's first State Architect and designed the Oregon Supreme Court Building and the Governor Hotel in Portland.) However, after the tragic death at sea of Dr. Port's son, the family moved to Los Angeles, never living in the home.

The home was sold to George and Willie Bingham in 1895 where they resided for almost three decades and developed extensive gardens and an orchard. It was sold by the Bingham's daughter to Clifford Brown who married Alice Bretherton in 1908; after the drowning death of Mr. Brown in 1927, Alice continued living there and commissioned well-known Salem landscape architects Elizabeth Lord and Edith Schryver to further enhance the four-acre estate.

Alice began calling her home Deepwood after a children's book favored by her sons; when the formal gardens were nearly complete, Alice took legal steps to ensure the enduring name.

She later married Keith Powell (widower of Alice Bingham Powell) who was the daughter of George and Willie Bingham) and lived there until they could no longer care for the property.

The City of Salem acquired the property in 1971, attaining placement on the National Register of Historic Homes in 1973.

Nominal admission price; home and gardens are available for private events (rental).

new name and banquet facilities. The lengthy menu is excellent and full of curry, Szechuan and garlic options in vegetable, rice and noodle dishes combined with meats (chicken, beef, seafood, emu, lamb and pork) and prepared with mild, medium, hot or super-hot spice levels. The results are interesting, flavorful (without chemicals like MSG) and attractively presented. Special dietary requests such as gluten-free are honored to nourish the soul and body. Hard-working Kwan is always on the job taking only four days off each year: Memorial Day, Independence Day, Thanksgiving and Christmas! One of Kwan's many talents is deboning a chicken with a meat cleaver while blindfolded!

LA CAPITALE

508 State St SE   503/585-1975
Lunch: Mon-Sat; Dinner: Mon-Sat   lacapitalesalem.com
Moderately expensive

In a bistro presided over by owner **David Rosales** and Chef **Richardo Antunez**, diners are treated to a large menu of delights, many with a French accent. You'll find a charcuterie offering of assorted cured meats with rustic bread, onion soup gratinée, baked snails with puff pastry, quiche or deliciously crisp pommes frites served with sea salt and several sauces. A number of salads and sandwiches might include an open-faced Dungeness crab offering with chives and gruyere cheese, duck or pork confit. Wonderful dinner entrees feature beef, poultry, fish or shellfish incorporating fresh Northwest elements. This popular watering hole has eight local and Belgian beers on tap and a selection of local wines. Whatever time you visit, you may catch snippets of conversations from Oregon legislators and lobbyists whose government house is a short walk away.

MADRONA HILLS ACE HARDWARE

706 Madrona Ave SE   503/763-6323
Mon-Sat: 7 a.m.-8 p.m.; Sun: 9-6   madronaacehardware.com

Head to the hills, Madrona Hills Ace Hardware, that is, for hardware, yard and garden, paint and do-it-yourself project needs. The expert staff is ready to dispense advice for clogged drains, electrical projects and paint selection, along with the nuts and bolts to keep a home and yard looking fresh. Common and unique outdoor plants and garden accessories are attractively displayed in garden-like settings and porchscapes. The store's exquisite gift section is original, well-displayed, fun to browse and inspires creativity. Don't miss their splendid Christmas department; even Santa gives it two thumbs up. Indeed, Ace is the place!

MARCO POLO GLOBAL RESTAURANT

300 Liberty St SE   503/364-4833
Lunch, Dinner: Daily   mpologlobal.com
Moderate

This aptly named restaurant enjoys spacious quarters in downtown Salem. Proprietors **Jackey and Cathay Cheung** serve a full-slate of Chinese-Asian fare, European specialties such as pastas and raviolis, vegetarian and vegan offerings, tofu entrees and American favorites such as burgers; gluten-free selections are also available. Garlic green beans with choice of chicken, prawns or beef and the Marco Polo special crispy pan-fried egg noodles loaded with chicken, BBQ pork and shrimp with a substantial portion of good-for-you vegetables are especially satisfying.

ORCHARD HEIGHTS WINERY

6057 Orchard Heights Road NW   503/391-7308
Lunch: Mon-Sat; Brunch: Sun   orchardheightswinery.com
Moderate

Looking for a relaxing place to bring your family and friends for Sunday brunch? This winery, tasting room and cafe sits amidst a five-acre Gewürztraminer vineyard. An ideal afternoon combines a bucolic drive through West Salem's orchards, vineyards and farmland with a break here for lunch of homemade soup, bread and caramelized pear salad. You may want to repeat the drive on a Sunday for their tasty brunch. You'll find outstanding omelet and pasta bars, build-your-own waffles, breads and pastries, breakfast burritos, fresh seasonal fruits, cheeses and Orchard Heights' wines. An assortment of Island Princess Tropical wines start with a dry white wine mixed with juices (pineapple, passion fruit and mango). Owners **Gwen and Michael Purdy** also own a Hawaiian macadamia nut orchard and chocolate factory specializing in Island Princess gourmet chocolates and confections using macadamia nuts and Kona coffee beans. Needless to say, they carry an impressive line of the sister company's Hawaiian delights in the well-stocked gift shop.

THE ORIGINAL PANCAKE HOUSE

4685 Portland Road NE	503/393-9124
4656 Commercial St SE	503/378-0431
Breakfast: Daily: 6-2	originalpancakehouse.com
Moderate	

Founded in Portland in 1953 by **Erma Heuneke** and **Les Highet** and long a Frank family favorite, The Original Pancake House now boasts 116 franchised locations from Hawaii to New York. Whether you call them pancakes, griddlecakes, flapjacks or hotcakes, the menu offers almost every concoction of pancake imaginable: buttermilk, potato, buckwheat, sourdough, Swedish or wheat germ finished with fruits, nuts, bacon or other goodies. Add crepes, waffles, egg dishes, omelets, cereal and specialties such as the Dutch Baby (a light double-decker sort of pancake filled with lemon, whipped butter and powdered sugar) and, man oh man, you have breakfast for everyone. Other Oregon locations are in Portland, Bend, Redmond and Eugene; menu items may vary by location.

RIVERFRONT PARK
SALEM'S RIVERFRONT CAROUSEL

101 Front St NE	503/540-0374
Daily (seasonal hours)	salemcarousel.org
Nominal	

A.C. GILBERT'S DISCOVERY VILLAGE

116 Marion St NE	503/371-3631
Mon-Sat: 10-5; Sun: noon-5	acgilbert.org
Nominal	

WILLAMETTE QUEEN

200 Water St, City Dock	503/371-1103
Days and hours vary	willamettequeen.com
Nominal to expensive	

What is now a beautiful downtown greenspace along the Willamette River was formerly industrial ground for a flour

BURIED TREASURE

Experienced restaurateurs, **Janet and Martin Bleck**, pulled up Miami stakes in 2008, moved to Oregon, "the most beautiful state in the nation," and opened **Subterra - A Wine Cellar Restaurant** (1505 Portland Road, Newberg; 503/538-6060; subterrarestaurant.com). As the name suggests, this white-tablecloth, affordable restaurant is an underground affair (underneath the **Dark Horse Wine Bar** (503/538-2427) adding to the wine cellar mystique that shrouds this entire area). The seasonal menu is extensive with tasty and imaginative land and sea and pasta options for lunch and dinner, served with bread made on-premises; small plate offerings; wine bar, too. Diners are reminded to save room for freshly-made desserts that change on a whim. Lunch Monday through Friday, 11:30 a.m. to 5 p.m.; dinner, daily from 5 p.m.

mill and more recently Boise Cascade's paper and cardboard-manufacturing plant. In the mid-1980s the City of Salem purchased the property and cleared the way for a carousel, heritage village, an amphitheater, covered pavilion, boat dock and miles of walking and biking paths. One lasting vestige of the industrial past is a large pressurized "acid ball" which held acids for processing wood chips. A five-year endeavor transformed it into an artistic world globe depicted through 86,000 hand-crafted tiles. A trip to the park is not complete without a ride on the locally hand-carved indoor carousel where 46 horses and friends prance to calliope music. The nonprofit, hands-on children's museum is named for Salem-born **A.C. Gilbert**, an Olympic athlete, creator of the erector set and a prolific inventor. The museum features three historic Victorian-style houses filled with interactive exhibits. The Imagination Station features many of Gilbert's toys and inventions as well as a scale replica of Riverfront Park. On the north end of the park is a defunct railroad bridge that is now a popular pedestrian walkway across the river to West Salem and through Wallace Marine Park. Salem's only sternwheeler is serenely docked along the river until she ventures out for excursions, lunch and dinner cruises and special events. Plans are underway to connect the southern terminus of the park with Minto-Brown Island Park; the result will open a continuous network of paths and trails bypassing busy downtown traffic. Recreationists and families enjoy these activities and numerous events and festivals throughout the year. This is a spectacular example of how community volunteers pulling together can make great things happen in their hometowns.

WILLAMETTE HERITAGE CENTER AT THE MILL

1313 Mill St SE	503/585-7012
Mon-Sat: 10-5	willametteheritage.org
Tours: nominal	

MISSION MILL CAFE

Lunch: Mon-Sat	503/763-1266
Inexpensive	missionmillcafe.com

DANNER & SOLI — ANTIQUES AND COLLECTIBLES

Mon-Sat: 10-5   503/586-0232

There are several "oldests" and "onlys" at this history complex that began in 1896 as the Thomas Kay Woolen Mill, a forerunner of the famous **Pendleton Woolen Mills**' label. Restored, refurnished and moved to the manicured grounds are the oldest remaining frame houses in the Northwest (the Jason Lee House and Methodist Parsonage), Salem's oldest single family dwelling (the John D. Boon house) and Pleasant Grove Church (the oldest remaining Presbyterian Church in Oregon). The mill, which closed in 1962, is the only woolen mill museum west of Missouri and was the last direct water-powered factory in the U.S. when it closed. In 2010, Mission Mill Museum Association merged with the Marion County Historical Society and established library, archives and collections divisions to oversee the combined collections and provide a vision for the future. The Center has created fabulous interpretive displays harkening back to the time when blankets and textiles were made at the mill. A rushing millrace and the thump-thump sound of looms is part of the re-created working ambience. Self-guided tours for individuals and small groups and guided tours for larger groups are available. Inside the warehouse building, **Danner & Soli** is a fine gift shop with textiles, Pendleton blankets, antiques and gifts for the home, garden and person; **Mission Mill Cafe** is convenient for lunch, afternoon tea and fresh baked pie; a visitors center and a few other businesses use the Mill for their enterprises.

WILLAMETTE VALLEY CHEESE CO.

8105 Wallace Road NW   503/399-9806
Tues-Sat: 10-5   wvcheeseco.com

Always on the lookout for good cheese, I found Boerenkaas (raw milk aged Gouda) at this delightful cheesery with certified organic pastures and production facilities. This operation makes all-natural, handcrafted cheeses from a decades-old recipe. In addition to Boerenkaas they produce cheddar, fontina, Gouda, creamy Havarti, jack, mozzarella and brie. Many cheeses are enhanced with herbs, spices or blueberries, then smoked and aged. You will also find their products at upper-end markets and seasonal farmers markets throughout Portland and the Valley.

WILLAMETTE VALLEY FRUIT COMPANY

2994 82nd Ave NE   503/362-8678
Mon-Fri: 7-6; Sat: 9-5   wvfco.com

A relatively new retail store offers an up-close glimpse into an incredible pie-making operation. Twenty or so folks produce thousands of pies that are sold locally and shipped throughout the western states (and beyond via amazon.com). Up to 30 local growers funnel fruits through this family-owned business to be used in not only pies, but cobblers, jams and jellies, freezer jams, honey, syrups and fruit snack bars. The store offers other gourmet products, seasonal fresh produce, gift and garden items, frozen packaged fruit, baked goods, milkshakes, lunch fare and more. Call by 8:30 a.m. to pick up a pie baked fresh for you that afternoon. A much-anticipated Harvest Festival with corn maze and Christmas events are held at this rural locale between Salem and Silverton (check website for extended seasonal hours).

WORD OF MOUTH NEIGHBORHOOD BISTRO

140 17th St NE   503/930-4285
Breakfast, Lunch: Daily   wordofsalem.com
Moderate

A friend said her dying wish would be a heaping platter of

Word of Mouth's crème brûlée French toast. What's not to love; thick slices of challah bread with a caramelized crunchy topping, ordered a la carte or with eggs and bacon. Until closing in mid-afternoon, **Becky and Steve Mucha** turn out seductive breakfast winners such as prime rib Benedict, the incredible flying biscuit (buttermilk biscuit, fried chicken, fried egg, melted cheese, bacon and sausage gravy with breakfast potatoes), omelets, hash (veggie, corned beef or prime rib) and housemade sausage. Lunch service begins at 11 with soups, chowders, fresh salads (spinach, chicken bistro or chopped chicken), burgers and hearty specialty sandwiches with a nice assortment of sides. There is almost always a waiting line for a table on the enclosed front porch, at the bar or in the main floor dining areas at this small house. Don't tell your cardiologist about your cholesterol overload!

OREGON BOUNTY

From the fertile Willamette Valley soil to the far reaches of Eastern Oregon row crops and all the Oregon landscape in between, Oregonians love the fresh fruits, vegetables, meats, dairy, nursery stock and crafts that appear at farmers markets. For a great reference list covering Oregon from east and west to north and south, see **oregonfarmersmarkets.org**.

SCOTTS MILLS

DOMAINE MARGELLE
20159 Hazelnut Ridge Road   503/873-0692
Moderate   domainemargelle.com

Many wineries around Oregon are located in spectacular settings, but it would be hard to beat this location in the scenic Cascade foothills. Sublime La Bastide (country farmhouse) provides an elevated rustic respite on 30 wooded acres across from the vineyard proper. This vacation home sleeps six to eight comfortably in three bedrooms (larger parties can be accommodated). Though rustic, amenities are plenty; fireplace, elevated patio, modern kitchen (wine cooler and copper bar), washer and dryer and two bathrooms (one with antique lounging tub) plus outdoor Koi fish ponds, barbecue grill and firepit. Top-notch pinot noir and pinot gris boutique wines are bottled under the Margelle label; private personalized wine tastings and winemaker dinners by prior arrangement.

SILVERTON

THE CHOCOLATE BAR

202 N Water St   503/873-3225
Tues-Sat: 11:30-5   silvertonchocolateboxshop.com

This boutique is all about my favorite food — chocolate. You'll find well-known, made in Oregon brands like Moonstruck, Euphoria, Goody's, Extreme, The Brigittine Monks and others all under one roof in Silverton's historic district. Buy these luscious chocolates by the piece or as many as you wish; custom gift baskets and boxes are no problem. The folks here will skillfully design a chocolate buffet or favors for weddings, showers, anniversaries and other celebrations. Dairy-free and vegan chocolates, chocolate sauces and gourmet hot cocoa, as well as dessert wines and ports are also featured. Bet you can't eat just one piece!

EDWARD ADAMS HOUSE BED & BREAKFAST

729 S Water St   503/873-8868
Moderate   edwardadamshousebandb.com

In one of Oregon's most picturesque towns, this inn is as snug as you will be in one of the three lovingly restored bedrooms. Built by Swedish master craftsman Magnus Ek, the 1890 home is a Silverton Heritage Landmark. The home features antiques throughout, including a 1920 Steinway grand piano and vintage furnishings. Updated private baths are individualized with a whirlpool tub in the octagonal turret, vintage tub or a walk-in shower; all are stocked with sumptuous bathrobes and towels. Mornings start with a silver tray of coffee and tea set outside your bedroom door, followed by a delightful breakfast of homemade goodies, fruits and varying entrees (special dietary needs can be accommodated) in the dining room.

THE OREGON GARDEN

879 W Main St   503/874-8100, 877/674-2733
Daily: May-Sept: 9-6; Oct-April: 10-4   oregongarden.org
Nominal to moderate

THE GORDON HOUSE

503/874-6006
Tours by reservation   thegordonhouse.org

OREGON GARDEN RESORT

895 W Main St   503/874-2500
Moderate   moonstonehotels.com

Plan a day or two in the Silverton area and include time to admire the gardens, waterfalls, ponds and fountains at The Oregon Garden. Since its opening in 2001 (I was one of the founders), more than 20 themed gardens (Northwest Garden, Silverton Market Garden, Children's Garden, Amazing Water Garden, Pet-Friendly Garden, Rose Garden, Home Demonstration Garden, Tropical House, wetlands and more) have been developed. Each season brings new vistas with blooming annuals, perennials, trees and shrubs. In addition, this is a prime venue for concerts, festivals, weddings and a full spectrum of special events on the grounds or in the J. Frank Schmidt Pavilion. Between April and October, a tram conveys visitors throughout the 80 glorious acres. Overlooking the Garden is the Oregon Garden Resort which includes a full-service, moderately-priced restaurant with tables situated for diners to enjoy the expansive Valley views. The Resort also features full-service **Moonstone Spa** and the Fireside Lounge which hosts live music every evening. Several Northwest-style buildings contain 103 guest rooms; all include private patios or decks and fireplaces. The Gordon House, Oregon's only Frank Lloyd Wright designed home, was relocated 24 miles to showcase at The Oregon Garden. The design concept is "Usonian," characterized by an open floor plan, cantilevered roofs and floor-to-ceiling windows.

SEVEN BRIDES BREWERY AND TAP ROOM

990 N 1st St   503/874-4677
Thurs, Sun: 11-9; Fri, Sat: 11-11   sevenbridesbrewing.com
Lunch: Inexpensive; Dinner: Moderate

Enjoy lunch and dinner at this fun brewery and tap room. Try the small plate selection with a flight of beer or wine or full meals of salads, sandwiches, burgers, tacos, steaks and other land and sea items. Unlike most breweries and pubs, they do not, nor will they ever have, a deep fat fryer. The brewery's name comes from the seven daughters of the three partners, who realized they'd better make some dough to pay for upcoming weddings. They refined their home brew hobby and started the microbrewery that celebrated its first bottling in 2010 and created seven signature beers, one named for each of the seven daughters (no pending nuptials planned for the young gals aged 5 to 18). Local is something they strive for every day, from hops to beef and cheese. Since they hope to have the local folks of Oregon support them, they feel that they darn well better do the same! Seven Brides' beers are also sold in growlers and bottles and at select retailers.

SILVER GRILLE

206 E Main St   503/873-4035
Dinner: Wed-Sun   silvergrille.com
Moderate

Well-known Chef **Jeff Niziek** is in command of this charming and intimate contemporary bistro. His travels and experiences have honed his desire to offer patrons fresh and savory Willamette Valley cuisine. Appetizers, salads, entrees and fabulous desserts are artistically plated, each as pleasing to the eyes as to the stomach. The menu is peppered with local ingredients and healthy fruits and vegetables from sources like nearby Steffen Farms. Attractive and delicious starters may include Dungeness crab bisque and a salad of poached pickled pears, blue cheese and organic field greens. Seasonal entrees are prepared for hearty winter appetites or lighter summer dining; a vegetarian choice is always tempting. Chef Jeff's multi-course wine dinners are a superb way to sample his culinary talents and world-class wines from the Valley's best wineries.

SILVERTON INN & SUITES

310 N Water St   503/873-1000
Inexpensive to expensive   silvertoninnandsuites.com

Silverton Inn & Suites lends its presence to the community heartbeat. In 2005, **Elaine and Doug DeGeorge** purchased the dated Nordic Motel; they completed a total redesign and remodel in 2006, adding an elegant two-story lobby with a massive fireplace. A stay in one of the 18 accommodations may bring a quaint European town to mind rather than Silverton, Oregon, U.S.A. All suites (one, two or three beds; one or two bedrooms) are outfitted with full kitchens or kitchenettes. Each room is named after a portion of Silverton's rich history. For additional glimpses of the town's history, wander through town to view the dozen or so colorful murals.

SPRINGFIELD

MCKENZIE ORCHARDS BED & BREAKFAST
34694 McKenzie View Dr   541/515-8153
Moderate   mkobb.com

On the lower McKenzie River, just 15 minutes from Eugene, is this ADA-accessible, modern accommodation with five guest rooms; four rooms offer tranquil river views. Each evening wine and hors d'oeuvres are served as guests regale one another with accounts of fly-fishing, bicycle touring or day trip excursions. Pampered overnighters are on the receiving end of hosts **Karen and Tom Reid**'s culinary expertise for morning breakfasts; if you'd rather stay in and enjoy the solitude, inquire about light evening bistro fare. Check with the Reids for a seat at their popular cooking school held at the inn; hands-on demonstrations (elegant but easy, French, Mexican, Italian, etc.), paired wines and a delicious dinner with fellow classmates are combined for a great evening.

ST. PAUL

FRENCH PRAIRIE GARDENS
17673 French Prairie Road   503/633-8445
Seasonal days and hours   fpgardens.com

The Pohlschneider family has operated this gem for more than 20 years. Through the years it has morphed from a self-service fruit and vegetable stand into a country experience on a working farm. A great farm-fresh option is the 18-week Community Supported Agriculture program. Each week harvest boxes are

FICKLE FATE

An Oregon president? The word around the Miami 1968 Republican convention was that **Mark Hatfield**, then a young senator from Oregon, was a favored candidate for President **Richard Nixon**'s VP choice. Early on, the Miami newspapers heralded, "It is a Nixon-Hatfield ticket." The conservative delegates did not like the possibility, however, and let it be known. The night of the selection, Nixon was surrounded by his closest aides, including Reverand **Billy Graham** (who was Hatfield's greatest promoter). Alas, after a back-and-forth telephone game all night to the Hatfield camp ("Yes, he is." "No, he isn't."), Governor **Spiro Agnew** was announced as Nixon's choice. Had fate been in his corner, Mark O. Hatfield would have become president when Nixon was disgraced and resigned with the Watergate fiasco.

packed with a wondrous assortment of farm fresh produce; add an optional basket of French Prairie's baked goods for a yummy sweet treat. Fresh produce is sold in the farm market as are homemade fruit pies, muffins, cookies, scones and coffee cakes (March to mid-December) and nursery products in the spring and summer. Fun festivals herald the first crop of strawberries, the fall harvest and other family-oriented gatherings. Especially enjoyable with Mother Nature's spectacle of fragrant blooming flowers and ripe produce, garden dinners (local meats, produce, brews and wines) are a big hit May through September. Call for details and reservations.

STAYTON

GARDNER HOUSE CAFE AND BED & BREAKFAST

633 N 3rd Ave   503/769-5478
Cafe: Tues-Sat: 8-3   gardnerhousebnb.com
Inexpensive

You'll find Stayton a charming small town not far from **Silver Falls State Park**, a jewel of our state park system. Proprietors

Loni and James Loftus operate this classic Queen Anne Victorian turned into a cozy spot for breakfast, lunch or tea. Breakfast, served until 11, has plenty of egg combination plates, scones, crumpets and pancakes (your appetite determines the number you order). Salads, sandwiches, homemade soups and seasonal specials such as mac and cheese, pizzas and pot pies satisfy lunchers. Afternoon tea is also served (11-3, reservations required) with a delightful array of teas, fresh fruit, savory tarts, assorted finger sandwiches or scones. Talented Loni has won over 100 awards at the Oregon State Fair for her baked items. Some of those pies, cakes, cheesecakes, cookies and muffins are also in the cafe. An overnight stay in the private cottage won't break the bank; breakfast is delivered to your room or you may opt to eat in the cafe.

TURNER

WILLAMETTE VALLEY VINEYARDS
8800 Enchanted Way SE   503/588-8894, 800/344-9463
Tasting room: Daily: 11-6
Restaurant: Daily: 11:30-5   wvv.com

Since 1983, **Jim Bernau**, founder of award-winning Willamette Valley Vineyards, has worked to become a premier viticulturist and promoter of classic Oregon wines from the Willamette Valley appellation. Through exhausting toil, he cleared an old plum orchard which was overgrown with obnoxious Scotch broom and meticulously tended pinot noir and pinot gris plants, even hand watering with thousands of feet of garden hose. Now, hundreds of thousands of motorists pass the elaborate WVV estate vineyard on a picturesque hillside, just east of I-5, south of Salem. A new restaurant features fresh Northwest cuisine. Named the 2011 Winery of the Year by both *Wine & Spirits* and *Wine Press Northwest* publications, Jim's vision is bearing the fruits of his long labor. Wines are sold worldwide and have been spotlighted by celebrity chefs and served at White House dinners. Stop in for a tasting and tour and survey the expansive western view toward the Coast Range or make WVV headquarters for a fabulous event. Jim is a super fellow and very generous to his community; I am honored to call him friend.

VENETA

OUR DAILY BREAD RESTAURANT

88170 Territorial Road   541/935-4921
Mon, Tues: 7-3; Wed-Sat: 7 a.m.-8 p.m.;   ourdailybreadrestaurant.com
Sun: Brunch: 10-1, Dinner: 4-8
Breakfast, Lunch (inexpensive), Dinner (moderately expensive)

Our Daily Bread is a suitable name for a restaurant and bakery in a renovated country church near Fern Ridge Reservoir. The dining area is especially cheery with sunlight streaming through the stained glass windows and backyard seating is perfect on a warm summer afternoon. The extensive breakfast menu offers good ol' American standards: bacon, eggs, rustic red potatoes, hotcakes and more scrambles and omelet combinations than you can shake a stick at. Lunch customers have the usual choices of soups, salads and sandwiches on housemade bread, plus wraps and specials. Prime rib, steaks, chops, pastas, seafood and chicken are filling dinner entrees; sweet meal-enders are fresh from the bakery. Brunch is served buffet style with plenty of the bakery's muffins, pastries and other goodies. A small country store sells locally-grown and -made products, gift baskets, mixes, wines, soaps and body products.

VIDA

VIDA CAFE

45641 McKenzie Hwy   541/896-3289
Daily: 7-7 (June-Sept till 8)
Inexpensive to moderate

Head up the McKenzie River for an out-of-the-way spot to find good home cooking in a fun and friendly atmosphere. If you are looking for low-calorie, low-fat options, it's probably best to keep right on driving; signature items are the Frisbee-size hotcakes, a "monster" burger and from-scratch pies and cobblers. A point of interest is the nearby historic **Goodpasture Bridge**, the second longest covered bridge in Oregon.

WILSONVILLE

DAR ESSALAM
29585 SW Park Pl, Suite A   503/682-3600
Lunch: Mon-Thurs; Dinner: Mon-Sat   daressalam.org
Moderate

Abdellah Elhabbassi was born and raised in Morocco, immigrating in 1985 to Denver where he met and married his wife, Dee, who comes from Iowa. Intent on going back to Abdellah's roots and operating a Moroccan establishment, they moved back to Morocco in 1999 to study the cuisine. Now in Wilsonville, Dee is the chef and infuses fine North African spices and other exotics at Dar Essalam, which means "House of Tranquility." From the hummus supreme (their signature honey hummus topped with roasted red peppers, capers, feta and black olives and served with warm pita bread) that you might choose for a lunch starter to a variety of kabobs or a famous gyro, you won't be disappointed. Dinner offers a choice of meat tajines combined with savory, sweet or spicy options (gluten-free and vegetarian menu also). Interesting dessert options include the Casablanca dessert, buttery filo layers stuffed with fruit, dusted with powdered sugar and toasted almonds, then topped with vanilla ice cream.

FAMILY FUN CENTER & BULLWINKLE'S RESTAURANT
29111 SW Town Center Loop W   503/685-5000
Hours vary   fun-center.com
Ticket prices vary

Pack up the offspring and their buddies for a day of fun, food and merriment at this amusement attraction along I-5. Kids invariably point it out, followed by the appeal to stop and play. Outdoor activities include miniature golf (two courses), go-carts, bumper boats, batting cages, a climbing wall and a ropes course. Laser tag, cyber roller coaster, an arcade and play areas for the three and older set are indoors, especially handy for rainy days. After working up appetites, your brood will enjoy inexpensive burgers, pizza, salads, sandwiches and other kid-friendly favorites or re-energize with ice cream and milkshakes. This is a popular birthday party locale for kids of all ages.

WOODBURN

AL'S GARDEN CENTER
1220 N Pacific Hwy   503/981-1245
Mon-Fri: 10-6; Sat, Sun: 9-6   als-gardencenter.com

A visit to one of Al's Garden Center's three locations is a springtime ritual for folks far and wide. Al's is family-owned and operated by **Jack Bigej**, one of the nicest and most knowledgeable nurserymen in the biz. Nursery stock prevails, but plenty of other quality merchandise is attractively presented such as planters, patio accessories, household decor and women's apparel. Al's friendly helpers in Woodburn, Sherwood (16920 SW Roy Rogers Road) and Gresham (7505 SE Hogan Road) are easily spotted by their signature purple shirts. They are ready to dispense advice to turn a brown thumb into a green one! Store hours vary slightly according to the season.

WOODBURN COMPANY STORES
1001 Arney Road   503/981-1900, 888-664-7467
Daily   woodburncompanystores.com

Since the doors opened in 2007, this very attractive, well-planned outlet mall has been wildly successful; 2011 saw record sales and traffic. Frequent special events and big sales draw huge crowds, evidenced by the cars lined up to exit I-5, especially on holiday weekends. Shoppers from the Northwest and Canada target WCS for great deals and tax-free shopping at 98 stores (adidas, Columbia Sportswear, Cole Haan, Bose, Nike Factory Store, Nine West, Fossil, Helly Hansen, The North Face and dozens more). Six buildings are bursting with bargains in family clothing, footwear and accessories, housewares, luggage, fragrances, garden goods, electronics and fine jewelry. It's no wonder that this is one of Oregon's top tourist attractions: great retailers, a visitors information center, kids' play area with tree house and assorted eateries. Shop on!

Highest state office

Starting with my Great Uncle **Julius Meier**, who was elected to the governorship (1931-1935) as the first (and only) Oregon Independent, I've had the opportunity to meet and to get to know many of our state's succeeding governors. While results and personalities vary, it is an exceptional group of individuals who put public service at the forefront of their lives. Julius Meier was the busy head of the **Meier & Frank Co.**, reluctantly turned politician at the urging of Republicans who were unhappy with the elective choice before them when the original candidate (George Joseph) died between the primary and the general elections. Meier brought a tough, organized mind to the job, which included establishing the **Oregon State Police** as one of his priorities.

Meier was followed by **Charles Martin** (1935-1939), **Charles Sprague** (1939-1943), **Earl Snell** (1943-1947) and **John Hall** (1947-1949), none of whom I knew, except Sprague. Charles Sprague was a crusty Salem newspaper publisher, a keen observer of local, national and international events (he wrote a daily column) and a former Salem First Citizen.

Douglas McKay (1949-1952), a Salem car dealer, was a popular figure who went on to serve as Secretary of the Interior in the Eisenhower administration. **Paul Patterson** (1952-1956) was an unexciting "don't-rock-the-boat" administrator. **Elmo Smith** (1956-1957), from Ontario, joined those who didn't complete a term. (Political genes sometimes run in the family, proven by Elmo's son, **Denny Smith**, who served in the U.S. House of Representatives and also made a gubernatorial run against John Kitzhaber.) **Robert "Bob" Holmes** (1957-1959), from Astoria, was an excellent communicator and effective governor who started a state economic development program among other accomplishments.

Mark Hatfield (1959-1967), a legendary figure in

Oregon politics, was one of our state's most successful politicians, serving two terms as governor and five terms in the U.S. Senate (as well as during pre-gubernatorial days, serving as Secretary of State and a representative in the Oregon House). Next in line was colorful **Tom McCall** (1967-1975), a bigger-than-life former television commentator. Aided by an exceptional staff, McCall's administration focused on the Bottle Bill and keeping Oregon's beaches in public hands. (People often ask about the Hatfield-McCall relationship. Answer: Not close. Hatfield was a carefully studied student; McCall, a flamboyant loose cannon.)

Former State Treasurer **Robert "Bob" Straub** (1975-1979) was a keen businessman, but lacked strong staff support; nevertheless, he was an able CEO, suffering from constant comparison to the popular McCall.

Straub was defeated in his second-term run by rug merchant **Vic Atiyeh** (1979-1987) who presided over the state during bleak economic days, quietly earning kudos for his no-nonsense leadership. (Atiyeh enjoys the historical retrospect of being more popular today than he was as governor.)

The **Neil Goldschmidt** (1987-1991) story is not only a personal tragedy for all involved, but also a public one. Brilliant, charismatic and visionary, he could have been President of the United States (he served as an outstanding Secretary of Transportation in the Carter administration).

Barbara Roberts (1991-1995) is the only woman to serve as governor, a gifted public speaker and enthusiastic Oregon booster for many worthwhile causes. (She continues in this realm.)

Dr. **John Kitzhaber** (1995-2003) served two consecutive terms and later ran for an unprecedented third (2011-) term. His medical education took him to Roseburg's emergency room where he became politically involved and proceeded to become a strong Oregon Senate President and clear advocate for medical, educational and environmental reform. Extremely intelligent with a true western presence (usually decked out in blue jeans), he won a close race for his third term and has become more popular in his ensuing tenure.

After Kitzhaber's first terms, a thoroughly fine and decent man and former marine, **Ted Kulongoski** (2003-2011), served in the midst of the Iraq and Afghanistan wars and made it his tribute to attend the funeral services of over 120 Oregon servicemen and women killed during his time in office. Kulongoski ably served Oregonians in all three branches of state government over his professional lifetime, a modern record.

Despite human failings (we all have), these men along with our lone woman leader, represent devoted, honest, exemplary service on behalf of our state.

DID YOU KNOW ...?

... that during **World War II**, six shipyards in the Portland area (five in Portland, one in Vancouver), mainly run by the Kaiser organization, completed 1,189 vessels and converted 20 more for wartime use.

... that Portland real estate tycoon and former theater owner, **Tom Moyer**, was once a champion amateur boxer?

... that three Oregon destinations have been named among the "World's Best" by top travel magazines? (**Tu Tu' Tun Lodge** on the Rogue River, the **Stephanie Inn** at Cannon Beach and **The Allison** in Newberg).

... that **Crater Lake** (at 1,943 feet deep) is the deepest lake in the United States?

... that **Lake Billy Chinook** (at the intersection of the Metolius, Deschutes and Crooked rivers) not only offers houseboats to visitors, but also is the source of much of Oregon's famous crawfish?

Your notes

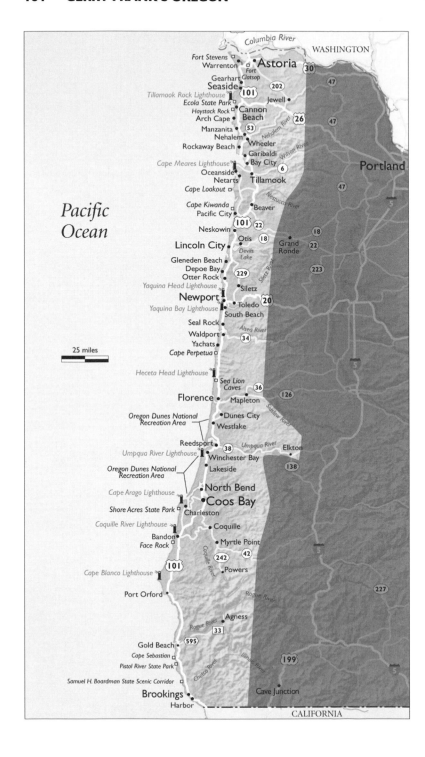

WASHINGTON

Columbia River

Fort Stevens
Warrenton
Astoria
Fort
Clatsop
Gearhart
Seaside
101
202
Jewell
Tillamook Rock Lighthouse
Ecola State Park
Haystack Rock
Cannon
Beach
Arch Cape
Manzanita
Nehalem
Rockaway Beach
Wheeler
Garibaldi
Bay City
Oceanside
Netarts
Tillamook
Cape Meares Lighthouse
Cape Lookout
Cape Kiwanda
Pacific City
Beaver
Neskowin
101
22
Otis
18
Lincoln City
Devils
Lake
Grand
Ronde
Gleneden Beach
Depoe Bay
Otter Rock
229
Yaquina Head Lighthouse
Siletz
Newport
Toledo
20
Yaquina Bay Lighthouse
South Beach
Seal Rock
Waldport
Yachats
34
Cape Perpetua

Heceta Head Lighthouse
Sea Lion
Caves
36
Florence
Mapleton
126
Oregon Dunes National
Recreation Area
Dunes City
Westlake
Reedsport
38
Umpqua River
Elkton
Umpqua River Lighthouse
Winchester Bay
Lakeside
138
Oregon Dunes National
Recreation Area
Cape Arago Lighthouse
North Bend
Coos Bay
Shore Acres State Park
Charleston
Caquille River Lighthouse
Coquille
Bandon
Myrtle Point
Face Rock
242
42
Powers
101
Cape Blanco Lighthouse
227
Port Orford

Rogue River
Agness
Rogue River
33
Gold Beach
595
Cape Sebastian
Pistol River State Park
199
Samuel H. Boardman State Scenic Corridor
Brookings
Cave Junction
Harbor

Pacific
Ocean

25 miles

Portland

Nehalem River
Wilson River
Nestucca River
Siletz River
Alsea River
Siuslaw River
Coquille River
Chetco River
Illinois River

30
47
47
26
47
6
18
22
223
5
5
5

CALIFORNIA

3. Oregon Coast

AGNESS

SINGING SPRINGS RESORT

34501 Agness Illahe Road
Lodge: Seasonal
Inexpensive

541/247-6162, 877/330-3777
singingspringsresort.com

If you're looking for a true Oregon getaway, think about Singing Springs Resort. You can arrive by car (about an hour northeast of Gold Beach), but it's more fun to take a commercial jet boat from Gold Beach. Clean and comfortable cabins that accommodate two to four guests are popular with families, hikers and fishermen and available throughout the year. The lodge is open between May and mid-October. Continental breakfast is included with an overnight stay and a lunch buffet and sandwiches are also available. The all-you-can-eat dinner buffet (July and August) features Southern fried chicken, barbecued pork loin, freshly-baked biscuits and all the trimmings. Meals in the off-season are optional with prior arrangement. Plan ahead if you want to book a fishing guide. The Rogue River is spectacular!

ARCH CAPE

ARCH CAPE INN & RETREAT

31970 E Ocean Lane   503/436-2800, 800/436-2848
Moderate to very expensive   archcapeinn.com

This romantic chateau is sure to elicit plenty of oohs and aahs. The inn is well-appointed, service extremely gracious and the experience nearly magical. Nine rooms and one suite are appointed with European-style furnishings, soft pillows, fine linens and Aveda bath products. Relaxing, oversize soaking or Jacuzzi tubs in private baths and gas fireplaces in most rooms enhance this get-away-from-it-all location with ocean and garden views. Overnight stays include a three-course gourmet breakfast with locally foraged ingredients and fresh-from-the-kitchen-garden produce and herbs masterfully woven into an ever-changing menu. Other pleasant touches are afternoon wine and light appetizers and in-room refreshments as well as Wi-Fi and choices from a movie library. You and your partner will want to plan a return visit even before you depart.

ASTORIA

ASTORIA COLUMN

2199 Coxcomb Dr   503/325-2963
Daily   astoriacolumn.org

Put one foot in front of the other, take a few deep breaths, and before long you're climbed the 164-step spiral staircase up to the observation deck of the Astoria Column where the rewards are magnificent views of the Columbia River, the Pacific Ocean, rivers, forests and communities. Kids get a kick out of launching balsa wood gliders (available in the gift shop) from this 125-foot tall Coxcomb Hill tower. The exterior depicts 14 early Oregon events (such as discovery of the Columbia River and the Lewis and Clark Exhibition) via magnificent murals which spiral the length of the column. The nonprofit Friends of Astoria oversee the tower's maintenance and were behind a major restoration project in 1995 and more recently a granite plaza and lighting. Can you imagine what the Astoria Column was like when it was erected in 1926?

LAND AHOY!

Eleven lighthouses dot Oregon's scenic coast; most have been restored and some are still navigational aids. While several are decommissioned, these iconic Oregon symbols were built to last, warning ship captains of imminent dangers in the midst of wild and wooly weather and are a testament to our state's rugged history. Most are open to the public and Heceta Head offers a B&B opportunity. From north to south:

Tillamook Rock: Cannon Beach

Cape Meares: Oceanside

Yaquina Head: Newport

Yaquina Bay: Newport

Cleft of the Rock: Yachats, private

Heceta Head: Florence

Umpqua River: Reedsport

Cape Arago: Charleston

Coquille River: Bandon

Cape Blanco: Port Orford

Pelican Bay: Brookings, private

BAKED ALASKA

1 12th St   503/325-7414
Lunch, Dinner: Daily   bakedak.com
Moderate

Over a decade ago **Jennifer and Chris Holen** settled upon their current Astoria location for a full-service lunch and dinner house. You'll find all tables placed to capture a view of the Columbia River. Soups and clam chowder are homemade; order by the cup or bowl or in a freshly-baked sourdough bread bowl (the latter is a throwback to Chef Chris' days in Alaska selling the satisfying combination out of a utility trailer). Eclectic choices make up the lunch menu: tacos, chicken pot pie in a cast iron skillet, sandwiches and burgers, pastas and entree salads based on fish, seafood and meats as the main ingredients. Appetizers are primarily from the ocean; Dungeness crab cakes and pancetta-wrapped wild prawns are always good. For dinner, ranch and ocean choices are served in combination or on their own; build your three-course *prix-fixe* meal from designated items. And for dessert, Baked Alaska (a smaller version is named Half Baked Alaska) or a seasonal sweet. There's more: a fully stocked lounge and private dining rooms for groups. Next door, **Mise en Place** (503/325-3554) is the source for cooking supplies, demonstrations and cooking lessons.

BLUE SCORCHER BAKERY CAFE

1493 Duane St   503/338-7473
Daily: 8-5   bluescorcher.com

Artisan breads, almond bear claws, other pastries and handcrafted seasonal and organic foods are the bread and butter at this bakery. Cakes in a variety of delicious flavors are available by special order. Fresh, quality ingredients make the difference; eggs, produce, honey, flowers and coffee are from local suppliers. Families come for healthy breakfasts (heartier choices on weekends) and lunches of soups, salads, pizzas, calzones and sandwiches made on Scorcher bread. An interesting sideline is a magazine stand holding about 60 titles for browsing and purchase.

BRIDGEWATER BISTRO

20 Basin St   503/325-6777
Lunch: Mon-Sat; Dinner: Daily; Brunch: Sun   bridgewaterbistro.com
Moderate

In a fabulous venue right on the water you can feast upon small bites, salads and seafood dishes (like chili-lime prawns or pan-fried Willapa Bay oysters). If you're not in the mood for fish, steaks, bison and fowl preparations may be more to your liking. Swedish meatballs, pork tenderloin, roasted garlic bulb and crab-scargot are among the dozen or so small plates and combined with housemade soup or salad make a tasty dinner. Sunday brunch offers a bit of everything good such as eggs and oysters, hash, seafood cakes, sandwiches and burgers (over 80% of the menu is gluten-free). Bridgewater is so named for its location under the Astoria-Megler Bridge on the Columbia River; waterfront dining inside or out affords spectacular vistas.

OREGON VISTAS

What is the most scenic drive in Oregon? Given our state's geographical beauty, that's a hard point to ponder, but Highway 101 from Bandon south to the California border is certainly one of them. The spectacular coastal views are memorable, a sight no one can forget. Be sure to stop and smell the roses at the numerous state parks along the way. Ideas for fantastic drives through official scenic corridors and byways that crisscross our state are outlined at: oregon.gov/odot/hwy/scenicbyways/driving_guide.shtml.

CANNERY PIER HOTEL & SPA

10 Basin St	503/325-4996, 888/325-4996
Moderate to expensive	cannerypierhotel.com

Situated on 100-year-old pilings and jutting out into the mighty Columbia is this hotel that was once the Union Fisherman's Cooperative Packing Company. A far cry from the former commercial structure, this boutique hotel (38 rooms, eight suites) has private balconies, gas fireplaces and in-room mini-fridges, microwaves and dining tables. With a nod to the area's Scandinavian heritage and fishing industry, the complimentary continental breakfast features Finnish delicacies; wine and lox are served each evening. If you need a lift around town, you may be chauffeured in a classic car or head out on your own to explore the area on one of the hotel's vintage loaner bikes. Other amenities include a hot tub, sauna, exercise room, free Wi-Fi, day spa and library. For the ultimate experience, book the Pilot House penthouse (two bedrooms, hot tub, guest bath, full kitchen, living and dining rooms and two decks). Pet packages include treats and necessities to care for your canine travel companion.

THE CELLAR ON 10TH

1004 Marine Dr	503/325-6600
Tues-Sat: 10:00-5:30	thecellaron10th.com

Over 4,500 bottles of local, national and international wines are in stock in this historic perfect-for-wine underground shop; over

70% of the libations are from the Northwest. Proprietor **Mike Wallis** will help pick just the wine you want. Also find wine-related linens and table pieces, international gourmet foods, spices, sea salts, stemware and accessories. Weekly wine tastings, Saturdays between 1 and 4, feature a new winery, varietal or wine region each week. The shop remains open when cruise ships are in port.

CLEMENTE'S

1198 Commercial St	503/325-1067
Lunch, Dinner: Tues-Sun	clementesrestaurant.com
Moderate	

Seafood is the main attraction at many coastal restaurants. Having had my share of fish and chips during years spent at Cambridge University in England, I know a good dish of this fabled offering. Clemente's rates very well, indeed. But, that's only the beginning at this beautiful restaurant, light and bright with soaring ceilings and local art. Owners **Lisa and Gordon Clement** change the menu seasonally; local, wild and healthy foods are harmoniously balanced with vegetarian and beef dishes. A sampling of choices: cioppino, raw bar selections, organic beef (steaks or burgers), spaghetti marinara, a *prix-fixe* dinner for two people or three-course chef's choice. Conscious of their carbon footprint, the Clementes buy local whenever possible and promote reusing, recycling to-go glass jars and composting to-go containers.

COLUMBIA RIVER MARITIME MUSEUM

1972 Marine Dr	503/325-2323
Daily: 9:30-5	crmm.org
Inexpensive to moderate	

Land at this museum for fascinating exhibitions of Northwest maritime artifacts and collections. Anchoring the east end of the property is Pilot Boat *Peacock*, decommissioned in 1999. Learn about the role she played for over 30 years transporting bar pilots between Astoria and ships navigating the world's most dangerous river bar (more than 35,000 trips—impressive!). The Lightship *Columbia* is docked at the pier and self-guided tours are included with paid admission. Roam the ship for glimpses of crew and officers' quarters, mess deck, radio room and galley and imagine the crew's desolate life when stationed five miles off the mouth of the Columbia riding out frequent treacherous storms. Other vessels, nautical equipment, historical memorabilia and interactive displays are spread among six galleries and the Great Hall.

DRINA DAISY

915 Commercial St   503/338-2912
Lunch, Dinner: Wed-Sun   drinadaisy.com
Moderate

Lovers of ethnic food will enjoy the comfort food with an Old World twist at this Bosnian restaurant. The taste is very Euro-Mediterranean with cabbage rolls and goulash. Many entrees are slow-cooked and braised to perfection and served with fresh and pickled vegetables and tasty breads. Dishes are savory but not too spicy, traditional baklava is pleasingly sweet. Drina Daisy is derived from the name of a southern Bosnia river, the location of the chef's prior restaurant and Daisy is the owner's mother.

GRANDVIEW BED & BREAKFAST

1574 Grand Ave   503/325-0000, 800/488-3250
Inexpensive to moderate   grandviewbedandbreakfast.com

Try the Grandview, a unique Victorian mansion with ten attractive, individually decorated, affordable rooms; all but one have private baths. A few rooms connect to form two-bedroom suites. Delicious breakfast is served each morning in the Bullet Turret with views of the river and numerous Astoria landmarks. The home is located in a hilly area full of picturesque historic homes.

HOME BAKERY CO.

2845 Marine Dr   503/325-4631
Tues-Sat: 6-5   astoriacinnamontoast.com

Since 1910 the Tilander family has provided Astoria with authentic Finnish baked goods. Third generation, **Kathy and Jim Tilander**, continue to use traditional family recipes for breads, doughnuts, pastries, pies, cakes, apple fritters, prune tarts, cookies and dozens more baked goods. Holiday spreads are extra special with their oh-so-good Scandinavian holiday breads. For a taste from the past, try their famous cinnamon toast. Its popularity dates back to Finland in the 1800s and also became a staple for Astorians and local fishing fleets due to the long shelf life. Sweet coffee bread is toasted, liberally sprinkled with cinnamon and sugar and packed in two-pound boxes (also sold online). Enjoy any of these sweets and coffee at the bakery or to go.

HOTEL ELLIOTT

357 12th St   877/378-1924
Inexpensive and up   hotelelliott.com

The once quiet city of Astoria has come back to life in a big way. A prime example is the five-story Hotel Elliott, originally 68 rooms when built in 1924. A three-year major renovation to this classic beauty in the early 2000s enlarged guests' quarters and whittled down the number of rooms and suites to 32. The facelift created a boutique hotel restoring the turn-of-the-century elegance with the addition of modern conveniences. Designer bathrooms feature heated tile floors and plush terry robes. Signature beds are extra comfy and furnished with goose down pillows and custom duvet covers. HDTVs, free high-speed Internet and Wi-Fi are standard amenities. More luxuries await in the suites: custom-mantled gas fireplaces, cedar-lined closets, handcrafted cabinetry and Jacuzzi tubs (varies according to suite). The Presidential Suite is fit for a king: two stories with private access to the rooftop terrace, fully-furnished kitchen, living and dining rooms, two bedrooms and memorable views of the city and river. Complimentary breakfast is offered in the expanded lobby and a wine bar is upstairs. Dining and shopping are steps away from the front door; don't miss the **Astoria Sunday Market** (astoriasundaymarket.com) mid-May to Mid-October on 12th Street.

JOSEPHSON'S SMOKEHOUSE & SPECIALTY SEAFOOD

106 Marine Dr   503/325-2190, 800/722-3474
Mon-Fri: 9-5:30; Sat: 9:30-5:30; Sun: 10-5   josephsons.com

Josephson's celebrates the better part of a century of family ownership specializing in seafood. Stop in for fish and seafood that has been smoked, canned, made into jerky and sold fresh or fresh-frozen. The deli offers lunch fare of chowders, salmon burgers and smoked seafood dishes; eat inside, on the deck or pack your choices into a basket or cooler for a picnic. The premium products are made from #1 grade seafood and natural ingredients and are free of preservatives, dyes and unhealthy additives. Likely you've encountered their products in leading retailers or read about them in numerous magazines and major newspapers. They do a whale of an online business and ship the best of the Northwest worldwide; catalogs available.

OLD TOWN FRAMING COMPANY

1287 Commercial St   503/325-5221
Mon-Fri: 9:30-5:30; Sat: 10-5   oldtownframing.com

Dulcye Taylor's frame shop is not just for a fine showing of frames, but also for the outstanding collection of greeting cards—everyday, all-occasion and appropriately inappropriate. Although they specialize in custom framing, a nice selection of ready-made frames and local and regional artists' limited edition prints and photography are in stock. Old Town Framing participates in downtown Astoria's **2nd Saturday Art Walk**, a popular event featuring refreshments, entertainment and interesting exhibits.

PILOT HOUSE

1 14th St   503/289-9926, 888/683-7987
Expensive   astoriapilothouse.com

Ship ahoy! An elegant three-bedroom vacation home is available on Pier 14 of Astoria's historic waterfront which is upstairs (no elevator) from the Columbia River Pilots station. This location gives a catbird seat to the pilots who masterfully guide ocean-bound or arriving ships right outside your windows all day long. Guests will appreciate the state-of-the-art electronic access and quality of the furnishings; many are maritime artifacts. Up to eight adults are accommodated in the spacious quarters that include three bedrooms, three bathrooms, a complete kitchen, living and dining areas and gas fireplaces in all bedrooms and the living area. Master bedroom guests enjoy a private balcony and bathroom Jacuzzi tub. Rates vary according to season and length of stay and are adjusted for couple-only occupancy. Operating seasonally, a **Riverfront Trolley** stop is right outside the front door.

SILVER SALMON GRILLE

1105 Commercial St   503/338-6640
Lunch, Dinner: Daily   silversalmongrille.com
Moderate

The Fisher Building has seen restaurants come and go since it was built in 1924. Today, salmon reigns at **Laurie and Jeff Martin**'s restaurant. The lounge's antique bar (acquired in the 1950s) is a remnant of the Thiel Brothers restaurant operation at this location. The elaborate 130-year-old beauty is constructed of Scottish cherry wood that was shipped around Cape Horn in the 1880s. As the story goes, its first Astoria home was in Anna Bays Social Club, a house of ill repute in this fishing town. Now in a more refined setting, it is the lounge's centerpiece. Joining salmon dishes on the lunch menu are halibut and chips, Willapa Bay oyster stew, London broil, a variety of sandwiches (San Francisco melt – turkey, bacon, tomato, avocado, onions and cheese on sourdough bread, dipped in egg and grilled), wraps, soups and clam chowder. A half dozen or so salmon entrees headline the dinner selections plus halibut (topped with Dungeness crab, cheese and a cream sauce), more seafood, steaks, pastas and chicken. Lighter appetites

NORTH OF THE BORDER

I am stepping outside of the state border just across the Columbia River from Astoria to mention The **Depot Restaurant** (depotrestaurantdining.com) in Seaview, Washington, and **Pelicano Restaurant** (pelicanorestaurant.com) in Ilwaco. The Depot is set in a century-plus-old train station; along with other delicacies from an international menu, you'll find local oysters for which this area is famous. The food is exceptionally well-prepared, and the greetings are wonderful! Pelicano provides waterfront dining from an inspiring seasonally-changing menu. Take it from your author, a wandering foodie, you will find great food and service to match at both of these dining destinations.

will appreciate specialty salads (tropical prawn, seafood Caesar or Cobb, smoked salmon spinach) for lunch or dinner; also low-carb and vegetarian entrees. The fine dining is matched with an impressive selection of fine wines and choices from the saloon. An assortment of mouth-watering sweets is presented on the dessert tray; sure to please are Swedish cream with marionberry sauce or Bananas Foster, flambéed in the dining room. Keep up the super job, Laurie and Jeff.

SUPPLE ROCKERS

1590 Lexington Ave   503/325-5619
Mon-Fri: 8-5   supplerockers.com

If you or family members are passionate about baseball, a unique rocking chair from Supple Rockers may be a fine addition to your home or in the man-cave. Made with six Marucci or genuine Louisville Slugger bats and laser engraved with "ticket stub" backs, each rocker is one-of-a-kind. Seats are made with premium leather and hand-sewn baseball stitch detail. Choose from dark or natural white ash bats; light or dark brown, black, red or white seats and dark brown, tan, black or red stitching; all custom. **Kim and Dan Supple** take great pride in their family-owned Oregon business.

T. PAUL'S URBAN CAFE

1119 Commercial St   503/338-5133
Lunch, Dinner: Mon-Sat   tpaulsurbancafe.com
Moderate

T. PAUL'S SUPPER CLUB

360 12th St   503/325-2545
Lunch, Dinner: Mon-Sat
Moderate

Two diverse menus distinguish the two T. Paul venues. The Urban Cafe's menu offers salads, sandwiches, quesadillas, pastas and beer and wine. Down the street and around the corner, the Supper Club serves seemingly fresh-off-the-dock seafood plus pastas, chicken, steaks and all-natural beef half-pound burgers. Entree-size salads are creative and make a meal on their own. Beer, wine and cocktails from the full bar add to the supper club ambience.

Both restaurants feature live music every weekend. T. Paul's is also known for fabulous homemade desserts, many are from grandma's tried-and-true recipes.

WET DOG CAFÉ & ASTORIA BREWING COMPANY
144 11th St   503/325-6975
Breakfast, Lunch, Dinner: Daily   wetdogcafe.com
Moderate

The Wet Dog's American-style menu appeals to families out for a casual meal. Sandwiches and over 30 kinds of burgers (beef, fish, chicken, vegetarian, turkey, bison) are top dog on the lunch and dinner menu. Starters consist of classic bar food; lighter fare includes salads, homemade soups and chicken or fish baskets. Steak and seafood entrees are served with fries and coleslaw (full meal potato and

---

KIDS' ACTIVITIES: THE COAST

Astoria
Columbia River Maritime Museum (503/325-2323, crmm.org)

Florence
Sandland Adventures (541/997-8087, sandland.com): March to December
Sea Lion Caves (541/547-3111, sealioncaves.com)

Gold Beach
Jerry's Rogue Jets (800/451-3645, roguejets.com): seasonal

Newport
Hatfield Marine Science Center (541/867-0100, hmsc.oregonstate.edu)
Oregon Coast Aquarium (541/867-3474, aquarium.org)

Port Orford
Prehistoric Gardens (541/332-4463)

Tillamook
Tillamook Cheese Factory (503/815-1300, tillamook.com)

vegetable options after 5). Now to the on-site brewing company, beers are handcrafted and most names play off the canine theme. A fair-weather outdoor deck along the riverfront is amazing on sunny days.

BANDON

ALLORO WINE BAR & RESTAURANT
375 2nd St SE · 541/347-1850
Seasonal days and hours · allorowinebar.com
Moderate to expensive

Veer off Highway 101 into Old Town for great Italian fare. Chef **Jeremy Buck** and wine steward **Lian Schmidt** honed their restaurant experiences in Florence, Italy. The wine list pays homage to Northwest and Italian wines with several available by the glass. Local seafood and meats, fresh seasonal produce and imported specialties are combined into delicious fish stew, braised lamb shank and grilled salmon. From the appetizer menu, choose from antipasto, oysters on the half shell, salad with crab and avocado and soups. Pasta dishes feature fresh seafood, vegetables and herbs; a hearty New York steak preparation is always an option. Call ahead for seasonal hours and reservations.

B HOME TEAK FURNITURE CENTER
49667 Hwy 101 · 541/347-4410
Tues-Sat: 8-4:30 · bhome-bandon.com

Dress up your yard, deck or patio with classy teak outdoor furniture. Here you'll find well-made tables and chairs, bar stools, benches (cushions, too) and lounge chairs. Teak is ideal for the wet and humid Oregon coast as it is low maintenance and becomes more beautiful as it weathers. The longevity of teak is 70-plus years.

BANDON DUNES GOLF RESORT
57744 Round Lake Dr · 541/347-4380
Daily · bandondunesgolf.com

Visionary entrepreneur and golf enthusiast, **Mike Keiser,** made his fortune in the Midwest in recycled paper. Playing golf around the world and especially in Scotland, Mike was inspired when he came to the Oregon Coast and found a wee bit of the Old Country on Oregon's south coast near Bandon. Thus, Bandon Dunes was born on the shelf of the Pacific Ocean. (That's the short version; never mind that it took several years of dedication to the project and untold millions of dollars; the rest of the story is that Mike Keiser put Oregon and Oregon golf on the world map while giving a huge boost to the local and statewide economy in terms of both jobs and tourism dollars.) Mike hired the best architects and experts in links golf and added the most capable GM he could find in **Hank Hickox** who had already made his mark at Salishan and other resort properties. Bandon Dunes today offers four 18-hole courses (Bandon Dunes, Pacific Dunes, Bandon Trails, Old Macdonald), each unique and challenging, with more courses in the long-range plan. Food and drink are served in several unique restaurants; fine Northwest cuisine and exquisite wines, casual lounges, a Scottish-style pub and day-long casual dining (hours vary by season). Comfortable, luxurious lodge, inn and cottage accommodations are designed for singles, couples and foursomes (rates vary). Resort amenities include shuttle service between lodging, courses, restaurants and lounges; a business center in the lodge; fitness center; well-stocked pro shops and daily golf clinics. This is a fantastic only-in-Oregon golf experience.

THE LOFT

315 First St SE   541/329-0535
Lunch, Dinner: Seasonally; Brunch: Sun   theloftofbandon.com
Moderate

For stunning views and casual fine dining, head to the upper level of the High Dock building in Old Town. This family operation puts chef **Kali Fieger** (trained at Le Cordon Bleu College of Culinary Arts in Portland); Kali's brother **Reid Verner**, business manager and mom, **Caryn Fieger**, the artistic director, baker, prep chef, dishwasher and mom-about-the-kitchen, together to carry the restaurant business down the generational line from Caryn's grandparents. Not surprisingly, this coastal dinner house features seafood, but not exclusively; all meals are built around seasonally available fresh bounty. Plates are beautifully presented and attractively garnished. Try the crab bruschetta appetizer if it's offered on the changing menu. The 12-layer chocolate hazelnut praline dobos torte is made in-house like most of the offerings; if the sweet potato bread pudding is on the menu, go for it.

LORD BENNETT'S

1695 Beach Loop Dr   541/347-3663
Lunch: Fri; Dinner: Daily; Brunch, Lunch: Sat, Sun   lordbennett.com
Expensive

Chef/owner **Rich Iverson** keeps locals and tourists coming back for wonderful steaks and seafood that are cooked to perfection and accompanied by soup or salad, starch and fresh vegetables. Delicious pasta dishes may be made with crab, scallops, prawns or without for vegetarian preferences. Appetizers are mainly of the ocean-going variety; soups and salads are fresh and made with healthy ingredients. Lunch standouts are Kobe beef burgers, entree salads and crab enchiladas; other selections include sandwiches and various entrees. Weekenders will find lunch fare plus brunch items such as crispy crepes, sweet potato pancakes and egg platters. The location affords magnificent views of Face Rock, sunsets and the crashing Pacific below the parking lot. (Banquet facilities; live music on weekend evenings.)

LOTUS GROTTO GIFTS

140 E 2nd St   541/347-9322
Daily

Listen for the chimes when you're poking around Old Town; the sound will lead you right to this great shop. There is an unbelievable array of wind chimes, essences, cards, mugs and Thai silks. Owner **Penny Green** shows her good taste throughout; that, along with reasonable pricing makes Lotus lots of fun for eclectic browsing for local and imported gifts, jewelry, souvenirs, clothing and on and on.

MISTY MEADOWS JAM AND JELLY PRODUCTS

48053 Hwy 101   541/347-2575, 888/795-1719
Daily   gotjam.com

Jam lovers must make a stop at this family-owned and -operated farm where second generation **Traci and Mike Keller, Jr.**

offer just about any kind of jam to top your morning toast. In addition to jams, you'll find marmalades, syrups, jellies, fruit butters, no-sugar-added items, seedless offerings, super honey, pepper jellies, barbecue sauces and salsas. Most all products are Oregon-grown and have been since they began business in 1971. Some of the interesting products include tayberry jam, local cranberry jam and syrups, rare or hard-to-find jams (salal and chokecherry) and wild huckleberry jam. Retail activity is in a new, larger building next to the familiar roadside stand; phone, mail and Internet orders are also welcome.

TIFFANY'S DRUG STORE
44 Michigan Ave NE   541/347-4438
Daily: 9-9

What may be the best wine shop on the Southern Oregon coast is in the Bandon Shopping Center. Yes, that's right, a drug store with an inventory of more than 4,000 bottles of fine wine, with a great showing of both Oregon and international offerings. Some bottles fetch up to $400! An impressive selection of everyday goods includes cosmetics, clothing, toys, a huge selection of Red Heart yarn, games, pet supplies, craft beers, sporting goods, kitchen gadgets (OXO, Krups, Wüsthof, William Bounds) and small appliances, food and snacks, books, gourmet foods (Chuck's canned seafood, olive oils, dipping oils, balsamic vinegars), household supplies, office supplies and a smattering of this and that. The full-service pharmacy (541/347-9457) maintains shorter hours and is closed on Sunday.

TONY'S CRAB SHACK & SEAFOOD GRILL
155 1st St   541/347-2875
Lunch, Dinner: Daily   tonyscrabshack.com
Moderate

Owner **Tony Roszkowski** takes good care of customers at his restaurant and next-door **Port O' Call**. Crab (of course) is the main attraction on the menu—whole with drawn butter and in crab cakes, sandwiches, pasta, salad and cocktails. Fish tacos are superb; worth noting is the lack of a deep-fat fryer in this establishment resulting in healthier options. Salmon is smoked on-

---

WHALE'S TAIL

For decades on Yachats' south end, "Bazalgette" (so named by sculptor, **Jim Adler**) the whale has been reliably spouting off during daylight hours every 60 seconds. Take a car break and let the kids time the spouts coming from the earthen body with a metal fluke.

---

site and delicious in sandwiches and salads. Speaking of fresh—Tony rents crab rings for folks to catch their own (cleaning and cooking available) from Weber's Pier or other local hot spots. Port O' Call also carries fishing essentials—rods, licenses, tackle and bait. In case you get skunked, Tony always has fresh ocean fare on the menu.

BAY CITY

PACIFIC OYSTER
5150 Oyster Dr   503/377-2330
Daily   pacseafood.com

Monday through Friday this division of **Pacific Seafood** processes nearly 10,000 pounds of oysters. The oyster shucking process is interesting to watch. It involves brute force, finesse and a certain twist of the wrist before triple washing and sorting. The retail counter and restaurant are open year-round; a summer outdoor seafood market features dozens of fish varieties. Nestled on Tillamook Bay, this picturesque setting has picnic tables available for outdoor dining. Inside, diners will find ocean-fresh dishes like cioppino, fish and chips, crab Louis salad, clam chowder, shrimp, steamer clams, sandwiches, entree plates and oyster shooters from the retail counter. If it swims nearby, you're likely to find it at this visitor-friendly operation.

TILLAMOOK COUNTRY SMOKER
8250 Warren Ave   503/377-2222, 800/325-2220
Daily: 9-5   tcsjerky.com

Tillamook County is famous for not only cheese and ice cream, but also for jerky and other meats hot out of Tillamook Country

Smoker. From humble beginnings more than 50 years ago, **Art Crossley** started selling jerky and smoked meat sticks from his small meat market. Today, the third-generation business produces thousands of pounds of meat snacks that are sold in the store and on the Internet and shipped around the world. Teriyaki beef jerky is especially tasty. Nuts, sausage and other meat products are assembled into gift packs, including a military care package.

BROOKINGS

BEACHFRONT RV PARK
16035 Boat Basin Road   541/469-5867
beachfrontrvpark.com

If your family likes RV camping, this Port of Brookings-Harbor facility offers parking on the beach, a rarity on our state's coastline. Spaces are available year round, daily or weekly; reservations accepted. RVers have a choice of pull-through or back-in spots, ocean or river views and partial or full hook-ups; tent sites are also available for those who wish to rough it.

PANCHO'S RESTAURANTE Y CANTINA
1136 Chetco Ave   541/469-6531
Daily: 11-9:30   panchosalsa.com
Moderate

Pancho's is the place to go in this north-of-the-border town for south-of-the-border fare. Start with an ice-cold margarita (an excellent selection of tequilas), choose your favorite flavor (classic, strawberry or exotic) and munch on Pancho's Salsa Rubio and chips. Authentic dishes are homemade from family recipes using quality, fresh ingredients (no lard). A nice selection of chicken, seafood, vegetarian, beef and pork dishes and combinations is offered.

WHALESHEAD BEACH RESORT
19921 Whaleshead Road   541/469-7446, 800/943-4325
Cabins: Inexpensive to moderate
Restaurant: Breakfast, lunch, dinner: Daily   whalesheadresort.com
Moderate

Here's a unique stay. Cottages and cabins accommodate two

to ten guests and have forest or ocean views; each unit is privately owned (amenities and furnishings vary). RVers enjoy terraced pads with concrete or cedar decks, restrooms, showers and utilities. Within the resort confines are a laundromat, market and full-service restaurant. Breakfast choices are plentiful and hearty and lunches consist of big salads, fish and chip baskets, burgers and specialty sandwiches. Dinners emanate from the corral or ocean depths; gourmet or lighter fare—just right after a day exploring the beach or Redwoods (just south of Brookings). Whaleshead Beach is accessed through a 700-foot tunnel.

CANNON BEACH

BISTRO RESTAURANT   (closed – July 2012 fire)
263 N Hemlock St   503/436-2661
Dinner: Daily (winter: Thurs-Mon)
Moderate

You'll need to venture off the beaten sidewalk for this cozy, romantic restaurant. The brick walkway and patio are utterly charming, especially when abloom with flowers. One of my all-time favorites is the savory salad of organic greens, pears, walnuts and blue cheese as the perfect prelude to deliciously prepared seafood and beef entrees. Reservations are recommended to secure a table in this wee little cottage turned regional-American fare restaurant. The servers are especially accommodating.

BRONZE COAST GALLERY
224 N Hemlock St, Suite 2   503/436-1055
Daily: 10-6   bronzecoastgallery.com

Art is big in Cannon Beach, and among the best galleries is Bronze Coast. Owner **Kim Barnett** operated an Eastern Oregon art foundry prior to opening this premier establishment. Kim possesses an in-depth knowledge of the bronze casting process. Original paintings and photography, limited edition bronze sculptures and giclée reproductions are exhibited by over 40 regional, national and international artists. Frequent city-wide art events and festivals occur throughout the year.

BRUCE'S CANDY KITCHEN

256 N Hemlock St   503/436-2641
Daily   brucescandy.com

About four decades ago, Vicky Hawkins, an Englishwoman who was the editor of the Cannon Beach Gazette, asked **Bruce Haskell** whether he might be able to make the peppermint Bah Humbug candies she joyfully remembered from her childhood in England. Bruce's now mixes more than 200 pounds of this delicious seasonal (autumn and winter) treat. Family-owned and –operated since 1963, the fourth generation continues Cannon Beach's sweet tradition with salt water taffy (30 flavors, regular and sugar-free), hand-dipped chocolates (60 varieties) and assorted brittles, popcorns, caramels, hard candies and other favorites. Who can resist a purchase at this store with the distinctive clickity-clack of the taffy cutting and wrapping machine and aroma of homemade confections?

CANNON BEACH BOOK COMPANY

130 N Hemlock St, Suite 2   503/436-1301
Daily: 10-6 (weekends and seasonally till 8)   cannonbeachbooks.com

Legendary proprietor **Valerie Ryan** provides a charming and knowledgeable book resource, ably assisted by a friendly and equally knowledgeable staff. If you like who-dunits, there are plenty; latest *New York Times* best sellers, check here first; children's bedtime stories, a wonderful assortment and well-loved classics, you'll find them here, too. In essence, all types of books are in stock or can be specially ordered and quickly delivered. Other quality merchandise includes unique greeting cards, journals, sassy reading glasses, eco-friendly reusable bags, book lights and art supplies so you can release your inner artist on the beach. This is one of the better independent bookstores left in the state.

CANNON BEACH SPA

232 N Spruce St   503/436-8772, 888/577-8772
Seasonal days and hours   cannonbeachspa.com

After a hike in Ecola or Oswald West state parks, book an appointment and pamper yourself at this luxurious spa or slip next door to the decadent **Chocolate Cafe**. The spa offers a variety of massage, hydrotherapy, skin care and foot treatments. Total packages include seaweed, volcanic clay or aromatherapy applications to rejuvenate the body and soul. Treat yourself at the Chocolate Cafe dedicated to exquisite Moonstruck chocolates and other candies from France, Belgium, Switzerland and Ghana. An over-the-top shake is made from melted chocolate — oh my! Desserts, hot chocolate and French press coffee are equally tempting; even the cafe's walls are a rich chocolate brown. Your body and your tastebuds will thank you for stopping by these indulgent shops.

CENTER DIAMOND

1065 S Hemlock St   503/436-0833
Daily: 10-5   centerdiamond.com

Another gem in this laid-back community is a store chock-full of fabrics, patterns, books and gifts especially for quilters and textile artists. The large selection of fabrics includes seashore, maritime and Asian designs, batiks and other colorful prints and solids. Sources of inspiration are beautiful ready-made wall hangings and quilts; workshops and classes will help your creativity along.

DRIFTWOOD RESTAURANT & LOUNGE

179 N Hemlock St   503/436-2439
Lunch, Dinner: Daily   driftwoodcannonbeach.com
Moderate

For over 65 years, visitors have returned time and again to the Driftwood in downtown Cannon Beach for dependable service and good food. Ward off a chilly day with homemade clam chowder served in a sourdough bread bowl or opt for entree salads, burgers and sandwiches. Steaks are hand-cut, tender and a complete dinner with a choice of sides. Smaller portioned entrees, appetizers and homemade marionberry pies are also offered. Claim a spot on the massive front patio for lunch or dinner; you never know who will stroll past while you enjoy libations and a tasty repast.

EVOO CANNON BEACH

188 S Hemlock St   503/436-8555, 877/436-3866
Hours vary   evoo.biz

For the uninitiated, EVOO stands for extra virgin olive oil which is a central player in the dinner shows and hands-on cooking classes at

EVOO Cannon Beach. During the dinner shows, guests relax in the open kitchen/dining room watching as chefs prepare several courses and share recipes, techniques and wine pairing tips. Hands-on classes include artisan bread making, crepes, culinary fundamentals, omelets, pasta, pizza and more. Classes end with students eating the delicious results. Advance reservations required; private events welcome.

FISHES SUSHI & JAPANESE CUISINE

240 N Hemlock St   503/436-8862
Dinner: Daily   fishes-sushi.com
Moderate

Local restaurant duo **Sandy and John Newman** have another winner under their toques. This one is smack dab in the middle of Cannon Beach's main drag serving Japanese-inspired meat, vegan and vegetarian dishes; also sushi, sashimi, noodles, rolls, tempura and gluten-free items. Entrees include tasty teriyaki preparations and spicy tofu, which are served with rice and cabbage salad. Desserts are homemade and kissed with Asian flavors. Try ginger crème brûlée, saké sorbet or green tea ice cream. Japanese cuisine is new in Cannon Beach, but not to Chef John who worked at Silks Restaurant in San Francisco with Ming Tsai and Ken Oringer.

HOLY IMMUNITY?

Before Oregon's more recent days of legalized tribal gaming, gambling was illegal in our state. However, a few places (like the Gearhart Hotel) had several slot machines hidden in a back area. Episcopal Bishop **Benjamin Dagwell** spent much of his summers at the coast and liked to try his luck once in awhile. As the story goes, with his friend Reverend **Lansing Kempton** of Trinity Episcopal Church at his side, Dagwell was delighted to hear the rumble of a sea of coins tumbling his way. "Bishop, you won the jackpot!" announced Kempton in a loud voice. Dagwell's response was, "Don't ever call me Bishop in a situation like this!"

GIGI WILDE'S

231 N Hemlock St, Suite 101   503/436-0119, 800/695-7159
Daily: 10-6   rarediscovery.com

If you're looking for a special gift, poke around GiGi Wilde's shop for rare discoveries. Artists from around the states and foreign countries provide a variety of beautiful art for the home or office. Sculptures are created from stone, metal, wood, glass, resin or a combination of mediums. Brilliant kiln-fired and blown glass objets d'art and dramatic centerpieces are formed in seemingly every color of the rainbow. Unique watches, rings, necklaces and other pieces of wearable art are sure to catch the attention of discerning fashion-forward ladies and gents. Eye-appealing and vibrant displays are tempting.

HOUSE OF THE POTTER

232 N Spruce St   503/436-2504
Daily (seasonal hours)   houseofthepotter.com

Laura Stewart stocks the shelves with a variety of gifts, accessories, cards and books in addition to pottery by her son-in-law **Chris Johnson** and Blue Spruce Pottery (Bend, Oregon). You will find functional pottery, dinnerware, mugs and bowls as well as decorative raku pieces. Recently released, a new series of bronze sculptures by her late husband, Jay Stewart, is also featured.

IRISH TABLE

1235 S Hemlock St   503/436-0708
Dinner: Fri-Tues
Moderate

Crystal and Sean Corbin preside over this casual restaurant. Enter through the **Sleepy Monk** coffee house for seating at a large convivial table in the center of the dining venue (the Irish table), at smaller tables around the room or in the coffeehouse. The menu changes frequently with a selection of soups, salads or cheeses for appetizers. Irish stew (lamb and vegetables) is offered, as well as a vegetarian shepherd's pie (with wild mushrooms), plus a seafood dish and meat platter. My favorites are the chicken pastie (tender chicken and veggies in a buttery pastry with a creamy mushroom sauce) and delicious corned beef with potatoes and cabbage accompanied by warm Irish soda bread. Trifles, scones with homemade lemon curd and Guinness ice cream sandwiches stand out on the dessert menu. Servers are attentive and the menu has unusual appeal. Come early! It is usually crowded.

LUMBERYARD ROTISSERIE & GRILL

264 3rd St   503/436-0285
Lunch, Dinner: Daily   thelumberyardgrill.com
Moderate

The Lumberyard serves comfort food favorites in a spacious building that once served as the community's lumberyard. Pizza, burgers, sandwiches, seafood and grill items, housemade soups and fresh Dungeness crab salads are sure to please the whole family— kiddos to gramps. If you're really hungry or want to impress your friends, order the Lumberyard's Head Rigger Challenge. It is a 4x4 burger: four cheese-topped seasoned beef patties, served on a brioche bun with fries and beverage. If you finish it within the allotted 30 minutes, walk away with bragging rights, a T-shirt and recognition on the Head Rigger Wall of Fame. Smaller variations are easier to manage or order the 4x4 and share it with your party. The melted, gooey s'mores dessert, which is prepared in a cast iron skillet and delivered to your table, is fun for the family. Seasonal patio dining, ample indoor seating, capable service, historic signs, off-street parking and a full-service bar add to the appeal.

NEWMANS AT 988

988 S Hemlock St   503/436-1151
Dinner: Daily (winter: Wed-Sun)   newmansat988.com
Moderate to expensive

Newmans has been a French-Italian love affair for many a return diner. Husband and wife team **Sandy and John Newman** share restaurant duties; John is in the kitchen and Sandy minds the front of the tiny house with room for about 30 diners. White table linens, fresh roses and classy dinner music set the tone for the simple elegance. This gourmet eatery offers a three- or four-course chef's menu nightly, or order from exquisite a la carte selections (including vegan and gluten-free). With so many folks visiting this charming community, especially on weekends, it is a good idea to make reservations; also check for seasonal hours. A few of my favorites are lobster ravioli appetizers, marinated rack of lamb and an assortment of fine cheeses. John is a #1 chef!

THE OCEAN LODGE

2864 S Pacific St   503/436-2241, 888/777-4047
Moderate to expensive   theoceanlodge.com

The Ocean Lodge is a fabulous destination for romantic getaways, family vacations or a small retreat. Developers/ owners **Mike Clark**, **Tom Drumheller** and **Patrick Nofield's** vision for a 1940s-style beach resort is right on the mark. True to the name, this oceanfront property of 37 studios and suites is just feet away from a long stretch of sandy beach and familiar Haystack Rock is directly off shore; eight suites are adjacent to the lodge. The gorgeous lodge is warm, welcoming and staffed by the friendliest, most helpful team on the north coast. A crackling fire in the lobby's river rock wood-burning fireplace warms up chilly days and a coffee cart with oh-so-good fresh cookies is tempting. In the upstairs library and scattered throughout the lodge are informal seating areas and stacks of books begging guests to enjoy a quiet respite. The delicious, complimentary breakfast buffet is also upstairs; hot beverages are always available. Oregon artist **Andy Nichols'** breakfast room chandelier is spectacular depicting orange and blue tentacles and shells. Other glass pieces and local artwork adorn the lodge. Bathrooms are luxurious (Jacuzzi tubs in select rooms); guest accommodations are tastefully furnished with gas fireplaces, balconies, microwaves and snack refrigerators. At The Ocean Lodge, family-friendly includes the four-pawed member; view and non-view rooms are available as well as a pet wash area and special doggie amenities.

PIZZA À FETTA

231 N Hemlock St   503/436-0333
Lunch, Dinner: Daily   pizza-a-fetta.com
Inexpensive

Behind these doors are some of the best gourmet pizzas in the state. You will find hand-tossed, peasant crust pizzas, salads and soups, accompanied by a fine selection of Oregon wines. Toppings include Italian standbys (sausage, meats, optional cheese) as well as smoked basil chicken, crab and a half dozen vegetable combinations; order the whole pie of your choice or favorites by the slice. Sit in the main dining area or upstairs with superior service all around; catering, too. Owner **James Faurentino** has delighted patrons with hand-tossed pizzas since 1988. His next door **Bella Espresso** (503/436-2595) serves coffee drinks, beer, wine, other libations and gourmet desserts.

SLEEPY MONK

1235 S Hemlock St	503/436-2796
Fri-Sun: 8-4; Mon, Tues: 8-2	sleepymonkcoffee.com
Inexpensive	

Don't miss a superb cup of coffee at this organic tasting room. Beans are roasted on-site and also sold by the bag (served at area restaurants and hotels, too). Come evening, the adjacent restaurant, **Irish Table**, uses the Monk's space for additional seating.

STEPHANIE INN

2740 S Pacific St	503/436-2221, 800/633-3466
Expensive	stephanieinn.com

Not only does the Stephanie Inn have all the ingredients necessary for a really "luxe" vacation, it does it with a big smile. Guests enjoy superb service, comfortable rooms, a daily complimentary wine and cheese reception, spa treatment rooms, a multi-course buffet-type breakfast (Benedicts, homemade granola, morning-fresh baked goods and more), large well-fixtured bathrooms (including Jacuzzis and oversize towels) and wet bars with refreshments. The guest rooms and suites are luxuriously appointed and designed with privacy and relaxation in mind. A classy dining room serving excellent Northwest-inspired cuisine (moderate) is open nightly for overnighters and non-guests; reservations required. The multi-course *prix-fixe* menu is irresistible, available with a wine flight pairing. A la carte options include outstanding entrees such as filet mignon, Dungeness crab cakes, excellent appetizers and chocolate decadence cake. Haystack Rock and sunset views from the hotel grounds are breathtaking.

THE SURFSAND RESORT

148 W Gower St   503/436-2274, 800/547-6100
Moderate   surfsand.com

Location, location, location! Surfsand is steps away from Haystack Rock, adjacent to the **Wayfarer Restaurant and Lounge** and on the edge of Hemlock Street's eclectic, artsy shops, restaurants and galleries. Views are incomparable. Comfortable guest rooms are contemporary and appointed with luxurious bath amenities, Tempur-Pedic beds, gas fireplaces and modern technologies. Cabana service, ice cream socials, weenie roasts and kids' club activities are offered seasonally. Optional special packages are created with a host of extra goodies for beach bonfires, romance, celebrations and kids' birthday parties. Take a dip in the heated indoor swimming pool, play on the beach, relax, fly a kite or go for a bicycle or horseback ride (rentals nearby); the choices are seemingly endless.

WAVES OF GRAIN

3116 S Hemlock St   503/436-9600
Thurs-Tues: 7-3   wavesofgrainbakery.com

Hillary and Jason Fargo were drawn to the Oregon coast to set up a bakery where everything is impressively made from scratch. Sensitive to customers' needs, the Fargos showcase a few gluten-free and low-gluten products each day. The variety of baked goods turned out from this small cottage is amazing: biscuits, muffins, cookies, scones, cinnamon rolls, coffeecakes, bread pudding, cheese sticks, breads, quiches, granola, cheesecakes, brownies and bars, crème brûlée, tiramisu, truffles, tarts and cakes. Even Rover will be happy with the dog biscuits (also edible for his master). Wraps and a daily soup are available after 11 a.m. There's always something hot out of the oven.

WAYFARER RESTAURANT & LOUNGE

1190 Pacific Dr   503/436-1108
Breakfast, Lunch, Dinner: Daily   wayfarer-restaurant.com
Moderate to expensive

Choose buttermilk pancakes or a Dungeness crab cake Benedict for morning meals or the Dungeness crab mac and cheese (with Tillamook cheese curds) for lunch. A full dinner menu offers clams, fresh fish, house ravioli and tender Wagyu porterhouse steak. Starters (heavy on seafood options) make fine meals on the lighter side for lunch or dinner. Sit in the main dining room or bar and enjoy the view.

CHARLESTON

PORTSIDE RESTAURANT

63383 Kingfisher Dr
Lunch, Dinner: Daily
Moderate

541/888-5544
portsidebythebay.com

As the name suggests, this is a fishing port dinner house. The selection is wide and varied—steak any way you please, fresh catch (broiled, fried, poached, grilled), chicken specialties, satisfying pastas and smaller portions (for youngsters and oldsters). There are plenty of appealing appetizers including pickled herring, salmon with capers, deep-fried bar bites and homemade daily soups. An outdoor garden patio and solarium are alternatives to the dining room. The restaurant is also good for families and groups. When you're in this area, plan a visit to the botanical gardens at **Shore Acres State Park** especially beautiful between Thanksgiving and New Year's Day with thousands of holiday lights and decorations.

CLOVERDALE

SANDLAKE COUNTRY INN

8505 Galloway Road
Moderate

503/965-6745
sandlakecountryinn.com

The "Old Allen Place" farmhouse near Pacific City was constructed of red fir bridge timbers around 1900. It is now on the Oregon Historic Registry and is also a green lodging facility. Choose from three very comfortable suites and a private brookside guest cottage. All rooms have whirlpool tubs, refrigerators, fireplaces (wood, gas or electric) and private decks; each room is tastefully decorated in a different theme. Coffee, tea and a four-course breakfast are delivered to guest rooms each morning. The menu varies, but may include blackberry brûlée, baked or fresh fruit, hot egg dishes, crepes, roasted potatoes, meats and freshly-baked pastries and

LASTING LEGACIES

Oregonians can thank native son **John Gray**, who made his fortune as an entrepreneur at Omark Industries, for extending his influence to destination developments. Among other projects, Gray (Grayco LLC) is the genius and support behind two of Oregon's most successful recreational areas, **Salishan Spa Golf Resort** at the Oregon Coast and **Sunriver Resort** in Central Oregon. His quiet and significant philanthropic endeavors are also legendary.

breads. This is a small, quiet, relaxing retreat (no pets; children accommodated only in the cottage).

COOS BAY

BENETTI'S ITALIAN RESTAURANT

260 S Broadway   541/267-6066
Dinner: Daily   benettis.com
Moderate

For great Italian cuisine try **Tricia and Joe Benetti**'s first-class eatery featuring Italian dishes his grandmother used to make. The dinner house overlooks the Coos Bay boardwalk where diners can enjoy the comings and goings of ships, people and pets. Wine and cocktails are served in the upstairs dining room or downstairs in the full-service lounge. A tank of beautiful saltwater fish is a favorite feature. Popular dinner entrees include veal parmigiana, calzone, fettuccini alfredo, steaks, and outstanding spaghetti. Combo plates, daily specials and half-and-half platters are also enticing. It's hard not to fill up at the start with all-you-can-eat soup, salad and wonderful garlic bread.

KUM-YON'S

835 S Broadway   541/269-2662
Lunch, Dinner: Sun-Fri
Moderate

Kum-Yon's serves Japanese, Korean, Chinese and American dishes. Mongolian beef, bento boxes, chow meins and sushi are prepared with fresh crispy vegetables. The restaurant is family-friendly and good for groups; call ahead for takeout.

OREGON CONNECTION
(HOUSE OF MYRTLEWOOD)
1125 S 1st St   541/267-7804, 800/255-5318
April-Dec: Daily; Jan-March: Mon-Sat   oregonconnection.com

Known for years as the House of Myrtlewood, the new name more accurately reflects the mix of Oregon products: women's apparel and accessories, gourmet food items and fudge in addition to myrtlewood items. Myrtlewood is treasured for unique colors, grains and burls manifested in gorgeous bowls, trays, desk accessories, weather stations, one-of-a-kind tables and decorative accessories and gifts. The Wooden Touch Putter has been tried by some of the best golfers in our state, and reports are that it really does facilitate more accurate putting. Objects made from myrtlewood logs are cut, dried and turned on-site from the impressive stack of logs outside the building. Complimentary factory tours are open to the public. This is one of the oldest continuously working myrtlewood factories in this area, now owned and operated by a nonprofit agency serving the disabled.

DEPOE BAY

THE CHANNEL HOUSE
35 Ellingson St   541/765-2140, 800/447-2140
Moderate to expensive   channelhouse.com

This prime location overlooks the ocean and Depoe Bay channel where boats continuously enter and leave the harbor. The intimate contemporary inn has 16 beautiful rooms and suites with gas fireplaces and oceanfront decks. A natural color palate and understated elegant furnishings create a peaceful ambience sure to wash stress away. Select from wine, champagne or romantic packages which include a bottle of wine or champagne, etched glasses and Channel House robes; in-room massage service by appointment. Each morning, join fellow guests in the dining room for a complimentary continental breakfast before you explore other central coast communities.

SOUTH OF THE BORDER

Just a few hundred feet into California is the **Nautical Inn Restaurant** (16850 Hwy 101 N., Smith River, CA; 707/487-5006). Seafood is a specialty featuring crab cakes and clam chowder, plus mussels and fresh-catch halibut when available; you can find a great steak, pastas, salads and French onion soup, too, as well as housemade orange ginger crème brûlée and Bananas Foster. Topped off with a first-class view, friendly service and moderate prices, the Nautical Inn is a winner. You'll be in the heart of the Smith River region, where towering redwoods and magnificent campgrounds provide never-to-be-forgotten experiences.

LOOKOUT OBSERVATORY & GIFT SHOP

Cape Foulweather
4905 Otter Crest Loop   541/765-2270
Daily: 9-6 (winter till 5)   lookoutgiftshop.com

The Observatory and Gift Shop are perched atop a promontory, a staggering 500 feet above the ocean. A bit of history: In 1778 Captain James Cook discovered and named Cape Foulweather after encountering a severe Pacific storm. The name is still appropriate as frequent gales of 100 m.p.h. and higher roar across this headland. The building was constructed in 1937 and continues as an open-to-the-public lookout with a retail area of treasures (many are hand-crafted in Oregon) and displays of driftwood characters and ships' wreckage. No doubt about it, the views of migrating whales, nesting sea birds, sea lions, fishing fleets and other ocean-going vessels are magnificent. 2012 marks the shop's 75th anniversary.

TIDAL RAVES SEAFOOD GRILL

279 NW Hwy 101   541/765-2995
Lunch, Dinner: Daily   tidalraves.com
Moderate

There is nearly always a waiting line at Tidal Raves and it's not difficult to ascertain why. The view is spectacular from the picture windows overlooking the churning ocean below. The menu is varied, not fancy, well-priced and full of fresh seafood offerings like steamer clams, grilled shrimp, Dungeness crab cakes and Pacific oysters. Expect consistently good food with service that shines even though they routinely play to a full house; the serving personnel are uniformly efficient, gracious and extremely knowledgeable. Top off your meal with chocolate caramel-nut truffle cake or bread pudding with Kentucky bourbon sauce — then walk it off along the seawall to the historic **Depoe Bay Ocean Wayside** and whale watching center (oregonstateparks.org).

TRADEWINDS CHARTERS

118 Hwy 101   541/765-2345, 800/445-8730
Prices vary   tradewindscharters.com

If you want to get out on the water, here's a good option for fishing trips or whale watching cruises; Depoe Bay carries the title of "Whale Watching Capital of the Oregon Coast." Prime time viewing is December through May. Excursions are informative and fun for the family (practice shouting "Thar she blows!" beforehand). Tradewinds is the oldest charter company on the West Coast and offers a variety of fishing trips — bottom, salmon, tuna and halibut; some excursions include setting crab pots along the way; and vary between four hours and a full day. For this trip, practice shouting "Fish on!"

WHALE COVE INN

2345 S Hwy 101   541/765-4300, 800/628-3409
Expensive   whalecoveinn.com

RESTAURANT BECK

                                           541/765-3220
Daily (seasonal closures)   restaurantbeck.com
Expensive

This is a very special place! Guests enjoy fantastic vistas of the Pacific Ocean from private balconies. With seven suites, plus a three-bedroom "presidential suite," this luxury bed and breakfast features huge showers, patios with hot tubs and a continental breakfast. Competing neck and neck with the view is classy in-house **Restaurant Beck** (restaurantbeck.com). The evening's gourmet fare might be pork belly, halibut, pork brisket or some such local, in-season preparation. For a special occasion, splurge on the five-, seven- or nine-course tasting menu for your entire party.

ELSIE

CAMP 18 LOGGING MUSEUM AND RESTAURANT

42362 Hwy 26   503/755-1818, 800/874-1810
Breakfast, Lunch, Dinner: Daily   camp18restaurant.com
Moderate

If you're on the way to or from the north coast along Highway 26, you've probably spotted this roadside compound at milepost 18. The large log cabin restaurant and adjacent Old Time Logging Museum are the dreams of **Roberta and Gordon Smith** who built the place in the early 1970s and still operate it with the help of next-generation family. The hand-carved double-door entry is made of 4 ½ inch thick old-growth fir; the massive fireplaces are fashioned from 50 tons of local rock and the 85-foot ridge pole in the central dining room weighs in at 25 tons and contains 5,600 board feet of lumber. The plates match in scale, piled high with comfort food for logger-type appetites for breakfast, lunch and dinner (you'll pick up some logging lingo from the menu headings; for example, choker setters, riggin' boss and hot deck). If your sweet tooth needs a fix, the gigantic homemade cinnamon rolls are just the thing!

FLORENCE

1285 RESTOBAR

1285 Bay St   541/902-8338
Lunch, Dinner: Daily   1285restobar.com
Moderate

San Francisco-style Italian cuisine is served at this family-friendly trattoria in Old Town. Select a table inside or on the relaxing outside patio (seasonal). Especially tasty is anything with San Marzano tomatoes or locally-made sweet Italian sausage. Pizza and pasta are the mainstays, plus meats and seafood from the grill. The selection of early dinner specials changes weekly; prime rib is served every Wednesday.

BJ'S ICE CREAM PARLOR

1441 Bay St	541/902-7828
2930 Hwy 101	541/997-7286
Daily	

Most communities have a local ice cream parlor; Florence has two. One location is in Old Town, a delightful stop to enjoy a dish or cone while you're wandering in and out of the waterfront shops. The second location (also the ice cream-making locale) is on the north end of town, an easy turn off Highway 101 for a quick pick-me-up when you're on the road. Scoops are 14.2% butterfat, come in 48 hard-to-resist flavors (plus yogurt and sugar-free ice cream) and are also used in refreshing floats and malts.

BRIDGEWATER OCEAN FRESH FISH HOUSE AND ZEBRA BAR

1297 Bay St	541/997-1133
Lunch, Dinner: Daily	
Moderate	

The establishment's name is a mouthful and that's what you'll get at this Old Town eclectic dining house. Eclectic more in decor than menu, the African-themed bar and zebra-striped chairs make for a fun setting. Seafood is definitely the order of the day, though "land" options are available, too. Choosing becomes a bit problematic with chowder, cioppino, crab and salmon cakes, mussels and clams, fish and chips, various fish entrees and seafood sides, to red meat and fowl menu items. Enjoy the gratis shrimp cocktail that nicely arrives before dinner.

DRIFTWOOD SHORES RESORT & CONFERENCE CENTER

84416 1st Ave	541/997-8263, 800/422-5091
Moderate to very expensive	driftwoodshores.com

Uninterrupted sandy beaches are the main attraction at this hotel – the only oceanfront hotel in the Florence area. All rooms have oceanfront views and a balcony, deck or patio. Most guest rooms contain a full kitchen; mini-refrigerators and microwaves are furnished in standard rooms with queen beds. (Driftwood Shores experienced substantial damage during a January 2012 winter storm; at time of publication, repairs and renovations were underway.) **Surfside**, the moderately priced on-site restaurant, is open daily for breakfast, lunch and dinner. There are plenty of local and classic choices at each meal, plus pizzetas and Creole, Moroccan and other regional flavor-influenced entrees. If you are hankering for beef, garlic and rosemary roasted prime rib is served on Friday and Saturday evenings. Steaks, meatloaf, pork, chicken and lamb dishes are always offered.

EDWIN K BED & BREAKFAST

1155 Bay St   541/997-8360, 800/833-9465
Moderate   edwink.com

William Kyle, an area pioneer, built this 1914 Sears Craftsman home. Now a charming bed and breakfast accented with fine furnishings and antiques, there are six rooms with private bathrooms in the main building. **Laurie and Marv VandeStreek** prepare and serve a five-course gourmet breakfast to house guests in a historic dining room; fine china and crystal grace the table. A separate apartment with a full kitchen and living room accommodates up to four guests (breakfast on your own). There's plenty to do in Florence: fresh and saltwater fishing, whale watching, nearby dune buggy rides and shopping.

KITCHEN KLUTTER

1258 Bay St   541/997-6060
Daily

Kitchen gadgets, tableware and items to turn your home kitchen into a gourmet showplace are featured at this well-arranged shop. Bath products, gifts and other fun and unique items round out the appealing merchandise.

LA POMODORI RISTORANTE

1415 7th St   541/902-2525
Lunch: Tues-Fri; Dinner: Tues-Sat   lapomodori.com
Moderate

You can't go wrong at lunch or dinner in this small house which has been transformed into a fine Italian restaurant. Start with the garlic onion cheese bread as you peruse the expansive menu. Pasta reigns supreme with choices of prawns, seafood, pork, chicken, sausage, Italian vegetables and magnificent cream or tomato sauces combined into delicious dishes. Ribeye steaks are well-seasoned; other meats and seafood are grilled or prepared as picattas, scaloppinis, marsalas or with special sauces and ingredients. Appetizing sandwiches (Cubano, baked pastrami), soups, hearty salads and specials are served at lunch. A warm welcome is extended to both visitors and regular customers; reservations accepted.

LIGHTHOUSE INN

155 Hwy 101   541/997-3221, 866/997-3221
Inexpensive   lighthouseinn-florence.com

You'll find good value and friendly hosts at the Lighthouse Inn. While there have been sales and renovations over time, the inn has been one family's or another's venture since the 1930s (originally the Hotel Ragan). What endures is the location in the heart of town. Choose your accommodation (all non-smoking) from basic rooms to a family suite with kitchenette and fireplace, games and other creature comforts. Speaking of creatures, some rooms are pet-friendly.

LITTLE BROWN HEN

435 Hwy 101   541/902-2449
Breakfast: 7-2; Lunch: 11:30-2
Inexpensive

Voted by locals as serving the best breakfasts for miles around, the Little Brown Hen continues to do a bang-up job. Pop in for breakfast anytime. There's no skimping on biscuits and gravy, many egg incarnations, pancakes, Belgian waffles and French toast of several varieties. Lunchtime brings clam chowder, chili and other soups, salads, seafood dishes, burgers and moist pressure-fried (broasted) chicken. Tasty hand-sliced potatoes, covered with a secret seasoned-flour mixture and then deep fried, are referred to as "chirps."

LOVEJOY'S RESTAURANT & TEA ROOM

195 Nopal St   541/902-0502
Tues-Sat: 11-2:30   lovejoysrestaurant.com
Inexpensive to moderate

If it's an English-style meal that you desire, try Lovejoy's.

A TOAST TO BILL BADGER

Here's to Gearhart's unofficial mayor of the 1930s: an African-American man, railroad station master, chauffeur (in a horse-drawn wagon) for Portlanders on their coastal arrival and, above all, beloved citizen. "Bill" to some, "William" or "Mr. Badger" to most, he served on the city council (likely the first African-American to serve as a councilor in the state). His honorary mayor's title was permanent. He and his wife, Emma, also ran the very popular family-style Badger's Chicken Dinner Inn, serving the best southern fried chicken that I have ever tasted. (Adding to Bill's credit, Oregon was not a welcoming place for black Americans though discriminatory laws were repealed in 1926.)

For lunch, they offer cottage pie, pasties, savory sausage rolls, stuffed Dover sole, homemade soups, salads (pear, walnut and blue cheese is excellent) and other sandwiches and specials. The Royal Tea is a three-course affair with salads, a choice of delectable sandwiches (cucumber and cream cheese, bay shrimp and more), scones with Double Devon clotted cream, sweets and your choice of tea. The gift shop is the source for tea pots, accessories and imported English goodies for your pantry. **Judith and Liam Kingsmill** are the amiable couple tending to customers.

SAND MASTER PARK
5351 Hwy 101   541/997-6006
Seasonal hours   sandmasterpark.com

For a super memorable ride on the famous Florence dunes, grab a sandboard. If need be, instruction, equipment rental and sales are offered. For the thrill of a glide down the hill or hitting the jump ramps and rail slides, the only requirement is your feet and the desire for fun. The park offers more activities (March through December); zip lines and zip tours, helicopter rides, dune buggy tours, gardens, games and an RV park.

THE WATERFRONT DEPOT RESTAURANT

1252 Bay St   541/902-9100
Dinner: Daily   waterfrontdepot.com
Moderate

In a picturesque building that once housed the Mapleton train depot, this unpretentious restaurant has delicious offerings. The restaurant overlooks the Siuslaw River; the informal blackboard menu is appealing and the well-worn wood floors and cozy bar enhance the ambience. Seafood, especially the oyster stew and the crab-encrusted halibut, shines. You won't pay a fortune, and you'll be treated to freshly baked garlic French bread. Ask for patio seating on a warm summer evening to enjoy the river flowing by — delightful!

GARIBALDI

GARIBALDI HOUSE INN & SUITES

502 Garibaldi Ave   503/322-3338, 877/322-6489
Inexpensive to moderate   garibaldihouse.com

When Oregonians and visitors think of fishing, crabbing, clamming, whale watching, kayaking and such, Garibaldi House can serve as a great place to drop anchor. The 49 rooms and suites are professionally run as a B&B rather than a motel, offering hearty breakfasts and personal attention to customers' whims. An indoor heated pool, whirlpool, sauna and fitness center will add "ahhhh" to your coastal home away from home. Cookies and coffee, local cheeses and meats, popcorn and other snacks are available 24/7. Outdoor smoking, no pets. While you are in Garibaldi, take an excursion on the **Oregon Coast Scenic Railroad** (ocsr.net); seasonal schedule.

PIRATE'S COVE RESTAURANT

14170 Hwy 101 N   503/322-2092
Breakfast: Wed-Sun; Lunch, Dinner: Daily   piratesonline.biz
Moderate to expensive

The restaurant is situated to view fishing boats on Tillamook Bay, many laden with fresh catch. Perhaps your seafood dinner was on this morning's boat. Pirate's Cove is known for superb oyster stew; dinners and sandwiches are served with a choice of the stew, creamy clam chowder or salad. Steaks are excellent with the option of adding crab, seafood or other toppers. Lunch includes specials from the sea, burgers, sandwiches and salads with plenty of appetizer choices for lunch or dinner. Breakfast Benedicts and omelets are utterly delightful when made with crab, lobster or prawns. Dressed up pancakes, waffles, egg dishes and hearty biscuits and gravy should keep your motor running for several hours; take time to enjoy a second cup of coffee on the beautiful bay.

GEARHART

PACIFIC WAY BAKERY & CAFE

601 Pacific Way   503/738-0245
Bakery: Thurs-Mon
Cafe: Lunch, Dinner: Thurs-Mon   pacificwaybakery-cafe.com
Moderate

When I was a wee lad, my family would spend part of summers in Gearhart. We would leave our Portland environs for the low-key, charming, quaint coastal village and embark upon a summer filled with family, friends and activities. The season would start as soon as the school year was finished and end on Labor Day. Gearhart has retained its charm and draws visitors year round. **Lisa and John Allen**'s main street cafe/bakery is a favorite place to eat. Irresistible pizzas are built on handmade crusts. Traditional Italian pizzas are prepared on a tomato sauce base; Thai chicken, island ham and other pizza varieties benefit from special sauces. Homemade soups, sandwiches and entrees are served at lunch. Dinner starts with a basket of freshly baked breads and features full meals such as prosciutto wrapped scallops, ribeye steak, ravioli and lighter fare. The cafe's desserts, of course, are fresh from the bakery where they also bake cookies, pastries, savories and assorted breads.

GLENEDEN BEACH

CAVALIER BEACHFRONT CONDOMINIUMS

325 NW Lancer St   541/764-2352, 888/454-0880
Moderate   cavaliercondos.com

These units offer spacious family or double-couple accommodations with two bedrooms, two baths, fully-equipped kitchens, large living rooms with wood-burning fireplaces and open oceanfront decks. The 1,300 square foot units are right on the coastline with easy beach access, covered parking, heated indoor swimming pool, two saunas and recreation room with pool and Ping-Pong tables. One of the nice parts of visits with children is the large, exceptionally clean beach area, giving lots of room to run, roast weenies and marshmallows on the embers of a beach bonfire and build sand castles.

SALISHAN SPA & GOLF RESORT

7760 Hwy 101 N   541/764-2371, 800/452-2300
Moderate to expensive   salishan.com

From the time **John Gray** opened the lodge, I have been a frequent guest and great fan of this beautiful property, just south of Lincoln City. Gray sold it in 1996, and since then it

---

SHOW OFF!

The **Oregon Tourism Commission** is charged with the responsibility of encouraging residents of Oregon and domestic and foreign visitors to explore the wonders of our state. The nine dedicated commissioners with very capable CEO, **Todd Davidson** and his staff, do this with exceptional expertise and dedication. The commission has won a number of national awards for its professionalism and effectiveness. An annual hardcopy publication (*Travel Oregon*) and the website (traveloregon. com) provide a wealth of information on all aspects of our state's many attractions and advantages. Three e-newsletters (general, outdoors and culinary) are produced by the commission; subscribe at the website. The informational toll free number is 800/547-7842. Having served on the commission for a number of years (chair, 1996 – 2001), I wholeheartedly attest to the standard of information and help provided.

has survived several reincarnations. The highly-regarded Connor family of Eugene is the current owner and operator (son **Jason Connor** is the hardworking manager) and has spruced up some of the rooms, brought back the Sun Room coffee shop and done some much-needed refurbishing. The 205 rooms and suites are spread among 21 buildings; many overlook the golf course and forested areas from balconies and patios. Rooms are warmly appointed, reflecting natural Northwest elements with cozy seating areas for winter storm watching. For dinner, the signature dining room offers magnificent views of Siletz Bay and Salishan Spit to go along with featured fresh seafood and wines from the impressive wine cellars. Steaks are also available. The Sun Room starts the day with hearty and light breakfasts and continues serving lunch and dinner in a casual, family-friendly setting. Out at the clubhouse, **The Grill** satisfies golfers' pre- and post-round appetites with breakfasts, sandwiches, soups, salads and appetizers. Head across the highway to the **Shops at Salishan** where a variety of small, interesting businesses carry fashions, gifts, foods, home decor, accessories and works of art. A stunning spa was built several years ago on the estuary's edge, with an impressive array of health and pampering services. There is much to do at this legendary coast property.

SIDE DOOR CAFÉ

6675 Gleneden Beach Loop Road   541/764-3825
Lunch, Dinner: Wed-Mon   sidedoorcafe.com
Moderate

Brooke Price is a very hands-on person at her popular restaurant, working the floor, supervising the kitchen and making sure that her large facilities at the old Gleneden Brick and Tile Factory are kept in A-1 order. The evening menu features seafood salads and entrees (ribeye steak with oysters, fish, seafood, pork medallions) and also offers a great selection of pastas, quiches, steaks and several vegetarian items. Lunch soups, salads and quesadillas may also be ordered for dinner. Service is pleasant and informed. Sharing the space is **Eden Hall**, a large venue which accommodates live music and theater as well as private parties, exhibits and weddings (check website for schedule and prices).

GOLD BEACH

BELLA ROGUE BED & BREAKFAST

96265 N Bank Rogue   877/764-8308
Moderate   bellarogue.com

Rick Jackson's bed and breakfast is on prime property overlooking the majestic Rogue River. In the frame of the 1909 fly-fishing lodge, Rick has created a luxury suite and three other comfortable bedrooms with private baths. Restful, rustic simplicity is created by the use of soft hues, antiques, over-stuffed pillows and original artwork. Oregon woods are used throughout the charming building. Guests can expect breakfast every day; box lunches are available by request. Rick prepares reservation-only imaginative dinners and catering for guests and to the public on weekends. (He has owned and operated several area restaurants including Chives in Brookings and now hangs his toque at The Bridge in Gold Beach.)

THE BRIDGE RESTAURANT BAR & COFFEEHOUSE

94321 Wedderburn Loop   541/247-6465
Dinner: Wed-Sun; Brunch: Sun   thebridgerestaurants.com
Moderate

Rick Jackson took command of this dinner house, focusing on fresh fish, always with fresh salads, sometimes a great chicken breast with brie and hazelnuts, cioppino, steaks, prawns, beef filet tips, rack of lamb and other tempting entrees. He's mighty proud of margaritas made-to-order with freshly-juiced lemons, limes and oranges. A cafe menu offers reasonably-priced sandwiches and appetizers, lasagna, salads and more. Other options are nominally priced happy hour appetizers and pastas. This property is on the banks of the Rogue River, just beneath the landmark Isaac Lee Patterson Bridge.

EV'S HI-TECH AUTO AND TOWING SERVICE — CHEVRON

29719 Ellensburg Ave   541/247-7525
Daily

"May I clean your windshield? Check the tires and the oil?" All of this without a prompt? Seems unlikely these days, but when you're motoring through Curry County, fill 'er up at Ev's where real service is always provided. Additional services include towing, recovery, lock-out, jumpstart, snow and beach recovery services for autos, RVs and motorcycles. This place is a model for all service stations.

GOLD BEACH BOOKS

29707 Ellensburg Ave   541/247-2495
Daily   oregoncoastbooks.com

A Gold Beach treasure! You never know what you'll find in a large book shop and this store is no exception. The inventory encompasses well over 50,000 new and used books in every category. You're sure to find the latest tome from your favorite authors, classics, self-improvement and how-to books, travel guides and great reads for a day on the beach or curled up in front of a roaring fire. The Showroom Collection features first edition works, autographed books and rare collectibles. Frequent cultural events highlight local authors, artists, musicians and poets. Swing on by for specialty coffee and baked goods to enjoy while browsing the stacks of books.

INDIAN CREEK CAFÉ

94682 Jerry's Flat Road   541/247-0680
Daily: 5:30-2
Inexpensive

Located at the convergence of Indian Creek and the Rogue River, this small eatery just happens to serve great breakfasts and steaming hot coffee. It's not fancy, but you'll find pancakes and waffles with fruits, berries or pecans; pigs in blankets and fluffy omelets with hash browns or fried grits. Burgers and sandwiches (served with chips and baked beans, slaw or potato salad) are good for lunch as well as soups, salads and chili. Seating on the outdoor deck as weather allows.

JERRY'S ROGUE JETS

29985 Harbor Way   541/247-4571, 800/451-3645
Seasonal   roguejets.com
Prices vary

Back in 1895, the only way to deliver mail and freight to communities up the Rogue River was by mail boats. Now, over a century later, a 64-mile round trip follows the same route with your jet boat pilot delivering historical tidbits and lore along the way. Go a bit farther and take the exhilarating 80-mile whitewater round-trip excursion. Spend an unforgettable day when you travel 104 miles round trip to the wild section of the Rogue and Blossom Bar Rapids to experience the rugged wilderness and class II to III rapids. Trips include rest stops and lunch (separately priced). You're sure to see abundant wildlife, lodges, breathtaking scenery and be wowed by your pilot's stories, skills and knowledge. Jerry's also transports guests to lodges along the river. Daily departures from May 1 to October 15; museum and gift shop open all year. This is another must-do Oregon adventure.

NOR'WESTER STEAK & SEAFOOD

10 Harbor Way   541/247-2333
Dinner: Daily   norwesterseafood.com
Moderate

Your author enjoys harbor sights from the upstairs dining room. There is always activity—boats, seagulls, occasional harbor seals, fishermen and awesome sunsets. This fine dining house serves fresh local catch (as available) in appetizers, chowder, salads and generously portioned entrees, combinations and pastas. Steaks, lamb chops and chicken dishes are equally delicious; add prawns or oysters to a sirloin steak to create a land and sea platter. The Nor'Wester has a full bar, beer and wine selections plus menu offerings for the younger set.

ROLLIN' IN DOUGH BAKERY AND BISTRO

94257 North Bank Rogue Road   541/247-4438
Breakfast, Lunch: Tues-Sat; Brunch: Sun
Moderate

Owner and chef **Patti Joyce** oversees this casual, cozy eatery where Oregon-grown and organic products are preferred ingredients. She presents some of the area's most appealing value meals, from apple-brie omelets to strawberry crepes, or strata filled with sausage, bell pepper and Swiss cheese. My breakfast favorite is Patti's homemade biscuits with thick, creamy sausage gravy; coffee lovers will appreciate the bigger-than-normal cups of fresh-roasted joe. Imaginative bistro lunches are predicated on seasonal products; turkey sandwiches are always delicious. The baked goods are simply out of this world! In winter, Patti closes up shop between Christmas and mid-February.

SPINNERS SEAFOOD, STEAK & CHOPHOUSE

29430 Ellensburg Ave   541/247-5160
Dinner: Daily   spinnersrestaurant.com
Moderate

Gold Beach has a number of good dining spots and Spinners falls in that category as noted by the large, often-full parking lot. Salads are fresh and entree salads are, indeed, a full meal especially with the addition of chicken, prawns or oysters. Big burgers (including buffalo) and chicken main dishes are alternatives to seafood, steaks and chops. Varying seafood specialties may include lobster and crab cannelloni, fresh salmon roasted in leeks or a seafood choice combined with pasta. The dessert menu lists several varieties of pies, cakes and pastries—all homemade and delicious. You won't go away hungry!

TU TU' TUN LODGE

96550 North Bank Rogue   541/247-6664, 800/864-6357
Moderately expensive   tututun.com

For years one of my favorite R&R haunts has been **Tu Tu' Tun Lodge**. This is where I first encountered the twofold epitome of innkeepers, **Laurie and Dirk Van Zante**. While the Van Zantes are now happily retired from this demanding business, they put their heart and soul, blood, sweat, tears and treasure into building this unique respite. At the time of the announcement of the sale, special weekends were held exclusively for their numerous return clientele, many of whom visited annually. At the special dinners in the communal family dining room, that in itself is a TTT tradition, tears were shed by grown men and women in saying goodbye to the Van Zantes; the loyalty and love felt around the room honoring these two fine people was profound. This destination is now under the very capable management of owner **Kyle Ringer** and much to his credit, the rustic elegance and friendly ease still reflects the hospitality acumen and good taste that the Van Zantes instilled over decades. Most of the staff remained and continues to offer superb service. As always, when you go (and you should!), you'll be greeted as a friend as you enter this magical boutique river house, one of the best in the nation. The lodge's immaculate accommodations encompass two houses (one recently redone in magnificent style), two generous suites and 16 rooms all gorgeously appointed and include top-notch creature comforts. Fabulous breakfasts, lunches and dinners are optional (availability varies by season). I wholeheartedly recommend you experience TTT's gourmet cuisine at least once during your stay (reservations necessary). Every season brings a different perspective of the river and forest from superlative decks and landscaped outdoor spaces.

TURTLE ROCK RESORT

28788 Hunter Creek Loop   541/247-9203, 800/353-9754
Moderate   turtlerockresorts.com

If you are looking for a place for a casual family gathering, this resort might just fill the bill. There are 15 waterfront rental cottages,

---

TAKEOVER

In its early days, the **Gearhart Hotel** was furnished by **Meier & Frank**; with the bills left unpaid, the hotel fell into default and was taken over by the department store — much to the dismay of the M&F CEO, namely, **Aaron Frank**, my dad. He was furious to find bed bugs (and who knows what else) in the hotel, immediately ordering all furniture, linens — everything — removed and burned. Along with the hotel came the **Gearhart Golf Links** (gearhartgolflinks.com) where your author had his first sales job in charge of selling candy, ice cream and other snacks in the caddyshack; my sweet tooth, unfortunately, took over my good sense, and I ate up all the profits! (Today, **Jason Bangild** is the Director of Golf and likely has more reliable people on duty.) The Gearhart complex was later sold, and has been through a number of hands since. **Tim Boyle,** head man at **Columbia Sportswear** (columbia.com), is now the proud owner of this historic golf course. The hotel is now a venture of the **McMenamin** brothers (mcmenamins.com).

80 full RV hookups along Hunter Creek (three sites include hot tub, deck, barbecue), a vacation rental house which sleeps eight and eight tent sites. The group meeting room is equipped with a kitchen, exercise facility and more. The beach is nearby and this property offers horseshoes, kayaking, hiking, fire rings and a barbecue. There is a long list of amenities and activities such as complimentary Wi-Fi, potluck celebrations on most holidays, kayak rentals, laundry facility, store and abundant recreational opportunities.

HEMLOCK

BEAR CREEK ARTICHOKES
19659 Hwy 101 503/398-5411
Daily: 9-close (seasonal variations) bearcreekartichokes.com

You may not have heard of the small unincorporated community of Hemlock, but you may have stopped at or driven past this 20-acre farm about 11 miles south of Tillamook and 18 miles north of Neskowin. Fresh produce (from the farm and throughout the Northwest), a gift shop, farm kitchen (scrumptious apple dumplings and strawberry shortcake all summer; espresso drinks), greenhouse, display pond and the perennial crop of artichokes attract visitors from the Coast and Valley. The market stocks canned vegetables, preserves and gourmet goods prepared in the farm kitchen and assorted seasonal gourmet foods from other quality providers. Owner **Cindy Miles** heads up this enterprise where customers know they will find fun and unusual fruits and vegetables and fresh crab and oysters. The gorgeous hanging baskets and plants will perk up any yard or porch.

LANGLOIS

LANGLOIS MARKET
48444 Hwy 101 541/348-2476
Daily langloismarket.com

Midway between Bandon and Port Orford is a must-stop for world famous hot dogs. A "secret" mustard recipe makes these "top dog" among hot dog aficionados (other sandwiches are available).

The market is tidy and bright with various stuffed and mounted game animals hanging on the walls and from the rafters ostensibly keeping an eye on the merchandise. Super-friendly second-generation owner **Jake Pestana** stocks the shelves with staples, beer, local produce, snacks and local grass-fed beef from his brother's ranch.

LINCOLN CITY

BARNACLE BILL'S SEAFOOD MARKET
2174 NE Hwy 101   541/994-3022
Daily

An only-at-the-beach sight is the steam billowing out of massive cooking pots where just-caught Dungeness crabs are boiled until reaching a distinct brilliant red-orange hue. The succulent crustaceans are sold whole, by pieces or picked and ready to devour. Barnacle Bill's shrimp and crab cocktails are superb! Owners **Penny and Ron Edmunds** oversee the operation and son **Sean Edmunds** tends the smoker and turns out some of the tastiest smoked salmon around. Other fresh catch makes its way to the counter; convenient Styrofoam coolers are available to tote your delights to the beach or home. No credit cards.

BAY HOUSE
5911 SW Hwy 101   541/996-3222
Dinner: Wed-Sun   thebayhouse.org
Expensive

When **Stephen Wilson** took over the venerable Bay House in 2005, he knew he faced the challenge of keeping its excellent reputation intact. He rose to the test and also added a wine bar and cocktail lounge to the 1930s building which overlooks dramatic Siletz Bay. The gourmet menu is a standout on the Oregon Coast and includes seasonal items such as butternut squash ravioli, exquisitely prepared seafood, Piedmontese beef tenderloin and other Northwest tastes. If you'd like the chef to do the decision making, you won't be disappointed with the five-course tasting menu with recommended wine pairings from a superb wine selection. Sublime desserts include crème brûlée with housemade hazelnut biscotti and berry cobbler with a scoop of fresh vanilla ice cream. The adjoining bar features small plates and periodic live music.

THE COHO OCEANFRONT LODGE

1635 NW Harbor Ave   541/994-3684
Inexpensive to very expensive   thecoholodge.com

   Coho Oceanfront Lodge is a few blocks off busy Highway 101. This boutique-style hotel is a winning combination of ocean views, service, price and spacious accommodations. In the last few years guest rooms were restored and a new wing added to create 14 rooms and suites with decks overlooking the Pacific, jetted tubs, flat-screen TVs and fireplaces. Kids are sure to enjoy the unique suite created with them in mind. One room is furnished with bunk beds, a kid-size table and Wii or Play Station. Other features of the property are a heated indoor pool, sauna, Jacuzzi, on-site spa, continental breakfast, outdoor fire pits and more. The service-oriented Lee family and staff go out of their way to make guests feel welcome. The place is spotlessly clean and the beds are luxurious.

THE CULINARY CENTER IN LINCOLN CITY

801 SW Hwy 101, 4th floor   541/557-1125
                                                 oregoncoast.org/culinary

   Executive Chef **Sharon Wiest** oversees the menu of cooking demonstrations, hands-on classes and wildly popular cook-offs. Joining her are chefs who share a penchant for working with fresh bounty from Oregon's fertile land and waters. Recreational cooking sessions (pasta, cheese making, seafood) may last one to three hours or all day; multi-day courses may include canning, pickling or delve into one of many ethnic cuisines. **Rob Pounding** (the founder of this public-private partnership) is a frequent guest chef.

LOOKING GLASS INN

861 SW 51st St   541/996-3996
Inexpensive to moderate   lookingglass-inn.com

   Siletz Bay and a marvelous easily-accessible beach are in the historic Taft area on the southern end of Lincoln City and clustered with lodging, restaurants and shops. This inn is mere steps from the beach with incomparable bay and ocean views. Spacious studios and suites are nonsmoking and furnished with flat-screen TVs and kitchens; one suite is outfitted with a king bed, whirlpool tub and deck. Some one- and two-bedroom suites also include a gas fireplace and living area with sofa bed. Guests receive complimentary continental breakfast each morning. Several rooms are dog-friendly; Fido is sure to enjoy chasing sticks on the beach or playing in the waves.

MANZANITA

BIG WAVE CAFE
822 Laneda Ave   503/368-9283
Breakfast, Lunch, Dinner: Daily   oregonsbigwavecafe.com
Moderate

Carol and Brian Williams make a big deal out of breakfast! Whether you're heading out to catch the big wave or savoring alone time with newspaper in hand, you'll find just-right morning choices (also available all day) of daily specials, breakfast burritos, omelets, banana bread with fresh fruit and more. When weekends roll around, out comes the waffle bar with fresh fruit toppings, whipped cream and flavored syrups. Gourmet burgers, sandwiches, wonderful specialty salads and a handful of entrees are offered at lunch. The dinner menu focuses on steaks and seafood. Desserts like marionberry pie, chocolate cake and Bananas Foster are homemade and even better with a scoop of ice cream.

COAST CABINS
635 Laneda Ave   503/368-7113
Moderate to very expensive   coastcabins.com

There are coastal cabins, and then there are the accommodations at Coast Cabins. Six private cabins, which provide perfect escapes for those "wanting to get away from it all," are as charming as Manzanita itself. Units are one or two levels of varying sizes plus a modern ranch cabin. Tranquil comfort is achieved at this Zen-like property through intimate gardens, relaxing courtyard, cozy fire pit and wooded surroundings. Amenities differ among the quarters, full or convenience kitchens, outdoor jet spas, dry sauna, steam shower and wood or gas barbecues. The spa and modern ranch cabin are the ultimate in relaxation and romance.

THE INN AT MANZANITA

67 Laneda Ave   503/368-6754
Moderate   innatmanzanita.com

At the end of Manzanita's main avenue of appealing shops is a delightful inn. Four buildings (two to four units per building) are nestled on beautifully landscaped grounds amid coastal pine and spruce trees. Main and cottage building amenities include queen beds, jetted spa tubs, gas fireplaces and wet bars with a refrigerator. The north building is similar, with the captain-style queen bed situated in a curtained nook. Larger units are located in the Manzanita building; some kitchen facilities. The three-bedroom, two-bathroom penthouse is a home-away-from-home with full kitchen, partial ocean view and full amenities.

LEFT COAST SIESTA

288 Laneda Ave   503/368-7997
Lunch, Dinner: Wed-Sun   leftcoastsiesta.com
Inexpensive

If you're looking for great Mexican food with a healthy twist, check out **Lynn and Jeff Kyriss**'s establishment. Serving hungry customers since 1994, Left Coast has become a traditional "first stop" for visitors returning to the area. Burritos and tacos are assembled with a choice of tortilla, chicken or beef, organic refried or black beans and organic rice, plus veggies and freshly-made salsa available in three heat levels. Enchiladas are prepared with white or blue corn tortillas, one filling and topped with red or green sauce. Portions are large and tasty; kids' menu too. Unique to Left Coast is the bar of 100 to 200 hot sauces to sample or purchase: hot, hotter, hottest and grab the fire extinguisher!

NEHALEM

WANDA'S CAFE
12870 Hwy 101 N   503/368-8100
Breakfast, Lunch: Thurs-Tues (daily in summer)   wandascafe.com
Inexpensive

When you see a waiting line spilling onto the porch of a Nehalem establishment, you know you've arrived at Wanda's! Nevertheless, the personal, quick service is impressive. Wanda's specialties are big breakfasts (served all day), satisfying lunches and daily specials and a fine array of homemade pastries. Outdoor patio seating is great when Oregon's beach weather cooperates. You'll be tempted by glass cases filled with fresh and tasty goodies to take home.

NESKOWIN

HAWK CREEK CAFE
4505 Salem Ave   503/392-3838
Lunch, Dinner: Daily
Moderate

Another tiny Oregon coastal community has a small cafe with loyal repeat customers. The secret to the to-die-for pizzas is the combination of homemade dough and sauce, interesting toppings and baking to perfection in a wood-fired brick oven. Other favorites are burgers, sandwiches, salads served with garlic bread and homemade soups (perfect after a walk along Hawk Creek on a blustery day). Fresh Northwest fish, seafood, pastas and New York steak are well-prepared dinner choices. If you're there on certain holidays or during the busy season, the restaurant is open for breakfast. The atmosphere and service are extra-friendly.

NETARTS

LEX'S COOL STUFF
4955 Crab Ave   503/842-1744
Fri-Sun: noon-6

Who doesn't like cool? You can find some cool stuff at none other than Lex's eclectic shop. This busy lady scours the area for treasures that are nicely displayed inside and out. You're sure to linger as the background music provides great ambience and Lex offers customers free home-baked brownies (eight batches a day, made from scratch with Ghirardelli chocolate and Kahlua).

THE SCHOONER

2065 Netarts Bay Blvd   503/815-9900
Breakfast, Lunch, Dinner: Fri-Sun; Lunch, Dinner: Mon-Thurs
                                                          theschooner.net
Moderate

A remodel and expansion project changed the face of The Schooner which has been a Netarts fixture for over 60 years. A long table dominates the inviting dining room and glass windbreaks shield the outdoor deck from coastal breezes. The menu leans toward local ocean and farm products and wood-fired gourmet pizzas. The lounge serves classic and contemporary cocktails and area micro-brews; live music on weekends. Flavorful breakfast choices include chorizo sausage, seafood, vegetables and eggs combined into delicious scrambles, Benedicts, sandwiches and other fabrications.

NEWPORT

APRIL'S AT NYE BEACH

749 NW 3rd St   541/265-6855
Dinner: Wed-Sun   aprilsatnyebeach.com
Moderate

April and Kent Wolcott's Northwest-fresh farm-to-fork dinner house is a longtime favorite. Their variations of Mediterranean dishes are uniformly excellent. Breads and desserts are homemade; flowers, produce and herbs are grown on the Wolcott's Buzzard Hill Farm; and meats and seafood are selected for seasonal availability. That being said, a sample of offerings may include linguine with clams, chicken piccata or ribeye steak finished with gorgonzola brandy butter. Chef April assembles interesting nightly specials and Kent tends to the front of the house.

CAFE STEPHANIE

411 NW Coast St   541/265-8082
Daily: 7:30-3   cafestephanie.com
Moderate

Hearty breakfasts are served in an unpretentious building and it's always a good sign when locals fill the seats! Quiches, waffles, breakfast burritos and delicious homemade buttermilk pancakes are on the breakfast menu and priced right; kids' breakfasts are served with a freshly-baked scone. Lunch choices include soups, chowder, salads, sandwiches (whole or half) and fish tacos. Outdoor tables expand the limited inside seating capacity.

CANYON WAY RESTAURANT

1216 SW Canyon Way   541/265-8319
Lunch: Mon-Sat; Dinner: Fri   canyonway.com

Dozens of places along the coast offer crab cakes with a variety of additional ingredients and presentations, but none better than those served by **Roguey and Ed Doyle** at their bookstore/restaurant. These Dungeness delicacies are just the right size and consistency, and contain a great deal of crab meat. Homemade soups are another customer favorite; choices may include chicken curry, mushroom, cream of roasted garlic, New England-style clam chowder or soup du jour. Oyster or shrimp po' boys, Szechuan chicken pasta or fresh spinach salad are also good. Custardy bread pudding is made with homemade bread and topped with warm caramel rum sauce — very good and rich!

CAPTAIN'S REEL DEEP SEA FISHING

343 SW Bay Blvd   541/265-7441, 800/865-7441
Year round   captainsreel.com

Grab your fishing license, make a sack lunch, throw in rain gear (just in case) and sunscreen and head to Newport's waterfront to board one of four boats (six to 26 passengers) in Captain's fleet. Tackle and hot coffee are provided onboard. Depending on season and luck, you might pull in a prize halibut, albacore tuna, salmon or lingcod; even squid fishing is an option, along with bottom fishing. Most trips offer a crab combo opportunity. Excursions range from five to 18 hours (prices vary accordingly); check group and kids' discounts; fish filleting is available on the dock.

COASTAL CHARACTER

One of the central coast's favorite personalities is the longtime Depoe Bay owner and operator of **Gracie's Sea Hag** (theseahag.com), **Gracie Strom**. Aside from the food that fills any appetite, Gracie is especially known for her welcoming hospitality and playing the bottles; she has a great bar and can whip up tunes that people love to hear. Gracie has somewhat retired, but continues to leave an indelible mark on her community.

ELIZABETH STREET INN

232 SW Elizabeth St   541/265-9400, 877/265-9400
Moderate to expensive   elizabethstreetinn.com

Pampering touches are part of a stay at the Elizabeth Street Inn: cozy fireplaces, comfortable robes, hot breakfast buffet, private balconies and an indoor saltwater swimming pool. Oceanfront rooms look out onto the beach or north toward Yaquina Head Lighthouse. Choose from several accommodation types: queen, king or king Jacuzzi rooms and a spacious family suite; dog-friendly rooms also available. In addition to the complimentary breakfast, fresh cookies are set out in the lobby each evening and smoked salmon chowder is a hit on cool off-season afternoons. There is no shortage of nearby activities.

GREENSTONE INN

729 NW Coast St   541/265-2477, 800/480-2477
Moderate   greenstone-inn.com

With many innovative energy-saving alternatives, Greenstone is an apt name for this three-story earth-friendly oceanfront property. You'll even find some of the old Viking Cottage timbers recycled into the building. The 20 units offer balconies and gas fireplaces, an elevator, Wi-Fi and stairs that take you onto Nye Beach. Sustainable custom furnishings, an advanced plumbing system, twin peaks to maximize solar collection and a key-card docking system for empty-room energy savings are in all guest rooms; no landline phones, however.

KAM MENG CHINESE RESTAURANT

4424 N Hwy 101   541/574-9450
Lunch, Dinner: Tues-Sun   kammengchineserestaurant.com
Moderate

Kam Meng's features good home-style Chinese fare, with the added attraction of freshly caught seafood. You can gorge on Dungeness crab that comes in several dishes. Seafood, vegetarian, combination and grilled dishes are also popular. Artwork by owner **Huiya Chen** is displayed in the dining room; you may also hear her playing her beloved piano.

LA MAISON BAKERY & CAFE

315 SW 9th St   541/265-8812
Breakfast, Lunch: Daily   lamaisoncafe.com

This attractive yellow cottage sets the stage for what's inside. Fare is distinctly French: eggs Sardou, Chambord crepes, Provence omelets, croissant sandwiches and more; a glass of Champagne is a nice touch. *Tres délicieux* gourmet desserts are presented on fused-glass plates. Chef **Cliff Brown** uses local, organically-grown produce and eggs.

LOCAL OCEAN SEAFOODS

213 SE Bay Blvd   541/574-7959
Daily   localocean.net
Moderate

Seafood is always best fresh—and it's really fresh at this place. Products in the cases are tagged with specific information about the catch, the name of the boat and how and where it was caught. Only high-grade products are purchased, and the flavors show this advantage. Fish tacos, tuna kabobs, tuna wraps, plus salmon, halibut and crab are popular choices. (Only the French fries are deep-fried here.) Owner **Laura Anderson** runs a spotless restaurant with an open kitchen; as weather allows, roll-up glass doors are opened to bring the fresh ocean air into the dining area. The menu emphasizes a fine selection of seafood, including oyster shooters, steamer clams, Thai-style mussels, Dungeness crab and fishwives' stew (in a garlic and herb broth). A few non-fish options, kids' selections and homemade ice cream are also available.

OREGON COAST AQUARIUM

2820 SE Ferry Slip Road   541/867-3474
Daily   aquarium.org
Reasonable

The aquarium celebrated its 20th anniversary in 2012. Perhaps the best known resident was Keiko, the orca whale that starred in the movie *Free Willy*. Keiko arrived via UPS in 1996 amid much ballyhoo and wowed visitors until his rehabilitation was complete in 1998 when he was returned to his native Iceland. The vacancy at the aquarium was enormous in more ways than one. Keiko's tank was renovated to accommodate Passages of the Deep, an underwater exhibit, complete with a 200-foot-long glass tunnel where guests walk amid aquatic life. Fun and educational events include overnight stays to sleep with the sharks, a dive program with sharks and other fish, private parties and more. Within the 39-acre facility are 250 species, various exhibits (sandy and rocky environs, sea otters, seals and sea lions, nettles and a seabird aviary); many are hands-on. A full-service cafe offers food and beverages for active families and a coffee cart serves favorite coffee concoctions. The aquarium's book and gift shop is full of fascinating literature, colorful posters and DVDs about the marine environment and its inhabitants, plus treasures, art, clothing and ocean-themed gifts.

OSU HATFIELD MARINE SCIENCE CENTER

2030 SE Marine Science Dr   541/867-0100
Summer: Daily; Winter: Thurs-Mon   hmsc.oregonstate.edu/visitor

An ocean-related educational experience awaits you and your children. The visitor center (a Coastal Ecosystem Learning Center) is the public wing of Oregon State University's Mark O. Hatfield Marine Science Center and is managed by Oregon Sea Grant. This fascinating operation is part aquarium and part ocean laboratory. Learn about "habitat snatchers," aquatic invasive species (such as Asian clams and zebra mussels) that are an environmental threat to native wildlife, undersea volcanoes and whale migration. Fascinating exhibits include getting up close and personal with an octopus and other live marine animals, El Niño effects and interactive games and puzzles that demonstrate marine science concepts, offshore reef exploration and endangered species. A well-stocked bookstore has ocean and natural science-related books, videos and the like.

PANACHE

614 W Olive St   541/265-2929
Dinner: Thurs-Tues (daily in summer)   panachenewport.com
Moderate

Northwest cuisine is served in this fine-dining establishment adjacent to the Newport Performing Arts Center. **Linda and Tom Peddecord**'s charming old home is warm with a distinct Old World feel. Guests savor local seafood and meat made with interesting and seasonal organic foods as much as possible. How about seared rack of lamb, halibut encrusted with cranberries and hazelnuts or Wagyu sirloin steak for dinner? Small plates emphasize deliciously prepared seafood. Panache's signature dessert is a lemon and marionberry Napoleon—the icing on the cake!

PANINI BAKERY

232 NW Coast St   541/265-5033
Daily: 7-7

This is a good find for quick and casual lunches of soups, sandwiches and pizzas. Breads are out-of-this-world, especially the sourdough, and sweet and savory pastries are addicting. The pizzas are excellent and sold whole or by the slice. The Nye Beach location is on a charming street; opt for outdoor seating to enjoy the lovely coastal ambience while sipping organic coffee and munching on cookies or equally delicious baked goods. Get the bread while it is fresh!

SAFFRON SALMON

859 SW Bay Blvd   541/265-8921
Lunch, Dinner: Thurs-Tues   saffronsalmon.com
Moderate

Exceptional "from-scratch" cooking lends itself to exceptional entrees and desserts. Wild salmon takes a starring role in salads and entrees and in a sandwich with saffron aioli on the lunch menu. Local farms provide lamb, beef and chicken; produce is purchased at the seasonal farmers market and local fishermen supply the restaurant with in-season crab and seafood. Warm marionberry cobbler with ice cream is the signature dessert. Reservations suggested; seasonal hours in November.

SYLVIA BEACH HOTEL

267 NW Cliff St   541/265-5428, 888/795-8422
Moderate   sylviabeachhotel.com

Sylvia Beach Hotel has been known for some time as a most unusual bed and breakfast. Built a century ago, it opened as the New Cliff House and later became Hotel Gilmore before current owners **Sally Ford** and **Goody Cable** (with the assistance of friends) turned it into a novel beachside 20-room B&B with rooms furnished and named after renowned authors (Agatha Christie, Dr. Seuss, J.K. Rowling, F. Scott Fitzgerald). Room types are categorized as classic, bestseller or novel (all have private baths) and are designed for relaxation, reading and writing (you won't find TVs, Wi-Fi, telephones or other tech conveniences). Guests and non-guests are in for an informal and relaxed treat at **Tables of Content** where the Northwest cuisine dinner menu changes daily. The format is a bit unusual. When dinner reservations are made, diners are asked which of four entrees they prefer (seafood, poultry, meat or vegetarian). Seating is family-style with six or eight at a table; diners may enter into fun ice-breaker games to get acquainted with their tablemates. There is one seating each evening (6 p.m. during the winter and 7 p.m. on weekends, during the summer and holidays). Meals include tasty appetizers, a fresh salad, vegetable and starch with the main course, dessert and coffee or tea (beer and wine are optional). Group luncheons and special occasions are accommodated.

THE WHALER

155 SW Elizabeth St   541/265-9261, 800/433-9444
Moderate   whalernewport.com

The 73-room Whaler has great Pacific views from guest room balconies. Various units are equipped with fireplaces, wet bars and microwaves; all rooms offer Internet access and refrigerators. A continental breakfast is complimentary to guests with hot beverages and fresh popcorn available throughout the day.

Walk along the beach, visit Nye Beach or Old Town's excellent restaurants and shops or enjoy the indoor pool, spa and exercise facility. Four comfortable three- and four-bedroom homes with ocean views are also available. Owner **John Clark** operates a first-class establishment.

NORTH BEND

PORTA
1802 Virginia Ave   541/756-4900
Lunch: Tues-Fri; Dinner: Tues-Sat   portarestaurant.com
Moderate

Porta offers local dishes with a distinct Italian flavor. The stuffed portobello mushroom salad includes bay shrimp, pesto and asparagus and muffuletta is served as a panini sandwich. For dinner, second courses (risotto, pasta, pizza) suffice for smaller appetites, particularly when combined with a nicely-composed mixed green salad. Entrees (steak, chicken, lamb) are accompanied by housemade pasta, polenta cakes or gorgonzola potato hash. Seasonal options influence the menu.

OTIS

OTIS CAFE
1259 Salmon River Hwy   541/994-2813
Breakfast, Lunch, Dinner: Daily   otiscafe.com
Inexpensive

This, my friends, is a quintessential stop about five miles northeast of Lincoln City. The tiny, funky roadside diner is a must-visit for down-home cooking, especially breakfast. Toast is a big deal here; it is made from homemade black molasses bread. Loaves of black molasses, sourdough and pumpkin bread are available for purchase. Eggs and such are served with or without meats and with homemade hash browns (shredded baked russet potatoes). Sourdough or buttermilk pancakes (and waffles) are also popular; the kids' pancake version is made in the shape of a teddy bear face. Be ready to wait in line (even in the rain) and when your turn comes, join a community table for lively conversation.

> ## TRUSTWORTHY, LOYAL ...THRIFTY, BRAVE, CLEAN AND REVERENT
>
> From 1926 to 1958, **G.H. "Obie" Oberteuffer** was a father figure to thousands of boy scouts who summered at **Camp Meriwether** (cpcbsa.org) near Tillamook on the Oregon coast. Oberteuffer's influence as head of the scouting program in the Oregon region was instrumental in leadership development for many young men who later headed major Oregon institutions.

Hot and cold sandwiches, burgers, soups, salads and creamy clam chowder welcome a new wave of midday diners. Soup or salad, starch, vegetables and, of course, homemade bread accompany the comfort food dinners. My favorite Otis Cafe story involves former *New York Times* food critic **Bryan Miller**. He once chose this restaurant as his favorite during a gastronomical tour of Oregon!

OTTER ROCK

INN AT OTTER CREST
301 Otter Crest Dr
Inexpensive to moderate

541/765-2111, 800/452-2101

innatottercrest.com

OTTER CREST LODGE

Moderate

541/765-2094, 503/765-2326
ottercrestlodge.com

Decades ago, **T. Harry Banfield**, a major player in Portland's leadership during the mid-20th century, was among the first to build a vacation home at Otter Crest. Eventually the home was sold as Banfield spent more time as chairman of the Oregon State Highway Commission; the property developed as The Inn at Otter Crest, a vacation destination. Forests, waterfalls and wildlife surround this 27-building complex and views are spectacular from every guest room and vantage point. All units have wall-to-wall windows and private balconies. The restaurant is under new ownership; **Bruce Taylor** (publisher of the Salem Business Journal) opened **Otter Crest Lodge** in early 2012.

Guests and visitors are welcome to relax, socialize and watch migrating whales in the "ship-like" restaurant and lodge with 54 large windows. The Daily Coffee Shop is open for breakfast (all-you-can-eat pancakes and egg dishes) and lunch ("bootleg" clam chowder, burgers, salads). Complimentary pastries and beverages are served to guests each morning in the coffee shop. Dinner fare in the main dining room consists of pasta, ribeye steak and fish, a prelude to the evening's outdoor activities at the fire pit. There are abundant attractions and activities to keep everyone occupied for days.

PACIFIC CITY

COTTAGES AT CAPE KIWANDA
33000 Cape Kiwanda Dr   503/965-7920, 866/571-0605
Expensive   yourlittlebeachtown.com

Pacific City is home to Oregon's fleet of dory fishing vessels. It is quite a sight to watch the flat-bottom boats rush the waves out to fertile fishing grounds. These cottages have a catbird seat to the dories and Cape Kiwanda. The beautiful property consists of 18 two- and three-bedroom fractionally-owned cottages, also available for nightly rental. Units are cozy and outfitted with inviting contemporary furnishings; master bedrooms are situated to garner ocean views. Amenities and special features include heated bathroom floor tiles, gas fireplaces and barbecues, in-room Wi-Fi, beachfront decks and patios, covered parking and much more. The on-site concierge is friendly and helpful in locating massage and spa services, restaurants, special activities and filling other guest requests.

DELICATE PALATE BISTRO
35280 Brooten Road   503/965-6464, 866/567-3466
Dinner: Wed-Sun   delicatepalate.com
Moderate to expensive

Despite the rather ironic name, the bar conjures up a he-man half-pound Blue Mesa Ranch natural burger served on Grateful Bread brioche bun with housemade aioli and tomato ketchup. Other interesting choices include duck carnitas tostados, barbecue pulled pork sliders and an apple and gorgonzola salad. Superb bistro dinner choices include an Asian seafood bouillabaisse in coconut curry broth, herb crusted halibut, ribeye steak, oven-roasted rack of lamb and delightful seasonal selections; irresistible desserts are made in-house. Rare vintage wines and specialty drinks are served in both the bistro and bar. Sommelier **Matthew Williams** operates the bistro and his parents, **Patt and Geoff Williams, Sr.**, head up the family-owned enterprise including the 16-room **Pacific City Inn** (pacificcityinn.com) at the same location.

INN AT CAPE KIWANDA

33105 Cape Kiwanda Dr   503/965-7001, 888/965-7001
Moderate to expensive   yourlittlebeachtown.com/inn

Here is a friendly and attractive family-oriented facility. Each of the 35 rooms has a private balcony overlooking the ocean. Nice touches include Starbucks coffee in the lobby and guest rooms, complimentary newspapers, cozy gas fireplaces, pillow top mattresses and feather pillows, complimentary chocolates on arrival and free Wi-Fi. The Haystack Suite includes a living room, large bedroom and Jacuzzi tub with ocean view. Inquire about bicycle rentals to explore this delightful coastal community.

PELICAN PUB & BREWERY

33180 Cape Kiwanda Dr   503/965-7007
Breakfast, Lunch, Dinner: Daily   pelicanbrewery.com
Moderate

Long the hub of activity and good eating this pub enjoys a dramatic beach location. The place is a beehive of activity for breakfast, lunch and dinner, particularly with the on-premises brewery (tours available upon request) — Oregon's only oceanfront brewery. A huge menu gives diners choices of just about everything, from pork cutlet sandwiches to blackened salmon salads to gourmet pizzas. Pelican's own brews complement meals and are used in the preparation of numerous dishes (pale malt crusted salmon, Tsunami Stout pot roast, Scottish-style ale cakes for breakfast, beer-a-misu for dessert). Beer pairings are a specialty and so noted on the menu. Brewmaster **Darron Welch** masterminds three five-course brewers' dinners (reservations necessary) annually.

THE VILLAGE MERCHANTS
34950 Brooten Road   503/965-6911
Daily: 10-5   thevillagemerchants.com

Be sure to stop and browse at this amazing shop for an outstanding selection of goods for the person or home. Add to your wardrobe from a wide selection of contemporary women's clothing, handbags, unique jewelry and accessories. Lamps, accessories, furniture accent pieces, decorative objects, exquisite glassware, linens and tabletop items are tucked into every nook and cranny where they are beautifully and creatively displayed. Indulge yourself from the fine lines of bath products, candles and spa-type amenities. Tykes have a section all their own full of attractive clothing, games and lovable stuffed critters. This is also the source for all-occasion cards, Northwest wines, music, books and a little of this and that.

PORT ORFORD

HAWTHORNE GALLERY
267 6th St   541/366-2266
Daily   hawthornegallery.com

REDFISH
                                                    541/366-2200
Lunch, Dinner: Daily; Breakfast: Sat, Sun   redfishportorford.com
Moderate to expensive

REDFISH LOFT
                                                    541/366-2266
Moderate   redfishloft.com

Not that long ago entrepreneurs **Julie and Chris Hawthorne** in association with Chris' brother and sister-in-law, **Susan and Gregory Hawthorne**, developed an amazing oceanfront attraction. The gallery is fittingly named after the talented family, with an outdoor courtyard that draws enthusiasts to experience the beautiful artworks. One of the leading metal sculptors in the world, Albert Paley, exhibits dramatic iron and steel furniture and sculpted pieces, and over a dozen artists offer other compelling pieces. The gallery complex also has an upscale restaurant accented with striking art and a unique custom

SERVICE TO STATE

The Tymchuk family hails from Reedsport and has made its mark there as well as across the state. The late **Marlene Tymchuk** was the proud mother of Kerry and Keith and she set a high bar, being named Oregon's Teacher of the Year in 1980. Father, **Tom Tymchuk**, served as mayor; son, **Keith Tymchuk**, has served four mayoral terms (current term through 2012) for Reedsport citizens. **Kerry Tymchuk** is a well-respected politico known for his work with Representative **Denny Smith,** senators **Elizabeth and Bob Dole** and **Gordon Smith**; he is an accomplished writer and speaker (and 4-time Jeopardy champ); and executive director of the Oregon History Center.

bar. Brunch consists of egg dishes; lunch has soups, salads and sandwiches, including a superb mandarin cashew chicken version. Dinner is coastal cuisine with a French twist; meat and fish platters are complemented with excellent accompaniments. A single upscale lodging space is available upstairs from the gallery. Enjoy views from a soaking tub and slate balcony; a well-appointed living room with fireplace make the elegant Redfish LOFT one of a kind. This is a winning trifecta!

WILDSPRING GUEST HABITAT
92978 Cemetery Loop   866/333-9453
Expensive   wildspring.com

From its Port Orford hilltop location, this overnight gem is akin to staying in a private estate. Five beautiful cabin suites and the oceanview Guest Hall are nestled on five forested acres. Amble over to the Guest Hall for a tasty morning breakfast buffet; enjoy beverages, fruit, popcorn and chocolates anytime during the day; gaze at the Pacific while soaking in the open-air, slate jetted hot tub; or arrange for in-room spa treatments, guest bikes, hiking guides and other services. Luxurious appointments vary among the cabins; sliding doors separate the cozy living rooms from bedrooms. Furnishings include artwork, down comforters, antique and vintage pieces, oversize walk-in slate showers, massage tables, aromatherapy soaps and shampoos, refrigerators and a flat-screen

TV/DVD for movies (over 500 titles available in the Guest Hall library). No telephones, in-room cooking facilities or TV reception; however, guests are free to use a fully-equipped kitchen in the Hall. This small, eco-friendly property is a year-round destination for relaxation, picnics in the forest and walking the labyrinth.

REEDSPORT

SUGAR SHACK BAKERY

145 N 3rd St   541/271-3514
Daily: 3 a.m. to 7 p.m. (varies seasonally)   sugarshackbakery.biz

When you're passing through Reedsport, stop in for coffee and a doughnut, other sugary treats or a dish of ice cream to keep you going. The Bigfoot doughnut (chocolate and maple icings with whipped cream filling) is large enough to tame Sasquatch-size cravings! All delicious cookies, scones, cakes and candies are made from scratch. More substantial offerings include breakfast sandwiches and biscuits and gravy; soups and sandwiches are served midday until closing.

UMPQUA DISCOVERY CENTER

409 Riverfront Way   541/271-4816
Daily   umpquadiscoverycenter.com
Reasonable

Along the tidewaters of the Umpqua River, an interesting educational and cultural center with interactive, multi-sensory exhibits and programs is geared to families. Step back in time to experience life in a 1900s tidewater town, loggers' camp and salmon cannery; meet the early explorers such as Jedediah Smith; and see the culture of coastal Indian tribes. Take a simulated trail through the area's ecosystems guided by Rumpies (fantasy River Umpqua Elves) and slide down a hillside into a bear cave. There's much more to entertain and inform kids including a 35-foot periscope in the community room for capturing 360-degree views of the surrounding area. About three miles east of Reedsport, view a herd (at times over 120 head) of Roosevelt elk and other mammals, birds and carnivores at **Dean Creek Elk Viewing Area** (dfw. state.or.us/resources/visitors/dean_creek_wildlife_area.asp). Look for wildlife in marshes and meadows; good interpretive center.

SEAL ROCK

BRIAN MCENENY WOODCARVING GALLERY
10727 Hwy 101   541/563-2452
Summer: Daily;   woodcarvinggallery.com

Ultra-talented artist and owner, **Brian McEneny** makes incredible creations using driftwood, Port Orford Cedar, Manzanita roots, cypress, myrtlewood and other coastal woods. The fluidity of ocean life makes up the bulk of his menagerie, but you'll also find other animals, abstracts and Native American works. Pieces are finished to enhance distinctive wood grains. The two floors of the gallery are chock-full of Brian's small decorative pieces as well as impressive large carvings; intermingled are works by other Northwest carvers and master carvers. The gallery is closed Mondays and for six weeks during the winter; best to call ahead.

SEASIDE

BELL BUOY OF SEASIDE
1800 S Roosevelt Dr   800/529-2722
Daily   bellbuoyofseaside.com

When you are in Seaside, look for fresh Oregon Dungeness crab (whole or only crabmeat) at this family-owned specialty seafood store. A landmark neon bell buoy sign tops the building on the south end of Seaside. Fish is purchased right off the local fishing boats and sold fresh; salmon, albacore tuna, sturgeon and oysters are smoked and canned on-site. Gift boxes contain smoked and canned Oregon ocean delicacies (convenient online and phone orders, too); clam chowder and fish and chips are served at their next-door restaurant (503/738-6348).

GILBERT INN
341 Beach Dr   503/738-9770, 800/410-9770
Inexpensive to moderate   gilbertinn.com

This yellow and white Queen Anne Victorian beauty was originally built by former Seaside mayor Alexandre Gilbert; many of the Gilbert's furnishings have found their way back to the inn (Seaside's oldest surviving house). Each of the eight rooms accommodates one or two guests and is furnished with a queen-size bed, cable TV and private bath; the 1880's Room has a separate sitting room. The location is ideal for a romantic stay at the beach, close to the Promenade, shopping and restaurants.

MCKEOWN'S RESTAURANT & BAR

I N Holladay Dr   503/738-5232
Lunch, Dinner: Daily; Breakfast: Sat, Sun   mckeownsrestaurant.com
Moderate

This establishment features fresh seafood (good lager-battered fish and chips), tasty cottage pie, cedar-plank salmon, house cioppino, steaks and daily specials. Prime rib is featured on Friday and Saturday nights. A carving station and cooked-to-order omelet bar are highlights at McKeown's satisfying weekend brunch with various pastries, fruits, breakfast dishes, salads, meats and sweets. The latest addition is McKeown's Irish Bar.

RELIEF PITCHER

2795 S Roosevelt Dr   503/738-9801
Lunch, Dinner: Daily
Inexpensive to moderate

Superb burgers are found in an unlikely spot just south of town. The exterior doesn't have much curb-appeal, and the funky interior isn't anything to write home about. However, the Grand Slam burger, a half-pound juicy beauty topped with ham, egg, Tillamook and provolone cheese, along with cole slaw or fries makes up for the environs. Albacore tuna tacos, sandwiches and Reubens are also popular. Brews are available by the pitcher, glass or pint; full bar and wine offerings also.

SEASIDE CANDYMAN

21 N Columbia St, Suite 105   503/738-5280
Daily   seasidecandymaninc.com

The Seaside Candyman wants to sweeten your day. Choose from 180 flavors of salt water taffy, 72 Jelly Belly flavors, assorted chocolates, candy sticks, popcorn, ice cream, fudge and sugar-free confections. If you're not in the area, you can satisfy your taffy craving through the online candy store.

SEASIDE MOSTLY HATS
300 Broadway   503/738-4370
Daily   seasidemostlyhats.com

Seaside Mostly Hats is one of the most complete hat stores in the state. Located in the Carousel Mall, you'll find fun and dress hats for men, women and kids at reasonable prices in a variety of fabrics, styles and sizes. Depending on the weather, pop in to buy a rain hat or a straw hat. Some of the whimsical lids are made to look like fish or embellished with characters and attention-grabbing adornments; others come with synthetic hair attached.

SEASIDE OCEANFRONT INN AND RESTAURANT
581 S Prom   503/738-6403
Moderate   theseasideinn.com

A 14-room boutique inn and fine dining restaurant co-exist on the Prom among high-rises and grand oceanfront cottages. Themed guest rooms are creatively decorated along the lines of shells, timber, kites and bubbles with full or partial views of the ocean and mountains. The first floor restaurant, known to residents as **Maggie's on the Prom**, is favored by tourists, hotel guests and locals. Delicious lunch and dinner menus feature regional items such as Willapa Bay oysters and Tillamook cheese in addition to creatively presented seafood, beef and poultry preparations. Vegetarian and gluten-free diners will find several options; kids have their own choices. The view is incomparable from the Inn, restaurant and seasonal patio; restaurant days and hours vary by season.

TIPTON'S
319 Broadway   503/738-5864
Daily

George Tipton's attractive 2,500 square foot shop is a destination for classy home decor and holiday items. George has a discerning eye for warm Tuscan and French Country tabletop items, lamps, canisters, pictures, candles and soft goods. Don't overlook the case of delicious homemade chocolates (once the mainstay of the business). Delightful smells, nice background music (George is also a talented musician) and appealing merchandise blend harmoniously to create a pleasant ambience.

JOINT ISSUES

Primarily in pursuit of arthritis relief in its early days, the **Rinehart Clinic** (rinehartclinic.org) is a claim to fame in the tiny coastal town of Wheeler; the clinic will mark its 100th birthday in 2013. For a long while, medical care was provided to anyone in need for gratis, with over $800,000 charitably donated in support of the clinic. In addition to three generations of the Rinehart family offering arthritic treatments, one of the prominent names associated with the clinic for many years was **Dr. Harry Beckwith**, a Portlander who overcame a polio bout as a youngster to become an outstanding Oregon athlete. (Following the six degrees of separation theory, Beckwith's niece, **Caroline (Hoffman) Swindells**, is well known in her own right and as the wife of another prominent Oregonian, former U.S. Ambassador to New Zealand, **Charles "Butch" Swindells**.)

YUMMY WINE BAR & BISTRO

831 Broadway   503/738-3100
Thurs-Mon: 3-9   yummywinebarbistro.com
Moderate

Proprietor **Corey Albert** features an eclectic full dinner menu at his bistro in the old Seaside Fire Station West Bay parking garage. The emphasis is on Northwest ingredients with flavor influences from other countries and described under nifty appetizers, scrumptious soups and salads, tasty sandwiches and luscious main entrees. Happy hour comfort food is yummy and seasonally-changing wines are sold by the taste, glass or bottle. The establishment is decorated with what Albert calls "lowbrow art," by local artists. His email bulletins letting diners know of special events and dinners are very clever.

TILLAMOOK

BLUE HERON FRENCH CHEESE COMPANY

2001 Blue Heron Dr   503/842-8281, 800/275-0639
Daily   blueheronoregon.com

A 1930s Dutch Colonial barn houses this marvelous retail business that includes a deli and tasting room with fantastic cheeses, gourmet foods and wines. Products, tasty samples and gift items are arranged throughout the store suggesting attractive entertaining possibilities. The *pièce de résistance* is the cheese counter featuring the famous Blue Heron Brie with a selection of other fine cheeses; free samples provided. Another popular attraction is the wine tasting bar. For a nominal fee, sample five Northwest wines from four flights. At the deli, you can order lunch choices of homemade soups, chowder, salads and sandwiches on freshly-baked bread to eat at one of the comfy inside seating areas or for takeout. Outside, kids can get up close and pet farm animals or engage in other activities for the pint-size set.

LATIMER QUILT & TEXTILE CENTER

2105 Wilson River Loop   503/842-8622
Daily   latimerquiltandtextile.com
Nominal

This nonprofit working museum opened in 1991 and showcases textiles from the mid-19th century to the present. The former Maple Leaf schoolhouse building is home to a changing gallery, a research library and a fine gift shop where you'll find handmade items by local craftspeople, books, vintage fabrics, quilt patterns and other vintage and contemporary pieces. A self-guided Tillamook County Quilt Trail celebrates the county's rural heritage using painted wooden quilt blocks on historic barns built by Swiss and German immigrants. Watch the interesting weaving and spinning demonstrations or arrange for weaving, spinning, knitting, quilting and rug hooking instruction.

TILLAMOOK CHEESE FACTORY

4175 Hwy 101 N   503/815-1300, 800/542-7290
Daily (hours vary by season)   tillamook.com

Tillamook County Creamery Association was formed over a hundred years ago and continues to create high-quality dairy products and outstanding cheddar cheese from the original recipe. A free self-guided factory tour shows the fascinating cheese-making and packaging processes; visitors can peer through large viewing windows, engage in interactive kiosks and learn from informative videos. Tillamook produces over a dozen varieties of cheese in loaves, sliced or shredded which are sold at the on-site Tillamook Cheese Shop and stores across the country. Every flavor of Tillamook ice cream (34 in all, some only available here) is scooped into dishes and cones at the ice cream counter or used in milkshakes and sundaes; the enticing aroma of hot-off-the-griddle waffle cones permeates the retail and eatery areas. Other Tillamook dairy products are featured on the Creamery Cafe menu with items such as macaroni and cheese, grilled cheese sandwiches, burgers, salads and breakfast omelets. Before you leave, make a stop at the gift shop for souvenirs, gourmet food items and Northwest goods. A box of Tillamook chocolate hazelnut fudge (or any of the 40 flavors) is great to take along for munching in the car. Everything is delicious!

TILLAMOOK COUNTY PIONEER MUSEUM

2106 2nd St   503/842-4553
Tues-Sun: 10-4   tcpm.org
Nominal

This small museum has a large collection of over 48,000 artifacts and 15,000 photographs depicting the rich history of the north Oregon coast. Exhibits pertain to pioneers, Native Americans, the military, natural history and musical instruments plus the area's industries (logging, beaches, dairy). A popular addition is the late Senator **Mark Hatfield's** superb Abraham Lincoln collection, which once graced the walls of his Washington, D.C. office.

TILLAMOOK FOREST CENTER

45500 Wilson River Hwy   503/815-6800, 866/930-4646
Seasonal hours   tillamookforestcenter.org

Longtime Oregonians will remember the devastating fire in 1933 that ravaged nearly 240,000 acres of prime forest land, mostly in Tillamook County. (Smaller fires in 1939, 1945 and 1951 burned an additional 120,000 acres and are also considered part of the Tillamook Burn.) A massive reforestation effort included thousands of Oregon volunteers who helped plant more than 72 million Douglas fir seedlings in the area. An interpretive center owned and operated by the Oregon Department of Forestry is located near Jones Creek, 22 miles east of Tillamook on Highway 6. It offers fascinating, interactive exhibits along with a 40-foot tall replica of a fire lookout tower and a dramatic 250-foot-long pedestrian suspension bridge that leads from the building across the Wilson River to the nearby Jones Creek Campground and on to the Wilson River Trail. A classroom, theater and interpretive trails provide educational opportunities. This is an exceptional destination for exploration, outdoor learning and free family fun.

WALDPORT

SOUL VACATION RESORT
902 NW Bayshore Dr   541/563-7700
Inexpensive to moderate   soulvacationresorts.com

At one time, this resort property was crooner Pat Boone's dream. Now, completely renovated, this 83-room hotel is pet-friendly, offers free Wi-Fi and drop-in yoga classes. The location is on spectacular Alsea Bay and offers prime wildlife viewing. Choose from basic rooms and suites; some rooms have Jacuzzi soaking tubs. **Rumi Restaurant and Lounge** offers an exciting mix of traditional French modern cooking and contemporary American flavors that complement, and are inspired by the rhythm of the seasons. Menus are driven by fine ingredients from local farmers markets and quality purveyors. Rumi "food from the heart" is a dining experience that excites the senses with vibrant ambience and gracious service.

WARRENTON

OFFICER'S INN BED AND BREAKFAST
540 Russell Pl   503/791-2524
Moderate   officersinn.com

Here's a suggestion for a unique place to stay near the Fort Stevens and Battery Russell historic military site. Battery Russell (circa 1900) was built to protect the Columbia River entrance and was reactivated during WWII; it is the only place on our mainland to have been shelled by a Japanese submarine in WWII. Those structures are mainly intact and the gun batteries and tunnels are open for exploration. The residence itself was originally built in 1905 as a housing unit for military officers and their families and is furnished with antiques and military artifacts. Eight bedrooms are offered, all with private baths; family suites are available. Events are a specialty, with accommodations for dinners, weddings and business meetings. From the library, choose a made-in-Astoria movie (such as *The Goonies* or *Kindergarten Cop*) or other movie for in-room viewing or brush up on military history. Bicycle and hiking trails, beaches, Fort Clatsop, Astoria, fishing, clamming and crabbing are all nearby.

WHEELER

RISING STAR CAFE
92 Rorvik St   503/368-3990
Lunch: Wed, Thurs, Sat; Dinner: Wed-Sat; Brunch: Sun   risingstarcafe.com
Moderate

A bright spot in Wheeler is a charming blue house where the motto is "fresh food simply prepared with style." Bountiful lunches might include fresh fish of the day, cioppino or seafood chowder, large omelets, sandwiches, pasta and rice noodle bowls and as many local vegetables as possible. Dinner menus change daily based upon current sourcing and consist of fresh seafood, pasta and at least one meat item for the carnivores among us (vegetarians and special diets accommodated where possible). Entrees are accompanied by crisp salads and great desserts that are made daily. Reservations recommended; no credit cards.

WINCHESTER BAY

SPORTSMEN'S CANNERY & SMOKEHOUSE
182 Bayfront Loop   541/271-3293, 800/457-8048
Daily   sportsmenscannery.com

Owners **Steven Sanders** and **Brian Reeves**' catchy slogan pretty well sums up their business: "Catch what you can

CHOCOLATE!

My friends and readers know I am a chocoholic, so it wouldn't do not to mention some of Oregon's sweet players. You will find products from these fine purveyors around the state and nation.

Brigittine Monks: Amity; 503/835-8080; brigittine.org

Chocolates by Bernard: Lake Oswego; 888/829-6800; bernardcchocolates.com

Euphoria Chocolate Company: Eugene; 541/344-4605; euphoriachocolate.com

Extreme Chocolates: Salem; 503/581-6099; extremechocolates.com

Goody's: Bend; 541/385-7085; goodyschocolates.com

Ladybug Chocolates: Canby; 503/263-3335; canbychocolates.com

Lillie Belle Farms: Central Point; 888/899-2022; lilliebellefarms.com

Moonstruck: Portland; 800/557-6666; moonstruckchocolate.com

Puddin' River Chocolates: Canby; 866/802-2708; puddinriverchocolates.com

The Sycamore Tree: Baker City; 541/523-4840; sycamoregifts.com

Wallowa Lake Fudge Company: Joseph; 541/398-1780; wallowalakefudgecompany.com

and we'll can what you catch!" Not to worry if you are not a fisherman; canned, smoked and fresh fish and seafood are sold in the store or arrange for overnight shipping anywhere in the country. Gift boxes also include local and gourmet seasonings, jams and preserves. Delicious meals feature salmon, tuna, lingcod, oysters, prawns, crab or other fresh fish; the price is right and the setting memorable.

UMPQUA OYSTERS

723 Ork Rock Road   541/271-5684
Daily: 9-5:30 (winter: closed Wednesday)   umpquaoysters.com

Fresh oysters are a delicacy, especially those cultivated at the confluence of the Umpqua River and Pacific Ocean. **Cindy and Vern Simmons** operate their aquaculture farm using innovative oyster "curtains" that keep the shellfish suspended in the water, free of air and mud exposure. This method produces a cut-above quality of tasty morsels, shucked or in the shell. When you are at the retail shop, pick up perfect condiments and sauces, observe shuckers and inspectors as they process the catch and watch an informative video depicting the long-line growing system.

YACHATS

THE ADOBE RESORT

155 Hwy 101   541/547-3141, 800/522-3623
Inexpensive and up   adoberesort.com

The Adobe has been a popular respite on this stretch of the Pacific for several decades. All guest rooms are furnished with refrigerators, microwaves and other conveniences and have views of the ocean or mountains. Suites are outfitted with king beds, Jacuzzi tubs with ocean views, electric fireplaces and other amenities. It's no surprise that the resort is a favorite of families and groups. Appealing features include an indoor pool, children's pool, expansive lawn, accessible beach and tide pools, convenient pathway into town, pleasant lounge and meeting and banquet space (ideal for weddings). Seasonal hotel packages include breakfast or dinner in the award-winning ocean-view restaurant. Dinner entrees are moderately priced and deliciously prepared; same goes for early-bird dinner specials. There is a nice variety of beef, pork, fish and poultry offerings served by a friendly and efficient wait staff. This family-owned resort also welcomes canine companions.

EARTHWORKS GALLERY

2222 Hwy 101 N   541/547-4300
Daily   gocybervision.com/earthwork

Upwards of 150 Northwest artists are represented at this gallery and the sister location in Newport (859 SW Bay

Boulevard, 541/574-0802). Various fine-art pieces, sculpture, glass, baskets, clay, watercolors, jewelry and other selections are attractively arranged.

GREEN SALMON COFFEE AND TEA HOUSE

220 Hwy 101 N   541/547-3077
Tues-Sun   thegreensalmon.com

Next time you're in Yachats, skip the mini-mart coffee pot and instead indulge in a cup of wonderful custom-roasted coffee. If coffee is not your cup of tea, do opt for a pot of tea from the selection of teas and infusions. Fair trade and organic beans (eight seasonal selections) and teas (over 30 varieties) are sold in the retail store. Add a bit of sustenance with homemade breakfast pastries, scones and savories, hearty and delicious panini sandwiches or a smoothie, espresso or mocha drink. They also have magazines and books to buy or borrow from the locally-run book exchange.

HECETA HEAD LIGHTHOUSE BED & BREAKFAST

92072 Hwy 101 S   866/547-3696
Moderate to expensive   hecetalighthouse.com

Another unique Oregon experience awaits at one of the last remaining lighthouse keeper's cottages on the Pacific Coast. This year-round bed and breakfast has a capacity for 15; four rooms have private bathrooms and two rooms share a bathroom. The cottage has been restored to its original look and appointed with warm down comforters, antique furnishings and a fully-equipped guest kitchen. A nighttime view of the lighthouse is memorable, as is the seven-course gourmet breakfast prepared by innkeeper **Steven Bursey** and his highly-trained staff. Built about 1894, the lighthouse is one of the historic highlights of our state and one of the best-preserved lighthouses anywhere; a full renovation of the lighthouse is nearing completion.

PHOTO BY FRANK STERRETT, FORMER CHIEF OF PHOTOGRAPHY FOR *THE OREGONIAN*

Born Billy Gable in Ohio, the lanky young man later known as **Clark Gable** arrived in Oregon at age 21. He worked as a logger in Bend, sold neckties at Meier & Frank in Portland and acted with a troupe in Astoria before finally making it to Hollywood at age 23. (1938)

Portland's Great Flood of 1894. Row boats navigated Meier & Frank's store aisles.

STELLA VANE and BUCKLEY VEDIE · CHAMPION HEAVY HARNESS HORSES

Postcard from the Aaron M. Frank Farms stable showing Stella Vane and Buckley Vedie, world champion heavy harness show horses.

Aaron Frank addressing approximately 3,500 employees of the **Meier & Frank** store in Portland. An entire floor was cleared during the holiday season to serve a turkey dinner for all company co-workers. (circa 1952)

Aaron Frank, **Dick Frank** and Gerry Frank at groundbreaking of the Salem Meier & Frank store in 1953.

The first disaster wagon in the nation was built in Portland, Oregon, and donated to the city fire department by my father on March 15, 1939. Named after former Portland Fire Marshall **Jay W. Stevens,** the original wagon served as a mobile first aid station with apparatus far ahead of its time. Some 1,600 separate pieces of equipment from a completely-furnished operating table to multiple life-saving devices, advanced communication gear, movie camera, snowshoes and many other innovations filled the life-saving bus. A few years ago, the original wagon was located in Indiana, which instigated a serious exploratory effort to bring the historic vehicle back to its home city.

Rodeo performer, trick roper and actor **Montie Montana** made an appearance inside Meier & Frank's Portland store and rode an elevator to the 12th floor. (1955)

Meier & Frank, early store in Portland. (circa 1870-1880)

Former Portland **Rabbi Jonah Wise** and **"Aunt Rosie" White**. Who was "Aunt Rosie" White? One of the great ladies of early Portland, she lived more than a century ago in the City of Roses, most of it in a Benson Hotel suite. She played a mean game of poker with Oregon's powers-that-be of the day. She took a three-mile walk every morning with her companion, faithfully followed by her chauffeur who was at their service at the end of the walk to carry on with the day; during the walks she included mental exercise by reviewing memorized definitions of words she had read the day before in books, local newspapers and crossword puzzles. Even though slot machines were illegal, an Oregon official sent her one (at her request) for her personal use — a favorite pastime! She just happened to be my great-great aunt. Despite our family relationship, her familial title was used by many Portlanders.

The Frank family spent summers in **Garden Home**, eventually residing full time in the mid-1950s. My father built the house in the 1920s. The estate included a guest house, swimming pool and pool house, horse track and magnificent stables. The location was chosen for its proximity to the Oregon Electric railroad line where horses could be loaded and unloaded—what a sight and experience that was! Once an avid horseman, he lost interest after two tragedies in the 1930s. The first was a stable fire in Oakland, California, which claimed the lives of a number of his horses he was showing, followed that same year by an East Coast train wreck transporting the remaining horses to Madison Square Garden for a horse show in New York City. The stables were carpeted, immaculate and heated; nothing but the best for his pride and joys. Wondrous social events, successful charity fundraisers and years of memorable outings and celebrations enticed folks out to the location. For many years food was prepared in **Meier & Frank**'s downtown kitchen and was delivered by a caravan out to the parties, about an hour's drive in those days. Gone are those glory times; my dad's stables and my mother's beautiful gardens are now indelible memories. The property changed hands in the 1960s; now townhouses occupy portions of the land. Still standing sentinel are the original house, swimming pool, guest house and garage. An open area is a reminder of where horses were trained, ribbons were won and my formative years were spent happily riding my horse, Patsy.

My great uncle **Julius L. Meier** (1874-1937), Oregon's only Independent governor (1931-1935). He won election garnering more votes than the Republican and Democrat candidates combined. (photo circa 1880)

R.R. "Rube" Adams and wife Von Adams was a Portland legend in the merchandising and philanthropic fields. Von was Portland's #1 fashion model. Florist Tommy Lake looks on. (1952)

Aftermath of the 1959 explosion that rocked downtown Roseburg.

Rooftop fashion show and dance for area young people at Salem's Meier & Frank store. (1960)

Gerry Frank proudly displaying two of his scrumptious cakes outside **Gerry Frank's Konditorei**, his Salem cake shop and restaurant. (circa 1990)

Left to right: **Murray Kemp** (US Coast Guard), **David Eccles** (War Bond staff), **Forrest Berg** (Chas. F. Berg Inc.), **Paul Dick** (President, U.S. National Bank), **E.B. MacNaughton** (First National Bank), **Aaron Frank** (Meier & Frank) and **E.C. Sammons** (Chairman, Oregon War Bond Staff). Oregon set a record for bond sales in WWII, as did the Meier & Frank store. (1948)

Chester W. Nimitz, Fleet Admiral, USN, aboard the USS Missouri, Tokyo Bay, September 2, 1945 signing a document on the occasion of the Japanese Surrender.

Who was one of the most influential Oregon citizens of the last century? It was certainly **Glenn Jackson**: power company CEO, newspaper chain entrepreneur, rancher, former Air Force general, head of the Oregon Transportation Commission, friend and advisor to every governor of his time and much more. His genius? He was a conciliator, bringing divergent sides together to get things done for the greater good. He was unselfish, generous, an unforgettable character who sat at his desk (always with a pipe in his mouth) with his speaker phone on, holding court with leaders from throughout the state. He was a "second father" to me. (1962)

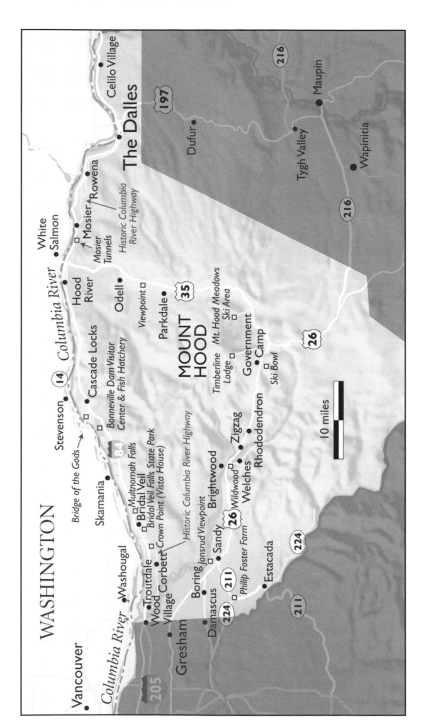

4. Columbia Gorge and Mt. Hood

MULTNOMAH FALLS
50000 Historic Columbia River Hwy   503/695-2372
Visitors Center: Daily: 9-5

MULTNOMAH FALLS LODGE DINING ROOM
Breakfast, Lunch, Dinner: Daily   503/695-2376
Moderate (breakfast, lunch); Expensive (dinner)   multnomahfallslodge.com

Multnomah Falls is Oregon's number-one visited natural attraction, a stunning site at any time of the year from below the falls, atop the trail or from the lodge. It is Oregon's tallest cataract and the second-highest year-round waterfall in the nation. **Simon Benson** donated the land and funding which led to the construction of the famed Benson Bridge; his magnanimous gesture led other private and public entities to join the project. The park was dedicated in 1915 and the lodge was completed in 1925. **Albert E. Doyle** (architect for the **Meier & Frank Co.** building in downtown Portland) designed the impressive stone and timber building, now home to a visitors center, snack and gift shops and a wonderful dining room. The cuisine is Northwest-inspired with fresh local ingredients and ideal for a romantic dinner for two or powering the body before or after hikes along the trail.

CASCADE LOCKS

BONNEVILLE FISH HATCHERY

70543 NE Herman Loop   541/374-8393
Mid-March to Oct: Daily: 7 a.m. -8 p.m.; Nov to Mid-March: Daily: 7-5
Free   dfw.state.or.us/resources/visitors/bonneville_hatchery.asp

The main attraction at this Columbia River hatchery at the mouth of Tanner Creek is **Herman the Sturgeon**. Herman is approaching his 75th birthday and packs 475 pounds onto his 11-foot boneless frame. The sturgeon interpretive center offers informational displays and sturgeon viewing. Guests may also walk to the rainbow trout ponds where they will see trophy-size trout, a visitor center for the spawning room and the historic incubation building. The Hatchery rears Chinook, Coho and Tule salmon and steelhead. An added bonus to a warm-weather picnic is observing birds of prey, songbirds, wading birds and waterfowl.

COLUMBIA GORGE STERNWHEELER

Cascade Locks Marine Park   503/224-3900, 800/224-3901
Seasonal days and times   portlandspirit.com
Expensive

Board this authentic triple-decker paddle wheeler for a memorable sightseeing excursion on the mighty Columbia. There

FRUITY TOOTY

Toot your horn in the heart of Oregon's most famous fruit orchards and accompanying scenic wonderland as you drive the official Fruit Loop (hoodriverfruitloop.com). It's about a 35-mile round-trip experience through hill and dale, forest and farmland, all with the iconic Cascade Mountains serving as a backdrop. The sheer beauty of this landscape is enough to make anyone catch their breath! There's something happening on the route most of the year with fruit stands, vineyard offerings, tours and various activities.

are a number of cruise options (two hours to a half-day) to appreciate the natural beauty and historic points of interest along this section of the Columbia Gorge. On board, enjoy Northwest cuisine.

CORBETT

VISTA HOUSE
Crown Point, 40700 E Historic Columbia River Hwy   503/695-2240
Nov-March: Sat, Sun: 10-4 (weather permitting);   oregonstateparks.org
April-Oct: Daily: 9-6

All adjectives synonymous with "magnificent" apply to the Columbia Gorge. If you drive the Historic Columbia River Highway, it takes you to the doorstep of the Vista House. Completed in 1917, this octagonal, cliff-top viewpoint was created as a comfort station. These were not just any facilities; the restrooms were outfitted in elegant marble and mahogany and continue in use today (follow the circular marble stairways to the lower level). An extensive restoration that culminated in 2006 brought this gem back to grandeur and now houses interpretive displays of this region's rich history, a gift shop and espresso cafe. The panoramic scene is among the most magnificent anywhere. The wind has been known to blow here; hang on to your hat!

GOVERNMENT CAMP

COLLINS LAKE RESORT
88149 E Creek Ridge Road   800/234-6288
Moderate and up   collinslakeresort.com

Open all year and geared for the outdoors, this resort is touted as providing luxury Chalets (4 to 10 people) and Grand Lodges (2 or 3 bedroom). **Mt. Hood Skibowl** owner, **Kirk Hanna**, is behind the master plan for this 28-acre parcel surrounded by the Mt. Hood National Forest. Snowmobiling, snowshoeing, cross-country skiing, sleigh rides, tubing and sledding are at your winter doorstep. Depart your basecamp via car to Summit or Meadows (or shuttle to Skibowl and Timberline), then enjoy the hot tub, heated pool or sauna — or simply cozy up to the fireplace on your return.   When the snow melts, guests may opt to explore the network of interpretive trails eventually leading to the village. Guests receive VIP discounts for outdoor recreation including three major ski areas and the **Mt. Hood Adventure Park** at Skibowl.

HUCKLEBERRY INN

88611 E Government Camp Loop   503/272-3325
Daily: 24 hours   huckleberry-inn.com
Cafe: Inexpensive to moderate
Lodging: Moderate

No matter the time of day, the Huckleberry Inn is open! Huckleberry hotcakes for dinner or at midnight? No problem, the full menu is served all day. Since 1966 this family-owned and operated restaurant has been a welcoming stop for folks looking for family-friendly dining in Government Camp. On ski season and holiday weekends the Huckleberry Inn opens its cozy, candlelit steakhouse with a steak and seafood menu. Fuel up for outdoor activities with a giant maple bar or fresh doughnut; better yet, treat yourself to a refreshing huckleberry milkshake or a slice of delicious homemade huckleberry pie, a la mode, of course. On-premise lodging includes 17 standard and deluxe rooms and a two-bedroom suite with a kitchen and bunk room (sleeps 14).

MT. HOOD SKIBOWL

87000 E Hwy 26   503/272-3206
Seasonal   skibowl.com
Fees vary by activity

Good family fun can be found on a visit to one of Oregon's best year-round resorts. Almost 1,000 acres of snow-covered topography affords alpine skiing (including the largest night-skiing terrain in the country), snowboarding, snowshoeing, cross-country skiing, sleigh rides, snowmobiling, day and cosmic tubing plus much more. Return in the summer to experience the **Mt. Hood Adventure Park** when it comes to life with over 20 mild to extreme attractions for all ages, including the alpine slide, scenic sky chair, bungee tower, zip line, Indy carts, batting cages, rock climbing wall, miniature and disc golf and mountain biking. The casual eateries offer welcome and satisfying breathers. This place is awesome any time of the year.

KIDS' ACTIVITIES: COLUMBIA RIVER GORGE AND MT. HOOD

Bridal Veil
Multnomah Falls (503/695-2372, oregon.com/attractions/multnomah_falls)

Cascade Locks
Bonneville Lock & Dam (541/374-8820, nwp.usace.army.mil/locations/bonneville.asp)
Sternwheeler Columbia Gorge (541/374-8427, portofcascadelocks.org/sternwheeler.htm): seasonal

Corbett
Vista House at Crown Point (503/695-2230, vistahouse.com)

Government Camp
Mt. Hood Skibowl & Adventure Park (503/272-3206, skibowl.com)

Hood River
Hood River WaterPlay (541/386-9463, hoodriverwaterplay.com)
Mt. Hood Railroad (541/386-3556, mthoodrr.com)

The Dalles
Columbia Gorge Discovery Center (541/296-8600, gorgediscovery.org)

Timberline Lodge
Timberline Lodge (503/272-3311, timberlinelodge.com)

RATSKELLER ALPINE BAR AND PIZZERIA

88335 E Government Camp Loop   503/272-3635
Mon-Thurs: 2-midnight; Fri-Sun: 11 a.m.-2 a.m.   ratskellerpizzeria.com
Moderate

Here's another winning combination on the mountain: a huge 13' projection screen, big beer and wine selections and super pizzas. Highly recommended dishes include the Original Rat pizza (pepperoni, Italian sausage and salami), beer-battered onion rings and classic burgers; or build your own pizzas and calzones. Satisfying food and beverages are served in the lounge, fireside in winter, outdoors in good weather and in the family-friendly section where kids are always welcome. General Manager **Tony Toupin** makes sure his fun-loving staff gives superior service.

HOOD RIVER

APPLE VALLEY COUNTRY STORE

2363 Tucker Road   541/386-1971
March-May: Sat, Sun; June-Oct: Daily   applevalleystore.com

For a taste of Oregon's world-famous fruit, make a trip to this small store. Start with a thick milkshake and wander the store to choose among jams, jellies, butters, syrups, sauces, pie fillings, mustards and mixes; sugar-free options are also available. Scratch pies are a mainstay, and don't forget to add Tillamook ice cream on top. Further up the road in Parkdale is **Apple Valley BBQ Restaurant and Catering** (4956 Baseline Drive, 541/352-3554) where the moderately priced specialties are smoked pork ribs, pulled pork and prime rib dinners on Friday and Saturday. Hours are 11 to 8, Wednesday through Sunday. The meats are smoked with local fruit woods, complemented by side dishes of pear cole slaw and apple-cider baked beans.

CELILO RESTAURANT AND BAR

16 Oak St   541/386-5710
Lunch, Dinner: Daily   celilorestaurant.com
Moderate

Local, organic and sustainable are the by-words at contemporary Celilo where great healthy foods are crafted. From the regularly changing menu, a bowl of housemade soup or hazelnut and blue cheese salad are tasty starters for lunch or dinner. A varied selection of lunchtime sandwiches is accompanied by organic mixed greens or fries. For dinner, beef, fish, pasta, poultry and pork options are expertly and creatively prepared to showcase the regional bounty; occasional wine dinners masterfully pair outstanding Northwest wines with Celilo's best menus. For dessert, local fruits are superb in delicious sorbets, tarts and cakes or you may prefer a cheese course with regional touches. Busy Chef **Ben Stenn** also conducts popular cooking classes.

COLUMBIA CLIFF VILLAS

3880 Westcliff Dr
Moderate and up

866/912-8366
columbiacliffvillas.com

A stay here yields ultra-comfortable digs and magnificent river and mountain views. Thirty-seven luxury rooms and suites rest above a 208-foot waterfall. Accommodations in this condominium hotel incorporate everything from European-style hotel rooms up to one- and three-bedroom adjoining villa and penthouse suites. Amenities vary by room and may include private decks (some look straight down the cliffs to the Columbia River), gas fireplaces, marble and tile walk-in showers, soaking tubs and gourmet kitchens. The layout and fabulous setting are perfect for retreats, romantic getaways and family gatherings.

COLUMBIA GORGE HOTEL

4000 Westcliff Dr
Moderate to expensive

541/386-5566, 800/345-1921
columbiagorgehotel.com

SIMON'S CLIFF HOUSE

Breakfast, Lunch, Dinner: Daily; Brunch: Sun
Expensive (dinner); Moderate (brunch)

The opulent Columbia Gorge Hotel opened in 1904 as a haven for guests traveling by steamboat. Highway promoter **Simon Benson** purchased the hotel in 1920 with dreams of grandeur to reward motorists journeying along the Columbia Gorge Scenic Highway. The hotel was home away from home to such distinguished guests as presidents **Franklin Roosevelt** and **Calvin Coolidge** and film legends **Myrna Loy**, **Jane Powell** and **Rudolph Valentino**. Through the years it fell in and out of prosperity, at one time functioning as a retirement home. Fortunately, a major restoration project propelled the hotel back to its stately beauty. There are 39 luxurious guest rooms furnished with either brass or canopy beds, all with views of the Gorge or vibrant manicured gardens. It is truly a romantic, restful destination.

Diners at **Simon's** have much to enjoy — starting with the magnificent view. Breakfast would not be complete without one of the pastry chef's special scones drizzled with "honey from the sky" (the practiced wait staff delights diners with high-dripping honey), although there are plenty of other breakfast choices. Soups, salads and hot or cold specialty sandwiches make a fine lunch, especially when served with the house potato chips. Dinner starts with housemade squaw bread, while leisurely enjoying appetizers and gourmet entrees fit for screen legends. The pièce de résistance is the Farmers Brunch; seven-courses beginning with champagne, progressing through a granola and yogurt parfait, scone, seasonal fruit, an assortment of cheeses, a choice of chef's entrees and culminating with coffee, pastries and petit desserts.

FULL SAIL BREWING

506 Columbia St   541/386-2247
Lunch, Dinner: Daily   fullsailbrewing.com
Moderate

In a building that formerly housed the Diamond Fruit Company, Full Sail Brewing operates a brewery, tasting room and pub. The cannery is gone, but the site is still bustling with dozens of skilled brewery specialists working full speed ahead at this independent, employee-owned enterprise crafting award-winning beers. Free brewery tours are conducted each afternoon between 1 and 4 with much-anticipated samples in the tasting room and pub after the tour. Brewery products are pleasingly used in the bill of fare: a lager-battered cod sandwich and stout-braised pork shoulder with Amber Ale barbecue sauce are served all day. Interesting sweet-tooth tamers are the Imperial Stout brownies and ice cream and Session Black Lager floats. The panorama from the roof-top deck across the Columbia to the Washington side of the Gorge is awesome, making this a great stop to unwind and savor brews and views.

THE GORGE WHITE HOUSE

2265 Hwy 35   541/386-2828
April-Oct: Seasonal hours   thegorgewhitehouse.com

Once a private residence and still surrounded by orchards, this Dutch Colonial Revival landmark offers five acres of cut

On the Washington side of the Columbia

The natural **Bonneville Hot Springs Resort & Spa** (bonnevilleresort.com) is just minutes up the Gorge from Portland. The geothermal water was originally enjoyed by Native Americans for medicinal purposes; today you can take advantage of the same healing and relaxing properties in the upscale spa and lodge facility; add hiking, biking, windsurfing or play a round on the minigolf course; on-site fine dining won't disappoint.

Joining iconic Oregon destination resorts such as Salishan and Sunriver, **Skamania Lodge** (866/399-7980, skamania. com) is another feather in developer **John Gray**'s cap. Just across the Bridge of the Gods at Cascade Locks, Skamania is a hop, skip and jump from Bonneville and offers river and mountain views, golf, horseback riding, spa and valuable R&R time away from it all. A recent makeover coincided with the lodge's 20th anniversary, updating the 254 Cascadian-style rooms. The Cascade Dining Room is a favorite special-occasion and brunch destination.

As you make your way farther east (from I-84, cross the Sam Hill Memorial Bridge at Biggs Junction), **Maryhill Winery** (maryhillwinery.com) and the **Maryhill Museum of Art** (maryhillmuseum.org) — and the Stonehenge memorial associated with the museum — are worth your time. **Samuel Hill** originally built the museum structure as his grand home and named it Maryhill after his wife, Mary; Hill built the Stonehenge replica as a monument to heroism and peace, honoring WWI servicemen of Klickitat County, Washington. The Columbia Gorge Highway, known now as I-84, is attributed to Hill's advocacy to "build a great highway so that the world can realize the magnificence and grandeur of the Columbia River Gorge." **Vicki and Craig Leuthold** established the Maryhill Winery in 1999, now a destination for fine wines, picnicking and world-class summertime concerts in the 4,000-seat amphitheater.

flower fields (picked or u-pick), gourmet foods, wine tastings, fresh fruits and vegetables, gifts, artwork and more. The converted original shop building houses the attractively displayed farmstand. Since **Camille Hukari**'s grandparents purchased the home in the 1940s, she spent a lot of time here. Now she and her husband, **Jerry Tausend**, are owners and hosts of this century-old, 31-acre working farm and tend to berry fields, grapes and an abundant orchard. It is a super special-occasion venue for reunions, weddings and such, especially with Mt. Hood and fields of flowers abloom in the background. Complete tours of the home are offered on Memorial Day and Labor Day weekends.

INN AT THE GORGE

1113 Eugene St   541/386-4429, 877/852-2385
Moderate   innatthegorge.com

Built in 1908, this Victorian beauty now functions as a comfortable bed and breakfast with five tastefully appointed rooms, all with private baths; one room has a secret passageway to the attic. Rates include a full breakfast served by innkeepers **Michele and Frank Bouche**, who use fresh, local produce in delicious, eye-appealing meals. In warm months, guests may take breakfast on the generous wraparound porch. If skiing at Mt. Hood Meadows is your destination, ask about discounted lift tickets. Three suites are equipped with kitchenettes and a separate bedroom; ideal for longer stays.

MOUNT HOOD RAILROAD

110 Railroad Ave   541/386-3556, 800/872-4661
Seasonal   mthoodrr.com
Expensive

All aboard for a fun and scenic ride! For more than 100 years this train has chugged through the picturesque Hood River Valley. Depending on the season, rail excursions depart from the Mount Hood Railroad depot for Parkdale near the base of Mt. Hood. Popular special events include murder mystery dinners, wine trains and a re-enacted train robbery. Especially for kids, the Polar Express heads to the "North Pole" in November and December. Food and beverages are available on all trips.

NORA'S TABLE

110 5th St   541/387-4000
Dinner: Nov-March: Tues-Sat; April-Oct: Daily   norastable.com
Expensive

Nora's Table offers small plates and main courses from the passionate cuisines of Italy, India, Mexico, Morocco and Spain and a Gorge-only wine and beer list. Whenever possible, the menu is based on produce from local farms and natural meats from nearby **Mountain Shadow Natural Meats**. The seasonal nosh plate provides a sample of many of these superb flavors: housemade beer crackers and pickles, brandied Teleme cheese and tomato chutney. Entrees may feature beef, fish, duck or lamb paired with curry, seasonal fresh vegetables and tantalizing sauces. Chef **Kathy Watson** prepares a five-course tasting menu for mid-week diners.

THE PINES TASTING ROOM

202 State St   541/993-8301
Wed, Sat, Sun: noon-7; Thurs, Fri: noon-10
(daily: Memorial Day to Sept)   thepinesvineyard.com

THE PINES COTTAGE

5450 Mill Creek Rd, The Dalles   541/993-8301

Boutique wines from **The Pines Vineyard** in The Dalles are offered in this tasting room and gallery where regional artists are featured under the watchful eye of art director **John Roz**. This winner is a great spot to while away an enjoyable afternoon or evening. The vineyard was originally planted by an Italian immigrant and has consistently yielded high-quality wine grapes. In 1982 the estate was revitalized and expanded and now accommodates overnight guests at The Pines Cottage. There are three bedrooms and a shared bath, kitchen and living areas; rent individual bedrooms or the entire cottage for your weekend getaway in the peaceful vineyard.

RASMUSSEN FARMS

3020 Thomsen Rd   541/386-4622
Mid-April to Mid-Dec: Seasonal hours   rasmussenfarms.com

Here is another good locale where you'll find plentiful quantities of local produce and flowers. **Dollie and Lynn**

Rasmussen operated their 20-acre farm for 65 years. Today **Julie and Patrick Milling** are lessees, running the place in the same family spirit. Luscious strawberries mark the beginning of the fresh fruit and vegetable season with plenty of special events as the seasons change. Sample pleasing temptations of preserves and other products before you buy. Autumn's Pumpkin Funland is very popular, especially the corn maze and pumpkin bowling. From their greenhouse, accent plants are available throughout the year and gorgeous hanging baskets in a full spectrum of varieties and colors are a summer specialty.

SILVERADO JEWELRY GALLERY

310 Oak St   541/386-7069
Mon-Sat: 10-6; Sun: 11-5   silveradogallery.com

In this inviting gallery you'll find wonderful pieces from nearly 100 artisans, including outstanding local talent. Designs are traditional and contemporary, casual and elegant and are handcrafted using gems, jewels, pearls and turquoise. Their aim is to provide customers the best and most exclusive handmade jewelry; by the looks of the colorful eye candy, I'd agree. It's a great place to buy a gift or indulge yourself.

STONEHEDGE GARDENS

3405 Cascade Ave   541/386-3940
Dinner: Daily (closed Mon in winter)   stonehedgeweddings.com
Expensive

This charming dinner house is situated on six acres of spectacular gardens and terraces at the end of a short gravel road. A fireplace, cozy tables and wood-paneled walls create a romantic setting indoors. The alfresco site is a popular wedding venue; the ceremonial area is cleverly framed with heart-shaped shrubbery. **Mike and Shawna Caldwell**'s gourmet menu features delicious specials such as authentic French onion soup, halibut and rack of lamb. Regular menu offerings include such tempting plates as a garlic mushroom dish, Thai-style crab cakes, spicy peanut chicken, steak Diane, wild salmon and pork scaloppini. Gluten-free gourmet entrees, housemade dinner rolls, stocks and sauces are another specialty. For dessert, try the flaming bread pudding topped with crème brûlée and served tableside.

HAVEN

Governor **Julius Meier** (my uncle) prized his **Menucha** (menucha.org; pronounced one of two ways: men-i-Sha or men-oo-Ka) summer home that still overlooks the Columbia River Gorge, now serving as a retreat center. Often visitors came to see Uncle Julius here. With a "peephole" in his private bathroom medicine cabinet, he looked into the living area at waiting guests to see if he wanted to receive them — or not! The opening is still there.

WESTERN ANTIQUE AEROPLANE & AUTOMOBILE MUSEUM

Ken Jernstedt Airfield
1600 Air Museum Road   541/308-1600
Daily: 9-5   waaamuseum.org
Reasonable

One of the largest collections of flying antique airplanes and operating antique automobiles in the country is housed in this fascinating museum. The museum showcases over 200 operable planes, cars, motorcycles, military jeeps and tractors. Volunteers are always tinkering on engines, polishing chrome and ensuring that the collection is in functioning order. For added enjoyment, plan a visit on the second Saturday of the month when proud drivers take the antique cars out for a spin (weather permitting) offering rides between 10:30 a.m. and 2 p.m. Allow plenty of time to partake in the monthly cookout and view the demonstrations.

MOSIER

10-SPEED EAST COFFEE HOUSE

1104 1st Ave   541/478-2104
Mon-Fri: 6:30-4; Sat, Sun: 7:30 a.m.-8 p.m.   10-speedcoffee.com
Inexpensive

When you're in need of a coffee (or more) pit stop along I-84, 10-Speed will hit the spot. Motorists and bicyclists fuel up on French-pressed coffee, artistically crafted espresso drinks, signature coffee drinks and organic tea, as well as organic juices and fruit smoothies. The cafe menu includes good-for-you organic sandwiches for breakfast or lunch, salads, wraps and freshly-baked pastries each morning. Take a few moments to appreciate the changing works of art. 10-Speed's small-batch roastery is in Hood River (1412 13th St, 541/386-3165).

THIRSTY WOMAN PUB
206 Main St

THE LITTLE WOMAN   541/490-2022
Dinner: Daily

THE BIG WOMAN   541/478-0199
Dinner: Wed-Sat; Brunch: Sun
Moderate   thirstywoman.com

In the tiny burg of Mosier are two side-by-side enterprises that make up the Thirsty Woman Pub. Little Woman operates from the renovated circa-1928 YWCA building; Big Woman is next door in a transformed home. If it is Sunday, the bonus is the brunch served from the Big Woman location. Confused? The enterprise is eclectic; to say the least — which makes it fun. The food is good and varies from pub grub to bordering on gourmet, the people are friendly, the setting is a treat and Wi-Fi is free.

Remember when?

Old-time, now defunct, restaurants played an important part in Oregon family histories:

• Baker's (now Baker City) **Blue and White Cafe** was famous for its forever 10-cent coffee and comfort food.

• Corvallis hosted **The Gables** for many years; the intimate atmosphere and excellent food made it a must-visit for generations of Oregonians.

• I always enjoyed the **Yankee Pot Roast** in Grants Pass; how difficult it is to find a place that serves this dish in its true form today!

• The **Pixie Kitchen** in Lincoln City was a much anticipated stopping place for youngsters and families; an added feature of the establishment was the **Pixieland Amusement Park**.

• The **Eastside Cafe** in Ontario was a popular place for meetings in Eastern Oregon, with the best Chinese food in the area.

• The best known fine-dining establishment in Pendleton, **Raphael's**, recently become history; many a great meal was enjoyed at this popular cowboy-country favorite.

• Longtime Portlanders will remember growing up with two eastside drive-ins, both famous for their juicy burgers and attractive carhops: **Yaw's Top Notch** and the **Tik Tok**. Two restaurants on Broadway in old-time Portland were named after their well-known owners: Larry Hilaire (**Hilaire's**) and Elston Ireland (**Ireland's**). A footnote: in Gold Beach, **Ireland's Rustic Cottages** (still open) served delicious plated meals brought to individual cabins where lucky diners ate by the fireplace (no connection to the Portland restaurant). Alas, the always crowded **Tea Room** at the downtown **Meier & Frank** store is long gone; the white-tablecloth dining room at the historic **Portland Hotel** was a special occasion place. A longtime favorite were the German pancakes dished up at **Henry Thiele's** at 23rd and Burnside. And who could forget the fabulous barbecued beef sandwiches (15 cents) at the downtown **Pit Barbecue**?

• The aroma and tastes at **The Barbeque Pit** in Salem are memorable, and so are evenings spent at **Morton's** in West Salem.

• On the way to the north Oregon Coast, the **Crab Broiler** was a very popular establishment, now a sad looking abandoned building, at the junction of Highways 26 and 101 near Seaside. Families stopped in for fresh crab and hear news of who they would see at the beach.

• A longtime favorite in Yachats, **Le Serre**, was an excellent eatery, with its hanging baskets and fabulous warm brie a cozy stop on a blustery Oregon Coast evening.

MT. HOOD

MT. HOOD MEADOWS
14040 Hwy 35   503/337-2222
Seasonal   skihood.com

Locals call it "Meadows;" the premier ski area on the mountain, with 2,777 vertical feet, 2,150 skiable acres, 11 lifts and the widest variety of skiing for all abilities from beginner to expert. When conditions cooperate, powder hounds will appreciate Heather Canyon, which can offer wonderful deep-powder experiences. The location on the southeast flank of the mountain is sunnier and more wind-protected than the south-facing slope, resulting in broader and more diverse downhill opportunities. As a day area so close to Portland (90 driving minutes away), weekends and school vacations can bring huge crowds; consider a mid-week visit. Energizing and delicious dining options in the South and North lodges include sit-down service at the **Alpenstube Restaurant** and **Vertical Restaurant and Sports Bar** and two quick, casual eateries. On the slopes, **Mazot** serves bistro fare at 6,000 feet and utterly awe-inspiring views. Additional services incorporate ski and snowboard schools and Nordic and demo centers. My older cousin, **Bill Rosenfeld**, was one of the

LOOK OUT BELOW!

Former U.S. Forest Service fire lookouts are available for seasonal (and low-budget) campouts. Amenities (bathrooms, cooking facilities, running water) vary by location. Here's a sampling for out-of-the-ordinary experiences (recreation. gov):

Flag Point Fire Lookout, Mt. Hood

Fivemile Butte Lookout, Mt. Hood

Quail Prairie Lookout, Kalmiopsis Wilderness in the Klamath Mountains

Green Ridge Lookout, Deschutes National Forest

Cold Springs Guard Station, Ochoco National Forest

original founders of Meadows. Now in his mid-90s, he frequently skis here. Perhaps you'll share a chair on the lift with him; if so, ask about the history, skiing and weather patterns on Mt. Hood — fascinating!

PARKDALE

OLD PARKDALE INN BED & BREAKFAST

4932 Baseline Road   541/352-5551
Moderate   hoodriverlodging.com

Three guest rooms are artistically decorated with Gauguin, Monet and O'Keeffe motifs; the latter two are suites with separate living rooms. All are equipped with flat-screen televisions, microwaves and refrigerators, access to Internet and a guest laptop and plush bathrobes. Breakfasts feature famous Hood River fruits and produce, served in the dining room or delivered to your room. The deck or picturesque gardens make tranquil morning coffee venues. The innkeepers have created several packages ranging from romantic seclusion to whitewater rafting and other local activities.

RHODODENDRON

A MAJESTIC MOUNTAIN RETREAT

Lolo Pass Road   503/686-8080
Expensive and up   amajesticmountainretreat.com

It is not a surprise that this secluded three-story log home was voted "Best cabin in the Northwest." All the creature comforts are here: plush towels and robes, 600 thread-count bed linens, a game room, fully-equipped kitchen (serving up to 24 people), dining and sitting area, individual iPod systems in each room, hot tub and a handcrafted two-story wood-burning fireplace. Owner **Becca Niday**'s handmade chocolate truffles are to die for! Two luxurious master king suites with en suite bathrooms and two queen bedrooms (one with a bunk bed, too) are strategically arranged in the home for maximum privacy. Mt. Hood, restaurants and year-round outdoor activities are only minutes away. (The exact address will be given upon reserving the retreat.)

ZIGZAG MOUNTAIN STORE & CAFE

70171 E Hwy 26   503/622-7684
Sun-Fri: 7-7; Sat: 7 a.m.-8 p.m.
Inexpensive

If you are in need of supplies in the Mt. Hood area, head for the Zigzag Mountain Store where you can complete your grocery and clothing list and enjoy a meal, too. The cafe cooks up feel-good favorites at breakfast, lunch and dinner with seating on the mezzanine or at tables overlooking the forest and creek. Cozy up to the stone fireplace with homemade bakery items and hot cocoa, or enjoy mac and cheese, beef stew, chicken-fried steak and always-popular pizza. Boysenberry cobbler with ice cream is a year-round temptation.

SANDY

THE HIDDEN WOODS BED & BREAKFAST

19380 E Summertime Dr   503/622-5754
Moderate   thehiddenwoods.com

Spend a memorable night or longer in a private two-bedroom log cabin with rustic charm and modern conveniences. The setting (ten miles east of Sandy) sets the mood for relaxation: beautiful gardens to stroll through, a trail to the nearby Sandy River, a contemplative trout pond and a deck with a hot tub and fire pit. Come evening, hunker down and unwind in front of the living room's rock fireplace and prepare your favorite dinner or snacks in the well-appointed kitchen. A splendid breakfast is served in the hosts' log home, a short walk from the guest cabin. (Cash or checks only; no children under eight years of age; no pets.)

JOE'S DONUT SHOP

39230 Pioneer Blvd   503/668-7215
Mon-Fri: 4 a.m.-5 p.m.; Sat, Sun: 5-5   joes-donuts.com
Inexpensive

Mmmm, doughnuts! On the way up to the mountain, stop in at this old-time hangout for a bracing cup of coffee to accompany the freshest apple fritters, maple bars and scrumptious doughnuts (the same doughnut production technology since 1974). Weekend customers often find

KABOOM!

When Mt. St. Helens erupted on May 18, 1980, your author and Senator **Mark Hatfield** were on a plane between Portland and Spokane. The view of the event and its aftermath went from spectacular to very gray; that aside, the problem was getting the senator, who was in Spokane for a college commencement speech, and me, out of the city. The volcanic ash brought transportation operations to a standstill, yet it was imperative that the senator be in Washington, D.C. the next day for an important hearing. To solve this vexing problem, I cajoled a taxi driver to take us (complete with masks and extra car filters) to Seattle to catch a plane. The tab (not paid by the government) was $415; I can only imagine what that trip might cost today!

themselves choosing from baked pastries like strudels, filled croissants, Danish and turnovers. Look for the recognizable red and white block front building, a local landmark.

SANDY SALMON BED & BREAKFAST LODGE

61661 E Hwy 26   503/622-6699
Expensive   sandysalmon.com

This 6,000-square-foot log building sits on a bluff some 60 feet above the confluence of the Sandy and Salmon rivers. Choose from four guest rooms with private bathrooms, including one with a Jacuzzi tub that could serve as a romantic bridal suite; some suites have outdoor decks, all feature native Oregon woods. The beautiful lodge hideaway also offers hearty breakfasts and plenty of recreation, including games around the comfortable stone fireplace, a theater room with a large 73-inch projection screen and a handcrafted pool table. Artistic wood carvings, a koi pond, waterfall and massive antler chandelier augment the interior of the lodge's ambience. The vistas around this five-acre setting are breathtaking and enjoyed from the relaxing decks or while fishing, rafting, hiking, mountain biking and skiing — all nearby.

TOLLGATE INN

38100 Hwy 26   503/668-8456
Breakfast, Lunch, Dinner: Daily
Moderate

For many Mt. Hood travelers, a hearty meal at the Tollgate Inn is a ritual when heading up or down the mountain. The menu selection is large and portions are satisfying. Their next-door bakery turns out copious quantities of breads, pastries, cakes, muffins and cookies. Pick a treat to pack along to your destination as well as a jar of jam or jelly from the gift shop. This is home-style cooking in a homey atmosphere complete with a big stone fireplace to warm your bones after a trek through the snow. A great place for Sunday breakfast any time of year!

THE DALLES

THE ANZAC TEA PARLOUR

218 W 4th St   541/296-5877
Tues-Sat: 11-4 (reservations suggested)   anzactea.com
Inexpensive to moderate

Tiny in size, but big in satisfaction describes **Bev and Alan Eagy**'s Australian tea spot, ideal for a restful and delicious midday stop. Start by choosing a teacup from the colorful collection, and then decide on one of the 100 varieties of fine teas. Sweet and savory treats are served with the one-, two- and three-course meals with favorites such as ANZAC (Australia-New Zealand Army Corps) biscuits, chicken almond tea sandwiches, scones, quiches and chocolate-dipped strawberries. A nice gift selection and private party space are wedged into the small 1865 building. Catering, specialty cakes and cooking classes keep the Eagys busy, as does the work-in-progress 1868 house next door that will eventually accommodate more guests.

THE BALDWIN SALOON

205 Court St   541/296-5666
Lunch, Dinner: Mon-Sat   baldwinsaloon.com
Moderate

James and John Baldwin originally opened this saloon in 1876 with the railroad and the mighty Columbia providing the brothers

Hotels of old

All around the state, yesteryear's renovated hotels still roll out the welcome mat for visitors far and wide:

Ashland
Ashland Springs Hotel (ashlandspringshotel.com)
Peerless Hotel (peerlesshotel.com)

Astoria
Hotel Elliott (hotelelliott.com)

Baker City
Geiser Grand Hotel (geisergrand.com)

Condon
Hotel Condon (hotelcondon.com)

Dufur
Balch Hotel (balchhotel.com)

Jacksonville
Jacksonville Inn (jacksonvilleinn.com)

Mitchell
Oregon Hotel (541/462-3027)

Prairie City
Historic Hotel Prairie (hotelprairie.com)

Prospect
Prospect Hotel (prospecthotel.com)

Wheeler
Old Wheeler Hotel (oldwheelerhotel.com), former location of the Rinehart Clinic

There are others, including **Portland's Embassy Suites** (embassysuites.hilton.com) where the historic **Multnomah Hotel** was formerly located.

with loads of business. The building has morphed through many entrepreneurial uses, and in 1991 **Mark and Tracy Linebarger** purchased and restored it, adding a pleasant outdoor patio. Now it's a great place to browse the acquired antiques and artwork while enjoying lunch or dinner. The large and varied menu of soups, salads, sandwiches, burgers, seafood, steaks and pasta dishes is fresh and homemade. Standouts are the French onion soup topped with Gruyere cheese and old-fashioned bread pudding with blueberries and whipped cream.

BIG JIM'S DRIVE-IN

2938 E 2nd St   541/298-5051
Lunch, Dinner: Daily   bigjimsdrivein.com
Inexpensive

Big Jim's has been *the* spot in The Dalles for high-quality food, fresh fruit milkshakes and "hamburgers made with love" for over 50 years. Hungry burger lovers have lots of flavors and sizes from which to choose as well as other sandwiches, fish and chicken baskets, homemade chili and clam chowder (Fridays), fries (seasoned or curly), tater tots and real onion rings (all sold solo or with a combo meal), homemade fry sauce and dozens of hard ice cream concoctions to quell hunger pangs. This local landmark offers inside dining, an enjoyable fresh-air patio during nice weather or drive-through service; call-in orders are welcome.

TELEVISION HISTORY

Oregon has had a number of pioneers who have left marks in the television industry. Among them, the late **Carolyn Chambers** of Eugene was founder and CEO of Chambers Communication Corporation, a business that she built from the ground up; **Don Tykeson**, also from the Eugene area, started his career selling TV advertising for KPTV in Portland; **Patsy Smullin** of Medford, learned the biz firsthand from her father, **William Smullin**, and continues to run a hands-on, far-reaching TV empire (KOBI). All these citizens as individuals have also shared their good fortunes with a variety of local and statewide causes.

CELILO INN

3550 E 2nd St   541/769-0001
Inexpensive and up   celiloinn.com

Oregon's Columbia River Gorge is as beautiful a place as you'll find anywhere. This recently updated circa-1950 motel makes a good base from its hillside perch. Accommodations with wondrous views range from a deluxe family suite (with both queen- and king-size beds), king suites, junior king rooms and queen rooms (non-view rooms). Morning pastries, granola and fruit are presented early mornings and a 24-hour coffee bar satisfies caffeine cravings. Other pluses are an outdoor patio with fire pit, fitness facility with a view, seasonal outdoor pool and wine tasting packages.

THE COLUMBIA GORGE DISCOVERY CENTER AND WASCO COUNTY HISTORICAL MUSEUM

5000 Discovery Dr   541/296-8600
Daily: 9-5   gorgediscovery.org
Nominal

Have you ever wondered how the Gorge was formed? Check out the Ice Age exhibit when you begin your journey through this beautiful museum adjacent to the Columbia River. Interactive displays depict the past; live birds of prey are featured in the center's raptor program. Learn how this area was shaped and influenced by early inhabitants, the Lewis and Clark expedition and settlers along the Oregon Trail. Catch a glimpse of Wasco County in a re-created setting. The location is magnificent in an award-winning building surrounded by wondrous vistas, trails, a pond and overlooks; don't miss the nature walk.

COUSINS COUNTRY INN

2114 W 6th St   541/298-5161, 800/848-9378
Inexpensive to moderate   cousinscountryinn.com

COUSINS RESTAURANT & SALOON

Breakfast, Lunch, Dinner: Daily   541/298-2771
Moderate   cousinsthedalles.com

One look at this welcoming complex beckons travelers to stop in for a meal or overnight respite. All of the rooms are outfitted with a refrigerator, microwave, DVD player and coffeemaker with a seasonal outdoor pool and hot tub also on site. In addition to 89 deluxe accommodations, eight rooms are enhanced with three showerheads in the large showers, fireplaces, patios, balconies and sundecks. Feel free to dip into the large jar of homemade cookies at the front desk where you can request a complimentary pass to The Dalles Fitness Club. A few steps away at **Cousins Restaurant** is an expansive menu of wonderful comfort food. Generous portions of homemade chicken pot pie, loaded chicken salad, old-fashioned meatloaf, pot roast sandwiches and fresh, gigantic cinnamon rolls are sure to please anyone in your party. Breakfast is served all day; a fun menu of appetizers and libations in the saloon satisfies the of-age group. As the name implies, this is a family-friendly place. Super accommodating **Tom Drumheller** is the outstanding proprietor.

COSTCO WHOLESALE

Costco Wholesale (costco.com) has changed the way the world shops! For many families, weekends begin with a trip to Costco to stock up for the week and to nibble their way through the store grazing on ample samples. From its beginning in Seattle, Washington, Costco has grown to more than 600 locations worldwide, over 400 in the U.S. alone, becoming the second largest retailer in this country. The 13 Oregon stores (Albany, Aloha, Bend, Clackamas, Eugene, Hillsboro, Medford, Portland, Roseburg, Salem, Tigard, Warrenton, Wilsonville) stock brand name and reliable private label appliances, sporting goods, automotive needs, office needs, family clothing, home goods and furniture, electronics and computers, health and beauty products, beer, wine and groceries. Top-quality meats are cut and packaged in stores, produce is always fresh and who can resist fresh-from-the-oven pies, cakes, cookies and pastries? Additional store services may include pharmacies, tire centers, fueling stations and food courts (love the Costco hot dogs!). Travel services, garage doors, flooring and much more, including cars, are added values to membership.

NICHOLS ART GLASS

912 W 6th St   541/296-2143
Wed-Sun: 10-6   nicholsartglass.com

Artist and entrepreneur **Andy Nichols** found his artistic dream niche in hot glass work and opened his gallery in 2007. You've likely seen his signature salmon pieces and other glasswork in galleries and installations throughout the Northwest. He is busy producing unique pieces in his 2,700-square-foot studio, where you can also custom order and/or buy direct. An example of Andy's larger scale work is a huge chandelier, best described as an abstract seascape, which hangs at **The Ocean Lodge** in Cannon Beach. On blustery Gorge days, this cozy gallery is warmed by a large stone fireplace. Displays are unique and interesting and an open viewing area gives onlookers the opportunity to see Andy and associates in action. Classes in glass blowing and art glass are offered throughout the year.

TIMBERLINE

TIMBERLINE LODGE

27500 E Timberline Road   503/272-3311, 800/547-1406
Moderate and up

CASCADE DINING ROOM

Breakfast, Lunch, Dinner: Daily; Brunch: Sun
Moderate to expensive

SILCOX HUT

Moderate   timberlinelodge.com

Mt. Hood is one of our state's most beloved and visited all-season attractions! Whether you ski, take a hike, enjoy a fabulous meal in the splendid dining room, spend the night or enjoy a day trip to Timberline Lodge, you won't be disappointed. The lodge was dedicated in 1937, a project of the Works Progress Administration (WPA), and is furnished with incredible handmade furnishings and hand-painted artwork, centered by a massive wood-burning stone fireplace. The **Cascade Dining Room** continues to serve first-class alpine cuisine in this National Historic Landmark. A tantalizing full menu is offered for breakfast, lunch and dinner. Oregon produce and products are highlighted with entrees such as elk sirloin schnitzel, braised lamb shank, chicken and a Northwest artisan cheese selection. Lighter fare is served at the lodge's other lounges and eateries. Overnighters will find cozy lodge rooms outfitted with handmade furnishings, modern necessities and wood-burning fireplaces in some rooms. Chalet rooms (outfitted with bunks to accommodate 2, 6 or 8 guests; shared bathrooms) are a fine option for groups and families. A larger chalet room, with private bath, sleeps 10. Situated farther up the mountain at 7,000 feet is a handcrafted stone and timber cabin, **Silcox Hut**, offering groups of 12 to 24 unique lodging, dinner, breakfast and round-trip transportation from the Lodge. An extra special indulgence at this restored rustic beauty is the monthly winemaker's dinners featuring Oregon vineyards, six-course gourmet fare and unforgettable snowmobile transportation between the lodge and hut. The ski area and lift

OREGON FACTORY OUTLET MALLS

Merchandise at these outlet centers is generally discounted 25% to 65% from retail prices, and special events and coupon books afford even deeper savings.

Bend Factory Stores (61334 S Hwy 97, Bend; 541/382-4736, mybendfactorystores.com): 20 stores, good savings

Columbia Gorge Premium Outlets (450 NW 257th Way, Troutdale; 503/669-8060, premiumoutlets.com/columbiagorge): 45 stores, minutes from Portland

Lincoln City Tanger Outlet (1500 SE East Devils Lake Road, Lincoln City; 541/996-5000, tangeroutlet.com/lincolncity): 65 well-known shops, plenty of parking

Seaside Factory Outlet Center (1111 N Roosevelt Dr, Seaside; 503/717-1603, seasideoutlets.com): 25 stores, NIKE and Pendleton outlets

Woodburn Company Stores (1001 Arney Road, Woodburn; 503/981-1900, woodburncompanystores.com): 98 stores and services, attractive buildings and beautiful flowers

network appeal to beginning and intermediate skiers. Palmer Snowfield offers summer skiing above the tree line, although much of the hill is reserved for summer racing camps.

TROUTDALE

CASWELL GALLERY

255 E Columbia River Hwy   503/492-2473
Tues-Sat: 10-5:30; Mon: by appointment   ripcaswell.com

Rip Caswell, who has been sculpting full-time for the past 20 years, took an interesting path to his career. Caswell studied animal anatomy in detail and was named best taxidermist in the nation in 1991. He went on to study human anatomy, and the rest, as they say, is history. His bronze pieces include a magnificent larger-than-life-size former Governor **Tom McCall** at Salem's Riverfront Park, two life-size elk at the **High Desert Museum** near Bend, an Iraq war memorial in Madras, an archway into the city of Tualatin and other installations in Oregon and Kansas. The artist's studio and gallery are also featured in Troutdale's monthly First Friday Art Walk.

SHIRLEY'S TIPPY CANOE

28242 E Columbia River Hwy   503/492-2220
Daily: 8 a.m.-11 p.m. (winter till 10)   shirleysfood.com
Moderate

An extensive renovation to this historic building created an enjoyable restaurant with an attractive outdoor dining spot. The menu is large and portions are plentiful. Breakfast consists of egg dishes with, among the usual offerings, housemade Italian or Polish sausage; prime rib hash; omelets with everything imaginable and freshly-squeezed juices. Sandwiches prevail on the lunch menu and are especially filling with freshly-cut French fries. Hungry beef lovers may opt for the 60-ounce ribeye or New York steak; other choices include fresh seafood, meat and pasta entrees. Jams, soups, salad dressings, sauces and desserts are homemade from old-fashioned recipes; try the Sloppy Sally cake (named for the process). Every Friday and Saturday night, the Tippy has live music; an outside barbecue and blues and jazz liven up summer evenings at this spirited restaurant on the banks of the Sandy River.

TAD'S CHICKEN 'N DUMPLINS

1325E Historic Columbia River Hwy   503/666-5337
Dinner: Daily   tadschicdump.com
Moderate

Every time I dine on chicken and dumplings, I recall long-ago family dinners. While Tad's is known for this stick-to-your-ribs dish, crispy fried chicken and chicken liver dinners have also enticed folks here for many years. You may also deviate to seafood, beef (liver and onions, too) and pasta entrees plus hearty salads. Dinners include a relish tray, soup or salad, bread and home-style green beans. A trip to Tad's merits a Sunday drive on this scenic highway along the Sandy River.

TROUTDALE GENERAL STORE

289 E Historic Columbia River Hwy   503/492-7912
Mon-Fri: 7:30-5; Sat, Sun: 9-5   troutdalegeneralstore.com

A visit to this store in the heart of Troutdale will take you back to a simpler time when mothers shopped and met friends on Main Street and kids came for after-school treats at the soda fountain. Browse through 7,000 square feet of nostalgic toys, decor and souvenirs or stop in for an inexpensive breakfast or lunch of biscuits and gravy, a Cajun meatloaf sandwich or a splurge from the ice cream counter. Weekends offer piping-hot smoked salmon chowder, a meal in itself, or pair with a great sandwich.

WELCHES

BARLOW TRAIL ROADHOUSE

69580 E Hwy 26   503/622-1662
Breakfast, Lunch, Dinner: Daily
Inexpensive and up

Since 1926 home-style cooking has been the mainstay at this historic log cabin which originally served as a general store and later became an inn. The name is derived from the famous Oregon Trail namesake toll road (circa 1846), constructed by Sam Barlow. For a hearty morning start, dig into mountain toast — Texas toast dipped in pancake batter, oats and frosted flakes, then deep fried.   Chicken-fried steak with all the accompaniments, homemade chicken cordon bleu and "the best burger on the mountain" are favorites at this rustic roadhouse.

THE RENDEZVOUS GRILL AND TAP ROOM

67149 E Hwy 26   503/622-6837
Lunch, Dinner: Daily   rendezvousgrill.net
Moderate (lunch), Expensive (dinner)

Where can you find raclettes? Right here at The Rendezvous. This tasty Swiss specialty is served as both an appetizer with cheese melted over Yukon gold potatoes and as a sandwich with Black Forest ham and potatoes. The menu selections are made to order with good options of housemade soups, salads and interesting sandwiches (muffuletta and grilled brie, pear and pepper bacon) for lunch. Well-prepared fish, seafood, beef and pork dinner entrees are complemented with seasonal vegetables that are given gourmet treatment. Specialty pasta entrees, on-request gluten-free breads and housemade ice cream round out the appealing menu.

THE RESORT AT THE MOUNTAIN

69010 E Fairway Ave   503/622-3101, 877/439-6774
Moderate to expensive   theresort.com

ALTITUDE

Breakfast, Lunch, Dinner: Daily
Moderate to expensive

What is now The Resort at The Mountain was Oregon's first golf resort in 1928 and has grown and prospered throughout the ensuing years. Two golf courses (Foxglove Nine and Thistle Nine) joined Pine Cone Nine, this region's oldest; each offers a distinct golfing challenge. Rooms, suites and large villas provide comfortable lodging options for couples or groups. The year-round restaurant, **Altitude**, is conveniently located near guest quarters and serves American and international favorites. Room service and additional casual eating venues are seasonally open in the spring and summer. A short trail leads to the activity center, spa, putting green, playground and more. This is a great getaway locale with leisure interests geared toward families: tennis, outdoor swimming pool (enclosed and heated seasonally), volleyball, bicycles, croquet, lawn bowling and badminton areas and rentals. Mountain sports and other activities are not far away.

WY'EAST BOOK SHOPPE & ART GALLERY

67195 E Hwy 26, Suite A   503/622-1623
Mon-Sat: 9-9; Sun: 11-8   wyeastonline.com

Owner **Sandy Palmer** keeps mountain readers stocked with all genres of current reading material with a focus on Northwest authors. Books are primarily new or gently used and discounted from the original price. Beautiful handcrafted items such as scarves, throws, high-caliber paintings and other gift items are throughout the store. Should you need to get down to business, there is a computer center with terminals for rent, printers, video conferencing capabilities, work space, free Wi-Fi, a shipping center and basic business services.

Your notes

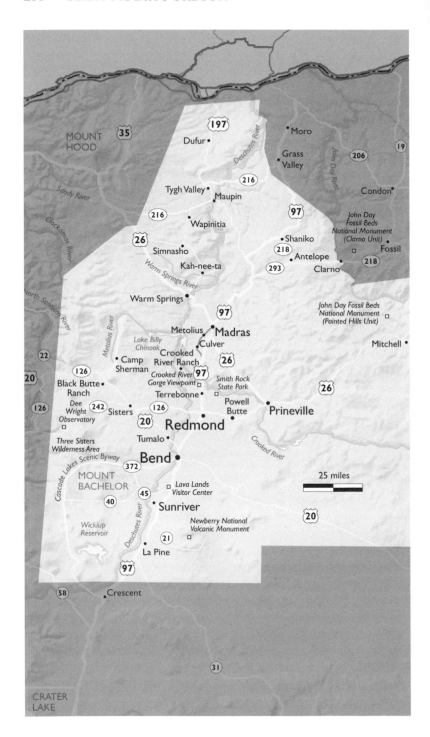

5. Central Oregon

BEND

900 WALL RESTAURANT

900 NW Wall St   541/323-6295
Dinner: Daily; Lunch: seasonal   900wall.com
Moderately expensive

This award-winning contemporary corner restaurant reminds me of Manhattan's lofts: long brick walls, high ceilings and industrial-style lighting. It is a popular watering hole accommodating diners with pizzas from the stone oven, steaks and other dinners. A nice small plate selection of shrimp grilled or "you peel" wild shrimp are super starters. On warm days, plan on sitting at an outdoor sidewalk table, people-watching and enjoying handcrafted cocktails, wine flights or other beverages.

ALPENGLOW CAFE

1133 NW Wall St, Suite 100   541/383-7676
Daily: 7-2   alpenglowcafe.com
Inexpensive to moderate

Alpenglow pledges to only provide the healthiest breakfasts and lunches using freshly-baked breads, dairy goods from Central

Oregon cows and other locally sourced items; no frozen or canned products are used in meal preparations. Wonderful breakfasts of fruit-stuffed French toast, pancakes, organic egg dishes, high-quality smoked bacon, chunky potato pancakes and more await. Quesadillas, housemade soups, salads, sandwiches and burgers will fill your stomach at lunch. Coffee is strictly organic and roasted locally. Grade A Vermont maple syrup, shipped directly from Greensboro, Vermont, is a tasty exception to local resources.

ARIANA

1304 NW Galveston Ave   541/330-5539
Dinner: Tues-Sat   arianarestaurantbend.com
Expensive

Upscale relaxed dining is the order of the day in this Craftsman bungalow. The European bistro menu has an ever-changing Mediterranean flair with such items as a spicy calamari appetizer, roasted beet salad, Spanish paella, grilled quail and an assortment of meat and seafood entrees. I heartily recommend the chocolate cake dessert, although the artisanal cheese plate comes in a close second. The outside patio will pique diners' appreciation for summer days. This is a beautiful choice for exceptional dining and professional service.

THE BLACKSMITH RESTAURANT

211 NW Greenwood Ave   541/318-0588
Dinner: Daily   bendblacksmith.com
Expensive

The historic Pierson's Blacksmith Shop is now a steakhouse, bar and lounge serving new ranch cuisine. Stone and brick walls, subtle lighting and leather upholstery create a casually-elegant ambience with cozy seating areas. The sophisticated comfort food meals are attractively plated with delicious accompaniments. At the top of the list is Not Your Mother's Meatloaf platter, everything good about your mother's best meatloaf kicked up a couple of notches (Condé Nast's *Travel and Leisure* named it to their best comfort foods list). Other not-to-be-missed dishes are cider-brined pork chops with mac and cheese, lobster corndogs and organic and natural steaks with bone marrow

KIDS' ACTIVITIES: BEND

Cascade Indoor Sports (541/330-1183, cascadeindoorsports.com)

Deschutes Historical Museum (541/389-1813, deschuteshistory.org)

High Desert Museum (541/382-4754, highdesertmuseum.org)

Mt. Bachelor Ski Resort (800/829-2442, mtbachelor. com)

Sun Mountain Fun Center (541/382-6161, sunmountainfun.com)

Wanderlust Tours (800/962-2862, wanderlusttours. com)

(sauced or simply grilled to perfection). Desserts are to die for, especially the show-stopping Fostered bananas split, prepared tableside. Executive Chef **Gavin McMichael** has practiced his trade around the world and brings his exquisite culinary skills and concepts to Central Oregon.

DESCHUTES BREWERY & PUBLIC HOUSE
1044 NW Bond St   541/382-9242
Mon-Thurs: 11-11; Fri, Sat: 11 a.m.-midnight; Sun: 11-10

deschutesbrewery.com

Moderate to moderately expensive

Many folks have ventured to the über-fun Public House to unwind after an outdoor day in Deschutes County, often times having to wait for a coveted table. The owner had designs on the next-door property long before it became available, and when it was, the wheels were set in motion to add a new section which ultimately doubled the capacity and diminished the long wait for a thirst-quenching brew and meal. Sausages and brewery pretzels with white Tillamook cheddar cheese and Black Butte Porter stone-ground mustard are made in-house. Wings and other bar snacks, sandwiches, salads and satisfying entrees are easily washed down with one of the dozen and a half year-round and seasonal brews and ales (also liberally used in menu items). While at the brewery, purchase a keg to go or fill a growler; bottled selections sold at retailers.

DESPERADO COUTURE
330 SW Powerhouse Dr   541/749-9980, 800/380-3994
Mon-Sat: 10-7; Sun: 11-7   desperadocouture.com

A visit to Desperado in the Old Mill District is a great place to shop for chic Western clothing, accessories, gifts and designer home decor by top Western couture designers. The styles are eclectic and influenced by Mexican, Spanish and Native American cultures. Owner **Joanne Sunnarborg** has rounded up brands such as Panhandle Slim, Double D, Liberty Boot Company, Old Gringo Boots, Silverado Home Western Decor and Johnny Was representing designer jeans, sterling silver belt buckles, exceptional clothing and much more.   These fashions are appropriate for everyday, special occasions and anytime in between.

DUDLEY'S BOOKSHOP CAFE
135 NW Minnesota Ave   541/749-2010
Mon, Tues, Thurs, Sat: 10-6; Wed: 10-8:30; Fri: 9-8:30; Sun: noon-5

Dudley's has become a community center of green recycling as a secondhand bookstore offering some 30,000 volumes. There are also new books by local authors as well as local artwork. The small first-floor cafe area serves coffee, tea and baked goods. The upper floor offers couches and comfy chairs. You'll find local musicians here on most Friday evenings. Dudley, the trusty springer spaniel belonging to shopkeeper Terri, is the namesake of this friendly bookshop.

ELK LAKE RESORT
60000 Century Dr   541/480-7378
Inexpensive to expensive   elklakeresort.net

It's hard to beat Central Oregon for some of Oregon's finest skiing, winter hiking and mountain relaxation. For a wintertime family treat, park your vehicle at Dutchman Flats and ski, snowmobile or take the Sno-Burbans to the resort. Most appealing are ten updated cabins with fully-outfitted kitchens. Three cabins are rustic — no power, water or amenities; bring your sleeping bag and other gear. The lodge functions as the activity hub with a store, equipment rentals (summer and winter sports) and dining room; live music on summer Saturdays. A new lodge has been discussed and on the drawing board for several years but no firm plans are in place. This retreat is open year round; winter is especially magical.

GREG'S GRILL

395 SW Powerhouse Dr   541/382-2200
Lunch, Dinner: Daily   gregsgrill.com
Moderately expensive

One of the most innovative and charming places to dine in Bend is in the busy Old Mill District at this Northwest lodge-themed restaurant. Relaxing views of the lazy Deschutes River and landscaped outdoor areas are framed by the floor-to-ceiling windows heightened by the soaring natural wood ceiling. Greg's could be called a steakhouse, but also offers almond and mesquite wood fire-grilled burgers, sandwiches, chicken, seafood and healthy salads and soups for lunch and dinner.

HIGH DESERT MUSEUM

59800 S Hwy 97   541/382-4754
Daily: Winter: 10-4; Summer: 9-5   highdesertmuseum.org
Reasonable

This place, originally conceived by **Donald M. Kerr**, is a Central Oregon treasure. Be sure to visit the exhibits and wildlife at this museum four miles south of Bend highlighting the natural and cultural resources of the High Desert. Meet raptors, porcupines, lynx, fox, otter and more live animals in natural habitat settings and in fun, educational programs. Kids love to explore the nature trails on 135 forested acres and learn through hands-on activities. Indoor and outdoor exhibitions feature historical characters portrayed live at a re-created 1880s town, working homestead ranch, a 100-year-old sawmill and outstanding collections of High Desert historic artifacts and Western art. Additional features include guided tours, play spaces for young kids, a cafe and Silver Sage Trading (the museum store). Parking is plentiful and convenient for tour buses, RVs and autos; the complex is ADA accessible and picnic areas are provided. Chipmunks and squirrels may be brazen in their quest for your picnic goods!

THE HILLSIDE INN

1744 NW 12th St   541/389-9660
Moderate   bendhillsideinn.com

This unique lodging offers an urban setting with a convenient location close to bustling downtown Bend. Proprietor **Annie Goldner**'s inn features a pond, waterfall and a nearby hot tub, perfect for unwinding after a busy day. Breakfasts are especially nice, healthy and flexible to address special dietary issues. Newly constructed in 1999, this is not an antique-filled country inn; it is light, bright and outfitted with contemporary furnishings and modern conveniences. The balcony suite overlooks the patio and pond while the ground-floor studio suite is complete with a fully-equipped kitchen and dining area, ideal for longer stays. Comforting amenities include silky robes, Turkish towels and luxury soaps and lotions. Shops, a park, bike trails and downtown Bend are easily accessible within a mile.

IDA'S CUPCAKE CAFÉ

1314 NW Galveston Ave   541/383-2345
Daily: 10-5 (Sun till 4)   idascupcakecafe.com

Thank you, Ida, for appealing to my insatiable sweet tooth! I could be here all day contemplating the perfect combination of cake and frosting flavors, about 80 in all, not counting the seasonal or rotating flavors. Request your favorite pairing or choose from pre-frosted regular size "kidcakes" or twice-the-size gourmet cupcakes. Special occasions are more distinct with these beautiful uniquely decorated treats. Other party-worthy options are personalized bundt cakes, small layer cakes and mini-cupcakes — just about bite size.

KANPAI SUSHI & SAKÉ BAR

990 NW Newport Ave   541/388-4636
Dinner: Daily   kanpai-bend.com
Moderate

For the best sushi in town, look to this westside restaurant for satisfying Pan-Asian cuisine using French techniques. Guests are assured that only locally-sourced, fresh, natural, hormone- and antibiotic-free meats and produce are used whenever possible. Talented instructors show diners how delicious Kanpai dishes are created and assist neophytes in selecting items from the ample menu including the area's largest selection of imported Japanese saké and beer, a full bar and wine.   A good-sized takeout list includes Nigiri and seared filet mignon. Kanpai!

MCKAY COTTAGE RESTAURANT

62910 O.B. Riley Road, #340   541/383-2697
Daily: 7-2   themckaycottage.com
Inexpensive to moderate

This stately bungalow cafe is the former 1916 home of pioneers **Olive and Clyde McKay**, whose son, Gordon, served in the Oregon Senate. It was relocated to this setting from its original location along Mirror Pond and splendidly restored. Enjoy award-winning comfort food breakfasts and lunches with a creative twist: Baja chicken hash stack, stuffed croissant French toast, Smith Rock "Benny" (a change-up on the usual eggs Benedict), mahi fish tacos, homemade soups, salads and sandwiches. Glorious cinnamon rolls and pecan sticky buns are made daily from scratch as are plump muffins, scones and a variety of desserts. Depending upon the weather, choose indoor seating next to the roaring fireplace or pleasant outdoor seating on the lawn.

MT. BACHELOR

13000 SW Century Dr   800/829-2442
                                                     mtbachelor.com

With an elevation of 9,065 feet, Mt. Bachelor is a major Cascade Range peak covering 3,365 feet of vertical drop from summit to base. It is one of the few peaks in the world that affords skiing the entire mountain 360 degrees off the top. Grab a trail map before you venture out; there is a network of 12 lifts (quads, triples and tubing) and 71 runs. Guests of all ages and levels of experience will find their Eden on the mountain from Dilly-Dally Alley for youngsters to the double black diamond extreme territory on the backside of the mountain for proficient skiers. Four lodges are conveniently placed on the mountain to refresh skiers, 'boarders, 'tubers, 'shoers and snow enthusiasts with food and drink. Other services include lessons; retail, rental and tuning shops; a demo center; childcare; guide service; sled dog rides; cross country skiing and snowshoe tours. Just in case, Bend Memorial Clinic Urgent Care has an outpost in the ski patrol building. For an entirely different perspective, head to the mountain in summer for activities including disc golf, spectacular vistas from the chairlifts and gourmet dinners at **Pine Marten Lodge**.

THE OXFORD HOTEL
10 NW Minnesota Ave   541/382-8436, 877/440-8436
Moderate   oxfordhotelbend.com

10 BELOW RESTAURANT AND LOUNGE
Breakfast, Lunch, Dinner: Daily   541/382-1010
Dinner: Moderate

Despite the sagebrush silver-gray that pervades the high desert of Central Oregon, Bend has gone green with a 59-suite, four-diamond boutique hotel dedicated to sustainable hospitality. It has all the amenities of a top-drawer hotel, combined with "green" bedding, selections from a pillow menu, plush bathrobes, premium organic toiletries, in-room French press coffee service and a state-of-the-art fitness center. Airport shuttle and cruiser bicycles (summer only) are complimentary to guests. Pet-friendly rooms are available; a nominal fee includes a size-appropriate bed for your canine, housemade treats and more. Three squares a day of "urban-organic" cuisine are offered on the lower level at **10 Below Restaurant and Lounge**. Offerings change to capture the essence of the seasons; room service is available. Sophisticated, contemporary luxury is a stunning addition to historic downtown Bend.

PAULINA PLUNGE
                                          541/389-0562, 800/296-0562
May 1-Sept 15: Daily   paulinaplunge.com

Take the plunge, the Paulina Plunge, for an all-downhill mountain biking adventure from Central Oregon's Newberry National Volcanic Monument. You'll drop more than 2,500 vertical feet on four one-and-a-half-mile segments and stop at up to six pristine waterfalls (two are natural waterslides where you can cool down and play). A couple of lively hikes are required to reach the falls, but they're easily achievable for tots to seniors. Experienced guides lead the charge and along the way impart insight into the local history, geology and archeology. A few details: catch a shuttle at Sunriver Resort for a 25-minute ride to the gathering spot. Included in the price are a bike, helmet and day pack (sack lunch and water bottle additional or bring your own). There's plenty of fine print; call or check the website for the minutiae and pricing.

PILOT BUTTE DRIVE-IN RESTAURANT

917 NE Greenwood Ave   541/382-2972
Daily: 7-7

320 SW Century Dr, Suite 410   541/323-3272
Daily: 7 a.m.-8 p.m.   pilotbutte.com
Inexpensive

Mention quality food, big portions and Bend drive-through and folks will know you're talking about Pilot Butte Drive-In, a local and visitor favorite since 1983. Burgers are just the way I like them: flavorful hand-pattied ground chuck, juicy and requiring several napkins. Variations to the basic burger are created with the addition of bacon, cheese, mushrooms, jalapenos, ham, guacamole, roasted garlic or a combo of the aforementioned fixings. The Pilot Butte burger is 18 ounces of beef; quite a mouthful! Plain or seasoned fries or onion rings and a float, freeze, shake or malt from the fountain complete the stop. Breakfast orders are also generously portioned.

PINE RIDGE INN

1200 SW Mt. Bachelor Dr   541/389-6137
Moderate to expensive   pineridgeinn.com

Perched above the Deschutes River Canyon is a boutique hotel overlooking the river, Farewell Bend Park and the Old Mill District. The location and superb views can't be beat! All 20 suites are well-furnished with gas fireplaces, private patios, plush king beds and mini-fridges. Overnight stays include complimentary cooked-to-order breakfast and evening reception with wine, Oregon microbrews and hors d'oeuvres. The well-tended property is beautiful; suites are spacious and relaxing, perfect for an R&R getaway.

PINE TAVERN RESTAURANT

967 NW Brooks St   541/382-5581
Lunch: Mon-Fri (summer, daily); Dinner: Daily   pinetavern.com
Moderate to expensive

Enterprising women (and men) and an interesting journey through time all add up to the legend of the Pine Tavern Restaurant. Founded in 1936, it has faithfully served Bend and its timber industry workers and their families, soldiers from Camp Abbot and tourists. The building overlooks picturesque Mirror Pond and has morphed through the years to accommodate additional customers and modern facilities. One expansion enclosed two gigantic Ponderosa pine trees in the Garden Room; the patio and garden were redesigned and are still part of the ambience. The menu features both classic and eclectic choices prepared with Northwest ingredients. Signature scones with honey butter are like manna from heaven; this is a traditional Central Oregon dining excursion.

PRONGHORN CLUB & RESORT

65600 Pronghorn Club Dr   541/693-5300, 866/372-1003
Expensive   golfpronghorn.com

Pronghorn is a superior getaway for golfers and non-golfers. Exquisite lodging includes 48 lodge units situated on the 18th hole of the Jack Nicklaus Signature Course. Junior suites consist of one bedroom and bathroom. Spacious two-, three- and four-bedroom units are furnished with gourmet kitchens, a home theater system and other technology, private patios and original art work. Personal concierge services (pre-stocked groceries, local activities, dining) are also available. All guests have access to the clubhouse, restaurants, fitness facility, sports courts, pools and complimentary shuttle between Roberts Field-Redmond Municipal Airport and other regional airports. The Nicklaus course is also open to the public while the Tom Fazio course is restricted to guests with a member-host from the club. Personal golf instruction with the latest technology is sure to help your game. The fine dining venue, **Chanterelle**, boasts a dramatic floor-to-ceiling fireplace with impeccable panoramic views of the Cascades. **Cascada** is the spot for a comfortable, relaxing repast; position your dining chair to capture the sunset or catch a game on a flat-screen TV. Order an internationally flavored Bloody Mary with breakfast or a signature cocktail and appetizers (baked brie, pot stickers, wild mushroom tortellini) later in the day. Burgers, pork tacos and the like are available all day; the dinner menu shines with New York steak, seafood, lamb and other outstanding entrees. Nestled in the heart of Pronghorn is casual and cozy **Trailhead Grill** for family-friendly, lighter fare, full bar with both inside and patio seating. (Restaurant days and hours fluctuate with the seasons.) This location is ideal for weddings, corporate retreats, special events and, of course, golf tournaments.

SCANLON'S RESTAURANT

61615 Athletic Club Dr   541/385-3062
Lunch: Mon-Fri; Dinner: Mon-Sat;
Breakfast, Lunch: Sun   athleticclubofbend.com
Moderate

The Athletic Club of Bend has done an outstanding job of providing the community a fine dining spot with its in-house Scanlon's Restaurant. It is open to the public and suitable for upscale dinners to happy-hour or game-day get-togethers. Designed for healthy lifestyles, the cuisine is fresh, organic and Northwest-influenced; nutritional information is noted on the menu. Interesting salads and sandwiches are excellent lunch selections. Seafood, meats, pastas, wood-grilled pizzas and delicious vegetarian dishes fill the dinner menu accompanied by full bar service, wines and microbrews. Sunday breakfast is a treat for the whole family, especially delightful enjoyed on the patio. The cafe is open daily for casual food: grilled sandwiches, smoothies, soups, salads and light breakfasts.

THE SPARROW BAKERY

50 SE Scott St   541/330-6321
Mon-Sat: 7-2; Sun: 8-2   thesparrowbakery.com

Owner **Whitney Blackman** and her business partner **Jessica Keating** specialize in rich French pastries and bountiful fresh salads. Their Ocean Roll (hand-rolled croissant dough filled with sugar, vanilla and cardamom) is a popular treat; *c'est magnifique*! Ask any repeat customer and they will heap accolades on other croissants, tarts, breads, cookies and breakfast sandwiches. A dilemma is what to order for lunch: a chicken waldorf, croque monsieur or Monte Cristo sandwich or savory quiche. This bakery is warm, cozy and friendly, just as a bakery should be; super lattes, too.

THE TUMALO FEED COMPANY

64619 W Hwy 20   541/382-2202
Dinner: Daily   tumalofeedcompany.com
Moderate

This steakhouse and saloon is a real Western winner! I almost expect to see horses tied up to the wide porch and ranch hands tipping back a beer while waiting for grub. Ease into the evening hours with a visit to the saloon for "Howdy Hour" drink and nibble specials or order Rocky Mountain oysters and other appetizers. Ample dinners are served family-style and accompanied by onion rings and salsa, salad, ranch-fried potatoes, house-baked beans, garlic bread and a sarsaparilla float or other meal-ending sweet or libation. Order from a hearty menu of steaks, seafood, fowl and combos; early "Sundown Suppers" offer great values. Tumalo Feed Company is family-friendly, has live music on Friday and Saturday evenings and is an enjoyable stop with great steaks, bar none.

THE VICTORIAN CAFE

1404 NW Galveston   541/382-6411
Daily: 7-2   victoriancafebend.com
Moderate

For locals, see you at "The Vic" means The Victorian Cafe, a Central Oregon institution for great breakfasts in a fun environment with commendable service. Traditional breakfast fare morphed into gourmet cuisine with the arrival of proprietor **John Nolan** in 2002. He reinvented the menu to offer about 20 descriptively-named omelets (The Green Hornet includes spinach, asparagus, jalapenos, scallions and avocados), eggs Benedict (Cuban ham, mango and black beans make up the Caribbean version) and potato specialties like the Apollonius

PROUD PUBLIC SERVANTS

The name Johnson is highly regarded in Oregon in the various areas where this talented Johnson family has lived and served. In Redmond, patriarch **Sam Johnson** was a successful land owner and lumberman, the generous sparkplug for numerous civic causes, state representative (serving seven terms) and, later, Redmond mayor. His highly intelligent wife, **Becky Johnson**, not only served as a WAVE (Women Accepted for Volunteer Emergency Service) in World War II, but was also a key player in educational circles during her lifetime. The family foundation generously supports worthwhile causes throughout the state. Daughter Betsy has continued the family tradition, serving in the Oregon House and Senate, representing the northern coast area with distinction. No one in public life, at least in this state, has quite the command of the English language as **Betsy Johnson**!

(linguica sausage, artichoke hearts, spinach, kalamata olives, red peppers and feta cheese). Legendary Bloody Marys and "ManMosas" (crafted with The Vic's private label champagne) put this full-service bar on the radar. About a dozen sandwiches (as a wrap or on bread), burgers and fresh salads entice the lunch crowd. The Vic is so popular, you may find yourself settling into an outside bench as you wait for your table.

WANDERLUST TOURS

541/389-8359, 800/962-2862
Prices vary   wanderlusttours.com

For a really cool experience in the Bend area, how about a visit to the Deschutes National Forest's Boyd and Skeleton Caves? Half-day tours take visitors beneath the area's desert floor. In winter, this outfit does a series of extraordinary experiences including snowshoeing by the light of a full Oregon moon and bonfires on the snow. Professional naturalist guides accompany groups; delicious desserts and warm drinks are added treats. For the 21 and older generation, hop on Wanderlust's Bend Brew Bus for a rollicking tour of four of the dozen or so local craft breweries, including samples and appetizers. Other tours consist of canoeing, kayaking, GPS Eco-challenge, volcano sightseeing, evening tours and special events; guides, transportation and appropriate equipment are furnished. Bring the wee ones and grandma; activities can be modified for the whole family!

ZYDECO KITCHEN & COCKTAILS

919 NW Bond St   541/312-2899
Lunch: Mon-Fri; Dinner: Daily   zydecokitchen.com
Moderately expensive

Barbecue shrimp served with a Southern grit cake is the hands-down favorite at this classy Cajun place. The Southwest Louisiana-inspired fare features étouffée, shrimp po'boy, artichoke and corn fritters and shrimp, Andouille and crawfish jambalaya. Other standouts are Acadian flatbread (you choose the toppings), Mama G's steak salad (avocado, tomato, chopped egg and blue cheese), sandwiches, pot pie and seasonal preparations made from scratch using fresh, quality ingredients. The Creole food is super and the atmosphere loads of fun; your toes will be a tappin'!

DUFUR

BALCH HOTEL

40 S Heimrich St   541/467-2277
Open seasonally   balchhotel.com
Inexpensive to moderate

Built in 1907 by rancher Charles P. Balch, the 1908 opening ads offered rooms for as little as 50 cents, promoting the fact that there was hot and cold running water in every room. Now the 18 rooms (five with private bathrooms) and one suite with en suite bathroom offer modern conveniences and still maintain comfortable prices. Gracious innkeepers **Samantha and Jeff Irwin** will start you on a day of exploring museums, wineries or cycling the back roads with a three-course breakfast featuring sweet and savory baked goods, strata and local seasonal fruit. You won't find an elevator, televisions or telephones, but there are chocolate chip cookies and special malty hot cocoa; Wi-Fi access, too.

Hometown theater

From the large venues that enjoy national troupes of the **Keller Auditorium** (auditoriumportland.com) and **Hult Center** (hultcenter.org) in Portland and Eugene to Ashland's highly-acclaimed **Oregon Shakespeare Festival** (osfashland.org) and Jacksonville's **Britt Festival** (brittfest. org), it seems talent is everywhere. We want to remember, too, small-theater settings, many of which have survived and thrived through hometown commitment. A good place to research particular auditoriums is **all-oregon.com/state/info/ theatre.htm**. Here are a few for your consideration when you are inspired for a cultural experience:

Astoria
Liberty Theater (liberty-theater.org)
Cannon Beach
Coaster Theatre Playhouse (coastertheatre.com)
Corvallis
Majestic Theatre (majestic.org)
Elgin
Elgin Opera House (elginoperahouse.com)
Eugene
The Very Little Theatre, Inc. (thevlt.com)
Klamath Falls
Ross Ragland Theater (rrtheater.org)
Lake Oswego
Lakewood Center for The Arts (lakewood-center.org)
Medford
Craterian Ginger Rogers Theater (craterian.org)
Portland
Oregon Children's Theatre (octc.org)
Salem
Historic Elsinore Theatre (elsinoretheatre.org)
Pentacle Theatre (pentacletheatre.org)
The Dalles
The Theatre Company of The Dalles
(thetheatrecompany.org)

LA PINE

PAULINA LAKE LODGE

Newberry National Volcanic Monument   541/536-2240
Moderate to expensive   paulinalakelodge.com

Adventurous Oregon travelers shouldn't miss this rustic lodge on the shores of Paulina Lake (23 miles south of Bend on Highway 97, then 12 miles east on Road 21) deep in the Deschutes National Forest. Depending on the season, enjoy fishing, boating, swimming, snowmobiling and tours, hiking and more. There are 200 miles of groomed snowmobile trails; bring your own or rent the big boy play toys on site. Vintage cabins are equipped with bathrooms, linens, firewood and kitchenware. Moderately priced, hearty full lunches and dinners are served in the 1929 log lodge; the famous prime rib is a Saturday night staple on the home cooking menu. A general store (summer only) is convenient to visitors for fishing licenses, food, clothing, equipment rentals, gas and oil, beer and groceries. This area's history is an interesting read.

MADRAS

GENO'S ITALIAN GRILL

212 SW 4th St   541/475-6048
Tues-Fri: 11-9; Sat, Sun: 8 a.m.-9 p.m.   genositaliangrill.net
Moderate

Madras for "authentic" Italian food? Yes, that and more at Geno's where the extensive menu features ingredients that are fresh and local as much as possible. The casual fare ranges from land to sea: lobster or meat cannelloni, chicken Giovanni, steaks and chops, assorted calzones, pasta dishes, gourmet and traditional pizzas and hearty hero sandwiches. Special attention is paid to providing great service and food. Weekend breakfasts lean toward traditional choices of omelets, pancakes, plus skillets, frittatas, gourmet pancakes and crème brûlée French toast.

MAUPIN

DESCHUTES CANYON FLY SHOP

LES SCHWAB IS #1

If there is one Oregon institution symbolizing the very best in customer service, it is **Les Schwab Tires** (lesschwab.com) with over 100 outlets in Oregon and 300 or more throughout other western states. Founded in Prineville in 1952 by a gentleman who understood the value of efficient, competent customer attention and good products, **Les Schwab** brought the same level of customer care to all outlets, largely through employee opportunity and empowerment. Personnel run, don't walk, to greet customers; they are clean cut and well trained; free flat repairs is routine policy; prices are competitive. Quite simply, Les Schwab keeps the bar set high for customer service and satisfaction.

---

599 S Hwy 197   541/395-2565
Mon-Sat: 8-6 (Sun till 4)   flyfishingdeschutes.com

John Smeraglio, fisherman and owner of this fly shop and guide service, shares his love of angling and the outdoors with others. John and his team teach the finer art of casting flies, offer customized guided float and non-float tours and stock high-quality brand name gear. They also share information on river conditions, fishing reports and fish counts. Throughout the year, look for seasonal product demos, clinics, lessons and more. Their customer-friendly motto is: "We guide; you fish!"

IMPERIAL RIVER CO.

304 Bakeoven Road   541/395-2404, 800/395-3903
Lodging: Inexpensive to moderate   deschutesriver.com
Restaurant (seasonal hours): Moderate

Hardworking entrepreneurs **Susie and Rob Miles** purchased this whitewater rafting and lodging operation in 2001. They added a full-service restaurant, quiet bar, 45-seat conference room, courtyard with fire pit, sand volleyball court, additional guest rooms and a photo shop to take digital pictures of everyone rafting this stretch of the Deschutes River. All 25 guest rooms have names and themes appropriate to the activities of the area, are well-appointed and include wader dryers. Try to plan your stay to coincide with restaurant hours. Angus beef is sourced from nearby Imperial Stock Ranch for burgers and steaks as well as lamb dishes; chicken, fish, sandwiches and desserts are also good. Well-trained personnel, whitewater rafting, great photo ops, superb fishing, guided upland bird hunting plus more are available.

POWELL BUTTE

BRASADA RANCH

16986 SW Brasada Ranch Road   541/526-6865, 888/322-6592
Moderate to very expensive   brasada.com

Just east of Bend, this high desert getaway offers Oregon native charm. Stay in a well-furnished Ranch House suite or a two- or three-bedroom Sage Canyon cabin. In addition to lodging, the welcoming Ranch House restaurant offers a full-service casual restaurant open for breakfast, lunch and dinner. The athletic center has an indoor lap pool, two outdoor pools and a giant slide. Take advantage of the full workout facility while children are busy in The Hideout, where activities abound. The semi-private Peter Jacobsen-designed 18-hole **Canyons Golf Course** is limited to members and resort guests. The full-service spa is open to the public and affords clients (and one additional guest) entrance into the private pool (no children). Biking and hiking trails are easily accessible on the 1,800-acre property as are horseback riding, whitewater rafting and fishing. Fine dining at the **Range Restaurant and Bar** opens to a panoramic view of the striking Cascades — enjoy a sunset meal and then move to the impressive fire pit. The changing menu is innovative, yet down-to-earth; most importantly, fresh, local ingredients are used to a large extent for this farm-to-fork experience. Enjoy other limitless R&R opportunities year round.

PRINEVILLE

BELLAVISTA BED & BREAKFAST

5070 SE Paulina Hwy   541/416-2400
Inexpensive   bellavistab-b.com

For fabulous 180-degree views of the Three Sisters and the

Cascades, try this hilltop bed and breakfast accented with furnishings from **Fulvia and Ben Guyger**'s Tuscan home. They will make you feel right at ease with two comfy bedrooms (one with a queen bed, the other two twins). The signature gourmet breakfast consists of orange-glazed sausage and apricot kabobs, eggs and fruit served on the sun deck or upper gazebo. The gracious hosts, unbeatable scenery and European elegance produce a memorable stay anytime of the year. (Credit cards not accepted.)

REDMOND

BRICKHOUSE
412 SW 6th St   541/526-1782
Dinner: Tues-Sat   brickhouseco.com
Moderate

One of Redmond's best restaurants is the casual fine dining Brickhouse in historic downtown. In addition to natural, hormone-free steaks you'll find crab, lobster, ahi tuna, fresh Alaskan salmon and halibut, white prawns and bivalves. Not to be overlooked are chops, chicken and pasta dishes, soups and nice meal-size salads. Cobbler a la mode is housemade as are other desserts and savory sauces. A sister Brickhouse in downtown Bend (803 SW Industrial Way, 541/728-0334) is open nightly for dinner.

SISTERS

ANGELINE'S BAKERY & CAFE
121 W Main St   541/549-9122
Daily: 6:30-6 (winter till 4)   angelinesbakery.com

Early morning coffee go-withs including muffins, scones, mighty cinnamon rolls, coffee cakes, bagels and anytime breads, cookies, brownies and more are baked from scratch here each day. Great salads, homemade soups, wraps, polenta pizza and specials make tasty lunchtime choices. Many of the items are vegan, gluten-free, agave-sweetened and/or dairy-free in response to the dietary demands of more and more health-conscious people; a strong emphasis is placed on raw foods and green smoothies. You can also find these flavorful baked products at Whole Foods markets, small health food stores and coffee shops in Central Oregon. Angeline's white rice bread makes super sandwiches.

ASPEN LAKES GOLF COURSE
16900 Aspen Lakes Dr   541/549-4653
                                                        aspenlakes.com

A short five minutes from Sisters is one of the best golf courses in Oregon. This ongoing Cyrus family project began in 1987 with the first nine holes completed in 1996 and the second in 2000. Natural elements were incorporated into the design and red cinders from the Cyrus property were crushed to fill the sand traps creating signature red sand bunkers. Restaurants operate seasonally; **Brand 33**, features Northwest cuisine, a mix of land and sea with fresh fruits and vegetables dotting the menu or relax over Sunday brunch. Sandwiches, burgers, appetizers, pizza and entrees are offered at **The Frog Pond**, the casual bar and lunch option. It is clear why Aspen Lakes is on many golfers "must play" list when visiting Central Oregon.

BLACK BUTTE RANCH
12930 Hawks Bear   541/595-1252, 866/901-2961
Moderate and up   blackbutteranch.com

With magnificent Central Oregon field and mountain vistas, the Black Butte Ranch setting is one of the most dramatic in the state. All manner of activities are available, including two 18-hole golf courses, tennis courts, swimming pools, 18 miles of bike paths,

---

FORE!

Perfectly matched for Oregon weather and golf's Scottish origin, **Seamus Golf** (seamusgolf.com) is an Oregon company going for a big swing with golf head covers. Owners **Megan and Akbar Chisti** source the woolen material from the Pacific Northwest and the covers are hand-cut and sewn in Oregon, keying on Scottish tartans. Not mass produced, individuals and golf courses can order family or other significant plaids or tartans for branding or simply to make a statement; if you'd like, customize with engraved images on leather trim.

stables, canoeing, fishing, snowmobiling and nearby superb winter skiing at Mt. Bachelor. In the early 1900s, the area was the home of the **Black Butte Land and Livestock Co**.; later the summer home of **Howard Morgan** and his family, members of the pioneer Portland Corbett dynasty. The 1,280 acres were then sold to **Brooks Scanlon**, a lumber firm; now homeowners own and oversee the property's management. **The Lodge Restaurant** is popular with residents, vacationers and those who simply come to enjoy dining in this rustic but upscale atmosphere.

BRONCO BILLY'S RANCH GRILL & SALOON

190 E Cascade Ave   541/549-7427
Lunch, Dinner: Daily   broncobillysranchgrill.com
Moderate

The Old West awaits at this Hotel Sisters' watering hole and family restaurant which dates back to the early 1900s. Don't miss the back bar built in the 1860s, a great piece that came around the Horn to San Francisco and then made its way to Central Oregon. The menu is typically Western, with crisp salads, their well-known Ranch Grill burgers, smokehouse dishes, baby back ribs, Mexican fare and more. The hotel no longer offers lodging; instead the upstairs quarters are used for private dining. There is a covered deck available for summertime events. You're likely to see plenty of authentic cowboys and city slickers here the second weekend in June for the annual **Sisters Rodeo** (sistersrodeo.com). Head on in for a cool beer, pardner!

DEPOT CAFE

250 W Cascade Ave   541/549-2572
Daily: 8-8 (winter: Wed-Sun: 8-8)   sistersdepot.com
Inexpensive to moderate

No matter the time of year, the town of Sisters sees a steady flow of traffic. It's long been a popular break for folks driving over the mountains on Highway 20 to walk the Western-style main street and peruse the shops, restaurants and boutiques. This rustic cafe makes everything from scratch with an emphasis on local ingredients. With that in mind, breakfasts (plate-size hotcakes) are large and inexpensive; so are the excellent lunchtime turkey club and other sandwiches. Dinner specials change weekly and may feature short ribs, steaks, salmon, beef pot pie, prawn fettuccine or chicken parmesan; beer, wine and cocktails are also at hand. Bread is homemade and you will want to save room for a delicious piece of pie (also homemade). Be sure to look up when you're inside to catch a glimpse of an electric train that continually chugs along an overhead track. The beautiful outdoor patio is restful in summer.

FIVEPINE LODGE AND CONFERENCE CENTER

1021 Desperado Trail   541/549-5900, 866/974-5900
Moderate to expensive   fivepinelodge.com

The FivePine Lodge caters to business groups who want five-star facilities in a small community. The state-of-the-art meeting facility also doubles as an intimate wedding, party and family reunion scene. Forget the briefcases and laptops and the luxurious accommodations become attractive for romantic stays; distractions are at a minimum. There are 24 cottages and eight lodge rooms outfitted with Amish-built hardwood furniture, tubs filled by a ceiling waterfall, gas fireplaces and large plasma screen TVs. Bookings include complimentary deluxe continental morning breakfast and hosted evening wine and craft beer reception. Borrow a free cruiser bicycle (seasonal) or play in the outdoor heated pool. The Sisters Athletic Club, where guests can take advantage of pursuing personal health and wellness and **Shibui Spa** (541/549-6164, shibuispa.com) for pampering treatments are on the FivePine campus. Guests are just a few steps away from food and entertainment at **Three Creeks Brewing** (541/549-1963, threecreeksbrewing.com) for handcrafted ales, lunch, dinner (sandwiches, burgers, steaks, pastas and other pub fare) and weekend breakfast. **Sisters Movie House** (541/549-8800, sistersmoviehouse.com) is adjacent; request discount tickets at the lodge's front desk. One could only hope to be snowed in over a long weekend.

HOODOO SKI AREA

Hwy 20   541/822-3799
Seasonal   hoodoo.com

At the summit of Santiam Pass is Central Oregon's original ski area. Skiers, sledders, 'boarders, 'tubers and snowbikers are all accommodated on beginning and expert runs at this family-friendly butte where the average snowbase is 10 to 15 feet. First-timers to Hoodoo will find convenient lessons and equipment rentals.   Part of Hoodoo's appeal is its proximity to the mid-Willamette Valley, affordability as compared to the larger ski locales, deep powder, 32 groomed runs and night skiing. There are over 800 acres of terrain, five lifts, a full-service lodge and the Autobahn Tubing Park with multiple runs (free tubes and cable tube tow with ticket purchase).

JEN'S GARDEN

403 E Hood Ave   541/549-2699
Dinner: Wed-Sun   intimatecottagecuisine.com
Expensive

Owners **Jennifer and T.R. McCrystal** converted a small 1930s-era cottage into a charming, warm dinner house. Choose from the *prix-fixe* or a la carte menus of extraordinary Southern French-influenced fare. The menu changes regularly depending upon fresh ingredients and seasonal favorites. Each dish is a masterpiece, beautifully plated and pleasing to the palate. Old World wines from a collection assembled by wine steward **Jamie Reynolds** ensure that a meal at Jen's is memorable, especially with wine flight pairing. Chef T.R. has won the Bite of Oregon Iron Chef competition and Jennifer makes superb desserts; together they produce the best fine dining in this area. Hours are seasonal and reservations are highly recommended.

THE LODGE AT SUTTLE LAKE

13300 Hwy 20   541/595-2628
Lodging: Inexpensive and up

THE BOATHOUSE RESTAURANT

Breakfast, Lunch, Dinner: Daily   thelodgeatsuttlelake.com
Moderate

I can smell the pines just contemplating a stay here. This comfortable destination was created in the style of the great old lodges of the West. The unusual treatment of each guest suite with Native American names, decor and symbols (New Moon,

Paths Crossing, Rain Drop, Big Mountain, Eagle Feather and Broken Arrow) makes the accommodations especially appropriate, particularly for those who treasure the grounds' colorful Native American history. To add to the charm, each suite has its own stone fireplace; some have hot tubs and all have spectacular views of the lake or forest. For a semi-roughing-it experience, book an inexpensive rustic cabin. You get a warm roof overhead, heat and electricity but no bathroom, running water, kitchen or other comforting amenities. You don't have to be a lodge guest to eat or stop in for a drink at **The Boathouse Restaurant**. This is Northwest-inspired fine cuisine (not campfire grub); selections may include housemade buffalo chili, pork molé, salads, sandwiches, steaks and more. The lake views from the restaurant are magnificent, too! Make plans ahead of your stay or on the spur of the moment to rent a kayak, canoe, boat, bike or peddleboat; take a three-and-a-half mile hike around the lake or simply enjoy a laid-back respite among the soaring pines at Suttle Lake. Naturally repopulating German brown and Kokanee trout entice fishermen; a project is underway to bring native Sockeye salmon back to the lake from the ocean to spawn. There is plenty more to do anytime of the year. This is the good life!

LONG HOLLOW RANCH

71105 Holmes Road   541/923-1901, 877/923-1901
March-Oct   lhranch.com
Moderate

If you're looking for a guest ranch experience with a bent toward "real," you'll find it at this historic Oregon ranch. With a history as a working ranch that goes back over a century, Long Hollow

---

PRINT MATTERS

It's not often that a periodical can successfully break into a tough print market, but Deschutes Media's **1859 Oregon Magazine** (1859oregonmagazine.com) has been enthusiastically received. Editor **Kevin Max** and his crew are producing an informative, professional publication, keying on our state assets of people and places.

offers guest activities associated with producing hay, running cattle and operating a large ranch. Choose from five guest rooms and a cottage, each offering different themes and short-term (per day) or weekly stays. The ranch operates on the American plan, which includes homecooked meals, lodging and many other things you might want to do, including horseback riding, fishing, cookouts, games, reading, playing the piano or mingling with other guests and ranch hands. History comes alive in the redesigned ranch that was once headquarters of the Black Butte Land and Livestock Company; remnants of the old ways are still evident. Check the website for pricing, restrictions and additional information.

SISTERS BAKERY

251 E Cascade Ave   541/549-0361
Daily: 5-5   sisters-bakery.com

Sisters Bakery is known for the freshest doughnuts in town. The glass case is chock-full of decadent pastries and eclairs, brownies, cookies, muffins, scones, breads, pies and cobblers all made from scratch and baked fresh daily. You can also find cheese sticks and marionberry biscuits (made with whole berries), artisan and sandwich breads, as well as soups, coffee drinks and pizzas. Cakes are beautifully decorated; choose from several cake, filling and icing flavors. Classic, all-butter croissants are baked at 7 every morning and filled with savory ingredients for breakfast-on-the-run, the bakery's own marionberry jam or just the way they are. The list of tempting delights is mighty long and everything is delish!

SISTERS DRUG AND GIFT

211 E Cascade Ave   541/549-6221
Daily: hours vary   pillboxinc.com

Aspirin to afghans, calamine lotion to candles; you get the picture! Ladies can spend hours perusing the fabulous gift department — a destination in itself. Shop for the latest totes from Vera Bradley, collectibles, kitchen necessities and accessories from the well-stocked Cook's Nook, Oregon-based food products, great home accessories, jewelry and one-of-a-kind gifts. The drug section will tend to your health needs with over-the-counter medications, prescription service and flu vaccines for residents and visitors alike. This classy, unique store may become your favorite boutique in Sisters.

SNO CAP ICE CREAM

380 W Cascade Ave   541/549-6151

Inexpensive

Long a central Oregon tradition, this tiny burger and ice cream joint showcases the fast food of yesteryear — thick ice cream shakes and tasty burgers and fries. Choose from shakes (over a dozen flavors), ice cream sundaes, corn dogs and assorted other basket meal options. There always seems to be a line out the door!

SUNRIVER

SUNRIVER RESORT

17600 Center Dr   541/593-1000, 866/930-2687

Prices vary   sunriver-resort.com

In 1965, Portland developers **John D. Gray** and **Donald V. McCallum** embarked on building this planned resort and residential community on property that once served as **Camp**

FROM THE GROUND UP

From very humble beginnings, **Fred G. Meyer** started a grocery operation in Portland, using his moniker, **Fred Meyer** (fredmeyer.com). The chain spread throughout the Northwest with 125 stores (now owned by Kroger, Inc.). Fred was very much a hands-on operator, constantly roaming the aisles of his stores greeting customers, checking the inventory (and ensuring customers and employees were not stealing from him!). Very generous to the Salvation Army during his lifetime, he left a large gift to establish the **Meyer Memorial Trust** (mmt.org), one of the nation's most significant charities.

There are 50 one-stop shopping centers in Oregon and Southwest Washington. Shelves are stocked with groceries and prepared foods (brand name and house brands), almost everything needed to keep a family and home running, specialty departments (pharmacy, electronics, fine jewelry, garden, home improvement, delicatessen, bakery) and in many locales Ticketmaster outlets, Starbucks coffee shops, banks and fuel centers.

Abbot, a WWII training facility. Through the ensuing years, the natural environment has remained protected while attaining the reputation as a casual yet luxurious destination for families, conferences and special events. Lodge Village guestrooms and suites are within walking distance to the main lodge, Great Hall and other meeting rooms. Either accommodation type includes free Wi-Fi, stone gas fireplace, private deck and provides access to the **Sage Springs Club and Spa**. Homes and condos are also available for short- or long-term rental. Resort amenities and activities are scattered throughout the enclave: equipment rentals, bike paths, six restaurants (varying fare, seasonal operating hours), retail shops, horse stables, four golf courses, airport, marina, and the 2012 debut of SHARC (Sunriver Homeowners Aquatic & Recreation Center), open to all guests. At the lodge, **Meadows at the Lodge** is open year round for breakfast and lunch (seasonal dinner service); the cozy **Owl's Nest** pub is open from 2 p.m. until closing. This is a family-friendly resort with something for everyone.

WARM SPRINGS

KAH-NEE-TA HIGH DESERT RESORT
6823 Hwy 8   541/553-1112, 800/554-4786
Moderate to expensive   kahneeta.com

INDIAN HEAD CASINO
3236 Hwy 26   541/460-7777
                    indianheadgaming.com

This resort, located along the Warm Springs River, is a fun destination for the entire family. The village is the hub of recreational activities including a glorious Olympic-size hot springs mineral pool and water slides, mini golf and **Spa Wanapine**. Lodging options range from village suites, RV parking spaces and tipis. Additional rooms are in the lodge (a half mile away, complimentary shuttle service), which also contains the convention center, restaurants and another pool. **Indian Head Casino** has relocated 11 miles down the road to larger quarters with expanded gaming areas and restaurants. **Cottonwood Restaurant** is top-notch (breakfast, lunch and dinner menus; buffet lunch Monday through Saturday, dinner buffet Friday and Saturday and Sunday brunch). The area boasts 300 days of sunshine a year; no assertions are made for casino gambling.

THE MUSEUM AT WARM SPRINGS

2189 Hwy 26   541/553-3331
Daily: 9-5 (seasonally adjusted)   museumatwarmsprings.org
Nominal

A beautiful museum on the Warm Springs Indian Reservation features collections and exhibitions of Pacific Northwest Native American ceremonial clothing, masks and ritual implements as well as baskets, beadwork, paintings, photographs and sculptures. Artifacts are displayed in permanent and changing exhibits; interactive exhibits come alive with colorful visuals and authentic audio recordings; a small amphitheater is outside. The museum, built in 1993 (Oregon's first tribal museum), is dedicated to preserving, advancing and sharing the cultural, traditional and artistic heritage of the Confederated Tribes of Warm Springs. The interpretive Twanat Trail is a recent addition; this quarter-mile trail has educational displays about the area's animals, birds, plants, water creatures, geology and history.

Get outdoors

There are more than 50 parks with year-round and seasonal campgrounds in the **Oregon Parks and Recreation** (oregonstateparks.org) system.   Most accept campsite reservations; others are first-come, first-served.   Day-use wayside, viewpoints and scenic bikeways and water trails are also a part of statewide offerings. Among the most popular parks:

CENTRAL OREGON

Bend
Pilot Butte State Scenic Viewpoint
Culver
Cove Palisades State Park
Terrebonne
Smith Rock State Park

COASTAL OREGON

Astoria
Fort Stevens State Park

Brookings
Harris Beach State Recreation Area

Cannon Beach
Tolovana Beach State Recreation Site

Coos Bay
Sunset Bay State Park

Depoe Bay
Boiler Bay State Scenic Viewpoint
Otter Crest State Scenic Viewpoint

Florence
Heceta Head Lighthouse Scenic Viewpoint
Jessie M. Honeyman Memorial State Park
Siuslaw North Jetty

Gold Beach
Samuel H. Boardman State Scenic Corridor

Lincoln City
D River State Recreation Site

Newport
South Beach State Park
Yaquina Bay State Recreation Site

EASTERN OREGON

Joseph
Wallowa Lake State Recreation Area

PORTLAND AREA

Portland
Tryon Creek State Natural Area

COLUMBIA RIVER GORGE AND MT. HOOD

Corbett
Crown Point State Scenic Corridor

WILLAMETTE VALLEY

Silverton
Silver Falls State Park

Senator **Mark Hatfield** in his Washington, D.C. office. He always had a clean desk. (1980s)

PERSONAL COLLECTION

Senator **Mark Hatfield**'s original Washington, D.C. staff. Left to right: **Eric Lindauer**, **Ray Underwood**, Hatfield, **Sam Mallicoat**, **Gerry Frank**, **Bill Swing.** (1967)

At left: Senator **Mark Hatfield**'s Washington, D.C. staff conducted a chocolate cake contest for Oregonians working on Capitol Hill; your author was the sole judge. **Antoinette Hatfield** shares a taste of cake with her husband. (1970s)

MORROW COUNTY HERITAGE MUSEUM

Looking north along Main Street after the June 14, 1903, flood in Heppner.

PERSONAL COLLECTION

Gerry Frank (left) and Hatfield (middle). Senator **Mark Hatfield** made an inspection trip of American installations in Antarctica (McMurdo, Byrd, Beardmore), representing the Senate Interior and Insular Affairs Committee. While there, the party met with Oregon State University marine biologists at the Palmer base and toured the Russian installation at Vostok. The penguins really fascinated Hatfield! (1970)

Keiko, the killer whale, at the Oregon Coast Aquarium (1996-1998). He was Oregon's most famous guest!

OREGON COAST
AQUARIUM

Left to right: **Amy Kerr**, Gerry Frank, **Katie Harman**. The
Miss America Pageant tapped Gresham, Oregon's Katie Harman
Ebner as its winner in 2002; following on the heels of Katie was Amy
Kerr McVey of Keizer, chosen as our 2002 America's Junior Miss.
These smart, talented (and, yes, beautiful) women made Oregonians
everywhere proud; both have gone on to married life and careers
and still call Oregon home. These were not the first two women to
bring such recognition to Oregon; **Cleo Maletis** (Mrs. Chris C.
Maletis, Jr.) of Portland was Mrs. America 1957. (2003)

GERRY LEWIN

Left to right: Former governors **Mark Hatfield**, **Victor Atiyeh**, **Neil Goldschmidt, Barbara Roberts** and **John Kitzhaber**; Governor **Ted Kulongoski** in Governor's office on the occasion of former Governor **Robert Straub**'s memorial service. (2002)

PERSONAL COLLECTION

Peter DeFazio, Denny Smith, Bob Packwood, Les AuCoin, Mark Hatfield, Neil Goldschmidt, Ron Wyden and **Bob Smith** at a Salem hearing. (1990s)

PERSONAL COLLECTION

Senator **Mark Hatfield**'s only "questionable political payoff" has been a longstanding anecdote in the annals of the Oregon State Fair. During his first run for the governorship, your author worked in the campaign. Having followed in my father's footsteps in more ways than one, I was (and am) a chocoholic; Mark told me that if he won, he would ask the Oregon State Fair Commission to appoint me the judge of the fair's chocolate cake contest. Mark did win and I was appointed to preside over the *Gerry Frank Chocolate Layer Cake Contest* where I've been the sole judge each year since 1959. From 1959's three entries to years of over 130, that's a lot of bites of chocolate cake (two bites of each)! (Secret to survival: a Pepto-Bismol "sandwich" — a good dose of the pink stuff before the contest and one immediately following!)

PHOTOGRAPH FROM SENATE REPUBLICAN CONFERENCE

Senator **Mark Hatfield's** Washington, D.C. staff. (circa 1970)

Senator **Mark Hatfield** on a Southern Oregon swing trip to meet constituents, taking a break and feeding apples to an elephant at the Wildlife Safari in Winston, Oregon. Hatfield posed on an elephant later; one can only imagine the condition of his pants at his next appearance!

PERSONAL COLLECTION

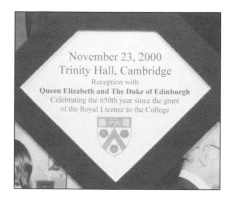

Photos taken at a lunch and reception at my alma mater, Trinity Hall, Cambridge University, England, celebrating the 650th year since the grant of the Royal License to the College. Top left: Master of Trinity Hall, Cambridge University, Gerry Frank, **Queen Elizabeth** and **The Duke of Edinburgh**. (2000)

*To Gerald Frank with best wishes
Bernard M Baruch
April 1965*

Bernard M. Baruch, New York banker and presidential advisor, conducted office hours on park benches in New York City's Central Park. He was an idol of your author who had the rare opportunity in 1962 to personally visit with Baruch in his New York apartment.

PERSONAL COLLECTION

LETTERS, TELEGRAMS AND STATION
KINGSTREE, SOUTH CAROLINA

may 8th
1962

LITTLE HOBCAW

My dear Mr. Frank,
              Let me
know when you are arriving
in New York where I shall be
on may 18th to June 3rd.
Then from July 20th till
October.
     I am looking forward to
meeting you
     Best wishes
              Bernard M Baruch

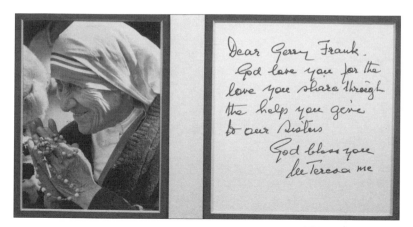

Mother Teresa and a personal note from her. Your author visited her numerous times in Calcutta, India, working on world hunger problems. (1975)

My late brother and his family: Dick, Jeff, Scott, Debbie, Skip, Paula (wife) and Michael Frank. (circa 1958)

Margaret Thatcher, Prime Minister of England (1979-1990), and Gerry Frank. (1994)

Former President **Ronald Reagan** and Gerry Frank at the White House, inauguration night. (1981)

Left, right: Devastation in the aftermath of the June 14, 1903 Heppner flood.

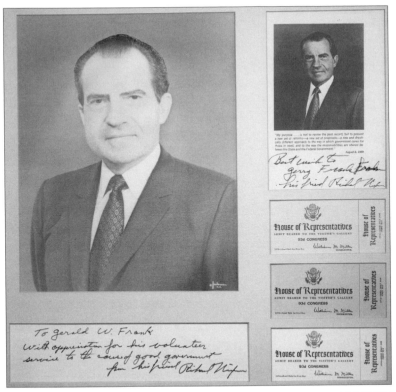

PERSONAL COLLECTION

At the time of President **Richard Nixon**'s scheduled 1974 impeachment hearings, tickets were printed by the House of Representatives for three different days and officially signed by William "Fishbait" Miller, then the Doorkeeper of the House. House members were incensed that a "mere employee" signed these documents, so all were ordered destroyed. Through a special friend, your author was able to extract three of these historic pieces prior to their disposal, probably a very few that are still in existence today. The hearings, of course, were never held, making these tickets especially memorable pieces of U.S. history. They now occupy space in my office, framed with the late president's photo. (1974)

President **Ronald Reagan**'s first inauguration. The only program copy in existence signed by Reagan's cabinet and all ceremony participants. The programs, invitation, tickets and photos are preserved and hang in my office. (1981)

INAUGURAL CEREMONIES PROGRAM

JANUARY 20, 1981

[signature]

The Joint Congressional Committee on Inaugural Ceremonies will escort the PRESIDENT-ELECT, RONALD WILSON REAGAN, and MRS. REAGAN; the VICE PRESIDENT-ELECT, GEORGE BUSH, and MRS. BUSH; the VICE PRESIDENT, WALTER F. MONDALE, and MRS. MONDALE from their respective residences to the White House as follows:

From the residence of the President-elect:

    PRESIDENT-ELECT RONALD WILSON REAGAN *[signature: Ronald Reagan]*
    MRS. NANCY REAGAN
    SENATOR MARK O. HATFIELD
    REPRESENTATIVE JOHN J. RHODES *[signature: John J. Rhodes]*

From the residence of the Vice President-elect:

    VICE PRESIDENT-ELECT GEORGE BUSH *[signature]*
    MRS. BARBARA BUSH
    SENATOR HOWARD H. BAKER, JR.
    REPRESENTATIVE ROBERT H. MICHEL *[signature: Robert Michel]*

From the residence of the Vice President:

    VICE PRESIDENT WALTER F. MONDALE *[signature: Wm Mondale]*
    MRS. JOAN MONDALE
    SENATOR ROBERT C. BYRD *[signature: Robert C. Byrd]*
    REPRESENTATIVE JIM WRIGHT

Speaker THOMAS P. O'NEILL and SENATOR CLAIBORNE PELL meet PRESIDENT JIMMY CARTER and MRS. CARTER at the White House.

From the White House, the order of automobiles will be as follows:

First Automobile: THE PRESIDENT *[signature: Jimmy Carter]*
    THE PRESIDENT-ELECT
    SENATOR HATFIELD
    SPEAKER O'NEILL *[signature: Tip O'Neill]*

Second Automobile: MRS. CARTER
    MRS. REAGAN
    REPRESENTATIVE RHODES
    SENATOR BYRD

Third Automobile: THE VICE PRESIDENT
    THE VICE PRESIDENT-ELECT
    SENATOR BAKER
    REPRESENTATIVE WRIGHT *[signature: Jim Wright]*

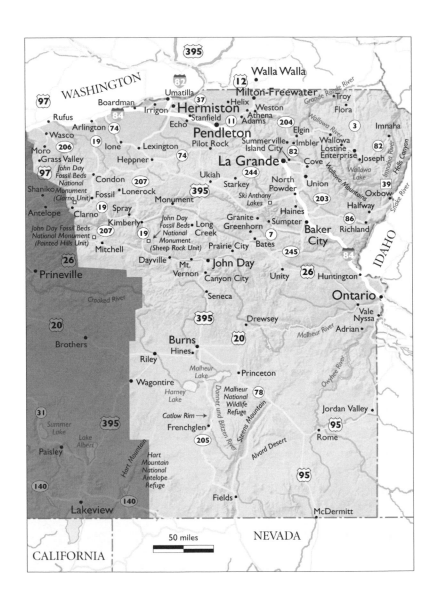

6. Eastern Oregon

BAKER CITY

BAKER HERITAGE MUSEUM

2480 Grove St   541/523-9308
March-Oct   bakerheritagemuseum.com

ADLER HOUSE MUSEUM

2305 Main St
Tours: Memorial Day to Labor Day

Baker County is a gold mine of history! At one time, Baker City was the third-largest city in Oregon and fastest-growing community in the West. Housed in the city's former natatorium, this building helps preserve the county's eclectic chronicles. Along with many artifacts, the **Cavin-Warfel Collection** of rocks, fossils and minerals, begun in the 1930s as a hobby of two Baker City sisters who continued their passion for 45 years, is housed here; the **Wyatt Family Collection** is an assemblage of some 2,000 agates, jasper and other rocks and gems. The **Adler House Museum** is also managed by the Baker Heritage Museum. Mr. Adler, a low-key gent, was very successful in the magazine distribution business and became a major benefactor to nearly every local cause. A lifelong bachelor, Leo died in 1993 at the age of 98 and left his $20 million fortune to his beloved community; the **Leo Adler Foundation** (leoadler.com) administers grants and scholarship funds. His Italianate home (circa 1889) has been restored to its glory days with period wallpaper, original furniture, artwork and light fixtures. It was my pleasure to meet with Leo now and then, especially with Senator **Mark Hatfield** during "swing" trips to Eastern Oregon. To conserve costs, Adler used only a small portion of his large home, never tending to its upkeep; we met in the rather shabby, darkened living room with heat only in the immediate area. Leo was one of a kind!

BARLEY BROWN'S BREW PUB

2190 Main St   541/523-4266
Mon-Sat: 4-10   barleybrowns.com
Moderate

Tyler Brown loves beer and in 1998 he combined his passion into a livelihood. Providing "small batch handcrafted beer, good food, good company, good times" is the basis of a Baker City mainstay eatery where you'll find plenty of comfort food along with award-winning beer to wash it down. Standout dinners include a one-pound rack of baby back ribs, shrimp and alligator pasta, steaks, salads and pub grub. Not unlike the iconic *Cheers* television show, everyone is likely to know your name — or get to know it should you venture in more than a time or two. Soon there will be two locations. Tyler and the Brown clan are expanding their operation with a second brewery and tasting room right across the street.

BELLA MAIN STREET MARKET

2023 Main St   541/523-7490
Daily: 7-7   bellabakercity.com

Be sure to check out the impressive selection of groceries plus gourmet foods, fine wines, kitchenware, gifts and good java drinks from the unique espresso bar (a massive 18-foot long, two-inch thick slab of slate). The shelves hold local and organic staples (eggs, bread, produce, lamb, beef), an extensive selection of cheese

KIDS' ACTIVITIES IN EASTERN OREGON

Baker City
National Historic Oregon Trail Interpretive Center (541/523-1843, blm.gov/or/oregontrail)

Dayville
Thomas Condon Paleontology Center (541/987-2333, nps.gov/joda)

Joseph
Wallowa Lake State Park (541/432-4185, oregonstateparks.org)

Wallowa Lake Tramway (541/432-5331 in summer, 503/781-4321 in winter, wallowalaketramway.com): seasonal

La Grande
Eagle Cap Excursion Train (541/963-9000, eaglecaptrain.com)

Princeton
Malheur National Wildlife Refuge (541/493-2612, fws.gov/Malheur)

and salami and Northwest, Italian, French, Thai, Japanese and Spanish favorites. Many of the gourmet foodstuffs are Baker City exclusives; gather up an assortment to include in a personalized gift (choose a basket, beautiful platter or whatever strikes your fancy) appropriate for any occasion. Kitchen necessities and accessories of all sizes and prices are great go-withs. There is sure to be a gadget, serveware, dishes or a special treasure to spiff up your kitchen, dining room or pantry.

CHARLEY'S ICE CREAM PARLOR

2101 Main St   541/524-9307
Daily

"Let's go to Charley's!" In this community, that familiar phrase leads customers to Basche-Sage Place at the corner of Main and Broadway. Stop in for a treat from early in the day until late into the evening and choose from a multitude of ice cream flavors, hot dogs, candies and espressos. Charley was indeed the confectionary's founder, no longer with us, but his name endures.

EARTH & VINE WINE BAR AND ART GALLERY
2001 Washington Ave   541/523-1687
Lunch, Dinner: Daily; Breakfast: Sat, Sun

For a "taste" of Baker City, visit this charming restaurant, wine bar and art gallery. You'll be impressed with talented local artists' showings and fine wines at reasonable prices. The menu offers good choices for lunch or dinner — homemade soups, sandwiches, salads, pizzas and pasta dishes; brunch specials include delicious homemade crepes and Benedicts. Coffee, desserts and other enticing goodies from **Sweet Wife Baking** (sweetwifebaking.com) are served all day. The gallery occasionally hosts live music performances.

GEISER GRAND HOTEL
1996 Main St   541/523-1889, 888/434-7374
Inexpensive to expensive   geisergrand.com

Center stage in Baker City's downtown is this elegant Eastern Oregon hotel with cowboy appeal. First opened in 1889, **Barbara and Dwight Sidway** undertook an unbelievable project in 1998 to restore this grande dame back to life. This historic landmark is an architectural jewel and charming with ornate mahogany, gleaming brass, crystal chandeliers in every room and leaded stained glass. Spend a memorable night in the grand Cupola Suite where you will enjoy impressive mountain views from your bed and luxuriate in the large, well-appointed bathroom. Other accommodations are also tastefully decorated and outfitted with amenities. Belly up to the mahogany bar in the **1889 Saloon** for sundown libations or dinner and enjoy local musicians and other entertainment. The classy **Palm Court** restaurant is surrounded by a mahogany balcony and basks under a stained glass ceiling. Fine dining entrees include meats, fish and seafood, in-house smoked meats and decadent homemade desserts. The Sidway's painstaking restoration has garnered prestigious awards; the Geiser is truly a sight to behold and appreciate any day of the year.

> ### BOOMERANG
>
> In the winter of 1933, arctic air slid into Northeastern Oregon, leading thermometers to plunge to -54 degrees in both Seneca and Ukiah. This remains Oregon's all-time recorded low temperature. The next day, the high was 45 degrees, resulting in an overnight swing of nearly 100 degrees in the same area!

PROSPECTORS FRONTIER INN

1917 Court Ave   541/403-4046
Inexpensive   prospectorsfrontierinn.com

Here is a practical B&B experience housed in the 1910 Ison Building (listed on the National Register of Historic Places). Two suites offer modern conveniences (like indoor plumbing, not to mention Wi-Fi) never dreamed of by the Strother Ison family whose 1862 travels from Missouri brought them to Baker City with the first wagon train. Virgil Ison completed the building for his medical practice and shared it with a brother-in-law's dental practice. **Marie and John Watson** purchased and renovated the building in 2005 and converted it to the current role as a B&B after a stint as a chocolate shop and bistro. Guests' quarters include the old doctor's and dentist's offices and den; shared bathrooms are down the hall (bathrobes provided). Room amenities vary, but may include a vintage record player, microwave and toaster or television with a selection of favorite movies. Breakfast in this turn-of-the-century landmark starts with freshly-baked cinnamon rolls followed by a fruit and yogurt parfait and a variety of quiches. Nearby are shops, eateries, galleries and loads of fascinating history (arrange for a customized carriage ride for an interesting back-then perspective).

THE SYCAMORE TREE

2108 Main St   541/523-4840
Mon-Sat: 10-6   sycamoregifts.com

Wrap up your gift list on Main Street! Sure to please any recipient are fresh flowers and fudge as well as an array of elegant gifts, home decor, religious items and an art gallery featuring local artists. Attractive vignettes showcase the merchandise and suggest eye-appealing arrangements. If you have a sweet tooth, make a beeline to the fudge counter for morsels of chocolate sensations or other interesting flavor variations, all made in the store by hand with quality ingredients.

BATES

BOULDER CREEK RANCH
72585 Middle Fork Lane   541/421-3031
Moderate   bouldercreekranch.net

Camp with a twist when you journey to Eastern Oregon's high desert country for the rare opportunity for kids (and kids-at-heart) to stay in an authentic Basque sheepherder's wagon. Sheepherders and their camps were a common sight in the 1800s, and now this ranch brings the Old West back to the forefront with this unique idea. The canvas-covered wagon has a full-size bed and offers a table with bench seating. Amenities? No power, no running water, no phone, no television — that's the point! Coupled with the authentic wagon, however, is a one-bedroom guest cabin immediately next door. With the cabin's modern-day facilities (bath, kitchen, woodstove), perhaps mom and dad will stay there and let the kids have a private adventure in the wagon (available except during winter months). Provisions are supplied to prepare a full ranch breakfast before you head out to explore the property or help with ranch chores.

BOARDMAN

RIVER LODGE AND GRILL
6 Marine Dr   541/481-6800, 888/988-2009
Lodging: Inexpensive   riverlodgeandgrill.com
Restaurant: Breakfast, Lunch, Dinner: Daily
Moderate

You might think that a stop at Boardman isn't worth the detour from I-84. Wrong. You would miss affordable lodging in a log and river-stone complex along the Columbia River in rooms that are tidy, clean and well-appointed. The riverside rooms and restaurant overlook the private rocky beach with incomparable views of the river. Whether you stay overnight or not, you'll get a good meal at the establishment's lodge-style restaurant. The menu changes seasonally but you can anticipate quality comfort food. Prices are family-friendly in the restaurant, too. Special hunting, fishing and golf packages combine accommodations with local activities.

BURNS

CRYSTAL CRANE HOT SPRINGS
59315 Hwy 78   541/493-2312
Inexpensive to moderate   cranehotsprings.com

Resting your head "in the middle of nowhere" is fun and a great way to better understand our diverse state. This is just such a quaint, atypical place where more adventurous travelers can hit the hay in a tent, use the available RV hookups or one of the establishment's five rustic cabins (mostly shared bathrooms). A three-bedroom apartment and three-bedroom home are also on site. Enjoy the great outdoors from the warm geothermal spring-fed pond or private soaking tubs in The Bathhouse, which also offers showers and restrooms; a nominal fee is charged for day use (daily, 9-9).

R J'S RESTAURANT
Hwy 20 E at Hwy 395   541/573-6346
Daily: 5:30 a.m.-7:30 p.m.
Inexpensive

For four decades, **Sonja and Bob McDannel** have run this quality operation where they proclaim, "Anything you want, any time of the day." The menu includes more than a dozen milkshake flavors, salad bar, hamburgers, popcorn shrimp, baked potatoes and a kids' menu. All burgers arrive with a hearty portion of fries (don't miss the super Swiss cheese and mushroom burger); breakfast is available throughout the day. There's plenty of parking for big rigs and oversize RVs at this Southeastern Oregon junction.

CANYON CITY

OXBOW TRADE COMPANY

303 S Canyon City Blvd   541/575-2911
Hours vary   oxbowwagonsandcoaches.com

Horse-drawn vehicles are an anomaly in this high-tech day and age. However, owners **Mary and Jim Jensen** build, buy and restore these conveyances for aficionados like themselves. In addition to other utility and pleasure vehicles are carriages, wagons, chuck wagons, sleighs, carts and an occasional hearse; you'll find high quality at fair prices. They also sell Amish-made harnesses, parts and accessories such as sleigh bells, cast iron horse heads, gears, lamps, steps and necessary accessories. Visitors are welcome, but call ahead to make sure someone is minding the shop; frequent auctions and shows are always a pull to add to their stock and locate hard-to-find pieces for customers.

DAYVILLE

THOMAS CONDON PALEONTOLOGY CENTER
JOHN DAY FOSSIL BEDS NATIONAL MONUMENT

Hwy 19, 9 miles north of Dayville   541/987-2333
Daily: 9-5   nps.gov/joda

The Thomas Condon Paleontology Center serves as a visitor center for the **Sheep Rock Unit** and encompasses a research lab, classrooms and large public areas for special exhibits showcasing over 50,000 fossils representative of more than 40 million years of geologic history. All fossils on display were found in the John Day Fossil Beds; look for rhino, giraffe-deer, camels, horses, bear-dogs, oreodonts and entelodonts, but no dinosaurs. Visitors from around the world enjoy the park's trails, overlooks and picnic areas as they marvel at the colorful formations. The park's headquarters are in the James Cant 1917 homestead dwelling; its history is an interesting read. Venture a bit farther to see two other components of this national monument: **Painted Hills Unit** (Hwy 26, 9 miles northwest of Mitchell) and **Clarno Unit** (Hwy 218, 20 miles west of Fossil). Don't even think about digging for fossils on these properties; instead, head to the town

ALWAYS BE PREPARED

It was a well-known fact among friends and colleagues that Governor (and later Senator) **Mark Hatfield** never passed up a chance to visit a convenient restroom. On one stop in a remote Central Oregon village, he heard a loud pounding coming from the inside of the only such facility (at a filling station) in the area. With his pocketknife at hand, Mark jimmied the lock, allowing the overly-excited gentleman to exit. Greatly relieved (in more ways than one), the individual (from out of state) was most impressed when he learned that his savior was none other than the senior senator from Oregon! Too bad he couldn't vote!

of Fossil where collecting is available to the public behind the high school (www.wheelercounty-oregon.com/fossils.html).

ENTERPRISE

ARROWHEAD RANCH CABINS

64745 Pine Tree Rd
May-Oct
Moderate

541/426-6420
arrowheadranchcabins.com

If you're staying a few days or longer, this ranch could provide just the right retreat. You can throw a horseshoe or two, bicycle (provided) the local country roads, meander the walking paths and observe the abundant flora and fauna. The one-bedroom Ruby Peak cabin provides 800 square feet of knotty-pine-paneled living, bed and bath space that accommodates up to four people. The white clapboard Wagon House cabin is slightly larger. Both cabins have full-service kitchens, overstuffed chairs, fine bed linens and down comforters making "camping" here first-class. The stately white peg-constructed barn (circa 1888) has been a favorite feature of the Wallowa County Barn Tour. Bring your horse for $10 a day; you provide feed unless pasture is available (no other pets, credit cards, telephone, television or smoking). Guests are treated to a box of handcrafted truffles from their **Arrowhead Chocolates** operation in Joseph (100 N Main Street, 541/432-2871).

BARKING MAD FARM AND COUNTRY BED & BREAKFAST

65156 Powers Road   541/215-2758
Moderate   barkingmadfarm.com

If you'd like a time-out from the kids, you'll love being pampered by **Diana and James Hunter** in their charming farmhouse. The working farm setting couldn't be more idyllic; grazing buffalo, alpine vistas, tranquil grounds and a short drive to Joseph and Wallowa Lake. Guest rooms are cozy, well-appointed and afford more glorious views. You're in for a treat each morning with a gourmet breakfast of huckleberry *palacsintas* (Hungarian crepes) with all the accoutrements, brioche French toast, homegrown and local fruits when available, house-smoked salmon, Wallowa

---

YOU COULDN'T MAKE THIS UP!

Beginning in 1981 until its collapse in 1985, the **Rajneeshpuram** episode unfolded before bewildered Oregonians' (and the nation's) eyes within a stone's throw of the tiny high desert rural community of Antelope (at one point renamed Rajneesh). The audacity of so-called spiritual power and the mega-money that followed provided almost daily newspaper exposés. The **Bhagwan Shree Rajneesh** with his 7,000 disciples, their unorthodox sexual practices, the fleet of Rolls Royces, the Bhagwan's spokesperson **Ma Anand Sheela** (Sheela Silverman) and other Rajneeshee characters, the bioterror attack through salmonella poisoning, attempted murders, wiretapping, arson — and more — were all fascinating topics. In short, the Bhagwan was deported back to his native India and the movement collapsed. A wealthy Montana businessman, **Dennis Washington**, purchased the 65,000-acre "Big Muddy" property in 1991 (now the Washington Family Ranch) where **Young Life** (younglife.org) operates a Christian youth camp within its borders using and adding to the magnificent facilities for learning and recreation.

County bacon and eggs and other delights. The entrepreneurial Hunters resided in various countries throughout the world before settling in to this region and fulfilling their lifelong dream of welcoming visitors to their own inn. On-site spa treatments (prior arrangements required) complete a weekend of indulgences.

ENTERPRISE HOUSE BED & BREAKFAST

508 1st South St   541/426-4238, 888/448-8825
Moderate   enterprisehousebnb.com

This circa-1910 Colonial Revival mansion is minutes from Joseph and Wallowa Lake and within walking distance to **Terminal Gravity Brewery and Public House** (terminalgravitybrewing.com). Relaxation beckons as guests approach the restored home, resplendent with white picket fence, a porch swing, stained glass, ornate woodwork and nostalgic wood-frame screen doors. Choose from five bedrooms or the Eagle Cap Suite which accommodates up to nine people. Proprietors **Judy and Jack Burgoyne** start each day with an impressive breakfast buffet of organic and locally grown products. On-site **Flying Cloud Gifts** (flyingcloudgifts.com) is worth your while, too.

LEAR'S PUB & GRILL

111 W Main St   541/426-3300
Daily: 7-2; 5 p.m.-close   learspubandgrill.com
Moderate

Husband and wife team, **Cathi and Steve Lear** combine forces in this Main Street family restaurant to dish up three squares daily along with a side of lively banter between themselves and customers. Chef Steve serves local products with an emphasis on Angus beef; check the chalkboard for daily specials. Don't miss hearty breakfasts consisting of Kahlua French toast, huervos rancheros or meat and egg pair-ups; bodacious burgers or real corned beef brisket Reuben sandwiches for lunch or dinner and great steak dinners. To go with your meal or just because, wet your whistle with local microbrews or your favorite drink from the full bar. You'll get your money's worth with good prices and quality food.

RIMROCK INN

83471 Lewiston Hwy   541/828-7769
Mon, Thurs-Sat: 9-7; Sun: 9-4   rimrockrestaurant.com
Inexpensive to moderate

The RimRock boasts a bar area, dining room and a magnificent outdoor deck that overlooks Joseph Canyon, 33 miles north of Enterprise. Almost everything, from salad dressings to breads and desserts is made from scratch. The lunch menu features large and fresh salads, panini sandwiches and burgers; dinner specialties include steaks and chicken. If it's Friday, then it is the Friday night fish basket; Saturday night's special is prime rib. All appetizers are of the battered and deep-fried variety. If you plan to stay in one of their three tipis, which sleep one to six people, bring your sleeping bag; mattresses, pillows, chairs and outdoor fire pits are provided. Other options include an RV park, packed lunches for day hikes and great hunting opportunities. After a night of roughing it, head inside for a hot, nourishing breakfast and homemade cinnamon roll, sure to quell growling stomachs for under $10.

YOU'VE COME A LONG WAY, BABY

After being discovered on a Florida beach and modeling for the cover of the first *Sports Illustrated* "swimsuit" issue in 1964, **Babette March Beatty** found her way to one of Northeastern Oregon's most picturesque places, the town of Halfway. (Check out this community on the Internet.) After forays as a chef and innkeeper, today Babette is an artist. If you don't happen to be in Halfway, see her work at babettesgallery.com.

FIELDS

ALVORD HOT SPRINGS

Fields-Denio Road
Always open

You'll be impressed by this remote attraction about 106 miles southeast of Burns on the edge of the picturesque Alvord

Desert. The spring's facilities, at an elevation of more than 4,000 feet, were remodeled a couple of years back; half of the man-made pool is enclosed by a wall above the ground. Water cools from 174 degrees at the source to a soothing 112 degrees in the three-foot deep pool. Access to the hot springs is free; you can expect a slight sulfur odor and a few bathers who prefer to leave bathing garb behind. A good source for detailed driving directions and a list of other Oregon hot springs is **soakoregon.com**.

FIELDS STATION

22276 Fields Dr   541/495-2275
Store: Mon-Sat: 8-6; Sun: 9-5   thefieldsstation.com
Cafe: Mon-Sat: 8-4:30; Sun: 9-4:30
Inexpensive

Are you among the smattering of Oregonians who have ventured to Fields? This small unincorporated community is 112 miles south of Burns taking Highway 205 (the highway becomes a county road, Catlow Valley Road, at the Roaring Springs Ranch). Nothing is more refreshing on a hot summer day along the dusty road than a huge milkshake or malt, made by hand the old-fashioned way and served in a frosty steel cup. The cafe is famous for its burgers; a half-pounder with chili or a double bacon cheeseburger. Breakfasts are equally satisfying and large. A most welcome sight for motorists running on fumes is one of the few gas pumps in the area; they also pump diesel and propane. If you're looking for a place to call it a night, super helpful **Sandra Downs** will put you up in one of the two two-bed rooms, or you may prefer to stay in the Old Hotel which rents as a single unit; RVers are accommodated in the adjacent facility. The store is the center of the community and stocks groceries, toiletries, necessary auto supplies, ice-cold beer (micros and domestic cans), other beverages and snacks; it contains a unique USPS Post Office and Oregon's smallest OLCC liquor store (with a full range of "snake bite medicine"). The epitome of Oregon's high desert is Steens Mountain for fishing, hunting and spectacular hiking and camping; be mindful of dangerous sudden weather changes.

FOSSIL

FOSSIL GENERAL MERCANTILE COMPANY

555 Main St   541/763-4617
Mon-Sat: 8-7 (till 6 in winter); Sun: 8-5

Readily known as "The Merc," this store has been reincarnated several times since its 1883 opening and still retains the feel of yesteryear. It's a godsend to those who live, work and play miles from city shopping opportunities for fabrics, clothing, groceries and sundry items.

SERVICE CREEK STAGE STOP

38686 Hwy 19   541/468-3331
Daily   servicecreekresort.com
Lodging: Inexpensive

In the midst of John Day Fossil Beds National Monument is Service Creek — population two. Six clean, themed guest rooms await individuals, families and groups. Rooms are outfitted with antiques and accessories appropriate to the theme; some have bunk beds for youngsters. An adjoining store carries all the travel necessities and the restaurant's menu includes most dishes the average family may want: hand-cut New York steaks, burgers, local produce and homemade soups and desserts (reduced hours in winter). Raft, pontoon boat, canoe and Tahiti inflatable canoe rentals, including shuttle service, are available. Also experience great hiking, ghost town exploring, wildlife, swimming, bass fishing and some of the state's best motorcycle roads. During the fall season, steelhead fishing is great on the John Day River. History buffs will love the stories of the 1920s lodge, which was once known as Tilly's Boarding House, convenient for those who made Service Creek a stage stop.

WILSON RANCHES RETREAT BED & BREAKFAST

16555 Butte Creek Road   541/763-2227, 866/763-2227
Year round   wilsonranchesretreat.com
Inexpensive to moderate

For an authentic Western retreat, book accommodations at **Nancy and Phil Wilson'**s 9,000-acre working cattle

KIND REGARDS

Senator **Mark Hatfield** made it a point to keep in touch with friends and constituents and took to heart their personal well-being. As Mark's friend and chief of staff, I was along on social calls to see former Governor **Oswald "Os" West** and the first appointed Oregon State Police Superintendent, **Charles "Charlie" Pray**. Both men were getting up in years; the appreciation by these men for such thoughtfulness was palpable. (Unfortunately, both also met their demise shortly after our visit and word got around that it might be the death knell if the senator paid a visit!) Another such story involved a staffer who was diagnosed with a serious disease as a young man. The man survived and years later the subject of his health came up when he was with the senator. Mark produced a card with names on it that he always kept in his pocket and said, "You've been on my prayer list ever since your illness."

and dude ranch. Up to 20 guests are housed in the 1910 Sears Roebuck Ranch House; each of the six pristine ranch-style guest rooms, some with private baths and fireplaces, is uniquely decorated. The fifth-generation Wilson's pioneer ancestors settled in Wheeler and Gilliam counties, choosing one of the most picturesque areas in Eastern Oregon for their homestead. There is plenty to do with multiple scenic horseback riding trails, fishing, birding, hiking, mountain biking and, of course, the **John Day Fossil Beds National Monument**. While Phil and Nancy regale visitors with tales of family history, a hearty full-course ranch-style breakfast is served in preparation for a memorable day in the beautiful Butte Creek Valley. Guests are invited to grill their own steaks and burgers for dinner. Rooms are outfitted with amenities befitting a nice hotel and guests have access to a movie library, books, games, TV/DVD and cowboy gear (boots, hats and saddle bags). Turn your stay into an occasion with optional activities, flowers, chocolates or other thoughtful touches.

HAINES

ENSMINGER HOUSE

46292 Rock Creek Town Road   541/910-6378
Moderate   ensmingerhouse.com

Built circa 1903 in the shadow of the Elkhorn range of the Blue Mountains by Frank Reilling is this three-bedroom home, great for family getaways anytime of the year. It is one of a few homes that survived the dam burst of 1917 in the Rock Creek area. Amy Ensminger purchased the home in the 1930s, giving it the Ensminger moniker. The house is currently owned by **Beverly and Ray Beach**, Amy's great grandson. Beautiful flowering trees and shrubs punctuate the spring and summer air, especially enjoyed on the new patio while grilling or chilling. Seasonal activities are an easy drive in any direction.

HAINES STEAK HOUSE

910 Front St   541/856-3639
Mon, Wed-Fri: 4:30-9; Sat: 3:30-9; Sun: 12:30-9   hainessteakhouse.com
Moderate

For Old West-style dinners, set your sights on the building with a chuck wagon above the entrance. This family-owned, Western-themed steakhouse has long been known for prime rib, Flame Kist Iron Branded steaks and extensive seafood offerings (lobster, crab, halibut, etc.). Start with the chuck wagon salad bar of fresh fixin's, homemade salads, chili, baked beans and cowboy bread. Quality steaks, seafood or combinations are sized to feed the hungriest cowpokes, petite appetites or young buckaroos. Folks from all over the world venture off the beaten track for dinner here; obviously the good word spreads.

T&T WILDLIFE TOURS

Seasonal   541/856-3356
                                              tnthorsemanship.com

An unusual opportunity for visitors to Northeastern Oregon is brought to you by owners **Susan Triplett** and **Alice Trindle**. Since 1990 they have hitched their Percheron team to a wagon for a narrated view of a herd of some 200 Rocky Mountain elk. Of

NEVER ASSUME!

Years ago I was pleased when asked to address the Chamber of Commerce Annual Awards banquet in Milton-Freewater (the pea capital of America). When I arrived at the banquet, I was impressed as to the fine detail these folks had thought of to welcome me; each chair in the large room had "M/F" plastered on it. Only later did I realize that it was not in recognition of **Meier & Frank** (our family department store), but a branding for city property!

the nine sites in the Baker Valley, T&T is the only feeding station at the base of the Elkhorn Mountains that provides this close-up viewing opportunity and the only place in Oregon that offers a horse-drawn experience to view the regal elk. It's advisable to call T&T to make sure that the team is up and running on the dates you'll be in the area. (Nominally priced tours typically run on the weekends between December and February and between December 26 and January 1.) The remainder of the year finds the ladies and their team conducting riding and trail clinics at their ranch or throughout the Northwest.

HALFWAY

INN AT CLEAR CREEK FARM

East Pine Road   541/742-2238
Moderate   clearcreekinn.com

When you're looking for a place to really "get away from it all," head to the northeast corner of our diverse state. This renovated farmhouse at Clear Creek Farm offers unique quarters near the Oregon Trail, halfway to the top of Eagle Cap. Five rooms and one family suite (all with private baths) are individually decorated a la turn-of-the-century. The full country breakfast is a relaxing affair, even more so watching deer and wild turkeys graze outside the dining room window. Seasonal fresh-from-the-orchard apples and pears are a special treat and the hosts are mindful of dietary needs (prior notification, please). You're smack dab in the middle of a working cattle ranch, surrounded by wildlife, trails, orchards and other delights. If fishing is on the agenda, there are bass- and trout-filled ponds, not to mention the Snake River running through nearby Hells Canyon and Brownlee Reservoir. Horseback riding, waterskiing, canoeing, bicycle tours, llama pack trips, day hikes and ranch chores are great activities during nice weather. With four feet of snow during the winter months, cross-country skiers and snowmobilers will think they're in seventh heaven (snowmobile rental available in-house). This gorgeous home is ideal for family getaways and mingling on the spacious wraparound porch.

JOHN DAY

KAM WAH CHUNG STATE HERITAGE SITE
125 NW Canton St   541/575-2800
May-Oct: Daily: 9-5   oregonstateparks.org/park_8.php

This unusual museum has roots back to the late 1800s when it became a social and religious center for the area's Chinese immigrants working the gold strikes. The building's seven rooms served as living quarters to Doc Hay and Lung On as well as their places of business. Hay was a medical practitioner specializing in herbal medicine and On was a merchant, labor contractor and immigration assistant. After a century of little notice, the building was deteriorating and the collections begged for preservation. In 2002, Oregon's then-First Lady **Mary Oberst** chaired the

QUIET GIANTS

Travis Cross was an unforgettable Portland and Salem operative, with an unbelievable memory and savvy political genius. He was mainly responsible for the success of **Mark Hatfield** in the early days; later he was a prime mover for the **Providence St. Vincent Medical Center** (providence.org) in Portland. The guesthouse for the hospital is lovingly named **The Travis & Beverly Cross Guest Housing Center** for families of patients to stay at very reasonable rates. And who was responsible for keeping Travis on target during his political days? None other than **Lilith PicKell**, one of the great quiet public servants of our state.

successful Kam Wah Chung capital campaign. As a result, an interpretive center and museum exhibitions chronicle the Chinese culture in Grant County. Thousands of interesting items from On's general store, Hay's medical supplies and furnishings used by the proprietors are on display. Entrance to the historic Kam Wah Chung building is by guided tour only which departs from the interpretive center.

JORDAN VALLEY

OLD BASQUE INN
306 Wroten St   541/586-2800
Breakfast, Lunch, Dinner: Daily
Moderate

The first Spanish Basques settled in the Owyhee Mountains in 1889 to tend sheep and ply their skills in what was then a predominantly Basque community. This restaurant's name continues to pay homage to those settlers, but the emphasis on Basque cuisine has waned; ethnic favorites chorizo sausage and homemade cabbage soup are still options, however. American fare such as burgers and fries, steaks, lamb and pork chops and a traditional breakfast menu prevail. Dinner entrees include salad, soup and bread (both homemade) served family-style for two or more. While you're in the heart of the Owyhees go whitewater rafting or hunting; view extraordinary wildlife and the nearby Pillars of Rome geologic formation. The nationally acclaimed annual Jordan Valley Big Loop Rodeo is held the third weekend in May.

JOSEPH

BEECROWBEE
1 S Main St   541/432-0158
Daily: 10:30-5   beecrowbee.com

Do you want to soothe winter-damaged skin? Try Oregon products from this outfit that handcrafts its bath and body items that not only lead to beautiful, healthy skin, but also nurture the spirit and mind. Beecrowbee sells mild soaps with different scents; lotion bars made with shea butter and various oils; bath soak, blended with natural salts; plus their own bath and body oils. The product line is complemented with five varieties of high-quality teas and unique teapots, soy wax candles and home decor. All these items and more are sold in their retail shop and online.

BELLE PEPPER'S BED & BREAKFAST

101 S Mill St   541/432-0490, 866/432-0490
Inexpensive to moderate   bellepeppersbnb.com

Gracious hosts **Pepper and John McColgan** look after their guests in the circa-1915 McCully Mansion. Picture perfect, the stately manse is surrounded by an acre of lawn and gardens alongside the Wallowa River. Each of the three guest rooms is named for past and present residents. The McCully room, the largest, boasts the original bathtub (refurbished), the Dawson room features a classic pedestal sink and the McColgan room has

---

SPOOKY!

Oregon has more ghosts and ghostly tales than you can shake a stick at, noting that we evidently have our share of paranormal activity statewide. Portland's **Pittock Mansion** and the McMenamin brothers' **Bagdad Theater** (many McMenamin holdings are touted to accommodate ghosts), Pendleton's **Eastern Oregon State Hospital**, the **Geiser Grand Hotel** in Baker City and the **Plunkett Center** at Southern Oregon University in Ashland all lay claim to in-house guest ghosts. Legends abound on the Oregon Coast. "Handsome Paul" is said to board at Astoria's **Liberty Theater** and when the Hotel Seaside (later renamed The Seasider) was torn down to make way for the current Shilo Inn, the resident ghosts vacated to inhabit Girtle's Restaurant (now the **Twisted Fish**) down the street. Our iconic lighthouses are no strangers to supernatural mysteries either. Each place ballyhooed with spirits has a unique story of who's who (boo!) and how these ghosts came into residence. If you are curious about this particular population, check out ghostsandcritters.com and other websites that are easily Googled.

a commanding view of the Wallowas and a private bath across the hall. Breakfast in the dining room features homemade breads, fresh fruit and a hot entree (often with eggs from their brood of chickens). Pepper is committed to minimizing their carbon footprint and instituted green practices that have been adopted by the lodging industry. Visit Joseph's charming art galleries, hike, hunt, fish or just sit back and breathe the fresh air.

BRONZE ANTLER BED & BREAKFAST

309 S Main St   541/432-0230, 866/520-9769
Inexpensive to expensive   bronzeantler.com

In a town known for its bronze foundries the Bronze Antler B&B, a 1925 Craftsman bungalow generously furnished with European antiques and furniture, is the perfect addition. Nourishing breakfasts are prepared by host **Bill Finney** while **Heather Tyreman** fills the bottomless cookie jar with daily goodies and makes delicious fresh desserts later in the day. Breakfast choices and times are somewhat flexible. Coffee and tea are brewing at 6 a.m. for early risers and to-go cups are provided for before-breakfast walkers if they head out. Bathrooms adjoin the three guest rooms and a suite with a king bed and additional amenities was constructed in 2008. The regulation-surface bocce court was installed in 2010.

CALDERAS

300 N Lake St   541/432-0585
April-Oct: days and hours vary   calderasofjoseph.com
Expensive

What a masterpiece! Renaissance woman **Nancy Young-Lincoln** and husband **Carl Lincoln** tore down a small shack and constructed a magnificent art nouveau building for their restaurant and retail enterprises. The building is a phenomenal work of art by local artisans; the centerpiece is the freestanding, hand-forged, spiral staircase. Nancy created the fused-glass pieces which are also prominently displayed in the gift gallery alongside an eclectic mix of merchandise including clothing. Hand-carved wooden dragons and mermaids adorn the two stories. The owners originally intended to open a small coffee shop, but more grandiose plans for a fine restaurant fell into place. Before dinner, start with wraps or cheese fondue followed by gourmet beef, chicken and seafood entrees. Everything is homemade and much of the seasonal fresh produce is grown on the owner's Little Sheep Farms in Imnaha. Seasonal backyard seating, frequent live music, vegetarian and gluten-free options and free Wi-Fi are nice features..

MAD MARY & CO.

5 S Main St   541/432-0547
Daily: 7-6   madmaryandcompany.com

Mary Wolfe, a fifth-generation Wallowa County local, launched her shop in 2003 on the main street of this artsy town. Her successful shop is a boon for residents and tourists to find just the right gift and is home base for toys, jewelry, gourmet food, home and garden accessories, a year-round selection of Christmas items and more. Across from the retail area is the 1950s-era fountain (with old time rock and roll tunes) for malts, milkshakes, sundaes (made to perfection), other creamy concoctions and good ol' hand-dipped ice cream; freshly baked goodies and a variety of sandwiches, soups and salads are also on the menu. Stop in early for a cuppa joe and a decadent homemade cinnamon bun or light breakfast.

KNOW YOUR GEOGRAPHY

Did you know that Oregon is the tenth largest state in the union and nearly 4 million people fit into our box-shaped (400 miles east to west; 360 miles north to south) state of just under 100,000 square miles?

VALI'S ALPINE RESTAURANT

59811 Wallowa Lake Hwy   541/432-5691
Dinner: April, May: Sat, Sun; Memorial Day-Labor Day: Wed-Sun
                                                         valisrestaurant.com
Moderate

Since 1974, family-owned Vali's has been Wallowa County's place for authentic Hungarian food. One entree is prepared for dinners (seatings at 5 and 7) and may include cabbage rolls,

---

A BIT FARTHER TO THE NORTHEAST

Just across the Eastern Oregon border near Pendleton, the **Marcus Whitman Hotel & Conference Center** (marcuswhitmanhotel.com) originally opened in Walla Walla, Washington on September 1, 1928. This historic hotel has undergone major renovations in recent years and still serves the city and area as a prime accommodation. Walla Walla has become a mecca for vineyards and, thus, wine-tasting enthusiasts flock to the region. Keep going north to the tiny town of Waitsburg where you'll find Southern comfort food at the **Whoopemup Hollow Café** (whoopemuphollowcafe.com). Forget about counting calories at this scrumptious stop.

---

goulash, chicken paprika, beef kabobs, schnitzel or grilled ribeye steak. Almost as tasty as the entrees are *langos* (Hungarian fry bread), sweet and sour cabbage and späetzle. Oh those desserts: homemade apple strudel, Black Forest cake, rum ice cream cake and exquisite seasonal goodies. The selection of beers, wines and cocktails is impressive. Near-famous homemade doughnuts are fresh on weekends between 9 and 11 (they frequently sell out early) or purchase European-style cold cuts at the summer-only takeout deli counter. Dinner reservations required; no credit cards.

WALLOWA LAKE LODGE

60060 Wallowa Lake Hwy   541/432-9821
Inexpensive to moderate   wallowalake.com
Seasonal

A trip to this gem in "Little Switzerland" offers a family adventure that will not soon be forgotten. This cozy retreat was built in the early 1920s and included an amusement park, bowling alley, dance hall, outdoor movie theater, horse-drawn carousel and other services accessed by boat across the lake. Much has changed except for the laid-back atmosphere and stunning views of the sparkling lake and Wallowa Mountains. Lodging options are all different and rustic; no in-room telephones or televisions (no pets or smoking either). The lodge's 22 rooms are seasonally available May through mid-October, as is the lodge's restaurant. In the off-season, the lodge hosts conferences and group events. Eight cabins are open year round; all are fully furnished, most have wood-burning fireplaces. When you go, be sure to ride the **Wallowa Lake Tramway** (wallowalaketramway.com) to the summit of Mt. Howard (May to October); a convenient cafe serves casual food and drink on the alpine patio. The views are breathtaking. Wear your hiking shoes and bring a jacket if you want to explore or walk down the mountain. There are plenty of hiking opportunities, including nearby Aneroid Lake.

LA GRANDE

HOT LAKE SPRINGS BED & BREAKFAST

66172 Hwy 203   541/963-4685
Moderate to expensive   hotlakesprings.com

Travelers along the Oregon Trail rested at Hot Lake 200 years ago. A hotel and essential services were under one roof in a wood structure built in 1864 and in the early 1900s, a 105-room brick building was completed to include administrative offices and guest rooms. Hot Lake Sanatorium occupied the third floor and became known as "The Mayo Clinic of the West;" the population of these two buildings numbered a whopping 1,000. A fire and the Great Depression all but wiped out the grandeur of the resort. For 70 years it played host to such endeavors as a WWII pilots' school, nurses' training center, nursing home, restaurant, nightclub and bathhouse before finally ending up in foreclosure. In 2003, **Lee and David Manuel** purchased Hot Lake and embarked on the ultimate extreme makeover (at that time there were no windows, floors or roof!). The resulting complex includes a history center (known for the largest Native American and military collection of its kind), collection of antique buggies and fire trucks, gift shop and bronze sculpture gallery, full-service spa and an artists' marketplace. Overnight packages vary from single accommodations with a shared bath to a two-bedroom suite with a private bath. All overnighters receive a gift of art (bronze by David Manuel or a print), tickets to on-site tours and nightly movies, a soak in the mineral springs and breakfast at in-house **Cackleberries**.

Magnoni's serves a light lunch buffet, offers full-service dining and a nightly dinner of all-you-can-eat pasta; banquet facilities are available. Here's another example of Oregon's wide-ranging history and perseverance.

THE POTTER'S HOUSE GALLERY & GIFT BOUTIQUE

1601 6th St   541/963-5351
Mon-Thurs: 9-7; Fri, Sat: 9-5   thepottershousegallery.com

Judy and Bob Jensen work at home from a 100-year-old Victorian beauty that also functions as their gallery and gift boutique. Each day you'll find Bob at the potter's wheel creating raku and decorative and functional stoneware pieces, all lead-free and safe in the microwave, oven and dishwasher. The Bob Jensen warmer would make a unique and thoughtful gift for your favorite cook or special order a full set of dinnerware. If you're crafty, schedule time to participate in making and firing a raku pot of your own design. Alongside Bob's raku in the gallery are sculptures, ceramics, prints, jewelry and photography by 20 or so local artists and craftsmen. A fine selection of boutique gifts include candles, regional gourmet foods, collectible figurines and cottage, Western and lodge decor items.

TEN DEPOT STREET

10 Depot St   541/963-8766
Dinner: Mon-Sat   tendepotstreet.com
Moderate

Hungry Eastern Oregonians and those who travel there have long appreciated this casual, yet on the upscale side, dinner house. Lamb meatballs with Jamaican dipping sauce, house specialty smoked salmon paté or a tasty combination of bites are beyond run-of-the-mill appetizers. Daily soups are homemade and taco and Thai entree salads are prepared with a choice of chicken or beef. Enjoy prime rib, generously portioned steaks and other meats, sandwiches, seafood and pasta. A lentil pecan burger, pasta with pesto and vegetarian dinners are pleasant choices for non-meat eaters. This corner brick building is a live music venue on Tuesday and Thursday evenings. Be sure to see the turn-of-the-century bar.

MITCHELL

SIDEWALK CAFE
204 Main St   541/462-3800
Breakfast, Lunch: Daily
Inexpensive

If you need to fuel your stomach in the distinctive Painted Hills area, the Sidewalk Cafe is friendly and accommodating with good food to boot. This down-home family-run eatery boasts four generations on the job. Folks come from far and wide to enjoy the cafe's homemade biscuits and gravy, with a sausage gravy recipe that's been offered for more than 30 years. Other daily selections include chicken noodle soup with a mini-bread loaf, chili and cornbread, apple cake with whipped cream and peanut butter pie, along with favorites like burgers. Old-fashioned hard ice cream

BED BATH & BEYOND

Bed Bath & Beyond (bedbathandbeyond.com) does things in a big way while still making every customer feel important. The quality is unquestioned. The service is prompt and informed. The selection is huge: sheets, blankets, rugs, kitchen gadgets, towels, dinnerware, hampers, furniture, lamps, cookware, kiddie items, pillows, paper goods, window treatments, wall decor, appliances and interesting gifts. Several locations have health and beauty departments; hours vary by location.

Beaverton — 12155 SW Broadway St, 503/644-6770
Bend — 63455 N Hwy 97, 541/389-4060
Corvallis — 1725 NW 9th St, 541/754-2262
Eugene — 95 Oakway Center, 541/685-2577
Gresham — 719 NW 12th St, 503/669-8888
Hillsboro — 18043 NW Evergreen Pkwy, 503/466-0775
Keizer — 6180 Ulali Dr, 503/304-0040
Medford — 1600 N Riverside Ave, 541/773-3697
Portland — 9918 SE Washington St, 503/258-1228
Tigard — 16800 SW 72nd Ave, 503/624-9242

milkshakes and malts are also on the menu. Trust the sign which advertises burgers, shakes, pies and more; if for no other reason, stop in for a coffee and pie break.

NORTH POWDER

ANTHONY LAKES SKI AREA
47500 Anthony Lake Hwy   541/856-3277
Seasonal   anthonylakes.com

Far from the megalopolis describes Anthony Lakes. Subject to snowpack, great family ski adventures await on uncrowded runs usually beginning in mid-November. At 8,000 feet you'll find light, dry snow, perfect for powder lovers, groomed cross-country trails, snowboard terrain and SnoCat tours to the back side of the mountain for awesome powder. Certified instructors are adept at teaching the entire family — youngsters, boomers and seniors. Start or end your day at the lodge with breakfast or lunch in the cafeteria or gather in Starbottle Saloon for a hot toddy and more fun times. As an aside, Governor **Mark Hatfield** and I had a hand in the early stage of development; a half century later it is still the "friendliest little ski area in America."

ONTARIO

MACKEY'S STEAKHOUSE & PUB
111 SW 1st St   541/889-3678
Sun-Thurs: 11-9; Fri, Sat: 11-10   mackeysonline.com
Moderate

Hardworking couple **Angie and Shawn Grove** honor their Irish heritage and ancestors in this establishment named after their grandfather, Thomas Mackey Grove. Irish fare it is, starting with Dublin potato skins (famous Malheur russets, no doubt), Guinness on tap and Killian's Irish Red. Traditional dinner fare includes Guinness glazed chicken, chicken with Jameson Irish Whiskey sauce, bangers and mash and shepherd's pie. Other options include steaks with the Mackey's traditional Irish rub, fish and seafood, sandwiches, daily fresh soups and interesting salads. Bring the whole family for dining upstairs or on the patio; the downstairs pub is "entertainment central" for the 21 and over crowd.

OXBOW

HELLS CANYON ADVENTURES
4200 Hells Canyon Dam Road   541/785-3352, 800/422-3568
Lodging, tours, charters: April-Sept   hellscanyonadventures.com
Lodging: Moderate

Hells Canyon is North America's deepest river gorge, carved by the Snake River on the Oregon/Idaho border and includes 215,000 acres of designated wilderness area. Jet boat tours provide dramatically different views of the north and south ends of the canyon — whitewater rapids and sheer rock walls or calm water and wide open terrain. Charters are available for steelhead, sturgeon, bass and trout fishing — great family outings. While camping under the stars is a romantic notion, if you're more attuned to a soft bed, try their lodge overlooking the reservoir. Continental breakfast is included (and lunch on some tours); however, the closest restaurants for lunch or dinner are at least ten miles down the road.

PENDLETON

HAMLEY & CO.
30 SE Court Ave   541/278-1100, opt. 1
Mon-Thurs: 9-6; Fri, Sat: 9-8; Sun: 10-4   hamley.com

Probably the most revitalized emporium in the eastern part of the state is Hamley's. Under the inspired ownership of **Parley Pearce** and **Blair Woodfield**, Hamley's, established in 1883, is back to its original glory and beyond. Expect outstanding selections of magnificent leather kits, belts, chaps, saddlery and tack; ranch and fashion apparel for the whole family; hats; silver jewelry, belt buckles and accessories and western gifts for the person or home. Custom saddles are made on site, true works of art and proudly used by generations of equestrians. Service is undeniably topnotch! During Round-Up week, the store is bursting at the seams with cowboys, cowgirls and rodeo fans looking to freshen up wardrobes

BULLS AND HORSES AND CLOWNS, OH MY!

Oregon has a long tradition of rodeos, the gem, of course, is the **Pendleton Round-Up** (pendletonroundup.com). Other well-anticipated shows on the summer circuit:

Joseph
Chief Joseph Days (chiefjosephdays.com): Joseph; fourth weekend in July

Molalla
Molalla Buckeroo PRCA Rodeo (molallabuckeroo. com): 4th of July weekend

Philomath
Philomath Frolic & Rodeo (philomathrodeo.org): second full weekend in July

Sisters
Sisters Rodeo (sistersrodeo.com): second weekend in June

St. Paul
St. Paul Rodeo (stpaulrodeo.com): Wild West Art Show, 4th of July weekend

or garner a professional cowboy's autograph. Hamley's mezzanine level accommodates one of the best collections of Western art that I've seen anywhere. The company's legacy of community support continues today and the Hamley name is synonymous with the **Pendleton Round-Up**.

HAMLEY STEAK HOUSE
8 SE Court Ave   541/278-1100, opt. 2
Dinner: Daily: 5-close   hamleysteakhouse.com
Expensive

HAMLEY CAFE
Daily: 8-4; Lunch: 11-3

Wranglers, Pendleton Whisky and dinner at Hamley Steak House! That, my friends, is the embodiment of an evening in

Pendleton. Hamley & Co. entrepreneurs **Parley Pearce** and **Blair Woodfield** have created a superb atmosphere for traditional, hearty ranch cooking and a not-to-be-missed saloon (open at 4 p.m. daily). The melt-in-your-mouth 14-ounce ribeye steak is bar none. Pop's pot roast and mom's meatloaf head the list of other home-cooking comfort food along with lamb chops, chicken and gravy and mac and cheese. Soups are homemade and sandwiches are more than a mouthful. Check out the surroundings for an original 18th-century bar, authentic tin ceilings, Old West artifacts and faultless local craftsmanship in every nook and cranny. Sandwiched between the Western store and steakhouse is the **Hamley Cafe**, a great quick stop for lunchtime soups, salads and sandwiches or coffee and pastries anytime. You'll be treated Western-style right with delicious food and faultless service.

MONTANA PEAKS HAT CO.

24 SW Court Ave   541/215-1400
Mon, Wed-Sat: 9-5   montanapeaks.net

Western wear is *de rigueur* for spectators, locals and cowboys at the Pendleton Round-Up. This popular retailer is dedicated to Western head gear. The array of felt hats would have pleased John Wayne, Tom Mix or Hopalong Cassidy; in fact, hat styles are named for these legendary characters. These folks shine when it comes to custom handmade cowboy hats — individualized by shape, fit, color and accessories. Might be best to call ahead if you're making a special trip to Montana Peaks; the owners practice random acts of kindness and take random days off.

THE PENDLETON HOUSE BED AND BREAKFAST

311 N Main St   541/276-8581
Inexpensive to moderate   pendletonhousebnb.com

Beauty and luxury co-exist in this 1917 French neoclassical and Italian inn. Amenities consist of fresh flowers in the rooms, home-baked treats, comfy robes, delicious breakfasts, afternoon wine and cheese, free Wi-Fi and parking and an operating Otis elevator to the guest rooms. Rooms are adorned with original wallpaper, heirloom Oriental rugs and antique furnishings. Relaxation awaits on the splendid front porch and balcony and in the wonderful

English garden. The location can't be beat — two blocks from historic downtown.

PENDLETON ROUND-UP
1114 SW Court Ave   541/278-0815
                                                 pendletonroundup.com

Let 'er Buck! That famous slogan and the saddle bronc rider astride a bucking bronc symbolize over 100 years of Pendleton's rodeo competition. This community comes alive the second full week each September for the Round-Up; schools close, businesses adjust hours, restaurants and saloons are packed and every possible lodging alternative is occupied to accommodate the thousands of competitors and spectators from around the country and world who descend upon Pendleton for an authentic taste of the Old West. Not only is lodging scarce, but performances play to sell-out crowds; make arrangements well ahead of time. Afternoon rodeos allow time for evening performances of the **Happy Canyon Indian Pageant and Wild West Show** and for entertainment and frivolity along Main Street (blocked off to vehicular traffic). Don't miss the Friday morning Westward Ho! Parade, Cowboy Breakfasts in Stillman Park, working tipi village or a visit to the Let 'er Buck Room (you must see this) under the grandstands. The prestigious Round-Up Association has received accolades for achievements over the last century. The community is richer in many arenas for the dedication and good works of its nearly 1,000 hardworking volunteers. This is one of my favorite annual events, best seen from a seat behind the bucking chutes. Let 'er Buck!

PENDLETON UNDERGROUND TOURS
37 SW Emigrant Ave   541/276-0730
Tours: Seasonal hours   pendletonundergroundtours.org
Reasonable

The influence of bootlegging, gambling, prostitution and Chinese inhabitants at the turn of the 19th century in Eastern Oregon is unknown to many. A walking tour through what was once the red light district entertains and informs tourists with character re-enactments and interesting tales of legal and illegal businesses and activities. Trained guides lead the curious (age 6 and over) along sidewalks, through tunnels and into historic buildings. You're sure to learn of a side of Pendleton not necessarily found in history books. One of the stops, a former bordello, now (legally) accommodates guests at the **Working Girls Hotel**.

PENDLETON WOOLEN MILLS

1307 SE Court Pl   541/276-6911
Mon-Fri: 8-6; Sat: 9-6; Sun: 10-5   pendleton-usa.com

In retail, nothing says quality and craftsmanship like Pendleton, weaving world-class blanket and apparel woolen fabrics under six generations of Bishop family leadership. The company's heritage in Eastern Oregon began in 1909. Indian trade blankets were the genesis and the tradition continues today in the same mill opened by the Bishop brothers. Take a free informative tour (offered four times daily). The shop is stocked with selections of familiar designs as well as commemorative blankets and throws, apparel for the family, home decor and gifts.

PRODIGAL SON BREWERY & PUB

230 SE Court Ave   541/276-6090
Tues-Sun: Lunch, Dinner   prodigalsonbrewery.com
Moderate

Good beer and good food. Those are the basic elements at Pendleton's first craft brewery smack dab in the middle of town. Ales, porters, stouts, hefs and seasonal brews are always on tap. Traditional pub fare, soups, salads and daily specials are made from scratch; the menu changes to incorporate seasonal regional ingredients. Save room for a delicious dessert — whoopie pie or chocolate and hazelnut tart laced with whiskey. The restaurant resides in a great old building, family-friendly with a children's room that features board games, a library and toys. The noise level adds to the buzz!

WILDHORSE RESORT & CASINO

46510 Wildhorse Blvd   541/966-1610, 800/654-9453
Lodging: Inexpensive to expensive   wildhorseresort.com

OREGON PARKS' SAINT

Respected in both Eastern and Western Oregon for his visionary accomplishments, **Samuel H. Boardman** remains a largely unknown historic Oregonian. Boardman homesteaded at the turn of the 20th century where, today, the town of **Boardman** is named in his honor. He later worked with the state doing road maintenance and went on to his appointment as the first superintendent (1919-1950) of the newly-created State Parks Commission; his mission was to protect roadside timber and develop a state parks system. Boardman is credited with acquiring, on behalf of the state, many of the park areas that are now enjoyed by thousands; there are others, but, from the north coast to the California border, many of our coastal parks were created under Boardman's vision and tenacity. The **Samuel H. Boardman State Scenic Corridor** in southern Oregon's Curry County is a tribute to his vision as the Father of the Oregon State Park System. Remember to say, "Thanks, Sam," as you enjoy our parks. (Within the corridor spanning a deep ravine, the 956 feet long, 345 feet high Thomas Creek Bridge (oregon.gov/ODOT/HWY/geoenvironmental/historic_bridges_coastal1.shtm) is Oregon's highest and a feat of accomplishment when it was built in 1961. The structure consists of three steel deck trusses, supported on steel frame towers on concrete piers.)

PLATEAU RESTAURANT
Lunch: Mon-Fri; Dinner: Daily
Moderate

Wildhorse Resort recently completed a major expansion including a ten-story hotel that boasts being Eastern Oregon's tallest building. Rooms and suites are comfortably furnished and attractively priced. Good restaurants, a nearby golf course, RV park, tipi village and various gaming opportunities make this a popular destination. **Plateau Restaurant** features farm-to-table cuisine with local ingredients best exemplified in the

Pendleton Whisky steak. Plateau is on the upper floor of the casino, where you'll not only enjoy one of the best Kobe beef burgers (white cheddar cheese, mushrooms, shallot ketchup, frizzled onions and hand-cut French fries) in the state, but also sweeping views of the Blue Mountains. Worth noting are Northwest wines, beers and special dining events. A sports bar, 24-hour cafe and buffet satisfy casual diners. What else to do? Take in a current flick at the five-screen Cineplex, turn the kiddos loose in the children's entertainment center or head across the parking lot to **Tamástslikt Cultural Institute** (541/966-9748; tamastslikt.org) for 10,000 years of living history.

WORKING GIRLS HOTEL
17 SW Emigrant Ave   541/276-0730
Inexpensive   pendletonundergroundtours.org

For a real Old West experience, stay in one of the hotel's four guest rooms or one suite operated by **Pendleton Underground Tours**. Through **Pam Severe**'s meticulous renovation in 1991, the Victorian style, hardwood floors, 18-foot ceilings and exposed brick walls remain. The circa-1890 hotel (formerly W.G. Hotel) has 21st-century indulgences (like heat and air conditioning); baths are extra large. Open year round; no children or pets. In case you're wondering, yes, this was once one of Pendleton's 18 "boarding houses" (bordellos).

PRAIRIE CITY

HISTORIC HOTEL PRAIRIE
112 Front St   541/820-4800
Inexpensive to moderate   hotelprairie.com

If you head cross-country on Oregon's designated Journey Through Time Scenic Byway, Prairie City is a likely stop. Guests are welcomed into nine rooms, including one full suite (with kitchen). Two rooms can create a suite effect; all rooms offer private baths. Built in 1905, the hotel has gone through several transformations, serving various business ventures from 1980 to 2005. In 2005 the current owners stepped in to create a cozy destination hotel and greeted their first guests three years later. Lining the walls are photos of local families, the area and its bygone mining, ranching and logging past. Free Wi-Fi and cable television are modern amenities; an on-site masseuse will ease away the day's sore muscles. A spacious lobby and welcoming backyard patio garden invite relaxation.

OXBOW RESTAURANT & SALOON

128 W Front St   541/820-4544
Lunch, Dinner: Tues-Sun   prairiecityoregon.com
Moderate

Carol and Phil Bopp offer lunch and dinner burgers, sandwiches, steaks, seafood and such. Do not miss the specialty of the house: Carol's homemade pies, made fresh daily and served with a scoop of hard ice cream. The original condition, antique bar (circa 1879) is quite a conversation piece where full-service drink options and a large selection of beers and microbrews are poured.

RIVERSIDE SCHOOL HOUSE BED & BREAKFAST

28076 N River Road   541/820-4731
Moderate   riversideschoolhouse.com

This unusual resting place offers two suites with separate entrances and private baths. Original chalkboards with a personalized message greet guests as they enter the former one-room schoolhouse; rooms are comfortable with classy furnishings. Innkeeper **Judy Jacobs** delivers the morning's bountiful gourmet breakfast at the appointed time with ample suggestions for a day full of local activities. Located on a working cattle ranch, visitors are treated to seasonal opportunities for great hiking, fishing, cycling, snowmobiling, cross-country skiing or horseback riding. The early 1900s schoolhouse is about a mile from its original location. Back then, students regularly rode their horses to class; the barn and hitching posts still stand. Peaceful surrounds include the John Day River meandering through the property, abundant wildlife and vistas of the Strawberry Mountain Range.

RUFUS

BOB'S TEXAS T-BONE
101 E 1st St   541/739-2559
Breakfast, Lunch, Dinner: Daily
Moderate

For more than 40 years the Baunach family has owned a familiar establishment in Rufus (midway between Portland and Pendleton with easy access off I-84), first as Frosty's, a local tavern. Long hours make Bob's a convenient dining stop for travelers and Gorge dwellers. Portions are generous, the salad bar items are fresh and the menu showcases hand-cut steaks, freshly-ground hamburger, family-recipe sausages, smoked chicken and ribs and seasonal Columbia River salmon. Weekend dinners feature prime rib. Daily lunch specials, homemade soups, hearty sandwiches and burgers give midday diners plenty to choose from including breakfast anytime of the day.

SUMPTER

SUMPTER VALLEY RAILROAD
211 Austin St   541/894-2268, 866/894-2268
Weekends and major holidays   sumptervalleyrailroad.org
Prices vary

The narrow gauge Sumpter Valley Railroad that once helped haul ore, lumber, freight and passengers met its demise with the march of progress. However, a dedicated group of volunteers revived this great iron horse ensuring that the whistle of a steam train continues to echo through this scenic valley, preserving another remnant of the past. Since July 4, 1976, the railroad has provided nostalgic weekend and holiday excursions through the rugged countryside. The approximate five-mile route from McEwen to the town of Sumpter ends at a reproduction of the original passenger station. Volunteers are the mainstay of this organization and have been since the inception of the tourist railroad. Along the way, restored historic equipment and artifacts from around the country are on display. A trip on the Sumpter Valley Railroad is a fun and affordable activity for the whole family.

Major Oregon disasters

Several calamities have affected our state; among them:

1903 — Heppner Flash Flood

A strong thunderstorm with extremely heavy rain created severe flash flooding along Willow Creek running through Heppner's town center. One-third of the city structures were swept away in a few short minutes, drowning 250 people.

1910 — Langlois Fire

The entire business district of Langlois, in Curry County, was wiped out by a fire that started in a livery stable, largely due to dry weather. Only a blacksmith shop and a soft-drink stand remained in the business area. (Langlois was also known then as Dairyville and it was the first town on the stage line from Bandon to Curry County.)

1922 — Astoria Fire

The business district of Astoria was destroyed, hundreds left homeless and property loss estimated at $15 million. The cause was a fire that started in a restaurant. Firemen resorted to dynamiting in a vain effort to stop the inferno.

1933 — Tillamook Burn (and 1939, 1945, 1951)

A fire ignited during a logging operation in the Coast Range and within two days, flames spread to 40,000 acres. Dry, strong east winds fanned the flames to a quarter of a million acres, burning huge, ancient stands of old growth Douglas fir. The front of fire was 18 miles long, and Oregon beaches had ash and cinders two feet deep for a 30-mile stretch. Over 13 billion board feet of timber was lost. Devastation by these fires helped bring about legislation for reforestation and improved forest practices.

1950 — January Snowstorms

Three massive snowstorms, with little time in between and accompanied by high winds, created chaos. A severe sleet storm followed the snow, then freezing rain, generating broken and fallen trees, highway mayhem and downed power lines.

Hundreds of motorists were stranded in the Columbia River Gorge. Record January snowfall totals (in inches) include: Albany (54), Astoria (39), Corvallis (52), Portland and Salem (32) and Tillamook (19).

1959 — Roseburg Blast

The accidental detonation of 6 1/2 tons of explosives destroyed all buildings within an eight-block city area. A truck loaded with dynamite and nitro carbo nitrate was parked overnight in front of the Garretsen Building waiting for delivery the next morning; that night the building caught fire and the explosive-laden truck remained unnoticed until moments before it detonated. Fourteen people were killed and another 125 injured. City damages were estimated at $10 to $12 million.

1962 — Columbus Day Windstorm

This quintessential Pacific Northwest windstorm killed 38 people and did $170 to $200 million in damage. Wind gusts reached 116 m.p.h. in downtown Portland. Cities lost power for two to three weeks and 50,000 dwellings were damaged; agriculture and livestock took a devastating blow. (In comparison, it's been noted that the amount of trees lost to this storm was nearly 15 times more than the 1980 eruption of Mt. St. Helens.)

1964 — Southern Oregon Flood

With over eight inches of rain in five days in the Medford area, the Rogue River quickly rose to flood stage, washing away houses, roads and bridges and killing 12 people. A new gas line across the river at Gold Hill was washed out, cutting service. Highways throughout the state were closed as high water and slides crippled travel and communications. It was a bleak Christmas for thousands of flooded-out Oregonians.

1996 — Willamette Valley Flood

Combined by four days of heavy rain, extended periods of bitter cold, low level snow packs and additional downpours, ground became saturated and runoffs flooded major rivers. Floods spread beyond the Willamette Valley to the Oregon

Coast and the Cascade Mountains.   Eight people died and nearly every Oregon county received a disaster declaration. Region-wide damage estimates exceeded $1 billion.

2007 — Vernonia Flooding

Heavy storms that impacted the Pacific Northwest flooded Rock Creek and the Nehalem River, washing out roads, destroying homes, cars and the communications infrastructure in the town of Vernonia. Hundreds of people in the town had to be rescued and evacuated.

Your notes

Gerry's Chocolate Cake

This is the recipe for your author's favorite chocolate cake. Enjoy!

CAKE

2 ½ cups all purpose flour
1 ½ tsps baking soda
1 tsp baking powder
½ cup cocoa powder
½ tsp salt
⅔ cup butter
1 ¾ cups granulated sugar
2 large eggs
½ cup water
1 tsp vanilla
1 cup buttermilk

FROSTING

1 6-oz pkg semi-sweet chocolate chips (about ¾ cup)
½ cup whipping cream
1 cup butter
2 ½ cups powdered sugar

(Have a bowl of ice ready)

Preheat oven to 350 degrees. Butter & flour two 9-inch cake pans. Line the bottom of each with parchment paper, then butter and flour parchment paper as well.

Sift together the flour, baking soda, baking powder, cocoa and salt. Set aside.

Cream the butter with electric mixer. Gradually add sugar and beat at medium speed for one minute. Add eggs, one at a time, beating one minute after each egg is added. Gradually add water and vanilla; beat for one minute. Do not over beat.

With the mixer on low speed, alternately add one-quarter of the sifted flour mixture, then one-third of the buttermilk; then another quarter of the flour mixture followed by another third of the buttermilk until both are completely added. Each time the flour mixture is added, continue blending only until the flour no longer shows, then add the next portion of buttermilk. Do not over beat.

Pour batter into the prepared pans and tap each once to settle. Bake for 30 minutes or until toothpick inserted in the center comes out clean. Cool the cakes for 10 minutes before inverting onto wire racks. Cool completely before frosting.

FROSTING: Combine the chocolate chips, whipping cream and butter in a double boiler over medium heat, stirring constantly until the mixture is smooth. Remove from heat. Whisk in the powdered sugar.

In a bowl set over ice, beat the icing with a wire whisk until the frosting holds its shape, about 10 minutes.

Makes one cake (10 to 12 servings)

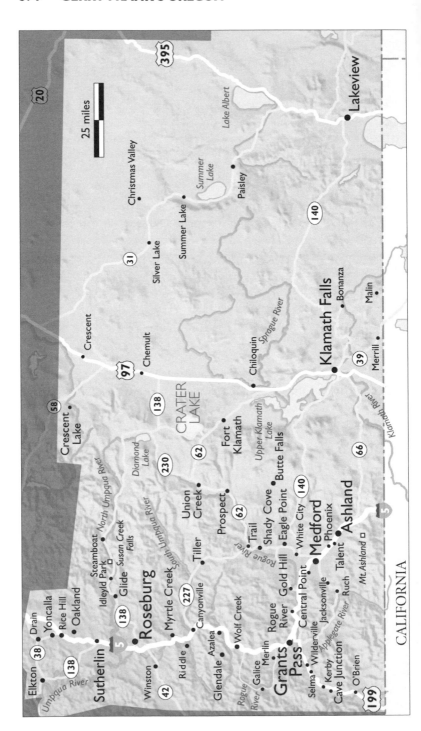

7. Southern Oregon

ASHLAND

A MIDSUMMER'S DREAM BED & BREAKFAST

496 Beach St	541/552-0605, 877/376-8800
Moderate	amidsummer.com

For a special occasion getaway, this classy 1901 Victorian may be the choice for you. In a quiet neighborhood within walking distance to downtown, you will be welcomed into your home away from home in a beautifully landscaped setting, with king-size beds and large private bathrooms. You'll be pampered with a spa tub and soft-as-silk robes, fireplace and wonderful linens. Relax in the common area, which includes a game room (and the only television on the property) with library, wet bar and tea service. **Lisa Beach** is the consummate host, offering gourmet breakfasts and anything else within her grasp.

AMUSE

15 N 1st St   541/488-9000
Dinner: seasonal   amuserestaurant.com
Moderately expensive

Chefs/owners **Jamie North** and **Erik Brown** have impressive culinary backgrounds, and it shows! North made original wedding cakes in Napa Valley and was a pastry cook at the legendary French Laundry restaurant; Brown also cooked at Napa Valley restaurants. The Northwest/French menu reflects their talents and utilizes fresh, seasonal ingredients. Green garlic soup or crispy veal sweetbreads with sunchokes, pistachio puree, black trumpets and smoked bacon are representative of starters. Flavorful seafood, steaks and roasted game hens are paired with wonderful relishes, butters, fresh produce and palate-pleasing accompaniments. By all means, order the beignets with crème anglaise and heirloom berry jam if they are offered—exquisite! This intimate, elegant restaurant has great service and a delightful summer patio (perfect for pre-theater dining).

KIDS' ACTIVITIES: SOUTHERN OREGON

Ashland
ScienceWorks Museum (541/482-6767,
    scienceworksmuseum.org)
Cave Junction
Great Cats World Park (541/592-2957,
    greatcatsworldpark.com)
Oregon Caves National Monument (541/592-2100,
    nps.gov/orca)
Crater Lake
Crater Lake National Park (541/594-3000, nps.gov/
    crla)
Gold Hill
Oregon Vortex (541/855-1543, oregonvortex.com)
Winston
Wildlife Safari (541/679-6761, wildlifesafari.net)

ASHLAND CREEK INN
70 Water St   541/482-3315
Moderate to expensive   ashlandcreekinn.com

Stunning blue shutters and awnings embellish the façade of this ten-suite boutique hotel set in a private park-like setting. Each suite is luxuriously decorated to commemorate an international area (Edinburgh, Marrakech, Normandy, Canton, etc.) visited by owner **Graham Sheldon**. Beautiful, über-comfortable rooms have a private entrance, balcony overlooking gurgling Ashland Creek and kitchen or kitchenette. Antiques, original artwork and jetted tubs vary among the units. Relax on the inn's deck and terraced gardens for breakfast or an afternoon glass of wine. Breakfast is a multi-course gourmet production and is served outdoors or in the elegant dining room. The location is handy to downtown shops, restaurants, nightlife and theaters.

ASHLAND SPRINGS HOTEL
212 E Main St   541/488-1700, 888/795-4545
Moderate   ashlandspringshotel.com

LARKS HOME KITCHEN CUISINE
Lunch: Mon-Fri; Dinner: Daily; Brunch: Sat, Sun   541/488-5558
Moderate   larksrestaurant.com

WATERSTONE SPA AND SALON
Spa: 236 E Main St   541/488-0325
Salon: 14 S 1st St   541/488-3700
                                          waterstonespa.com

Charm and elegance abound at this hotel listed on the National Register of Historic Places. Built as Lithia Hotel in 1925 and later named the Mark Antony, it was restored to grandeur in 2000 by owners **Becky and Doug Newman**. One look at the illuminated marquee and curved windows from the bygone era, and guests know that great care was given to the renovation. Guests are beckoned to a palm-filled conservatory and English garden featuring a wrought-iron gazebo and old-fashioned rosebushes. All 70 eclectically furnished and tastefully appointed guest rooms offer comfort and charm not found in modern hotels. Free parking and continental breakfast are included in the rates. On-site **Larks Home Kitchen Cuisine** serves farm-to-table gourmet, from-scratch comfort food with local organic components, housemade charcuterie and artisan cheeses. The chef is a master in showcasing Oregon wines and splendid seasonal ingredients delivered from local farms. Dishes such as homemade meatloaf, hearty soups and double-cut pork chops are popular. The pastry chef's creations include cocoa from Dagoba Organic Chocolates and berries from Pennington Farms. Nature-inspired **Waterstone Spa and Salon** is also part of this downtown resort, offering a full-service rejuvenating and beautifying menu. A variety of thoughtfully developed packages may include each of these elements and/or tickets to the Varsity Movie Theatre, the Oregon Shakespeare Festival, Oregon Chocolate Festival or lift tickets to Mt. Ashland.

BLUE GREEK ON GRANITE

5 Granite St   541/708-5150
Dinner: Daily; Lunch: Fri-Sun (summer)   bluegreekongranite.com
Moderate

Experienced restaurateurs **Gloria and Yiorgo Menedes** opened their restaurant in 2010. As the name suggests, Greek food is the feature; items such as souvlaki (grilled meat sometimes wrapped in pita bread with veggies and tzatziki — Greek yogurt, cucumber, garlic and mint), pastitso (lasagna), pilafi (creamy rice) and so much more are on the menu. Folks come from far and wide for their slow-cooked lamb shanks. The Menedes' aim is to bring healthful Greek cuisine using local organic growers and grass-fed protein to the table. Check the website for a schedule of frequent live entertainment featuring Broadway tunes presented by Oregon's musical theater performers.

CALLAHAN'S MOUNTAIN LODGE

7100 Old Hwy 99 S   541/482-1299, 800/286-0507
Moderate to expensive   callahanslodge.com

Callahan's full-service restaurant and lodge is a Southern Oregon landmark (established in 1947). The picturesque setting is tucked into a wooded canyon ten minutes south of Ashland just below Mt. Ashland Ski Resort and the Pacific Crest Trail.

> ## HARD WORK
>
> Oregon's early days saw an influx of Chinese laborers whose mark remains today. The **China Ditch Car Tour** (blm.gov) is a little-known 30-mile ditch excavated by the Chinese during the 1890s in Southern Oregon. A portion is set aside for walking tours as well as a 10½-mile loop drive.

Nineteen guest rooms are furnished with corner jetted tubs, wood-burning fireplaces and terraces with rockers to while away the afternoon; a few rooms contain kitchenettes and living rooms. Lodge amenities include a horseshoe pit, pool and shuffleboard tables and man-made rock waterfall features. Basic to fancy egg dishes are good choices for breakfast, included with lodging, and served with fruit and lodge-made pastries; crepes and pancakes are nice options. House-cut fries go well with lunch wraps and sandwiches. Kick back on the outdoor deck when the weather cooperates for a get-away-from-it-all stay. Moderately priced "Western mountain lodge" dinner entrees are sourced from pastures, freshwater and saltwater and are served with a signature hazelnut pear vinaigrette house salad and artisan bread. Appetizers are available at lunch and dinner. For a different dessert, try the baked banana split. The lodge is open 365 days a year with nightly live music at dinner. This beautiful location is a favorite of brides and grooms and ideal for small conferences and gatherings for up to 150 guests.

COUNTRY WILLOWS BED & BREAKFAST INN

1313 Clay St   541/488-1590, 800/945-5697
Moderate   countrywillowsinn.com

This charmer has all the atmosphere of bygone days but with comfortable, modern facilities. The original farmhouse was built more than a century ago and is now in its third decade as a B&B. Features include full country breakfasts, top-grade bed linens and magnificent views. Mt. Ashland skiing, theaters, hiking and biking trails and wineries are close at hand. Four guest rooms are in the main house. Three comfortable suites and a standard room with private porch are located in the renovated barn behind the house. A separate cottage has queen and twin beds, wet bar and private patio. Bicycles, a heated outdoor swimming pool and croquet and lawn bocce equipment are accessible in warm weather. Comfy seating is spread throughout the property, by the willow tree, in the den or sunroom and on the porch; enjoy a cookie and cup of tea – on the house, of course.

DRAGONFLY CAFE AND GARDENS

241 Hargadine St   541/488-4855
Breakfast, Lunch, Dinner: Daily   dragonflyashland.com
Moderate

Dragonfly is a great Ashland complement and is well attended by the pre-theater crowd. The cuisine is Latin-Asian fusion with such offerings as various "Buddha" bowls full of steamy lemongrass, coconut milk, noodles, veggies and more with an Asian twist; then there's marinated grilled salmon served with papaya-mango mint salsa, chicken tamales and flat-iron steak. If the baby back ribs are on the menu, though, look no further. These well-above average ribs are extra meaty and extra delicious, too; combined with deep-fried garlic plantain fries, it's a benchmark plate. Choose from coconut French toast, unusual pancakes, artichoke or avocado scrambles and other out-of-the-ordinary selections for breakfast. Soups and sandwiches, still with a fusion bent, come out at lunchtime.

GREEN SPRINGS INN & CABINS

11470 Hwy 66   541/890-6435
Moderate   greenspringsinn.com

No need to spend big bucks on faraway destinations with so many great places in our own state. This rustic retreat is about 25 minutes east of Ashland, and, as the name suggests, a relaxed atmosphere awaits. Amenities in the eight lodge rooms may include Jacuzzi tubs, private decks and a fireplace. You can also choose from five cabins, mainly powered by solar energy, that sleep up to six. Each is furnished with a Jacuzzi tub, fully-equipped kitchen, wood-burning stove, gas grill and large deck. The inn serves three square meals a day from a menu of great selections.

LOFT BRASSERIE & BAR

18 Calle Guanajuato   541/482-1116
Dinner: Daily   loftbrasserie.com
Moderate

Jacqueline and Jeremy Vidalo present an inspiring space offering contemporary American-French fare in their brasserie and bar. As much as possible, the food is organic, all-natural and sourced locally; made from scratch is the rule, not the exception. The full bar has a fun specialty cocktail list and features local and European wines (from the Rogue to the Rhine). Jeremy is the chef, with **Josh Vidalo**, his younger brother, serving as the sous chef; Jacqueline runs the front of the house. Starters might include steamed Penn Cove black mussels or chicken liver mousse; caramelized French onion soup is a must. Roasted beet salad and other greens top the salad selection. Other entrees include chicken, scallops, duck breast, lamb, steak frites and more. Enjoy enchanting alfresco dining overlooking Ashland Creek on a mid-summer night.

MARTINO'S/MACARONI'S
RISTORANTE AND LOUNGE

58 E Main St   541/488-3359, 541/488-4420
Lunch: Apr-Sept: Tues-Sun; Dinner: Daily   martinosashland.com
Moderate

If you choose outdoor seating at Martino's, you'll be as close as you can be to the Angus Bowmer Theatre without a ticket! Martino's is upstairs and Macaroni's is downstairs; owner **Marty Morlan** offers the same menu throughout the neo-classic house. You won't be disappointed with the Oregon smoked salmon ravioli served in a mushroom, basil and tomato cream sauce or the rigatoni carbonara made with applewood-smoked bacon. This location is handy for after-theater bistro fare, drinks and dessert (try the homemade Sicilian vanilla ice cream).

MORNING GLORY

1149 Siskiyou Blvd   541/488-8636
Daily: 8-1:30   morninggloryrestaurant.com
Moderate

Owner **Patricia Groth** presides over her breakfast and lunch establishment, a favorite of local families and visitors. Inside the 1926 Craftsman bungalow, you'll find some of the most unusual day starters imaginable. Think shrimp cakes with poached eggs and smoked tomato chutney or a steak omelet with mushrooms, red onions and spinach. Also expect whole grain pecan waffles, oatmeal pancakes and other such fare. Lunch service begins at 11 a.m. with interesting sandwiches and homemade soups and salads made with organic mixed greens. A chipotle flavored Bloody Mary or other libation from the full-service bar is sure to make you bright-eyed and bushy-tailed as you start your vacation or weekend day.

MUSIC COOP
268 E Main St   541/482-3115
Daily   musiccooponline.com

A hidden treasure awaits music lovers at this well-known store, one of the largest record outlets on the West Coast between Sacramento and Portland. There are over 20,000 CD titles, hundreds of box-set CDs and the largest selection of vinyl LPs in Southern Oregon. **Trina and John Brenes** have been in the business since 1975 and moved lock, stock and record to Ashland in 2001. Take a break from the Ashland stages to enjoy the great selection at the Music Coop, offering everything from rock, hip-hop, jazz, blues and folk to bluegrass and country music.

NORTHWEST NATURE SHOP
154 Oak St   541/482-3241
Mon-Sat: 10-6; Sun: 11-5   northwestnatureshop.com

Here you'll find a variety of educational books, hiking guides, bird amenities, cards and gifts, toys and information about the forests and waterways of our state. Treat the birds and wildlife in your yard to a new bird bath, fountain or feeder or accent your home with clocks and decorative pieces.

OREGON CABARET THEATRE
1 Hargadine St   541/488-2902
                                                     oregoncabaret.com

For an amusing evening, forget Shakespeare for a bit and book your party at the Oregon Cabaret Theatre. Five shows (over 270 performances) change throughout the year, but the intimate

---

NOT QUITE ROUGHING IT ON THE ROGUE

There is an enchanting mystique about Southern Oregon's Rogue River; along its calm-cum-whitewater corridor, remote privately-owned lodges, some accessed only by boat or on foot, dot its banks:

Black Bar Lodge (blackbarlodge.net)
Clay Hill Lodge (clayhilllodge.com)
Marial Lodge (541/474-2057)
Morrison's Rogue River Lodge (morrisonslodge.com)
Paradise Lodge (paradise-lodge.com)
Singing Springs Resort (singingspringsresort.com)
Tu Tu' Tun Lodge (tututun.com)

Rafters, hikers, fishermen and anyone with an affinity for the great outdoors will enjoy being on the Rogue.

---

venue stays the same. You can opt for dinner (or brunch) theater or you can go for the entertainment only. Desserts are served during intermission; place your order before the curtain goes up for famous Dick Hay Pie. (**Dick Hay** has been a workhorse during a 50-plus-year stint helping develop the Ashland theater phenomenon.) The 140-seat theater calls the former First Baptist Church home, magnificently renovated in the 1980s.

OREGON SHAKESPEARE FESTIVAL

15 S Pioneer St   800/219-8161
Seasonal   osfashland.org

Charming Ashland provides one of the world's finest venues to celebrate William Shakespeare along with other performing arts. By the numbers, OSF presents more than 780 performances to approximately 400,000 patrons contributing over $58 million to the local economy. The festival was established in 1935 and boasts the oldest existing full-scale Elizabethan stage in the Western Hemisphere. Throughout the eight-month season, eleven plays by Shakespeare and classic and contemporary playwrights are presented in three venues with varying seating capacities (270 to 1,190). People come from all around the globe, often an annual outing, to Ashland to experience Shakespeare and Southern Oregon. Take in historic Jacksonville and the summertime outdoor **Britt Festivals** (brittfest.org) while in the area. During busy summer months, lodging and restaurants also play to a full house.

PADDINGTON STATION

125 E Main St   541/482-1343
Daily   paddingtonstationashland.com

Paddington has been a Main Street fixture for nearly 40 years. You'll find three floors of eclectic merchandise — gadgets and goodies, toys, clothing, books, kitchen needs, women's fashions, toiletries, stationery, souvenirs and more. This is a fun spot anytime of the year.

THE PEERLESS HOTEL

243 4th St   541/488-1082, 800/460-8758
Moderate   peerlesshotel.com

THE PEERLESS RESTAURANT & BAR

265 4th St   541/488-6067
Dinner: Tues-Sat   peerlessrestaurant.com
Moderate

Historic accommodations are part of Ashland's claim to fame. The Peerless, built in 1900, is charmingly restored and located close to the town's central shopping and gallery core. Most rooms have *tromp l'oeil* painted ceilings or walls. Amenities include classy Italian linens and access to the Ashland Racquet Club offering full workout facilities. By the way, if you like large bathrooms, ask for the room with two claw-foot tubs. Relax in gorgeous guest rooms decorated with antiques or outside in the private gardens. Breakfast and complimentary evening sherry are provided between mid-February and November. Room service is available from the property's excellent next-door Peerless Restaurant where you'll also find delicious full dinners, tapas and nightly sampler plates.

PLAZA INN & SUITES

98 Central Ave   541/488-8900, 888/488-0358
Moderate   plazainnashland.com

This Shakespearean-theme boutique hotel offers 91 spacious rooms with various options and concierge service. A hot tub and 24-hour fitness center are available and rooms in the Cascade building are designated for guests with pets. Mornings begin with a continental breakfast and a snack welcomes guests "home" each early evening. Later (10 p.m. to midnight), a nightcap of freshly-baked cookies, milk and PB&J sandwiches are provided. The town's attractions are within easy walking distance.

SCIENCEWORKS HANDS-ON MUSEUM

1500 E Main St   541/482-6767
Wed-Sun; Daily: Summer   scienceworksmuseum.org
Nominal

For a treat, take the kids to this museum for fun activities that will help them understand energy, anatomy, chemistry and more. They can build a bubble around themselves in the Bubble Room, see their "pedal" energy push an electric train around its track and encounter optical illusions and crazy mirrors. There are nearly 100 interactive exhibits with live demonstrations and performances which change frequently.

STANDING STONE BREWING CO.

101 Oak St   541/482-2448
Lunch, Dinner: Daily; Breakfast: Sat, Sun   standingstonebrewing.com
Moderate

A pub with class resides in the former Whittle Garage Building and serves up microbrews, signature pizzas baked in a wood-fired oven and great food until midnight. The restaurant's display kitchen turns out an extensive menu with usual pub grub, plus lots more such as spinach salad with sea scallops, a po' boy made with blackened wild Alaskan salmon and lamb or buffalo burgers. Szechwan green beans are tempting appetizers. Entrees include flavorful ribs, steaks, fish, chicken and pasta dishes. There is plenty of seating, a back deck with mountain views and regularly-scheduled live music; kids are welcome. In 2011, Standing Stone ventured into farming to raise free-range cattle, chickens and sheep and will add produce and more to this lofty project thereby reducing their "forkprint."

WEISINGER'S OF ASHLAND

3150 Siskiyou Blvd　　　　　　　　541/488-5989, 800/551-9463
Tasting room: Summer: Daily; Winter: Wed-Sun　　　weisingers.com

Travel about four miles south of town to Weisinger's artisan winery and tasting room for quality wines and local cheeses at a scenic hilltop location. Sunsets and picnics go hand in hand with the mountain and valley views. A remodeled one-bedroom Craftsman-style bungalow is adjacent to the vineyard and is reminiscent of the saying, "a jug of wine, a loaf of bread — and thou" for a couple's perfect weekend — or week. The moderately priced cottage is equipped with a kitchen and private deck with hot tub and guests receive a welcoming cheese and wine basket, chocolate truffles and discounts in the tasting room.

WINCHESTER INN

35 S 2nd St　　　　　　　　　　541/488-1113, 800/972-4991
Restaurant: Dinner: May-Oct: Daily,
Nov-Apr: Wed-Sun; Brunch: Sun　　　winchesterinn.com
Inexpensive to expensive

Owners **Laurie and Michael Gibbs** have magnificently transformed four buildings and a hilly lot into one of Ashland's finest bed and breakfasts with gorgeous tiered gardens. Making his parents proud, **Drew Gibbs** is the Inn's general manager and certified sommelier. Top-drawer amenities in the house and cottages' 11 rooms and eight suites include down feather beds, pillows and comforters; luxury bed linens and Egyptian cotton towels; imported toiletries and guest phones with data ports, voicemail and complimentary Wi-Fi. Afternoon pastries are delivered to guest rooms, followed later in the evening with turndown service. A sumptuous two-course gourmet breakfast is included with an overnight stay. The nationally-recognized restaurant is excellent! Chef **William Buscher** has assembled a fine selection of small plates, soups, salads and entrees utilizing local and organic products; daily menus change according to season. Rack of lamb may be laced with vanilla bean; pork may be complemented by French triple

A PEN MIGHTIER THAN THE SWORD

Editor and newspaper owner (*Medford Tribune* and *Medford Mail* creating the *Mail-Tribune*), **George Putnam**, put his steely pen where his mouth was, standing up for right and truth at his own peril. The celebrated early 1900's case of an ax-throwing attack against Medford Mayor **J.F. Reddy** put Putnam on trial for libel when he wrote an editorial against the ax-thrower after a not-true bill came forth from the Grand Jury. Found guilty and fined $150, Putnam eventually gained a pardon from Governor **George Chamberlain**, which he rejected so his appeal could go forward; a new trial was directed, but never held. He sold his Southern Oregon newspaper interest and bought the Salem *Capital-Journal* in 1919, which he owned until 1953. From the capital city, he unwaveringly tackled the fervent Ku Klux Klan that was embedding itself into Oregon politics. In one statement, he ridiculed the secret KKK society by saying it was "senseless and silly public appearances in nightgown regalia." His Salem home caught fire on August 18, 1961, where he died.

cream brie mac and cheese; fish will be prepared to capture the utmost flavor; and homemade pasta choices may showcase creamy sauces and fine cheeses. Fresh scones accompany assorted brunch dishes (duck confit hash, pancetta omelet, classic eggs Benedict) or you may opt for the crepe of the day or duck fat pancakes with Meyer Lemon confit maple syrup. Reservations recommended.

AZALEA

HEAVEN ON EARTH RESTAURANT & BAKERY
703 Quines Creek Road   541/837-3700
Breakfast, Lunch, Dinner: Daily   heavenonearthrestaurant.com
Moderate

A slice of paradise is 30 minutes north of Grants Pass at exit 86 where **Christine Jackson** makes her restaurant and bakery a requisite visit for folks in Southern Oregon to find the tastiest baked goods and gigantic, melt-in-your-mouth cinnamon rolls (including a humungous family-size version). The restaurant is also noted for its home-style cooking. The restaurant's Oregon Apple Butter Farms Gift Store has locally made apple butter, superior jams and jellies, candy, honey, sauces, salsa and such.

CAVE JUNCTION

THE CHATEAU AT OREGON CAVES

20000 Caves Hwy   541/592-5020, 877/245-9022
Seasonal: May-October   oregoncaveschateau.com
Moderate

Built in 1934 by businessmen from Grants Pass, this historic lodge features 23 unique rooms. Standard and deluxe (accented with Monterey furniture) rooms contain either two double beds or one queen bed; family suites have two rooms and one bath. A focal point is a stream channeled from the Oregon Caves that runs through the dining room. Dinners include fish, beef, bison, pastas and other Northwest-influenced selections. The vintage coffee shop (where you can take a stool at the counter, order a malt and enjoy the nostalgic 1930s soda fountain) is open for breakfast, lunch and dessert. Oregon Caves memorabilia, snacks and gifts are sold in the Gift Gallery.

GREAT CATS WORLD PARK

27919 Redwood Hwy   541/592-2957
Feb-March: Seasonal hours   greatcatsworldpark.com
Reasonable

Africa and Asia are closer than you think. Great Cats World Park offers animal demonstrations and educational guided tours where the cats exhibit natural behaviors. You can get up close and personal with a variety of large and small cats on this ten-acre park. Resident felines include lions, tigers, leopards, serval, ocelots, lynx and more. Snacks are available at the gift shop.

OREGON CAVES NATIONAL MONUMENT

1900 Caves Hwy   541/592-2100
Seasonal: Spring through fall   nps.gov/orca
Nominal

Another of our state's great places to visit is tucked into the Siskiyou Mountains about 20 miles east of Cave Junction; the last ten miles are narrow, steep and winding (travel trailers and large RVs are not recommended beyond milepost 12). Expect snowfall late fall through spring. That being said, the incentives are magnificent marble caves of re-crystalized limestone, hiking, wildlife and nearby camping. Tours of the caves (fee applies) are seasonal and weather dependent; no fee to visit the surface trails and monument facilities. There are two visitor centers; one at the monument and one in Cave Junction.

OUT'N'ABOUT TREEHOUSE TREESORT

300 Page Creek Road   541/592-2208
Year round   treehouses.com
Moderate

Kids of all ages have the time of their lives at this unique treesort. This bed and breakfast in the trees has 13 treehouses (and three non-treehouses) complete with lavatories in the trees (and on the ground). Each has a specific theme and accommodates two, four or more people on one level or two. Furnishings vary and may include queen or twin beds and bunks, kitchenettes and tables and chairs. The loftiest unit is over 40 feet up a tree and accessed by swinging bridges and platforms. Throughout the 36 private acres are child-size forts, seven swinging bridges, six swings, 20 flights of stairs and four ladders; over a mile of zip lines; a swimming pool plus a menagerie of horses and chickens. You will not be bored when you go out on a limb for this adventure! Breakfast is included in the stay and is served in the main lodge. A full breakfast with multiple choices served mid-March through October; continental breakfast is offered the remainder of the year. Reservations are necessary to play out your Tarzan and Jane vacation; no TVs or landline phones.

CENTRAL POINT

ROGUE CREAMERY

311 N Front St   541/665-1155, 866/396-4704
Daily   roguecreamery.com

This creamery's origin dates back to 1933. In the 1940s, the Vella family supplied cheddar cheese to the war effort and was the first major supplier of cottage cheese in Oregon. Blue Cheese was added to the mix in 1957, the first produced in caves on the West Coast. Today under the leadership of **Cary Bryant** and **David Gremmels**, Rogue Creamery continues the tradition of award-winning blue and cheddar cheese made locally in Central Point. You'll find artisan cheeses, specialty foods, local wines and craft beers in the cheese shop. Each March, the annual Oregon Cheese Festival showcases products from Rogue Creamery and other Oregon cheese producers, plus beer, wine, baked goods and chocolates.

CHILOQUIN

LONESOME DUCK RANCH & RESORT
32955 Hwy 97N   541/783-2783, 800/367-2540
Moderately expensive   lonesomeduck.com

Debbie and Steve Hilbert preside over a scenic and fun retreat, combining many things for different family members to enjoy (kids love walking the llamas) and is good for business meetings, too. In a 200-acre setting on two miles of Williamson River frontage, the possibilities are especially attractive for those who enjoy the outdoor life. The Settlement Bed and Breakfast has two beautiful guest rooms. Two full-size log homes are also available, with two bedrooms, two full baths and a loft area with twin beds. The Arrowhead cottage, one of the original ranch houses, features a great stone fireplace, two small bedrooms, kitchen, living and dining rooms. There's a two-night minimum and off-season (November to mid-May) rates are half-price. Each cabin offers superb views. Fly-fishing is first-class, with guides available for half or full days. The Wood River, Klamath Lake, Agency Lake and the Sprague River are nearby; what a thrill to land a trophy rainbow trout! The ranch is near five Klamath Basin refuges, home to more than 430 wildlife species, along with some 250 bird varieties. Take a tour with the ranch manager, **Marshal Moser**, a wildlife biologist and naturalist. You can't help but enjoy the flora and fauna, enhanced by Marshal's expert knowledge. With easy access to Crater Lake, horse facilities, barbecues and kitchens in each unit, what more could you ask for? Photographers: this place is for you!

CRATER LAKE

CRATER LAKE NATIONAL PARK

541/594-3000
Seasonal   nps.gov/crla

CRATER LAKE LODGE

888/774-2728
Seasonal   craterlakelodges.com

Oregon's only national park brings visitors from around the world to take in the brilliant blue beauty from the caldera rim. The rim road is open until the snow flies, usually operating late-May through mid-October. The scenery is breathtaking as you wind your way around our nation's deepest lake (1,943 feet) encompassing views of two islands (Wizard and Phantom Ship), breathtaking scenery and wildlife. Visitors centers are located at the rim (typically open June to October) and year round at park headquarters. A concessionaire operates seasonal ranger-narrated boat tours around the lake and to Wizard Island. The beautifully renovated 71-room **Crater Lake Lodge** (circa 1915) and restaurant are open mid-May through mid-October. The restaurant features Northwest breakfast, lunch and dinner cuisine. Southwest of the lake, Mazama Village has a campground, cabins, camper store, fuel, restaurant and gift shop. Various fees apply for vehicles, bicycles and pedestrians entering the park. Allow plenty of time to experience this national treasure and enjoy the pristine surroundings.

EAGLE POINT

BUTTE CREEK MILL

402 N Royal Ave   541/826-3531
Daily   buttecreekmill.com

As owners, **Debbie and Bob Russell** are making their living and keeping history alive as operators of the last commercial water-powered flour mill west of the Mississippi. The mill has functioned since 1872 and is on the National Register of Historic Places. Today you can buy (on-site or online) flours, cereals, stone-ground mixes, grains and other products, organically and otherwise produced, and all of the highest quality. The mill's educational center (call ahead to see when they are milling) offers information on American history, science and technology, ecology and more. The mill is great for family picnics, business retreats, concerts and parties. The adjacent antique store, formerly a cheese factory, is full of the Russell's personal collection (for sale) and sports an old-time saloon and barber shop right out of the 1890s.

ELKTON

BIG K GUEST RANCH
20029 Hwy 138W   800/390-2445
Year round   big-k.com
Moderate

The Big K offers 20 comfortable cabins housing up to four people in each unit. Choose from packages for lodging only, meals and lodging or custom hunting and fishing outings. Breakfast, lunch and dinner are served in the main dining room. The 2,500-acre ranch has ten miles of Umpqua River frontage and is the ideal place for individuals or families to enjoy the outdoors. In conjunction with **Todd Harrington's Living Waters Guide Service**, year-round guided fishing trips, scenic jet boat rides and rafting trips are available. Take a guided horseback ride or bring your own horse to explore the ranch.

GRANTS PASS

CARY'S OF OREGON
413 Union Ave   888/822-9300
Mon-Fri: 9-5; Sat: 10-2   carysoforegon.com

When you're in Southern Oregon and mention the words "English toffee," the immediate response is Cary's of Oregon. From a long-standing family recipe, **Cary Cound** and his crew make some of the best toffee around—known for its light crisp texture and seven mouthwatering flavors. A factory store carries all sorts of hard-to-resist toffee treats and samples to tempt. (I'll let you in on a little secret: there is a kettle full of imperfect pieces at bargain prices.) The products are all natural and gluten-free. Not going that way? They ship toffee and gift packs nationwide.

SOARING HIGH

Explore Lake Abert (one of Oregon's largest bodies of water and home to a variety of water birds; no outlet, considered an inland sea) and the **Abert Rim** in Southern Oregon's Lake County, about 30 miles north of Lakeview (west of Highway 395). The impressive Abert Rim was discovered by Lieutenant John Fremont in 1843 and named for his commanding officer, Colonel J.J. Abert; the 30-mile, north-south fault ridge rises 2,500 feet above the valley floor. This area is to hang gliders what the Columbia River Gorge is to windsurfers. (Watch for bighorn sheep and other wildlife.)

FLERY MANOR BED & BREAKFAST

2000 Jumpoff Joe Creek Road   541/476-3591
Moderate   flerymanor.com

A bed and breakfast combined with an art studio is the Flery's unusual hosting formula. This attractive mountainside destination is near the Rogue River with three suites and two additional nicely decorated rooms, some featuring fireplaces and Jacuzzis. Guests enjoy a well-stocked library, and a piano is available for those with a musical flair. Original recipe, three-course organic breakfasts (many times with ingredients fresh from the home garden) feature innovative egg dishes. Guests are invited to experience the art studio where they may dabble in clay, paint, music, photography, writing or other creative art forms. Enjoy a walk or hike around the property to view the ponds, waterfalls and streams and perhaps catch a glimpse of the two resident black swans.

SUMMER JO'S FARM, GARDEN AND RESTAURANT

2315 Upper River Road Loop   541/476-6882
Breakfast, Lunch, Dinner: Thurs-Sun   summerjos.com

"From the ground up" comes to mind when thinking about this certified organic farm open from mid-February through December. Pizzas (and breakfast omelets) are inspired by world cuisine; salads and pastas are made with abundant fresh vegetables, many from Summer Jo's garden. Burgers are made with organic beef and include a choice of side (soup, salad, fries). Other tasty sandwiches are built on Summer Jo's housemade bagels. You, too, can buy fresh from the farmstand and area farmers markets.

TAPROCK NORTHWEST GRILL

971 SE 6th St   541/955-5998
Breakfast, Lunch, Dinner: Daily   taprock.com
Moderate

This beautiful lodge-inspired restaurant sits at the edge of the Rogue River along Highway 99. A man-made waterfall, wildlife sculptures and ample outdoor lighting are welcoming touches. The restaurant has seating for 300 inside, plus more on the wraparound deck and at the hand-hewn bar. The menu reflects its Northwest theme with farm-fresh egg dishes, salmon, Dungeness crab and other seafood, sandwiches, burgers, steaks and pastas. Salads are farm-to-table fresh and offered in two sizes. Start your morning with breakfast favorites of Dungeness crab cake Benedicts, berry French toast and flat-iron steak and eggs.

WEASKU INN

5560 Rogue River Hwy   541/471-8000, 800/493-2758
Moderately expensive

Even the pronunciation of this inn's name is welcoming: We-Ask-U Inn. This historic lodge has been home away from home for guests since 1924. Restoration to the lodge and the original A-frame cabin were completed in 1998 retaining the authentic feel and decor. Wireless Internet is complimentary and available throughout the property, including the 11 riverfront cabins and a three-bedroom river house. Accommodations are nicely appointed; stone fireplaces and Jacuzzi tubs in some cabins.

Additional amenities include a continental breakfast, afternoon appetizer reception and nightly freshly-baked cookies and milk. Hollywood legends such as Clark Gable, Carole Lombard and Walt Disney left Tinseltown behind to vacation at this tranquil Rogue River retreat.

WILD RIVER BREWING & PIZZA COMPANY
595 NE E St   541/471-7487
Lunch, Dinner: Daily

WILD RIVER GRANTS PASS PUB
533 NE F St   541/474-4456
Lunch, Dinner: Mon-Sat; Dinner: Sun   wildriverbrewing.com
Moderate

Bertha and Jerry Miller coalesced their pizza/deli with their Steelhead Brewery, and in 1994 Wild River Brewing & Pizza came into being. The main location is a family-oriented restaurant that features a showcase brewery and in addition to pizza, serves pasta, European-inspired classics, sandwiches and other meals. Down the street, the pub's friendly atmosphere is a good place to grab a pint and watch a sporting event on the big screen. They serve great burgers, pub fare and entrees from the full-service menu.

JACKSONVILLE

BRITT FESTIVALS   541/779-0847, 800/882-7488
                                                brittfest.org

Each summer, Peter Britt's estate, now a Jackson County park, comes alive with three months of concerts and performances under the stars. Britt was a 19th-century photographer and painter who also appreciated fine music, often enjoying concerts on the lawn of his house on a hill. Since 1952, concert-goers have flocked to Jacksonville and this spectacular outdoor setting to hear classical, folk, pop, country and blues musicians and comedians. The relaxed venue is dotted with patrons seated on the lawn (bring a blanket) and reserved seating near the stage. Various cultural and fun events occur in conjunction with the concerts; early purchase of single performance and season tickets is highly recommended.

DÉJÀ VU BISTRO & WINE BAR

240 E California St   541/899-1942
Dinner: Wed-Sun
Moderate

Chef **Bill Prahl** returned to this restaurant in the **McCully House Inn**'s garden room and patio after a 14-year absence, hence the name Déjà vu Bistro & Wine Bar. The emphasis is on local produce, cheeses, meats and wines from the nearby Applegate and Rogue valleys. The chef's grilled romaine salad is back in his repertoire and is a wonderful accompaniment to a la carte entrees. In lieu of a "greens" starter, you may opt for oysters, ahi or scallops from the raw bar or housemade soup. Palate pleasing dinner combinations include coffee-rubbed flat-iron steak and fingerling potatoes, duck breast with cauliflower puree, seared sea scallops alongside zucchini spaghetti or other main dishes creatively melding organic and seasonal meats and produce.

ELAN GUEST SUITES AND GALLERY

245 W Main St   541/899-8000, 877/789-1952
Moderate   elanguestsuites.com

This classy boutique lodging includes a first-floor art gallery. Three luxury suites are appointed with large flat-screen televisions, DVD players, modern tech conveniences and fully-equipped kitchens. Guests are sure to appreciate the secure covered parking, luggage elevator and original artwork enhancing the contemporary suites. A complimentary continental breakfast is offered at a nearby coffee shop. The gallery is open daily to guests and features frequent special exhibits.

GARY WEST MEATS

690 N 5th St   800/833-1820
Daily   garywest.com

For you carnivores, a break at this jerky factory and tasting room is fun and different from the usual snack stops. You'll be treated to tasty elk, bison and Angus beef samples. If you're in a buying mood, there are jerky samplers; a great selection of Oregon wines; baskets featuring wild game, sausage and other unusual gifts; hams and buffalo strips. Gary's grandparents were pioneers in the Applegate area. Grandma Ina Pursel rode horseback to reach the school where she taught; Grandpa Nelson Pursel, born in Jacksonville, hauled logs to the local lumber mill. Gary is well-schooled in the special flavors of old-time foods that make for memorable ranch meals.

GOGI'S RESTAURANT
235 W Main St   541/899-8699
Dinner: Wed-Sun; Brunch: Sun   gogis.net
Moderate

Brothers **Gabriel Murphy** and **Jonoah Murphy** pull much of the produce served in their restaurant from their small farm in the Applegate Valley. Intimate dining in chic environs is well-paired with international cuisine, which is made in-house using local organic ingredients as much as possible. For appetizers, try nori-wrapped ahi or crispy pork belly served with creamy polenta and pickled watermelon rind. Delicious potato side dishes accompany double-cut New York steaks and pork chops; non-meat, fish and fowl entrees are tasty alternatives. Brunch temptations include Benedicts (traditional or a cowboy version with steak), Dutch-style cinnamon apple pancakes, housemade corned beef hash and soups, salads and sandwiches served with house-cut potato chips. Outstanding service, fine wines and creative cocktails complete the impressive dining experience.

JACKSONVILLE INN
175 E California St   541/899-1900, 800/321-9344
Rooms: Moderate; Cottages: Moderately expensive   jacksonvilleinn.com

If you can secure a room during the busy Britt Festival season (or at any other time of the year), stay at this highly-acclaimed inn. This historic bed and breakfast, built in 1861, is tastefully decorated with period antiques and reproductions. There are eight rooms with private bathrooms at the inn. The original honeymoon cottage, a small restored historic house, is two blocks away; three replicated cottages, including the Presidential Cottage where President and Mrs. George W. Bush stayed, were built at the same location. Each is private and luxurious. Full breakfast is included with an overnight stay and served in the inn's dining room; choose from a variety of delicious favorites (housemade granola, waffles, hearty egg preparations and such). The inn presents a wonderful brunch each Sunday; start with champagne or sparkling cider and work your way through fresh fruit, house-baked pastries, eggs and meats and near-famous scalloped potatoes or select a special of the day. Lunch and dinner are served in the dining room and bistro as well as on a lovely garden patio (weather permitting); the wine list and gourmet menus are extensive. Dinners, expertly prepared with fresh, local seasonal ingredients, include the inn's special grilled chicken, veal scaloppini, fish and seafood, flavorful steaks, prime rib and more. Keep the restaurant in mind for off-site catering, banquets (private dining rooms are available) and picnic baskets to take to Britt Festival concerts. Proprietors **Linda and Jerry Evans** also operate the Wine and Gift Shop at this location, fully-stocked with over 2,000 impressive wine selections.

POT RACK
140 W California St   541/899-5736
Daily: 10-6   jacksonvillepotrack.com

This aptly named shop sells pot racks as well as pots, pans and cooking utensils to hang on the holders. You'll find other brand name cookware, bakeware, useful and obscure gadgets, colorful table accessories, table linens, aprons, cutlery, attractive gifts and items to inspire your culinary bent.

TERRA FIRMA
135 E California St   541/899-1097
Daily   terrafirmahome.com

"Fun stuff" describes the merchandise at this gift emporium. The main floor has a unique selection of some of this and some of that—soap by the loaf, candles, jewelry, hardware, housewares, home decor and affordable gifts for your home or best friend. A clearance area for furniture from their home and design location in Medford is located on the second floor.

TOUVELLE HOUSE BED & BREAKFAST
455 N Oregon St   541/899-8938, 800/846-8422
Moderate   touvellehouse.com

Hosts **Gary Renninger Balfour** and **Tim Balfour** offer a number of special amenities, including a heated swimming pool

---

WHEN A DOOR CLOSES, A WINDOW OPENS

JELD-WEN (jeld-wen.com) is an international window and door manufacturer with humble beginnings still headquartered in Klamath Falls, employing some 20,000 people worldwide. Founded by the late **Richard Wendt**, his son, **Rod Wendt**, not only presently heads the firm, but is also a significant force in dozens of major activities that help make Oregon a great place to live, work and play.

(summer only) guest refrigerators on each floor, a library and a guest computer. The six individualized guest rooms, all with private baths, feature luxurious beds and linens, air conditioning, CD players and Wi-Fi. Common areas in the Craftsman-style home are comfortably furnished for reading, playing cards or games, warming by the great room's sandstone fireplace or taking morning coffee. You may want to find your niche in the beautifully landscaped grounds for an afternoon siesta. Coffee and breakfast in the dining room start mornings off on the right foot; your hosts will accommodate special dietary restrictions (advance notice, please). Tea is available all day in the well-decorated period dining room; fresh homemade sweets are set out later in the day. This is a great "sleep" in a superb location.

KLAMATH FALLS

CRYSTALWOOD LODGE
38625 Westside Road   866/381-2322
Moderate   crystalwoodlodge.com

When you pack up the family, and the pet dog (or cat) begs to come along, it's no problem if the destination is Crystalwood Lodge. Near the south entrance to Crater Lake National Park and adjacent to the Upper Klamath National Wildlife Refuge, this lodge sits on 130 acres in the center of wonderful fly-fishing, canoeing, golf, hiking, horseback riding, cross-country skiing, snowshoeing, dog sledding and other outdoor activities. Crates (home-away-from-home pet houses) are provided in every room, a dog-washing facility is near at hand and pet day care is available. In lieu of meal service, guests have access to a fully-outfitted commercial kitchen facility, walk-in cooler, freezer and grill. Meeting space and catered gourmet meals are available to groups for reunions, retreats and workshops.

FAVELL MUSEUM OF WESTERN ART AND INDIAN ARTIFACTS

125 W Main St   541/882-9996
Tues-Sat: 11-4   favellmuseum.org
Nominal

Founder **Gene Favell** assembled this rich and fascinating collection prior to his death in 2001. You'll find both art and artifacts under one roof plus one of the finest collections of firearms in the West; many are miniature models. More than 100,000 Indian artifacts are shown including a huge set of ancient and authentic Indian arrowheads. The striking building houses galleries of figurines, art, prints and sculptures that are also offered for sale; additional features include Favell's fabulous art book anthology and a comfortable meeting room for public events.

THE KLAMATH GRILL AND PANCAKE HOUSE

715 Main St   541/882-1427
Inexpensive   klamathgrill.com

It's always fun to check out "where the locals go," and a good place to start in K-Falls is at this Main Street restaurant which is open for breakfast and lunch seven days a week. Pancakes (ten varieties), waffles, stuffed French toast, pigs in a blanket and egg dishes are breakfast staples. If you're in the mood for lunch, hot and cold sandwiches, burgers and salads are tasty options.

LAKE OF THE WOODS MOUNTAIN LODGE & RESORT

950 Harriman Rt   541/949-8300, 866/201-4194
Moderate   lakeofthewoodsresort.com

Ah, the great outdoors! Spend the day at the lake then head inside your cozy cabin to rest and rejuvenate for another day of fishing, waterskiing, hiking, scuba diving or winter activities. One- and two-bedroom vintage cabins have varying amenities (full kitchen or kitchenette, jetted tub, gas fireplace, screened porch). One-bedroom park model cabins have living rooms with a sofa sleeper or trundle bed, full kitchens and bathrooms; units may also have sleeping lofts, covered porches or bunkrooms. **The Lake House Restaurant** is open for breakfast, lunch and dinner and the **Marina Pizza Parlor** serves lunch and dinner (pizza, wraps, salads, sandwiches) daily during the summer season. In winter, the pizza parlor is open Friday through Sunday. A full-service marina is handy for boat rentals, fuel and moorage.

MIA & PIA'S PIZZERIA & BREWHOUSE

3545 Summers Lane   541/884-4880, 541/884-0949
Lunch, Dinner: Daily   miapia.com

Dozens of beers and ales are on tap at Mia & Pia's. The spot is the outgrowth of a family business started nearly four decades ago. Much of the equipment and hardware is reclaimed from their prior dairy business and is in daily use at the pizzeria and brewhouse. Thirty pizza varieties are available, or they're up for your own creations. Other good eats include appetizers, burgers, broasted chicken, spaghetti, soups, salads and sandwiches. These folks will bring their beer truck to your event for a never-to-be-forgotten party.

ROCKY POINT RESORT

28121 Rocky Point Road   541/356-2287
Seasonal: Apr 1-Nov 1   rockypointoregon.com

If you want to "rough it" but also enjoy a comfy bed and shower each evening, consider a stay at this resort, not far from either Medford or Klamath Falls on the Northwest shore of Upper Klamath Lake. You have a choice of cabins, guest rooms, RV spaces—even tent sites; rates vary. Reservations are strongly suggested for the resort's popular restaurant, especially for evening meals; open Memorial Day through Labor Day, Wednesdays through Sundays and weekends only in spring and fall. Overnighters are welcome to use the well-kept public restrooms, showers, laundry facilities and fish-cleaning station; pick up supplies at the marina store, where you can also rent a canoe or fuel your watercraft.

RUNNING Y RANCH

5500 Running Y Road   800/569-0029
Moderate and up   runningy.com

Running Y Ranch is Southern Oregon's premier full-service destination resort. Recently purchased by new owners, the resort has undergone $3 million in refurbishments, most notably in the Lodge (new guest rooms and a restaurant, **The Ruddy Duck**) which overlooks Payne Canyon. Vacation homes and chalets also received upgrades. Although the Arnold Palmer Signature Course is a huge draw, non-golfers have plenty to do: abundant fishing, birding, hiking, whitewater rafting and boating opportunities are close at hand. Winter visitors don't have to travel far for snowshoeing or skating at the Bill Collier Community Ice Arena. Additional amenities include the Sandhill Spa and a sports and fitness center with swimming pool.

LAKEVIEW

WILLOW SPRINGS GUEST RANCH

34064 Clover Flat Road   541/947-5499
Mid-May to Sept   willowspringsguestranch.com
Moderate

Driving through this region, I'm always impressed with the huge expanse of land, magnificent fertile fields and herds of cattle lazing around the open territory. To get a taste of life in Oregon's Outback, visit **Patty and Keith Barnhart** at their working cattle ranch. You'll be in the midst of a vast population of birds, squirrels, deer, antelope and other critters. With hundreds of miles of trails, you can ride horses or, if your timing is right, accompany ranch hands on a cattle roundup. Choose a gentle steed if you're a beginner or a more challenging mount if you're an experienced rider. Part of the fun at Willow Springs is the on-site-generated electricity, with various combinations of solar and wind power. And after a day on the range, you'll have no problem with an early "lights out." Accommodations are rustic cabins decorated with exceptional Western artwork, a sunporch just right for meditating and a wood-fired hot tub to soothe those weary cowboy and cowgirl muscles. Rates include hearty ranch breakfasts. Additional fees apply for authentic Dutch-oven cooked dinners, box lunches, horseback riding, guided rides or lodging and feed for your own horse.

MEDFORD

4 DAUGHTERS IRISH PUB
126 W Main St
Lunch, Dinner: Mon-Sat
Moderate

541/779-4455
4daughtersirishpub.com

The history of this establishment goes back to the early 1900s; it has been a barbershop, theater, billiards parlor and cigar club. Named for the owner's four daughters, this pub is appropriately furnished with a game room including pool and darts. The extensive menu includes small bites, soups and salads, burgers, beer-battered fish and chips, Guinness meatloaf, shepherd's pie and wonderful homemade desserts. Plenty of Irish drink specialties and beers are available.

38 CENTRAL RESTAURANT & WINE BAR
38 N Central Ave
Lunch: Mon-Fri; Dinner: Mon-Sat; Brunch: Sun
Moderate

541/776-0038
38central.net

This casual dining restaurant has a big-city vibe achieved through the use of exposed-brick walls, attractive interior decor and an enticing staircase to the upstairs lounge area. Comfort food with a twist and specialty cocktails are influenced by the seasons. What to order? Crispy calamari and duck quesadilla appetizers, champagne-battered fish and chips, buttermilk fried chicken, ribs and burgers. Other innovative cuisine choices include salads, pastas, steak and fish. 38 Central earned the Superior Cellar Award from *Oregon Wine Press* in 2011 and 2012. Wines from the Northwest and elsewhere are value-priced and won't empty your pocketbook. This is one of Medford's top spots!

DOWNTOWN MARKET CO.
231 E Main St
Mon-Fri: 9-6; Sat: 10-4

541/973-2233
downtownmarketco.com

Nora LaBrocca's love of food led her to open this downtown market. Brought up in Southern California, the LaBrocca clan raised beef, poultry and game birds for chic Los Angeles-area restaurants. The taste kitchen's lunchtime menu changes weekly and brings fresh soups, salads, sandwiches and more to the tables; beyond lunch, though, this place is a specialty food market and offers culinary classes, tastings and occasional family-style dinners. Two ground floor outdoor patios are pleasantly furnished to feel like a big city rooftop. Large outdoor grills are used year round to prepare panini sandwiches and other delicious offerings (men have been know to drool over these to-die-for grills). Summer picnic baskets are superb!

ELEMENTS TAPAS BAR & LOUNGE

101 E Main St   541/779-0135
Daily: 4 p.m.-late   elementsmedford.com
Moderate

In a historic downtown building you'll find great drinks from the full bar (including fabulous Spanish wines) to accompany outstanding food, crafted as much as possible from local produce. Try red grapes encrusted with Rogue Creamery smoked blue cheese and crushed pistachios or Spanish olives for cold plates; for warm plates, sea salt-roasted Marcona almonds with green beans or bacon-wrapped Medjool dates. Traditional Spanish paellas with vegetables and assorted meats and seafood are made to order from scratch, which allows adequate time to share tasty tapas.

THIS CHANGED OREGON HISTORY

In October 1947, during a flight to a goose hunt in Lake County, Governor **Earl Snell**'s second term ended in calamity. All on board were killed in a crash, including Snell, Senate President **Marshall Cornett**, Secretary of State **Robert Farrell, Jr.** and pilot, **Cliff Hogue**. Oregon state government was devastated, making it necessary to appoint the fourth in line (Speaker of the House, **John Hall**) to the governorship. Hall served only for about one year, losing the 1948 election to state Senator **Douglas McKay**. McKay was later appointed Secretary of the Interior by President **Dwight Eisenhower**.

POMODORI RISTORANTE

1789 W Stewart Ave   541/776-6332
Lunch: Tues-Fri; Dinner: Tues-Sat   pomodoriristorante.com
Moderate

Owners **Jeff Lindow** and **John Bartow** offer an appealing atmosphere in this green building with tomato-red doors. The extensive menu is Northern Italian and starts with a basket of warm bread accompanied by pesto butter. Burgers, salads, pastas and sandwiches are good lunch choices. It's difficult to pick a dinner favorite from the delectable pastas, seafoods, meat specialties and ribeye steaks prepared three ways; the veal scaloppini is terrific.

MERLIN

ROGUE WILDERNESS ADVENTURES

325 Galice Road   541/479-9554, 800/336-1647
Seasonal (Apr-Oct)   wildrogue.com

Owner-operator **Brad Niva** knows the Rogue River like the back of his hand and will help plan your float trip, ranging from a half-day to three- or four-day journey via inflatable kayak or raft through the Wild and Scenic Rogue River Canyon. Multi-day river, fishing and hiking trips include stays at wilderness lodges and wonderful meals. The scenery is indescribable and the experience is sure to create a favorite lifetime memory.

PROSPECT

PROSPECT HISTORIC HOTEL & DINNER HOUSE

391 Mill Creek Dr   541/560-3664, 800/944-6490
Inexpensive to moderate

Does putting your head on a pillow at a historic stagecoach-stop hotel sound intriguing? If so, this stop in Prospect is the closest full-service town to Crater Lake and the Rogue River. It is also the jumping-off point for many outdoor activities. Ten bed and breakfast rooms are in the Nationally Registered Historic Hotel; the full hearty breakfast is a delightful start to the morning. All rooms have private bathrooms, handmade quilts and period furnishings. Behind the hotel, 14 modern motel units are outfitted with TVs, coffeemakers, refrigerators and microwaves (some kitchenettes); these units are ideal for families and guests with pets. The dinner house is open May through October as well as most holidays and serves mouth watering dinners complete with salad, freshly-baked bread and dessert. **Karen and Fred Wickman** are the latest owners of the Prospect Historic Hotel which has its origins in the late 1880s. Karen oversees the dinner house and Fred is the jack-of-all-trades.

ROGUE RIVER

PHOLIA FARM
9115 W Evans Creek Road   541/582-8883
                                                 pholiafarm.com

Learn all you never knew about Nigerian dwarf dairy goats and the rich milk and cheese they produce at **Gianaclis and Vern Caldwell**'s farm. The dairy is off-grid, as is the Caldwell's home; alternative power sources (solar, micro-hydro generator and backup bio-diesel generator) supply electricity. The breed's milk is unique and boasts the highest butterfat of all goats; the Caldwell's herd averages 6.5% butterfat and 4.3% percent in protein, which translates into extraordinary Old World cheese. The farm works with **Wild River Brewing**, feeding spent brewers grain to the goats and using an ale bath during one of the cheese's aging processes. Classes are offered in cheesemaking and herdsmanship for novice goat owners. The farm is open to the public the second Saturday of the month and by appointment between December and February. Cheeses are available from the farm and at a few select retailers; whole wheels of cheese may be ordered directly from Pholia. It's best to call ahead if you are going to this off-the-beaten-path enterprise.

ROSEBURG

ABACELA VINEYARD AND WINERY
12500 Lookingglass Road   541/679-6642
Daily: 11-5   abacela.com

What pinot noir is to the Chehalem terroir of the Dundee Hills, other varietals match the dry, rocky soil in Southern

Oregon. **Hilda and Earl Jones** searched the U.S. from their Alabama home for the right growing climate, gave up careers in medical research and began learning more about Tempranillo grapes. The established vineyard and award-winning winery produce Tempranillo, Albariño, Syrah, Malbec and other varietal wines. Tastings are served in the new Vine & Wine Center which includes magnificent venues and elegant private tastings.

EAT IT FRESH!

Abundant water, rich and enriched soils, combined with Oregon's climate (moderate in Western Oregon to more severe on the east side of the state), the Pacific Northwest is blessed from A to Z (apples to zucchini) with an amazing variety of fresh fruits and vegetables. To name a few: apricots, asparagus, beets, blackberries, blueberries, broccoli, cantaloupe, cherries, corn, cucumbers, green beans, lettuce, mushrooms, nectarines, peaches, pears, peas, potatoes, raspberries, squash, strawberries, tomatoes, watermelon… Grow your own or frequent our many farmers markets for the freshest produce; most are available from mid-summer to fall. Our fertile lands have played mightily in the burgeoning interest in Oregon's restaurant scene, both for chefs and their clientele.

BRIX 527

527 SE Jackson St   541/440-4901
Breakfast, Lunch, Dinner: Daily
Moderate

A weekend trip to the Land of the Umpqua has plenty of activities for the whole family. In downtown Roseburg in industrial chic quarters, Brix 527 encompasses three buildings, all built in the late 1800s, which were joined together to incorporate a lounge and make way for nightly dinner service. The made-on-the-premises real crab cake Benedict is delicious. There is a baker's dozen of gourmet selections, including salmon and a version of the beloved Reuben sandwich, a la Benedict. Soups, sandwiches, salads and other delicious lunch specials complete the list.

DELFINO VINEYARDS

3829 Colonial Road   541/673-7575
Daily: 11-5   delfinovineyards.com
Cottage: Moderate

Terri and Jim Delfino's enterprise includes a one-bedroom guest cottage nestled in the picturesque 160-acre site; in-room breakfast basket (or fixings to make breakfast on your own schedule) and a bottle of Delfino Vineyards wine are included. During your stay, amble over to the tasting room, hike the wooded trails, soak in the hot tub, take a dip in the lap pool or snuggle up by the cottage's fireplace. For two couples or a family (no guests younger than 14, please), the cottage has a queen sofa bed. If a wedding is in your future, consider this location.

SILVER LAKE

COWBOY DINNER TREE

East Bay Road   541/576-2426
June-Oct: Thurs-Sun;   cowboydinnertree.net
Nov-May: Fri-Sun (seasonal)
Moderate

In the heart of Oregon's High Desert country this unique dinner stop is an experience! When you call (reservations are a must), place your order for either a top sirloin steak (think roast) or whole chicken; the trimmings, such as hearty

---

DID YOU KNOW?

... that the **Yaquina Head Lighthouse**, a very popular Oregon Coast landmark, is the state's tallest at 93 feet?

... that **James Beard**, one of America's most famous and prolific national cookbook authors, was an Oregon native?

... that the population of Oregon doubled several years after the highly successful **Lewis and Clark Centennial Exposition** (1905)?

soup, salad, beans, baked potato and homemade dessert, will make you happy you journeyed this far. Portions are gigantic! Connie and Don Ramage are a mighty team. Connie prepares homemade dinner rolls from a secret family recipe; on a busy evening, she'll turn out 80 pans of the melt-in-your-mouth bread. Among other tasks, Don prepares chickens and spice-rubbed steaks for the grill. If you want to call it a night at sundown, reserve one of the two rustic cabins (no TV or telephone); the package deal includes dinner. Interesting cowboy memorabilia accents the dining room and cabins. Credit cards not accepted.

STEAMBOAT

STEAMBOAT INN

42705 N Umpqua Hwy   541/498-2230, 800/840-8825

Moderate and up   thesteamboatinn.com

Although this charming retreat is known far and wide by fishermen, others will be just as engaged with the many attractions offered. For over a half-century, anglers have made Steamboat their base camp for some of the best steelhead fishing anywhere. The eight cabins and two suites on the river are breathtaking; the sounds of the rippling water will put even the most restless sleeper into seventh heaven. Also available (and particularly well suited for families) are five hideaway cottages and three 1960s three-bedroom ranch houses. The main building has a charming library and a huge dining table where the legendary fabulous family-style dinners are served. For over 20 years, great winemakers and wonderful chefs have combined their talents to provide remarkable winemakers' dinners at Steamboat Inn. Hikers can enjoy a multitude of waterfalls and wildlife on some of the most fantastic trails in Oregon. Proprietors **Sharon and Jim Van Loan** and **Patricia Lee** are gracious, friendly, guest-oriented hosts. Take some fly-fishing instruction, a whitewater raft trip or enjoy a relaxing massage. This is one of Oregon's best!

TALENT

NEW SAMMY'S COWBOY BISTRO
2210 S Pacific Hwy   541/535-2779
Lunch, Dinner: Wed-Sun (Nov-Feb: closed Sun)
Moderately expensive

You may need your glasses to find this spot! Venture off I-5 about three miles north of Ashland for one heck of a dining experience. For some 20 years **Charlene and Vernon Rollins** have been filling satisfied customers' plates with awesome food. Chef Charlene consistently produces healthy, organic meals, with homemade breads, entrees made with seasonal ingredients and amazing desserts; Vernon takes care of the front of the house. The restaurant's garden supplies herbs and vegetables; other local producers provide meats and such, including whole suckling pigs. The Rollins' talents have caught the eye of prestigious food magazines and Charlene has been nominated by the James Beard Foundation for her culinary accomplishments. Reservations are definitely in order.

WINSTON

WILDLIFE SAFARI
1790 Safari Road   541/679-6761
Daily   wildlifesafari.net
Nominal

Years ago, Senator Mark Hatfield and your author paid a visit to Wildlife Safari on one of our trips through Southern Oregon: I'll always remember that outing and the elephant that stole the show. This spectacular drive-through park continues to attract families to observe over 500 animals roaming natural habitat. Ninety species of large and small African, Asian and North and South American animals are showcased; to the delight of youngsters, many brush up next to visitors' autos! Before or after your safari, explore the village with unique animals, train and animal rides and a petting zoo, as well as a cafe, gift shop, kids' play area and gardens. Allow several hours to take in all the activities. This popular attraction is committed to research, education and conservation of wildlife.

> **HELP!**
>
> If you're ever in need of roadside assistance as you visit some of the great places in this volume, your **AAA** (oregon.aaa.com) membership can be a godsend. These folks are available 24/7 for vehicle and bicycle roadside service, among many other services. Help is also available through various insurance company policy riders and auto manufacturer programs with certain car purchases. They are great at travel planning, too. (Disclaimer: your author serves as a director for AAA Oregon/Idaho.)

WOLF CREEK

WOLF CREEK INN

100 Front St   541/866-2474
Breakfast, Lunch, Dinner: Daily   historicwolfcreekinn.com
Lodging: Inexpensive
Restaurant: Moderate

Decades ago, Wolf Creek Tavern was a stagecoach stop providing lodging and food. Through the ensuing years famous guests came to this bend in the road to rest, hike and enjoy Southern Oregon outdoors. Author Jack London and screen legend Clark Gable were frequent guests and have a room and suite named in their honor. A massive four-year restoration project ensued following the Oregon Parks and Recreation Department's purchase of the inn in 1975. Nine rooms are vintage 1920 and decorated with period pictures and furnishings; no TVs or telephones, although Wi-Fi is available. Private bathrooms are standard in all rooms and a full hot breakfast is served in the dining room. Heritage roses and 125-year-old fruit trees are scattered throughout the three-acre property. Today's travelers will enjoy satisfying comfort food in the warm dining room or on the outdoor patio. Live music and special events are scheduled throughout the year.

Index